Shojo Beat

VAMPIRE KNIGHT

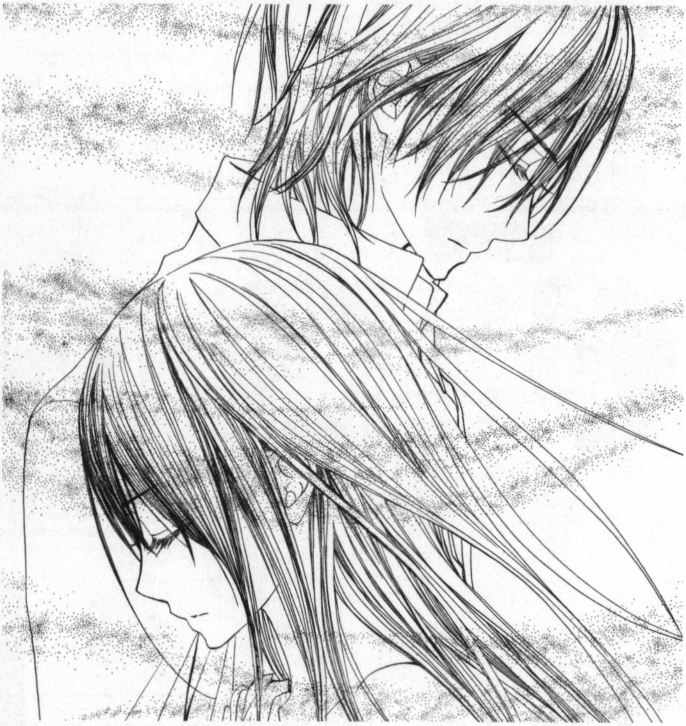

Story & Art by
Matsuri
Hino

Vol. 17

The Story of VAMPIRE KNIGHT

1 Cross Academy, a private boarding school, is where the Day Class and Night Class coexist. The Night Class—a group of beautiful elite students—are all vampires!

2 Four years ago, after turning his twin brother against him, the pureblood Shizuka Hio bit Zero and turned him into a vampire. Kaname kills Shizuka, but the source may still exist. Meanwhile, Yuki suffers from lost memories. When Kaname sinks his fangs into her neck, her memories return!

3 Yuki is the princess of the Kuran family—and a pureblood vampire!! Ten years ago, her mother exchanged her life to seal away Yuki's vampire nature. Yuki's Uncle Rido killed her father. Rido takes over Shiki's body and arrives at the Academy. He targets Yuki for her blood, so Kaname gives his own blood to resurrect Rido. Kaname confesses that he's the progenitor of the Kurans, and that Rido is the master who awakened him!

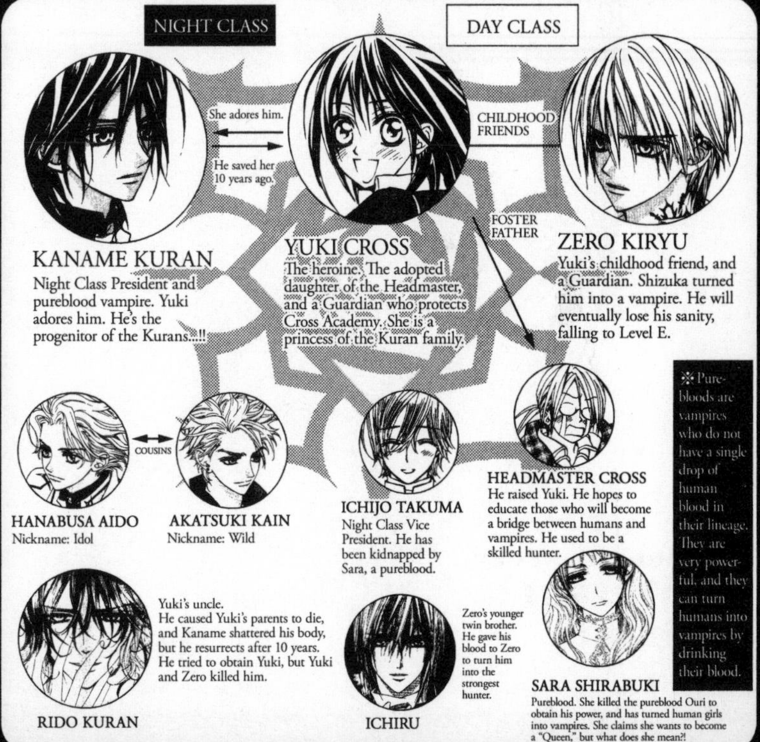

NIGHT CLASS
DAY CLASS
She adores him.
He saved her 10 years ago.
CHILDHOOD FRIENDS
FOSTER FATHER
KANAME KURAN
Night Class President and pureblood vampire. Yuki adores him. He's the progenitor of the Kurans...!!
YUKI CROSS
The heroine. The adopted daughter of the Headmaster, and a Guardian who protects Cross Academy. She is a princess of the Kuran family.
ZERO KIRYU
Yuki's childhood friend, and a Guardian. Shizuka turned him into a vampire. He will eventually lose his sanity, falling to Level E.
※Purebloods are vampires who do not have a single drop of human blood in their lineage. They are very powerful, and they can turn humans into vampires by drinking their blood.
COUSINS
HANABUSA AIDO
Nickname: Idol
AKATSUKI KAIN
Nickname: Wild
ICHIJO TAKUMA
Night Class Vice President. He has been kidnapped by Sara, a pureblood.
HEADMASTER CROSS
He raised Yuki. He hopes to educate those who will become a bridge between humans and vampires. He used to be a skilled hunter.
Yuki's uncle.
He caused Yuki's parents to die, and Kaname shattered his body, but he resurrects after 10 years. He tried to obtain Yuki, but Yuki and Zero killed him.
RIDO KURAN
Zero's younger twin brother. He gave his blood to Zero to turn him into the strongest hunter.
ICHIRU
SARA SHIRABUKI
Pureblood. She killed the pureblood Ouri to obtain his power, and has turned human girls into vampires. She claims she wants to become a "Queen," but what does she mean?!

4 Cross Academy turns into a battlefield. After fierce fighting, Yuki and Zero succeed in defeating Rido, but right after Zero points his gun at Yuki. No matter what their feelings are, their fates will never intertwine. Yuki leaves the Academy with Kaname, and the Night Class at Cross Academy is no more.

5 A year has passed since Yuki and Zero's parting. Kaname and Zero have become the representatives of each group respectively. Meanwhile, Sara Shirabuki begins to make suspicious moves by creating more servants of her own. Yuki tries to live together with Kaname, but he slays Aido's father and disappears. Yuki is taken captive by the Hunter Society and reinstates the Night Class at Cross Academy to maintain order.

6 Kaname continues to kill purebloods. Sara claims she is his next target and asks those at Cross Academy for help. Sara usurps Yuki's authority by giving the Night Class highly addictive underground blood tablets. Yuki gives her blood to the Night Class students to save them. Sara then takes interest in Zero and tells him there's something important he should know...

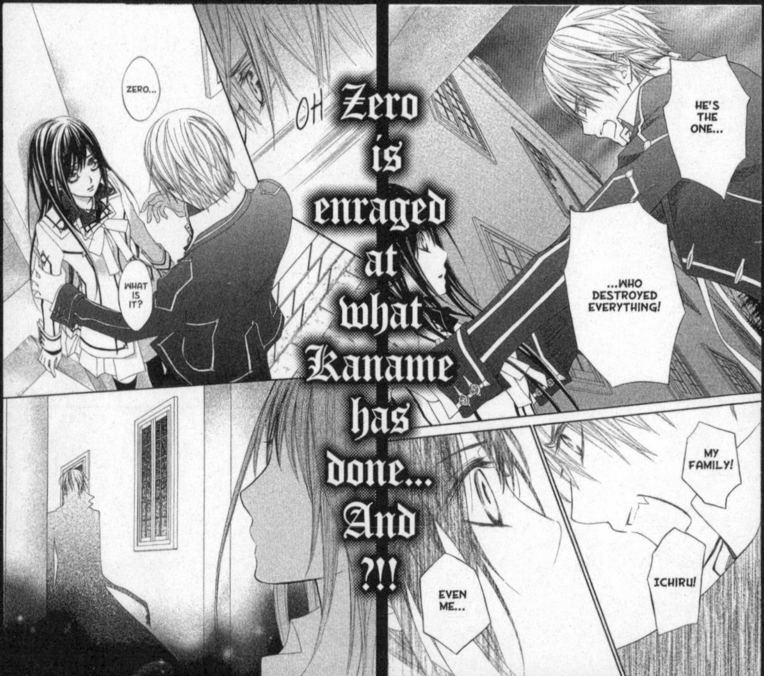
HE'S THE ONE...
...WHO DESTROYED EVERYTHING!
ZERO...
OH
WHAT IS IT?
Zero is enraged at what Kaname has done... And ?!!
MY FAMILY!
ICHIRU!
EVEN ME...

VAMPIRE KNIGHT

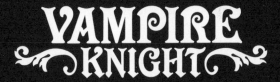

Contents

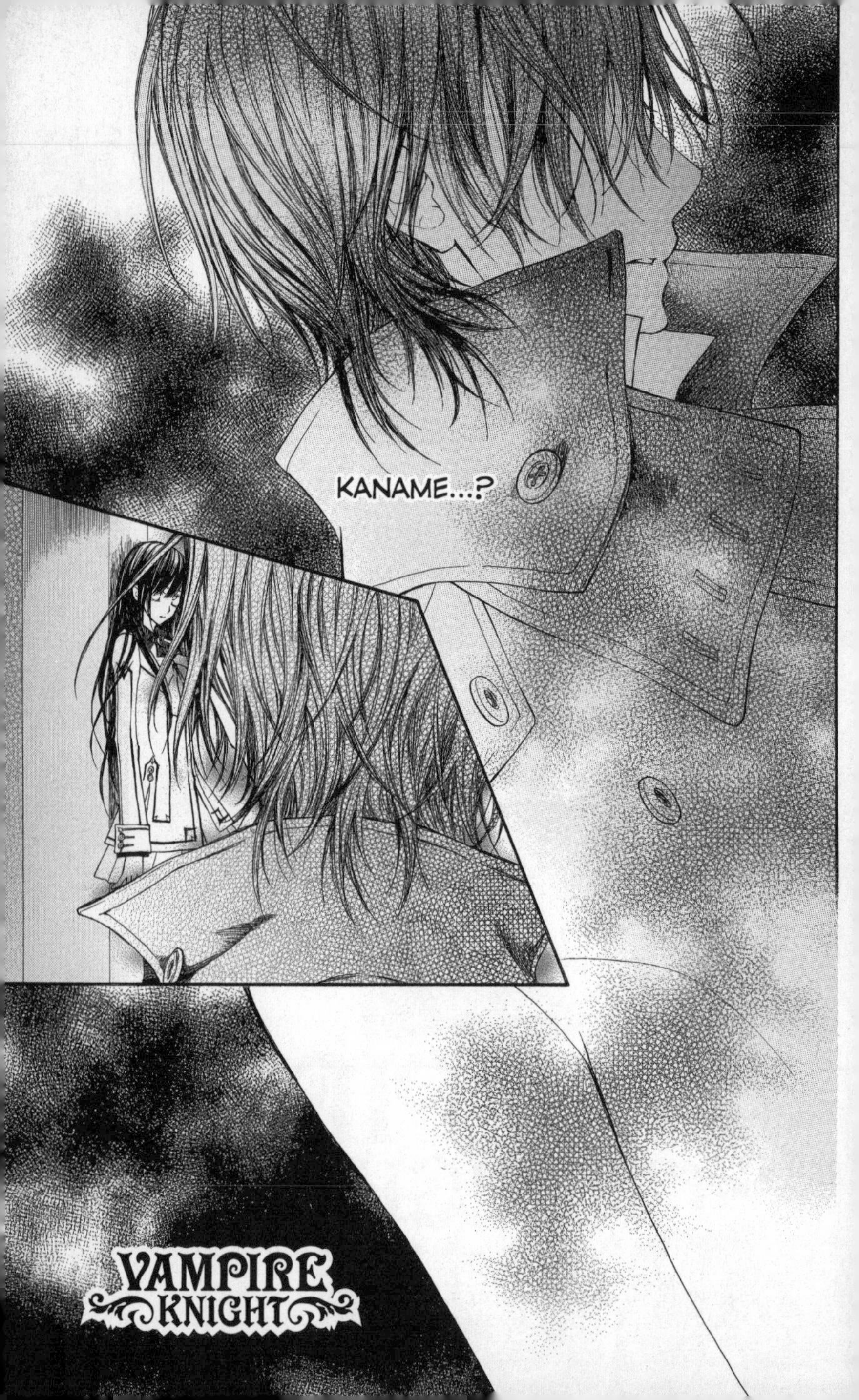
KANAME...?
VAMPIRE KNIGHT

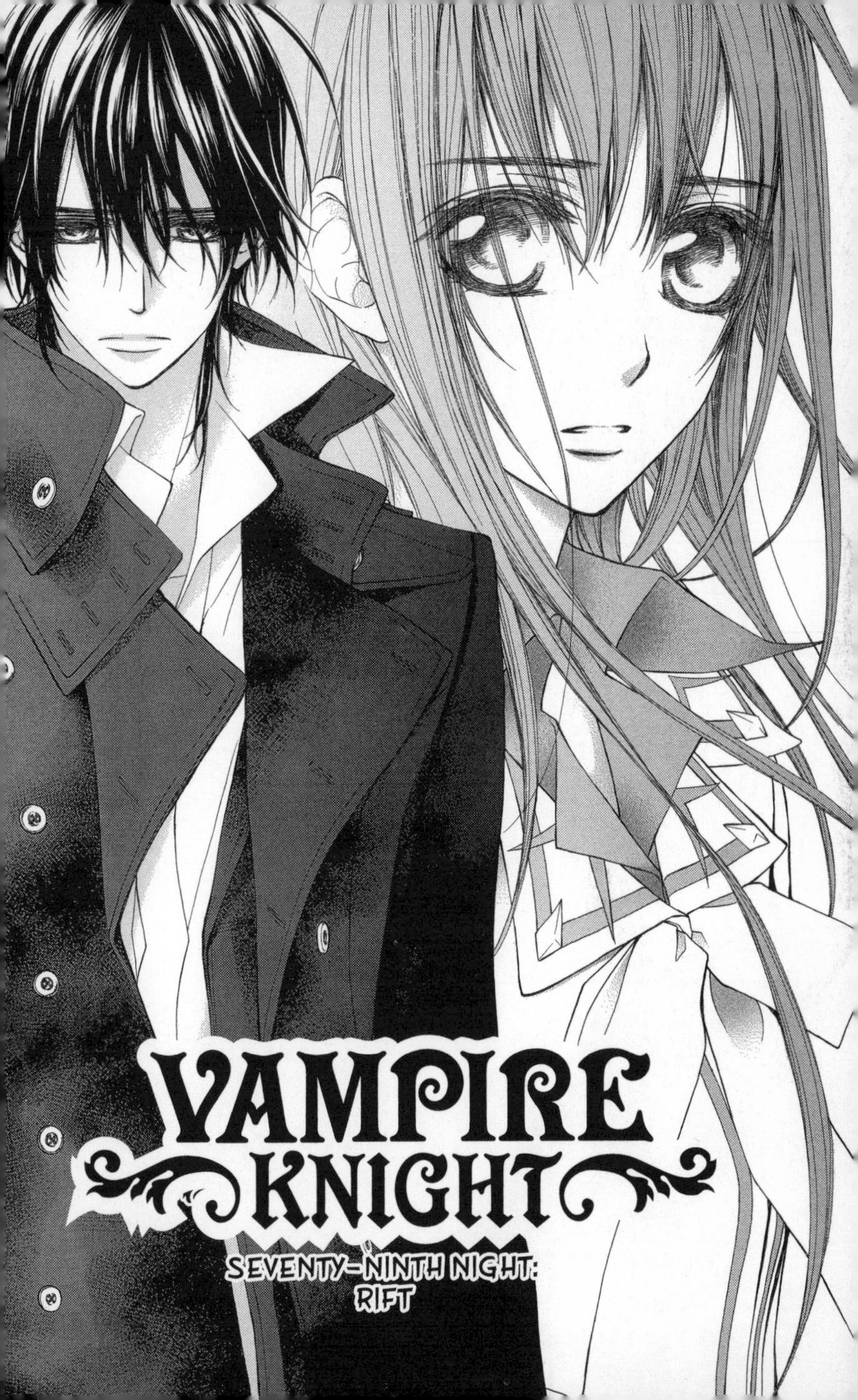
VAMPIRE KNIGHT
SEVENTY-NINTH NIGHT: RIFT

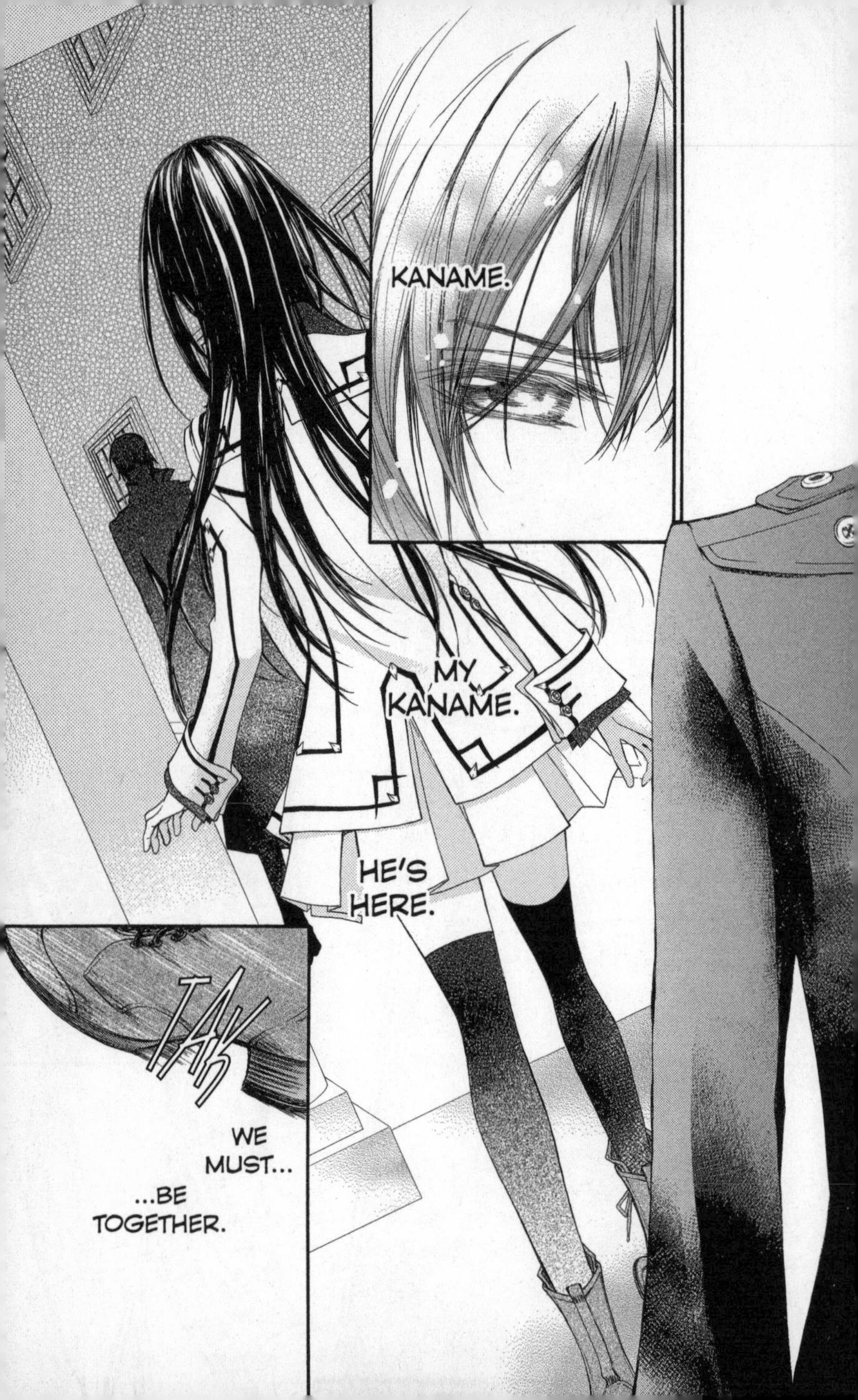
KANAME.
MY KANAME.
HE'S HERE.
TAK
WE MUST...
...BE TOGETHER.

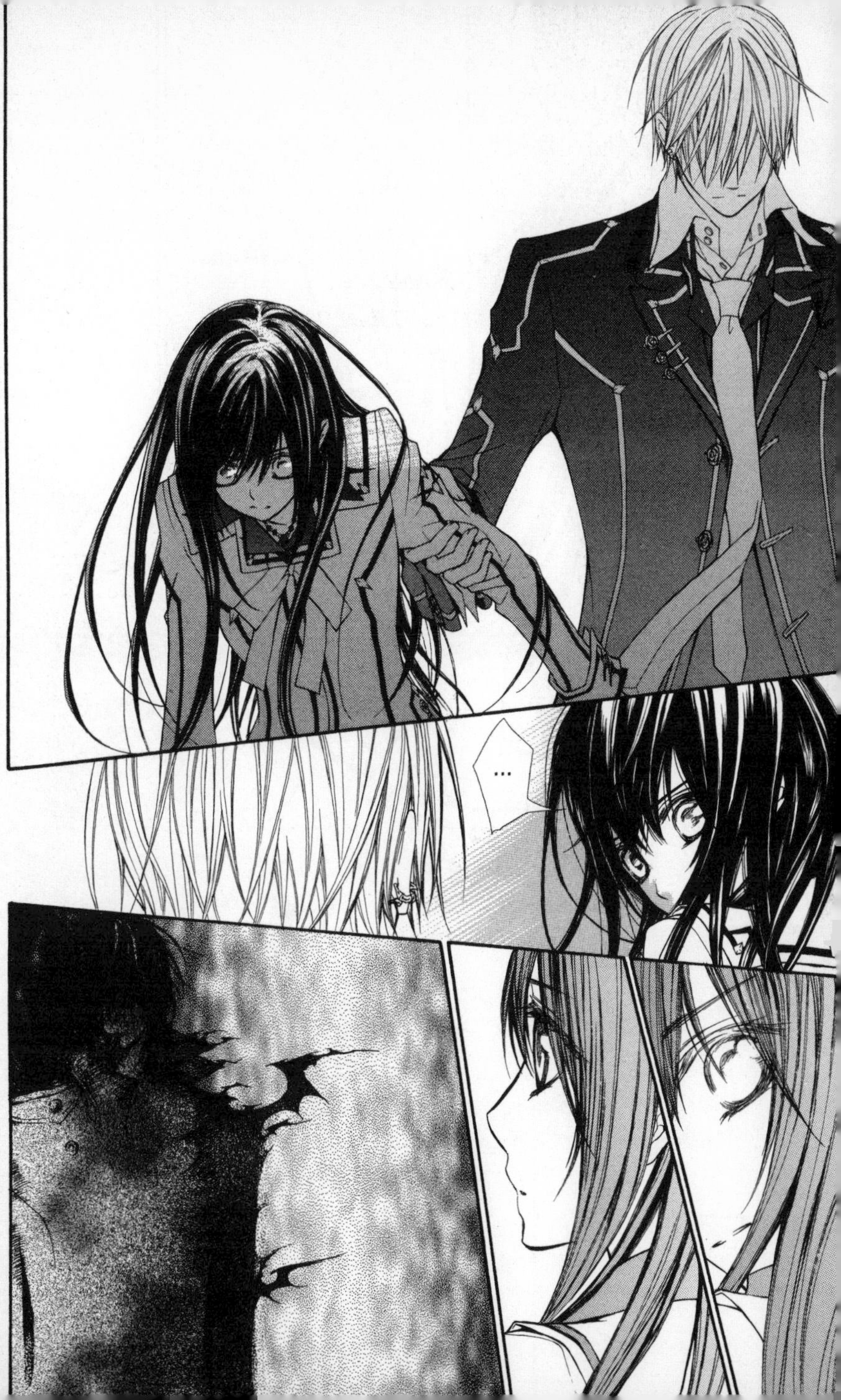
...

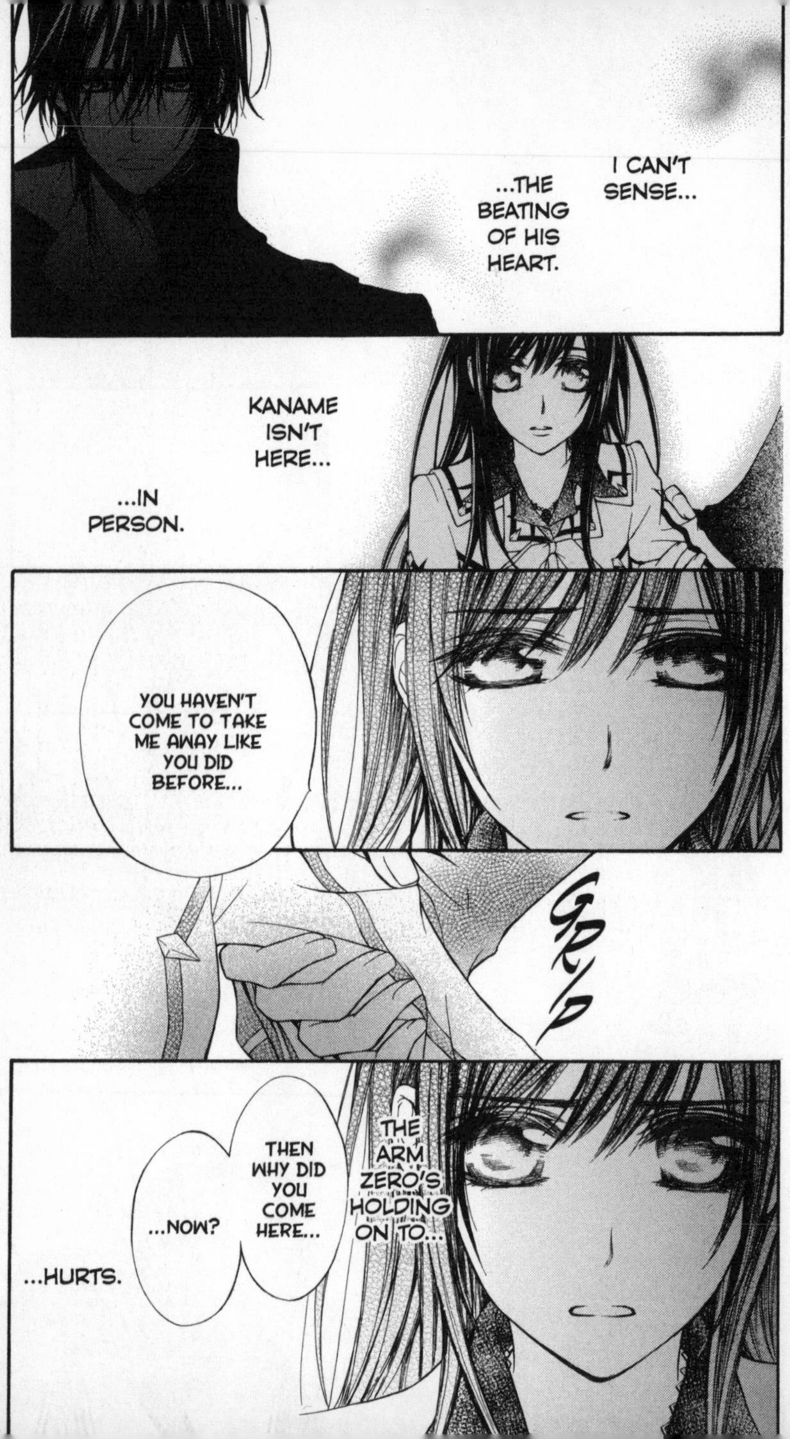
I CAN'T SENSE...
...THE BEATING OF HIS HEART.
KANAME ISN'T HERE...
...IN PERSON.
YOU HAVEN'T COME TO TAKE ME AWAY LIKE YOU DID BEFORE...
GRIP
THE ARM ZERO'S HOLDING ON TO...
THEN WHY DID YOU COME HERE...
...NOW?
...HURTS.

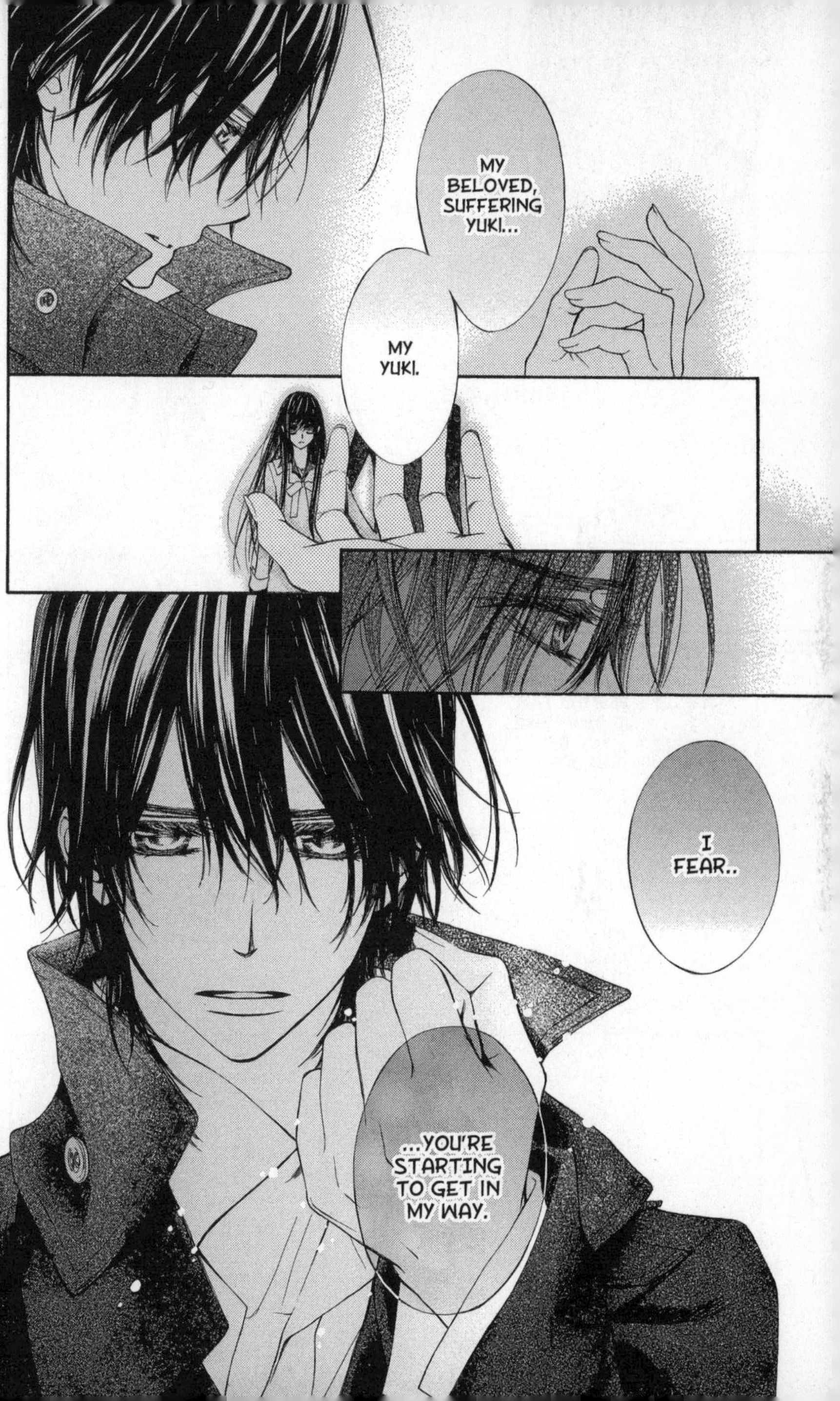
MY BELOVED, SUFFERING YUKI...
MY YUKI.
I FEAR..
...YOU'RE STARTING TO GET IN MY WAY.

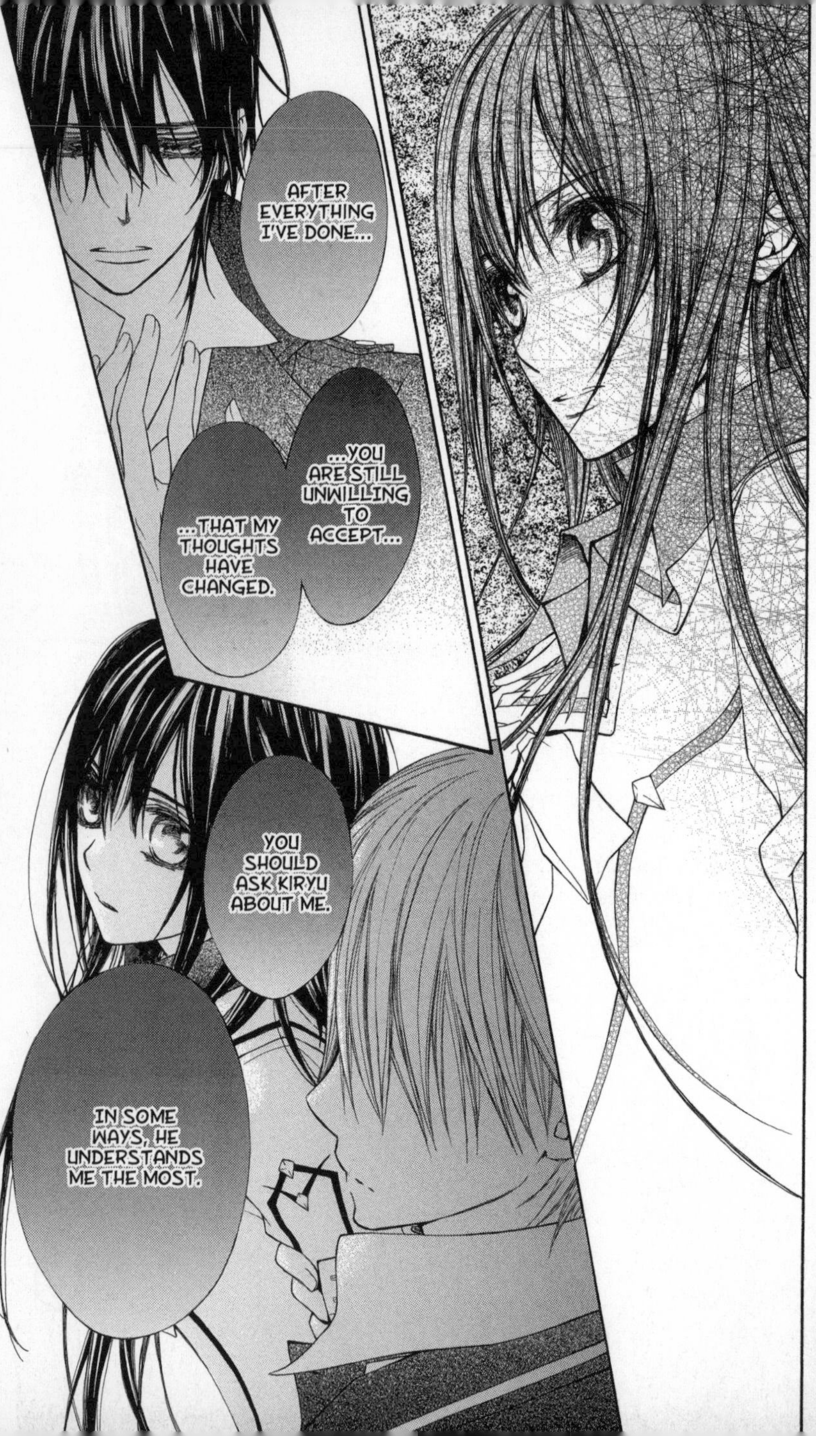
AFTER EVERYTHING I'VE DONE...
...YOU ARE STILL UNWILLING TO ACCEPT...
...THAT MY THOUGHTS HAVE CHANGED.
YOU SHOULD ASK KIRYU ABOUT ME.
IN SOME WAYS, HE UNDERSTANDS ME THE MOST.

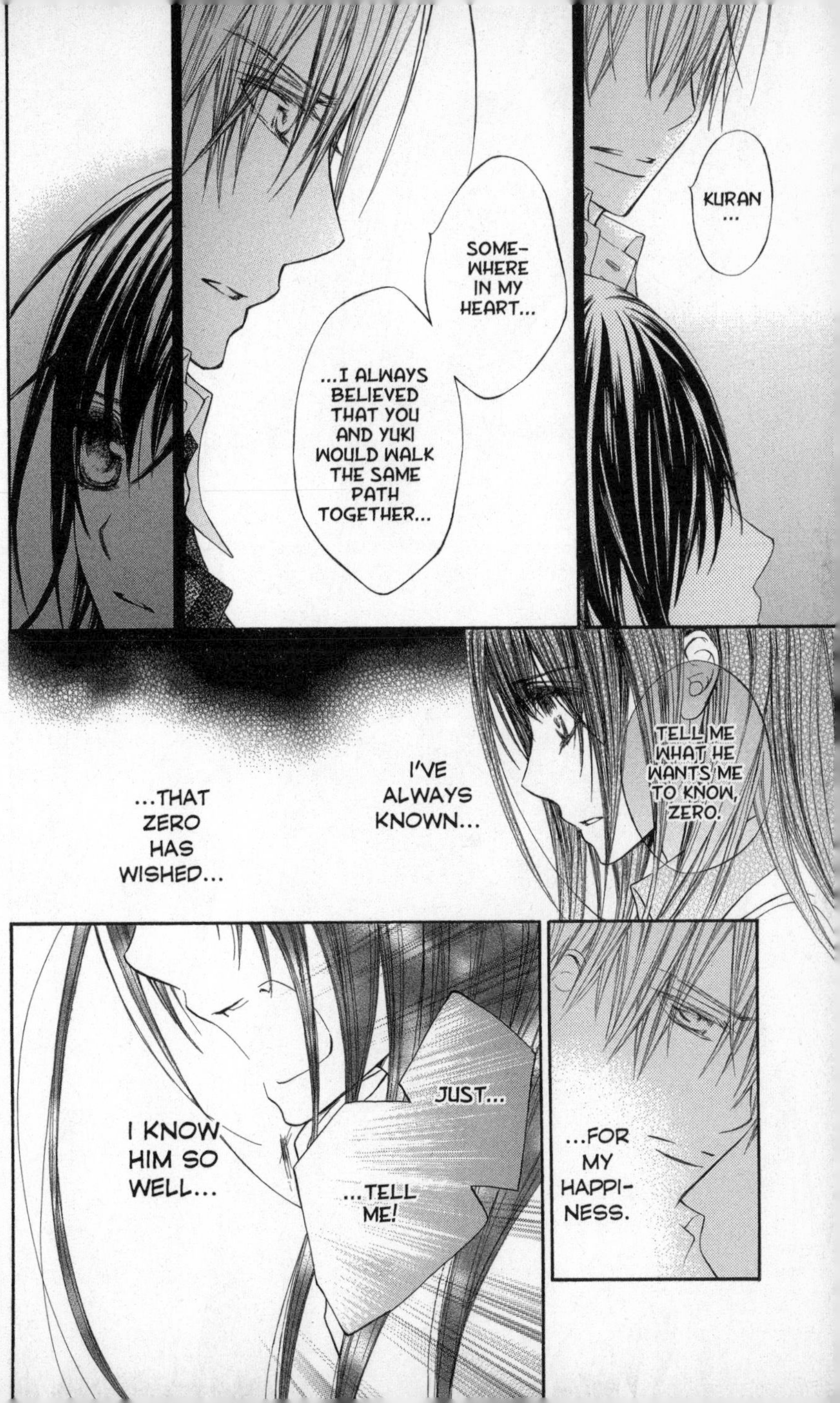
KURAN...
SOME-WHERE IN MY HEART...
...I ALWAYS BELIEVED THAT YOU AND YUKI WOULD WALK THE SAME PATH TOGETHER...
TELL ME WHAT HE WANTS ME TO KNOW, ZERO.
I'VE ALWAYS KNOWN...
...THAT ZERO HAS WISHED...
...FOR MY HAPPI-NESS.
JUST...
I KNOW HIM SO WELL...
...TELL ME!

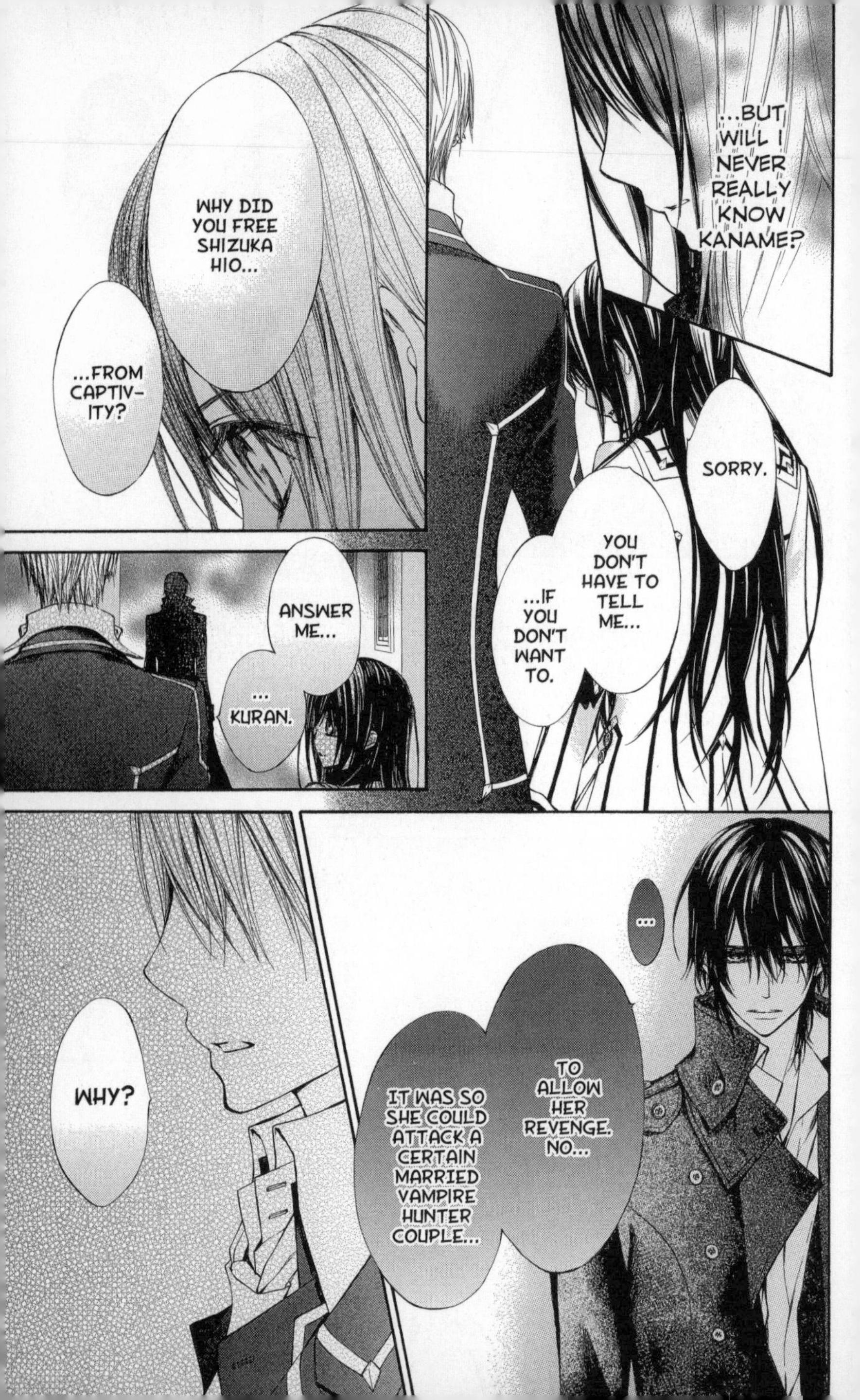
...BUT WILL I NEVER REALLY KNOW KANAME?
SORRY.
YOU DON'T HAVE TO TELL ME...
...IF YOU DON'T WANT TO.
WHY DID YOU FREE SHIZUKA HIO...
...FROM CAPTIV-ITY?
ANSWER ME...
... KURAN.
...
TO ALLOW HER REVENGE. NO...
IT WAS SO SHE COULD ATTACK A CERTAIN MARRIED VAMPIRE HUNTER COUPLE...
WHY?

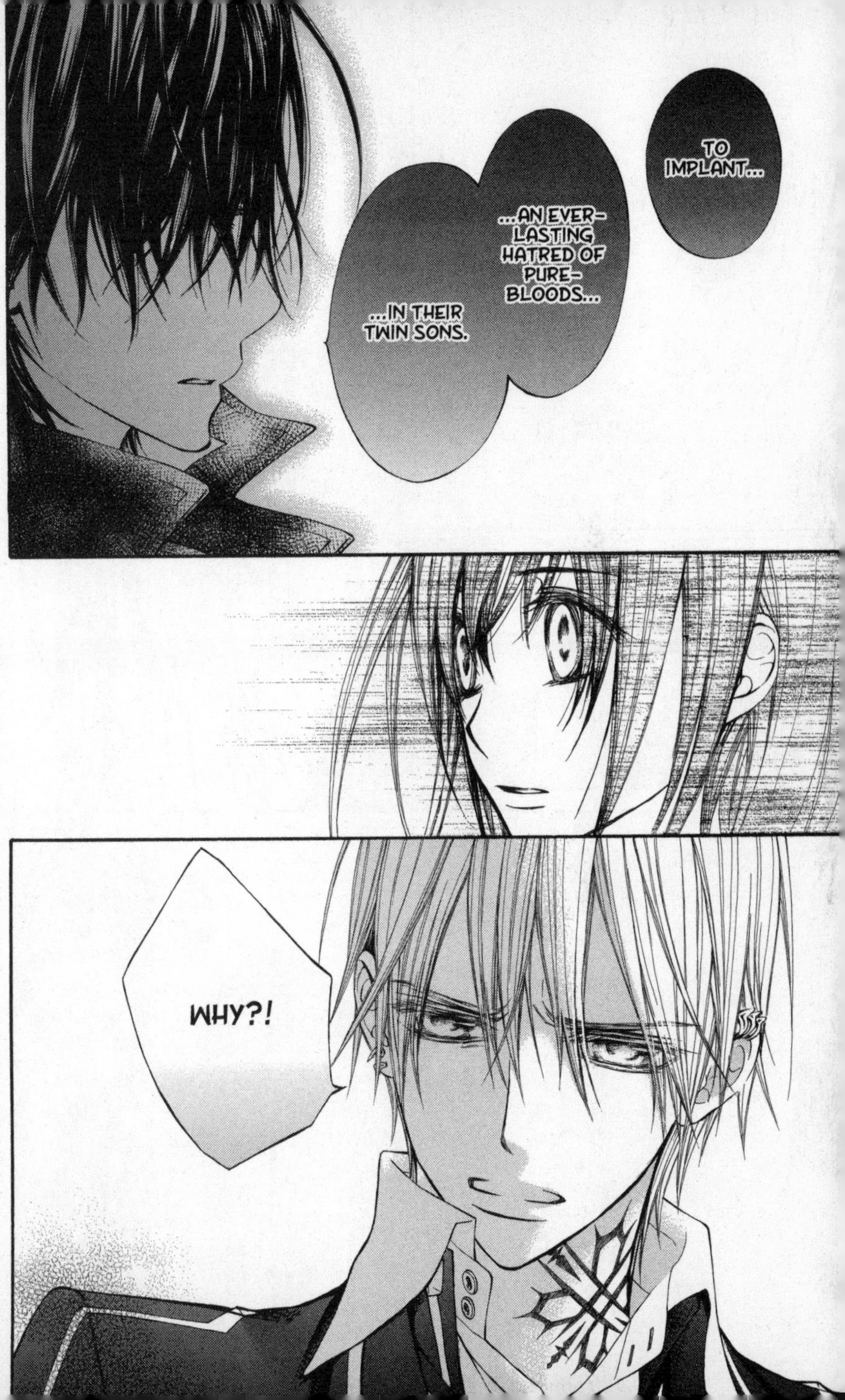
TO IMPLANT...
...AN EVER-LASTING HATRED OF PURE-BLOODS...
...IN THEIR TWIN SONS.
WHY?!

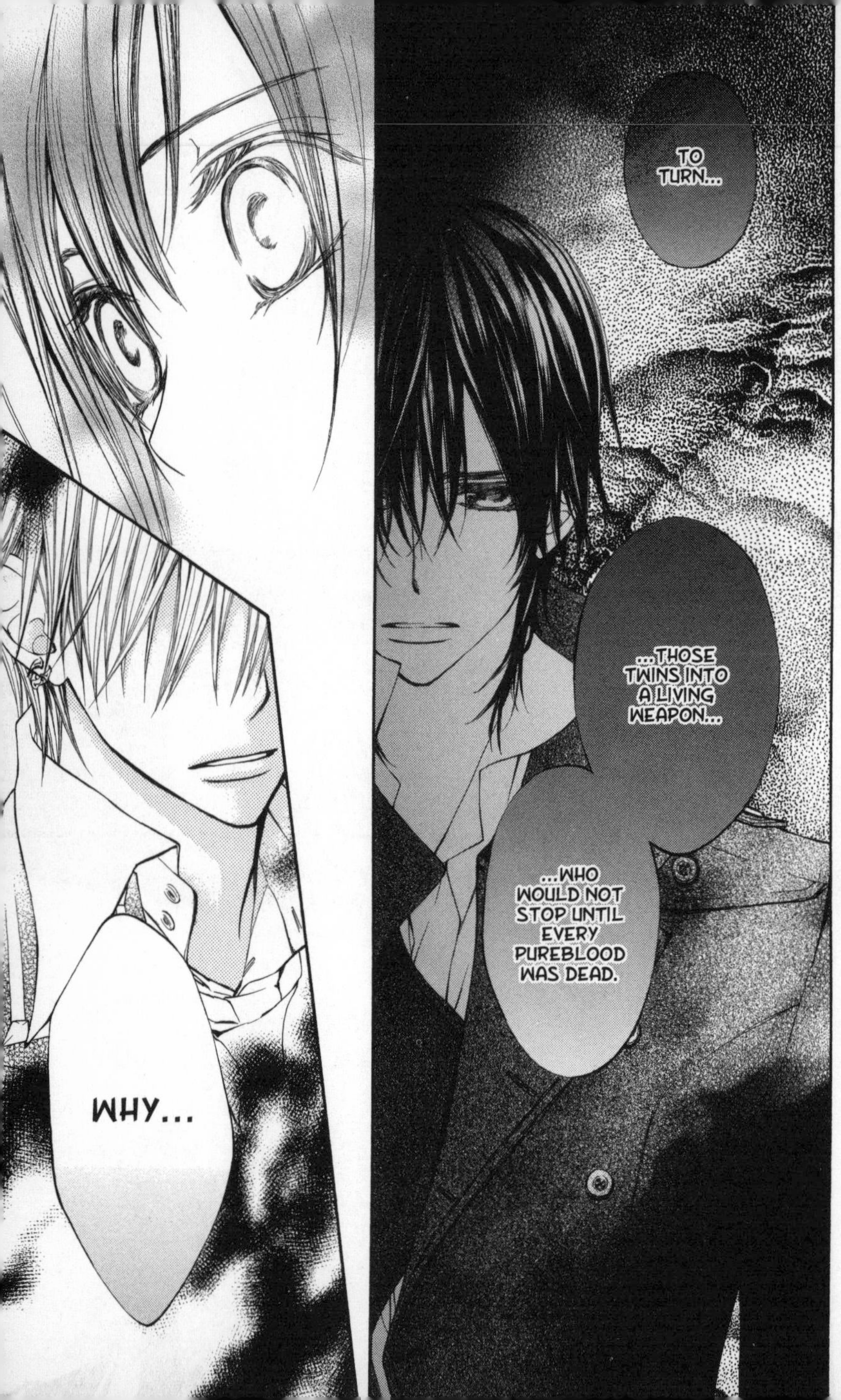
TO TURN...
...THOSE TWINS INTO A LIVING WEAPON...
...WHO WOULD NOT STOP UNTIL EVERY PUREBLOOD WAS DEAD.
WHY...

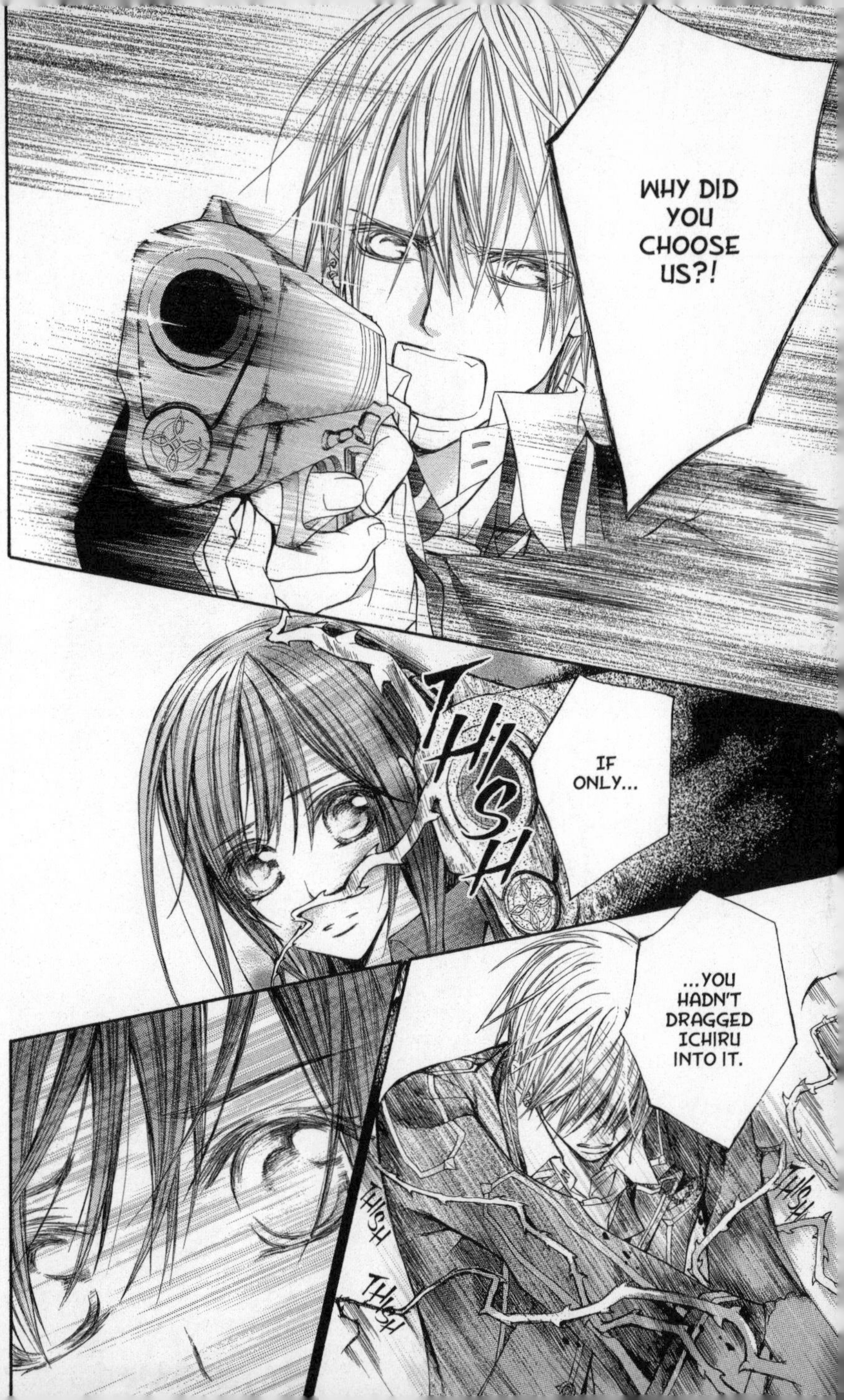
WHY DID YOU CHOOSE US?!
THISH
IF ONLY...
...YOU HADN'T DRAGGED ICHIRU INTO IT.
THISH
THISH
THISH

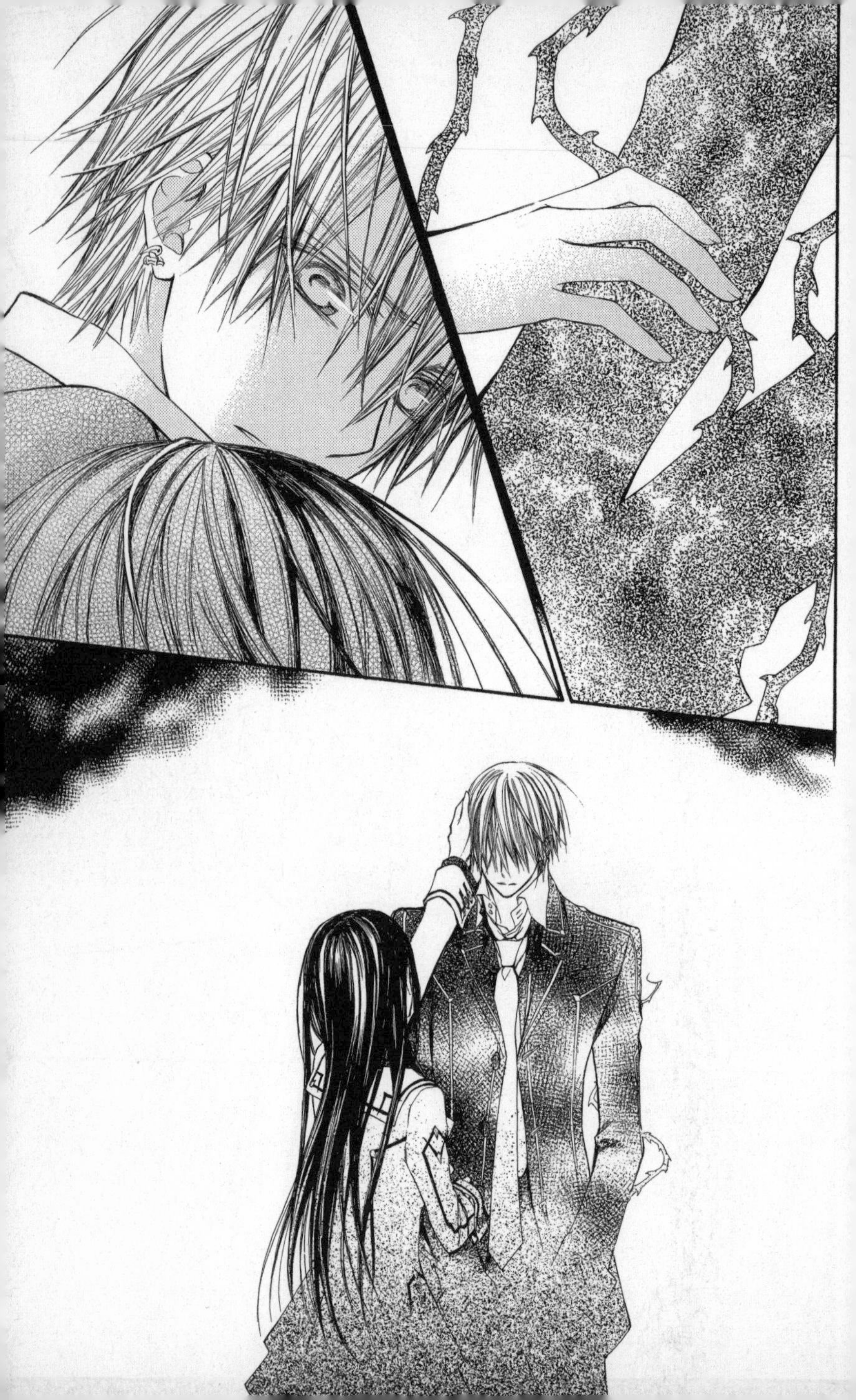

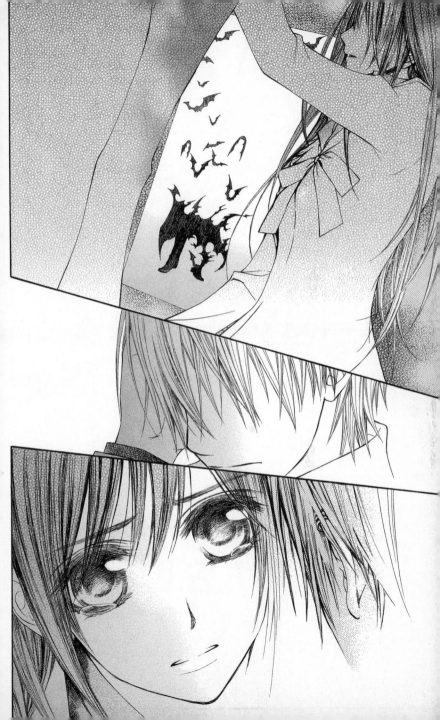

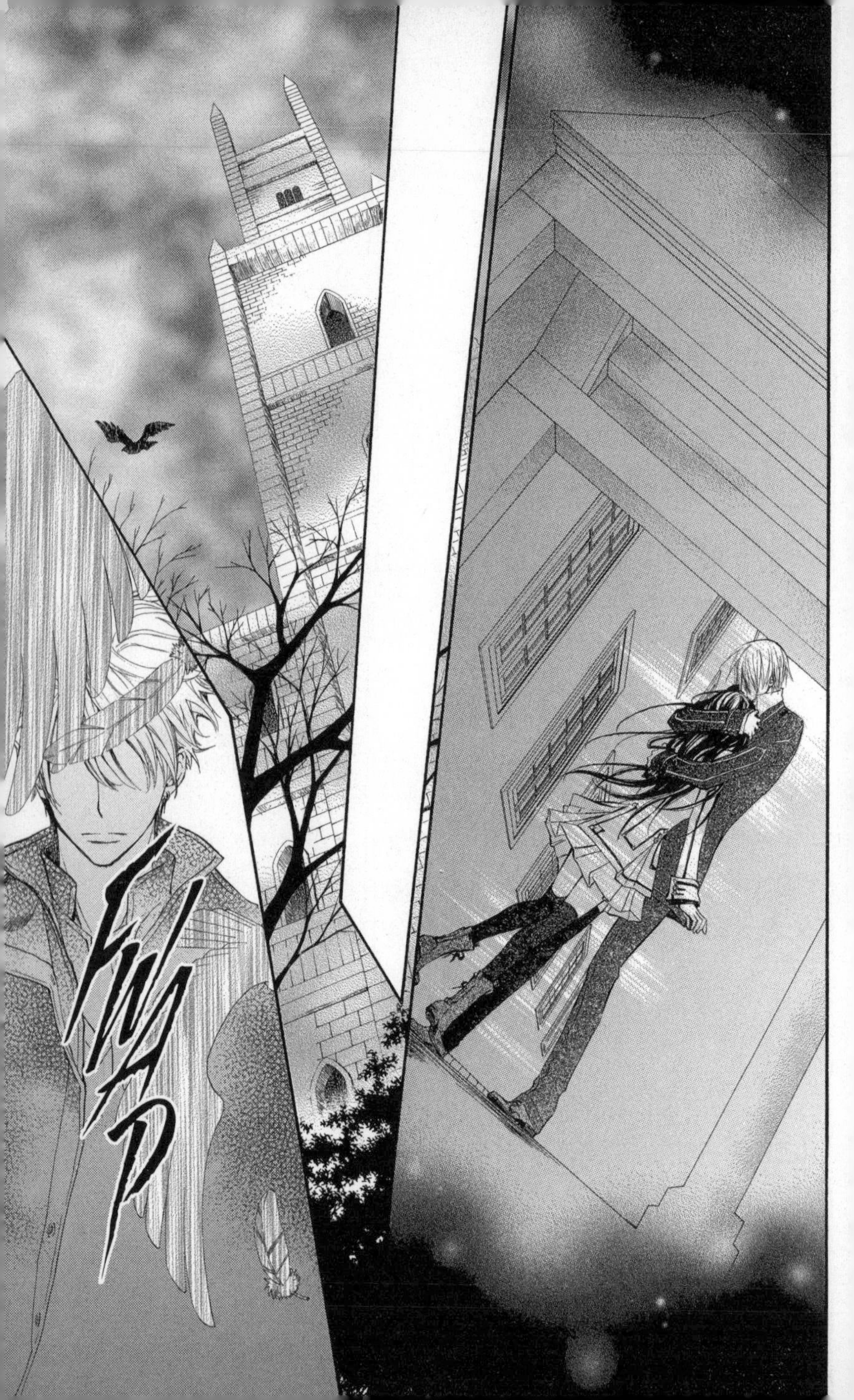
FLAP

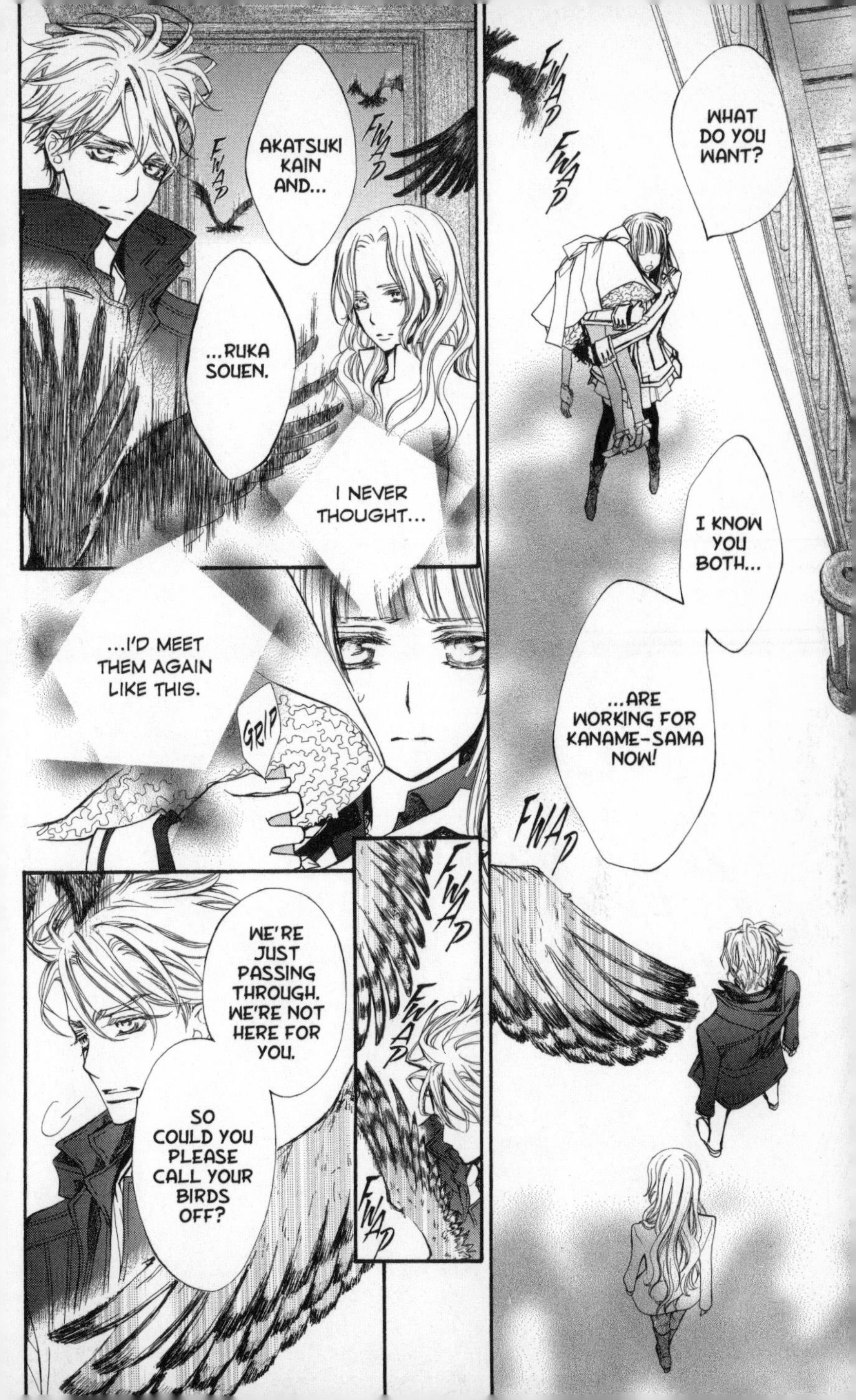
FWAP
FWAP
WHAT DO YOU WANT?
I KNOW YOU BOTH...
...ARE WORKING FOR KANAME-SAMA NOW!
FWAP
FWAP
AKATSUKI KAIN AND...
FWAP
...RUKA SOUEN.
I NEVER THOUGHT...
...I'D MEET THEM AGAIN LIKE THIS.
GRIP
FWAP
FWAP
FWAP
WE'RE JUST PASSING THROUGH. WE'RE NOT HERE FOR YOU.
SO COULD YOU PLEASE CALL YOUR BIRDS OFF?

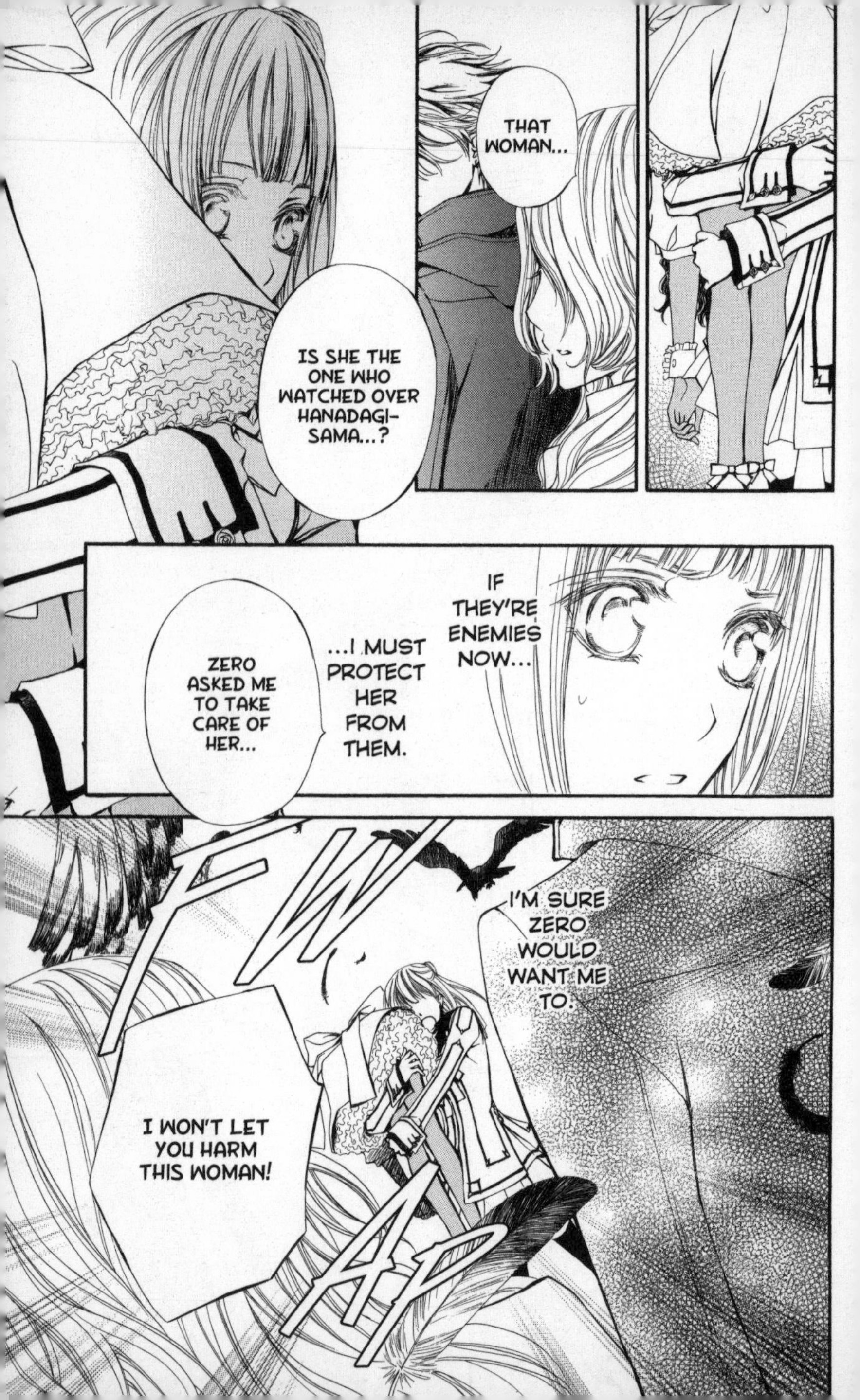
THAT WOMAN...
IS SHE THE ONE WHO WATCHED OVER HANADAGI-SAMA...?
IF THEY'RE ENEMIES NOW...
...I MUST PROTECT HER FROM THEM.
ZERO ASKED ME TO TAKE CARE OF HER...
I'M SURE ZERO WOULD WANT ME TO.
FWAP
I WON'T LET YOU HARM THIS WOMAN!

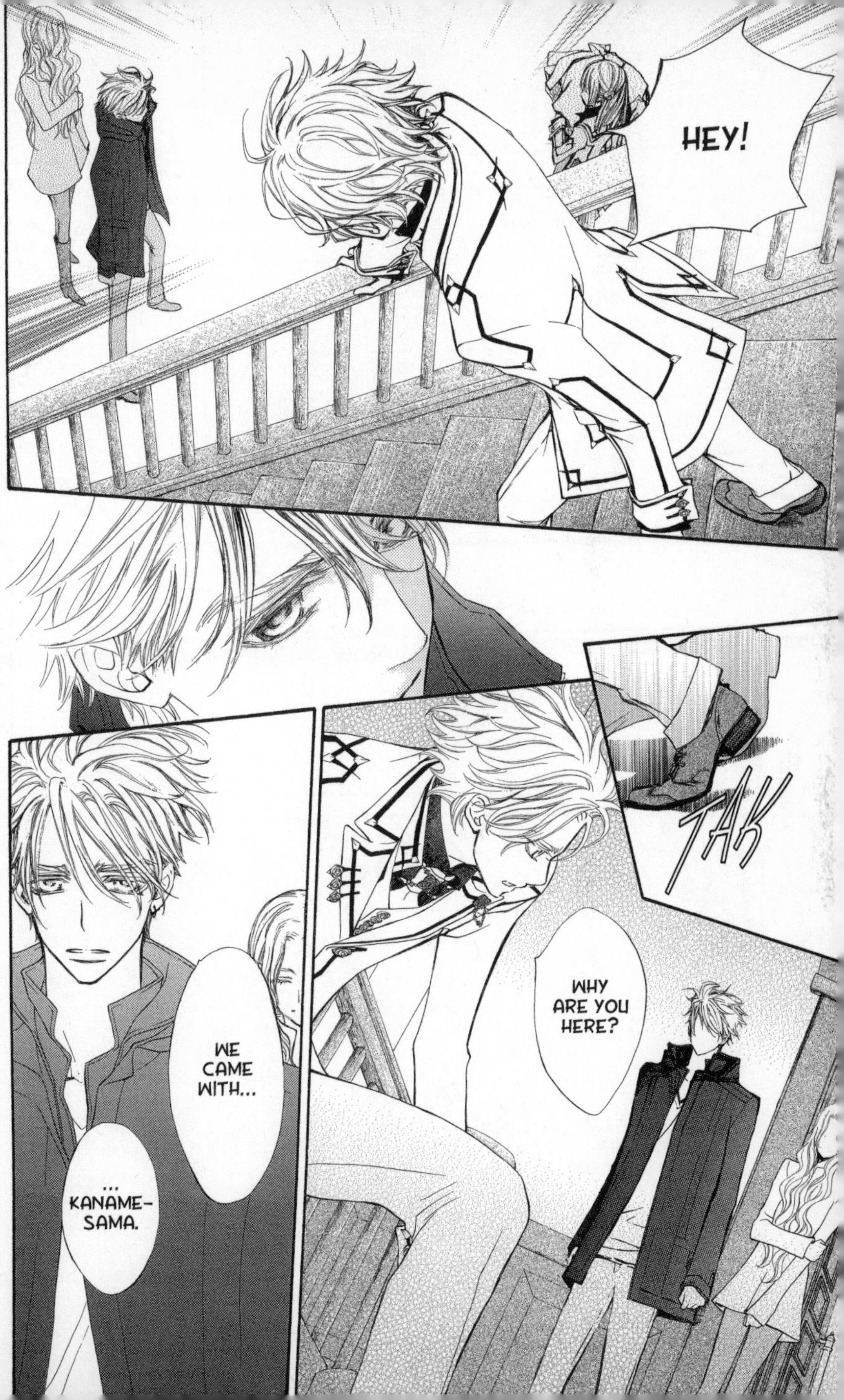
HEY!
TAK
WHY ARE YOU HERE?
WE CAME WITH...
...KANAME-SAMA.

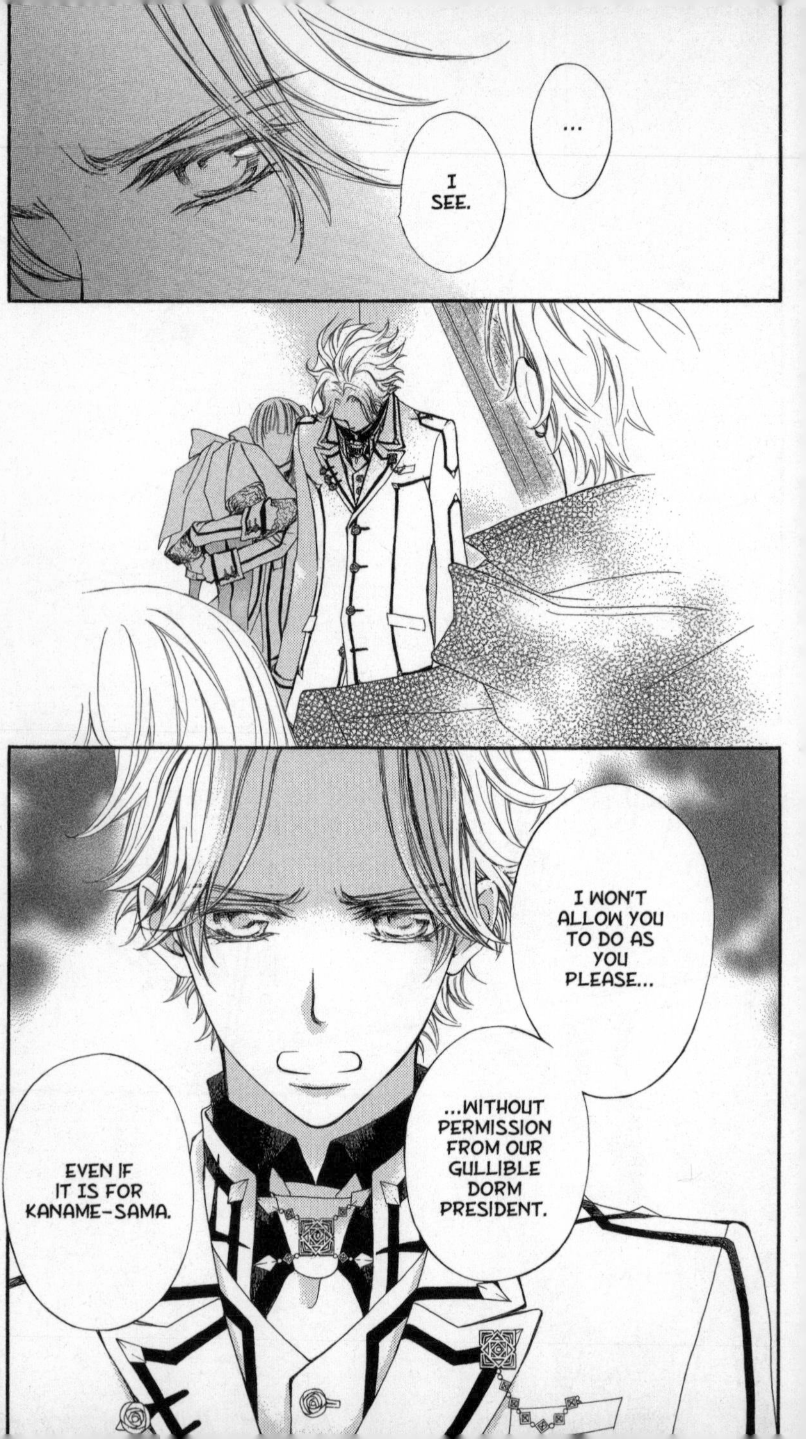
...
I SEE.
I WON'T ALLOW YOU TO DO AS YOU PLEASE...
...WITHOUT PERMISSION FROM OUR GULLIBLE DORM PRESIDENT.
EVEN IF IT IS FOR KANAME-SAMA.

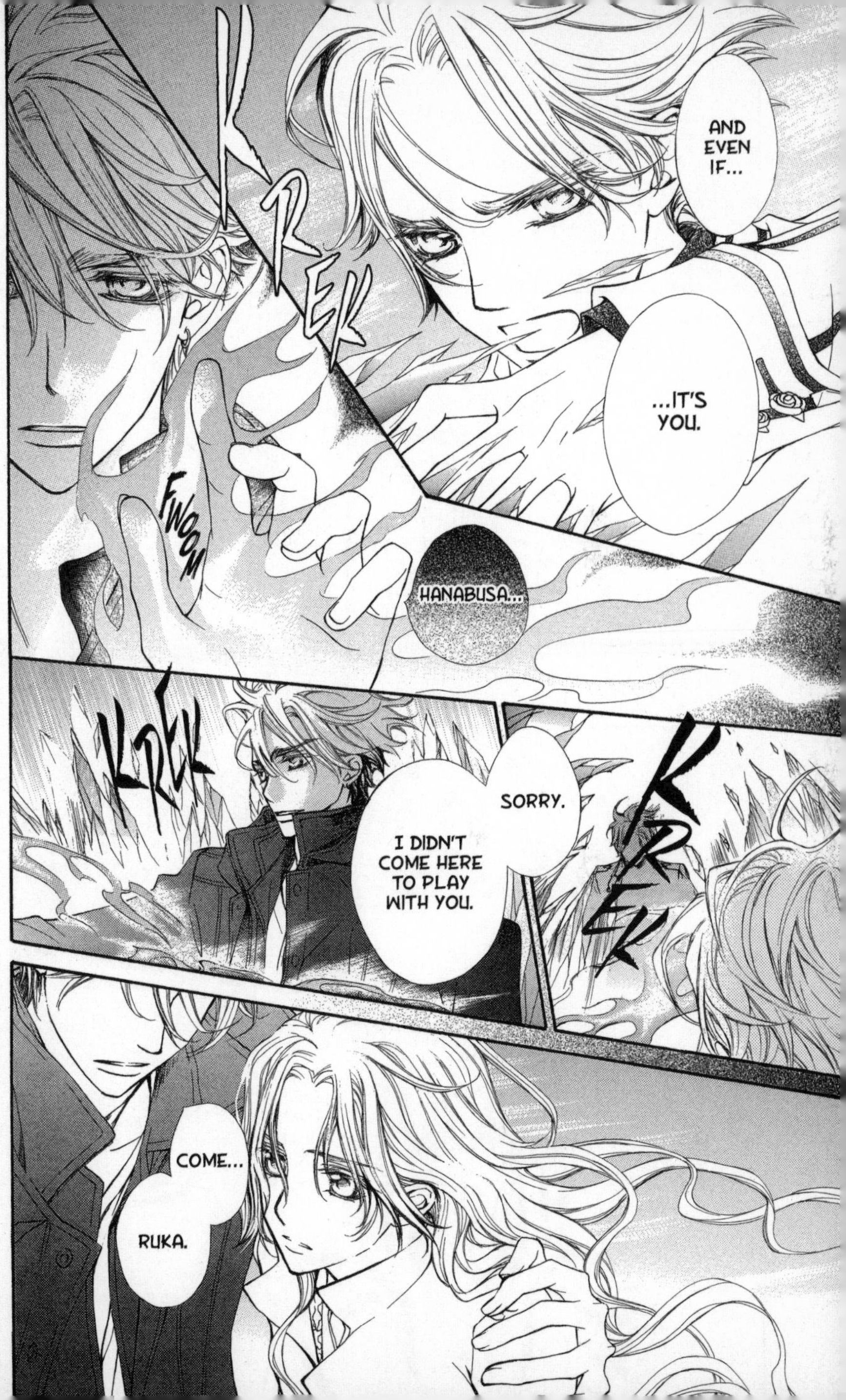
AND EVEN IF...
...IT'S YOU.
KREK
HANABUSA...
FWOOM
KREK
SORRY.
I DIDN'T COME HERE TO PLAY WITH YOU.
KREK
COME...
RUKA.

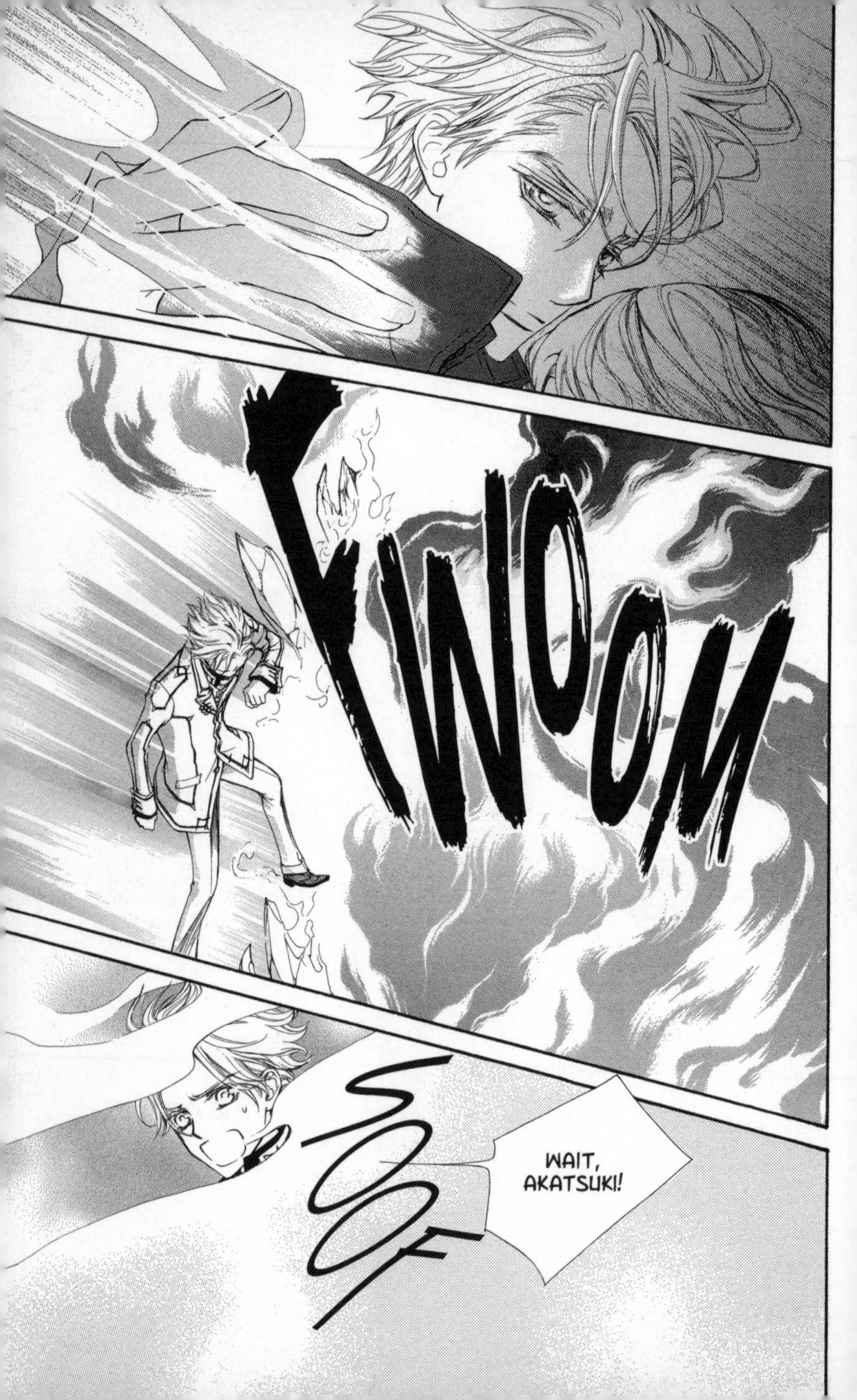
FWOOM
WAIT, AKATSUKI!
SWOOF

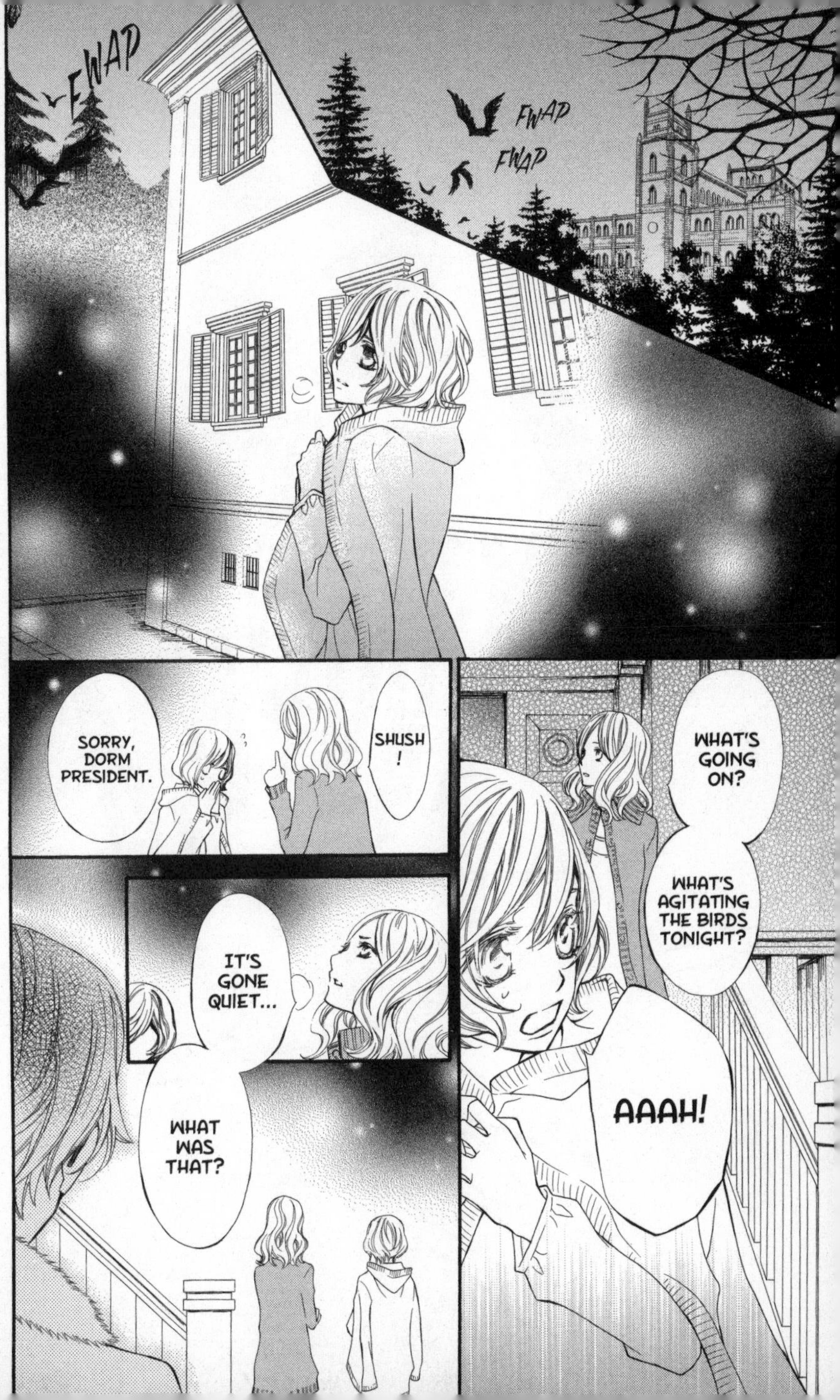
FWAP
FWAP
FWAP
WHAT'S GOING ON?
WHAT'S AGITATING THE BIRDS TONIGHT?
AAAH!
SHUSH!
SORRY, DORM PRESIDENT.
IT'S GONE QUIET...
WHAT WAS THAT?

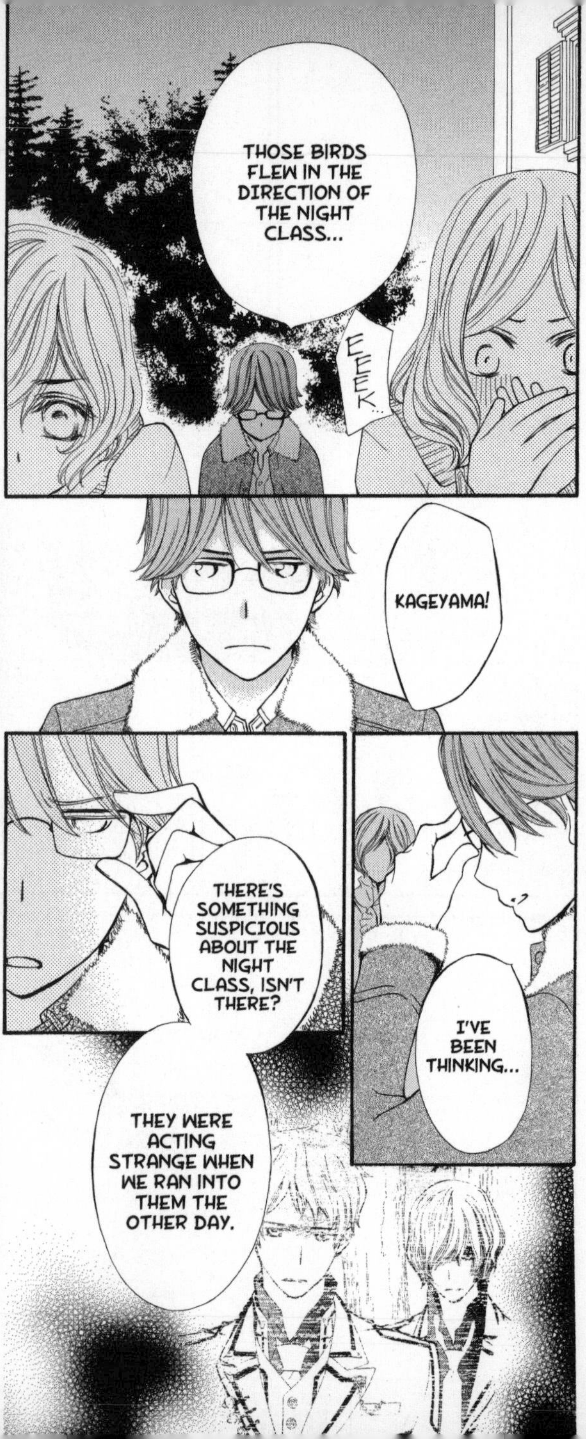
THOSE BIRDS FLEW IN THE DIRECTION OF THE NIGHT CLASS...
EEEK...
KAGEYAMA!
I'VE BEEN THINKING...
THERE'S SOMETHING SUSPICIOUS ABOUT THE NIGHT CLASS, ISN'T THERE?
THEY WERE ACTING STRANGE WHEN WE RAN INTO THEM THE OTHER DAY.

I

This is volume 17! Thank you for picking up this volume! The countdown for the final chapter of the series should be starting about now in LaLa magazine. To tell you the truth, the countdown already began inside me a while ago. After seeing the people around me working very hard, I too have been able to gather the strength I need to keep doing my best till the very end! There was quite a bit of room at end of this volume, but I wanted to channel all my energy into the end of this series, so I did not draw much bonus manga...

↓(continues)

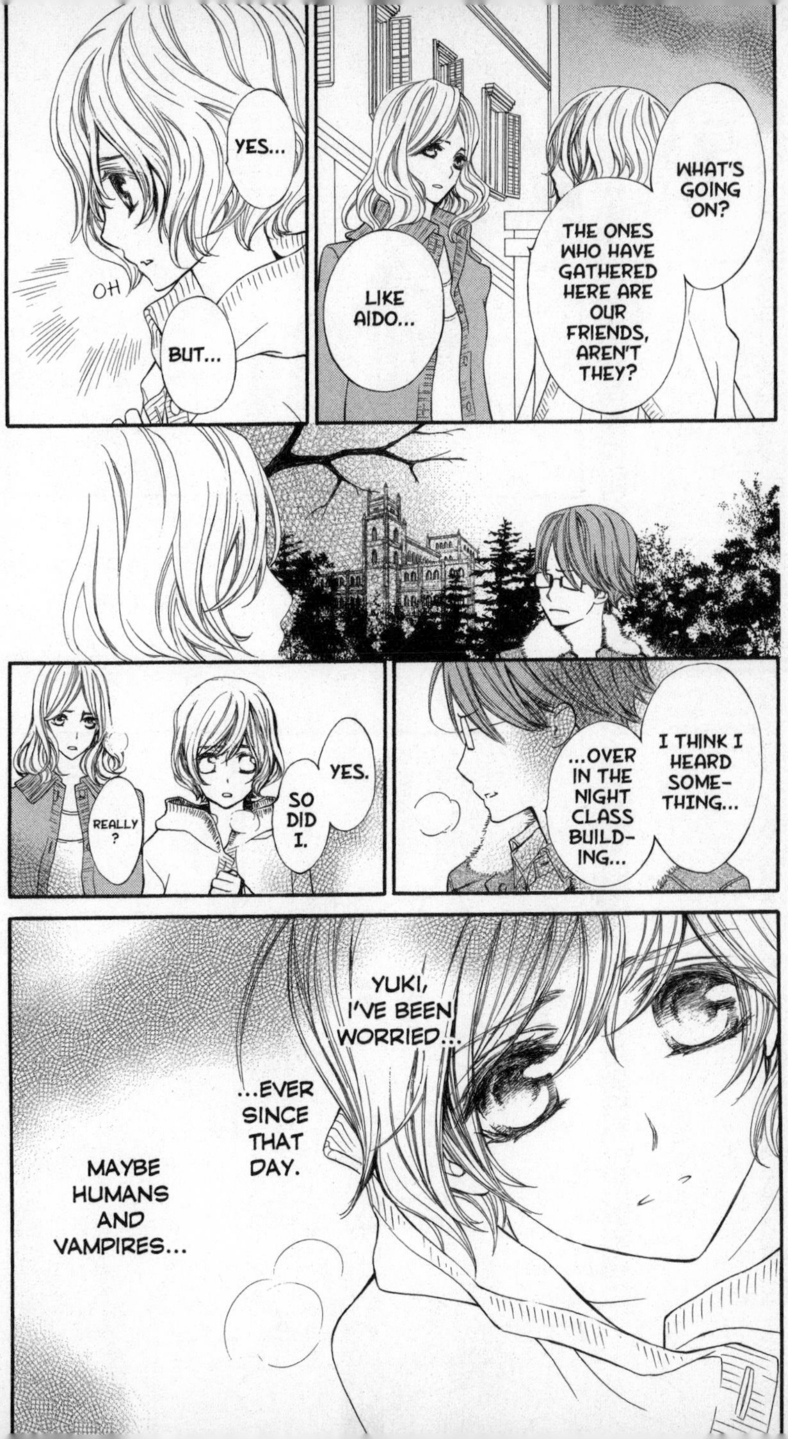
WHAT'S GOING ON?
THE ONES WHO HAVE GATHERED HERE ARE OUR FRIENDS, AREN'T THEY?
LIKE AIDO...
YES...
OH
BUT...
I THINK I HEARD SOME-THING...
...OVER IN THE NIGHT CLASS BUILD-ING...
YES.
SO DID I.
REALLY?
YUKI, I'VE BEEN WORRIED...
...EVER SINCE THAT DAY.
MAYBE HUMANS AND VAMPIRES...

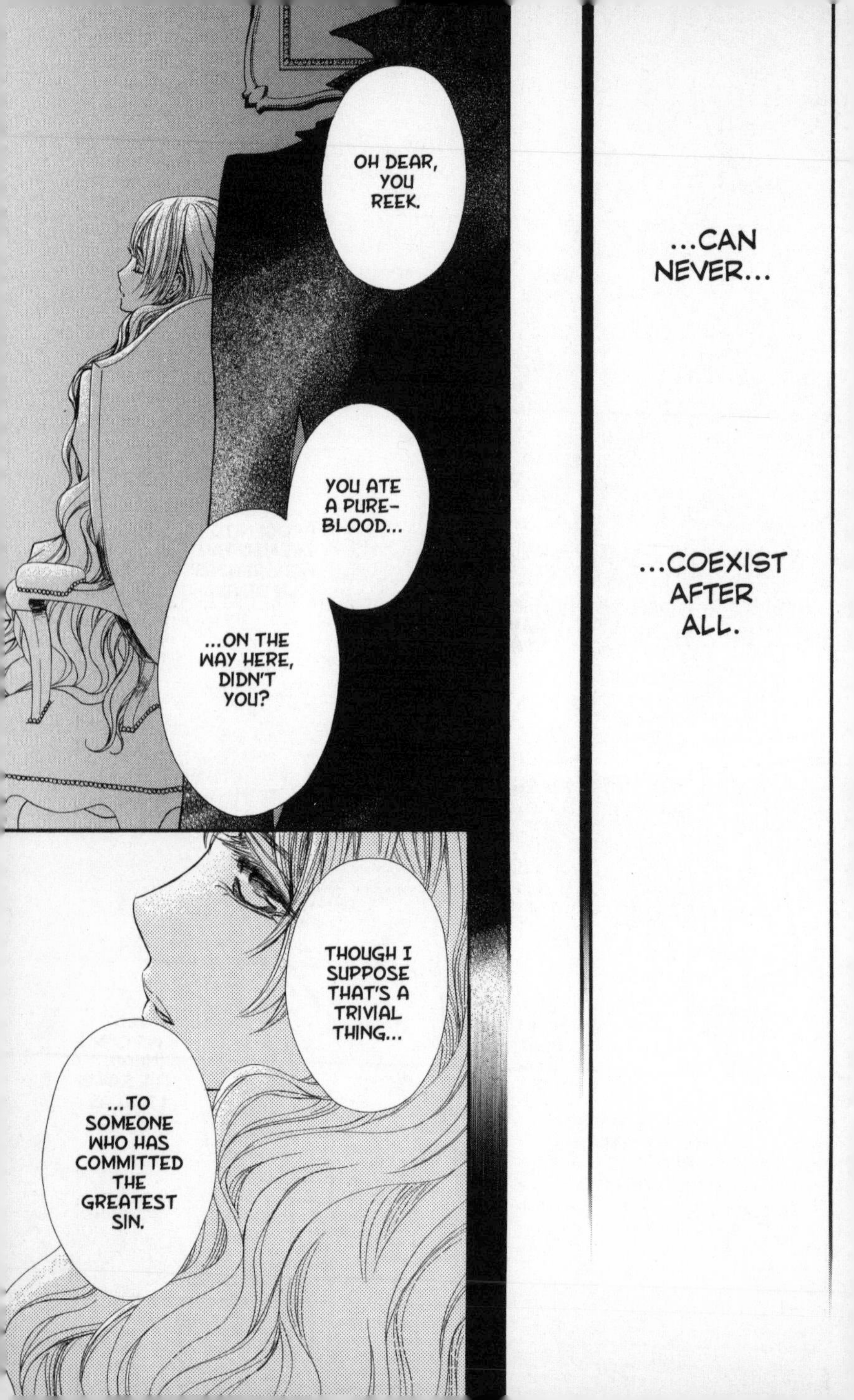
...CAN NEVER...
...COEXIST AFTER ALL.
OH DEAR, YOU REEK.
YOU ATE A PURE-BLOOD...
...ON THE WAY HERE, DIDN'T YOU?
THOUGH I SUPPOSE THAT'S A TRIVIAL THING...
...TO SOMEONE WHO HAS COMMITTED THE GREATEST SIN.

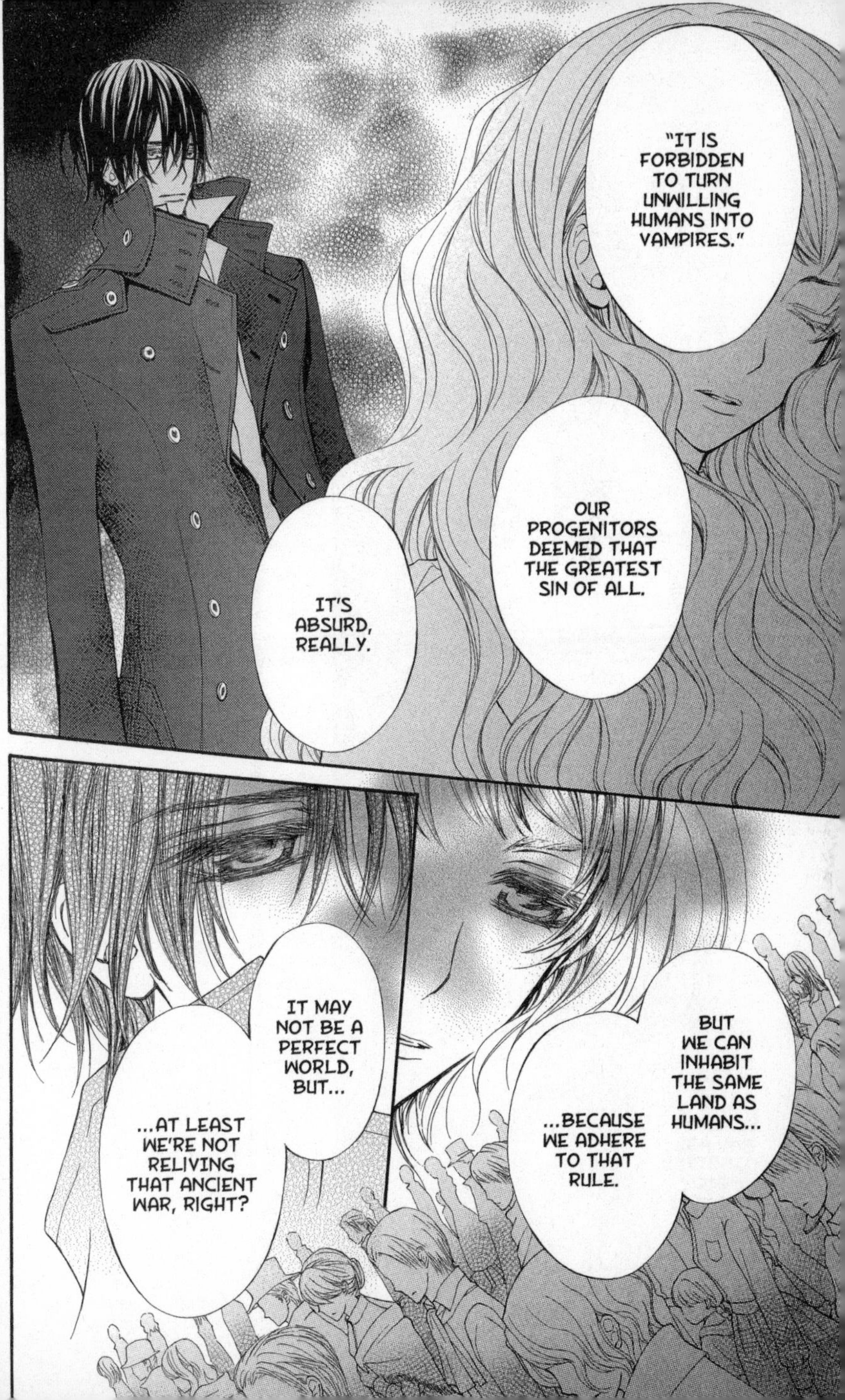
"IT IS FORBIDDEN TO TURN UNWILLING HUMANS INTO VAMPIRES."
OUR PROGENITORS DEEMED THAT THE GREATEST SIN OF ALL.
IT'S ABSURD, REALLY.
BUT WE CAN INHABIT THE SAME LAND AS HUMANS...
...BECAUSE WE ADHERE TO THAT RULE.
IT MAY NOT BE A PERFECT WORLD, BUT...
...AT LEAST WE'RE NOT RELIVING THAT ANCIENT WAR, RIGHT?

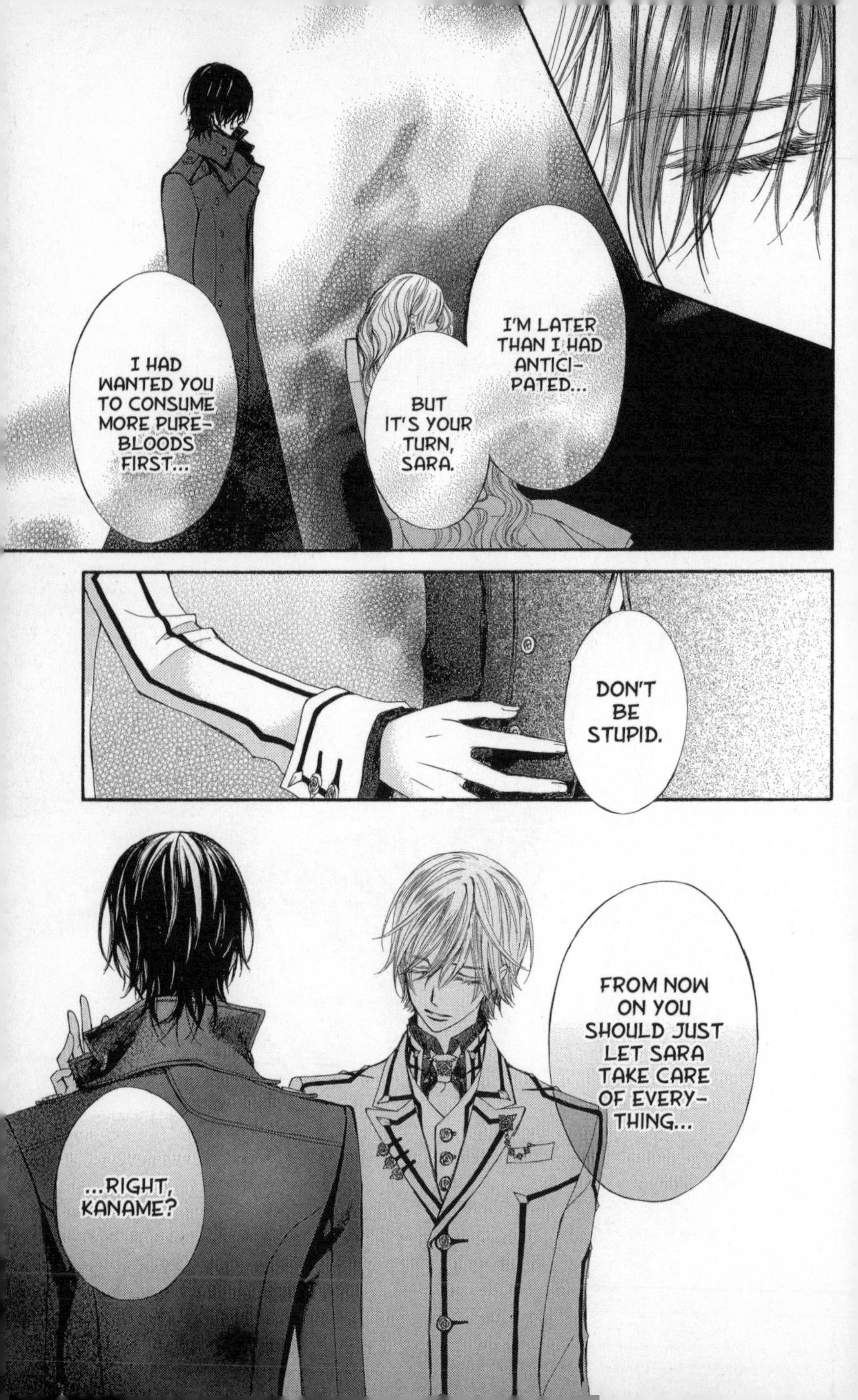
I'M LATER THAN I HAD ANTICI-PATED...
BUT IT'S YOUR TURN, SARA.
I HAD WANTED YOU TO CONSUME MORE PURE-BLOODS FIRST...
DON'T BE STUPID.
FROM NOW ON YOU SHOULD JUST LET SARA TAKE CARE OF EVERY-THING...
...RIGHT, KANAME?

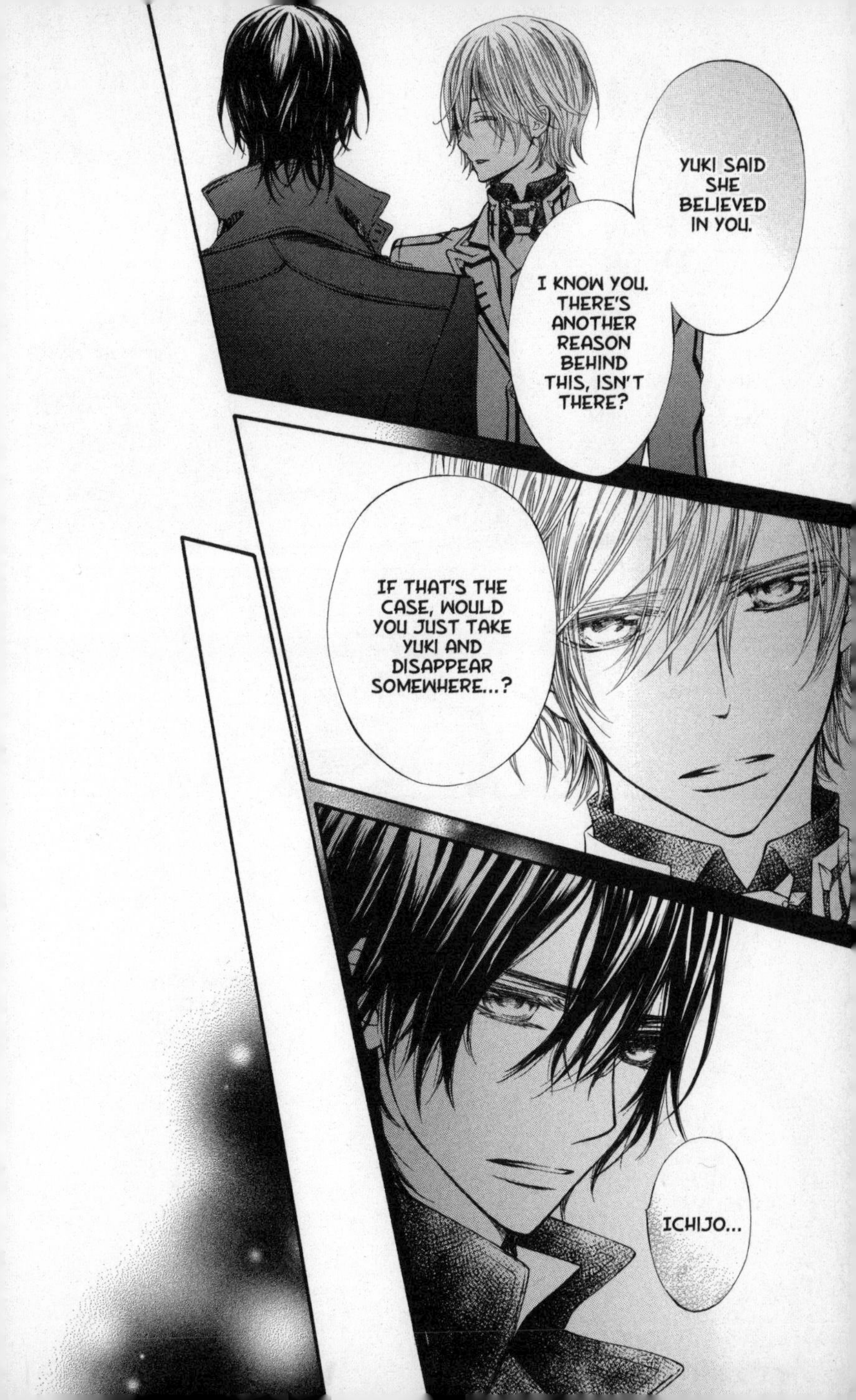

YUKI SAID SHE BELIEVED IN YOU.
I KNOW YOU. THERE'S ANOTHER REASON BEHIND THIS, ISN'T THERE?
IF THAT'S THE CASE, WOULD YOU JUST TAKE YUKI AND DISAPPEAR SOMEWHERE...?
ICHIJO...

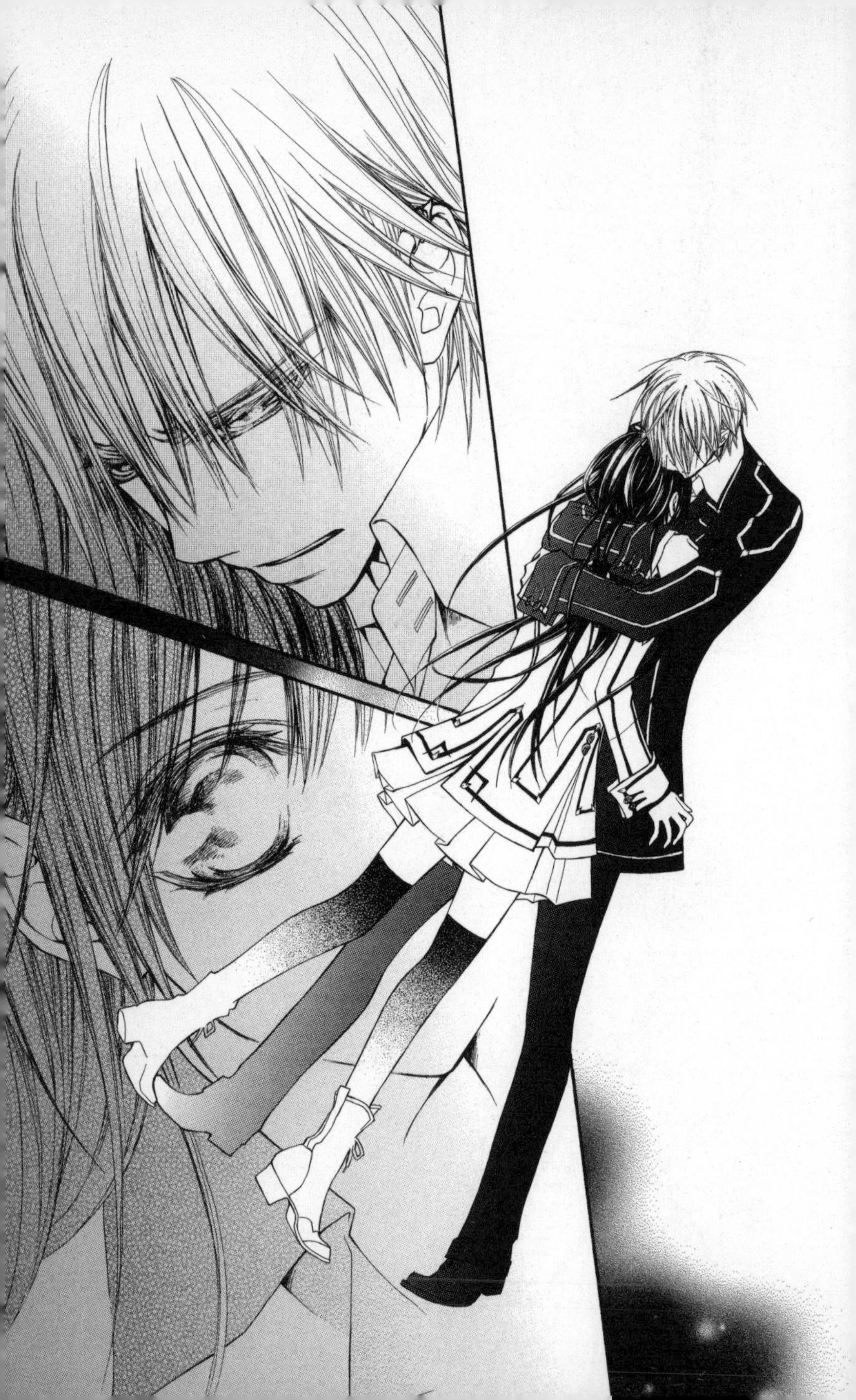

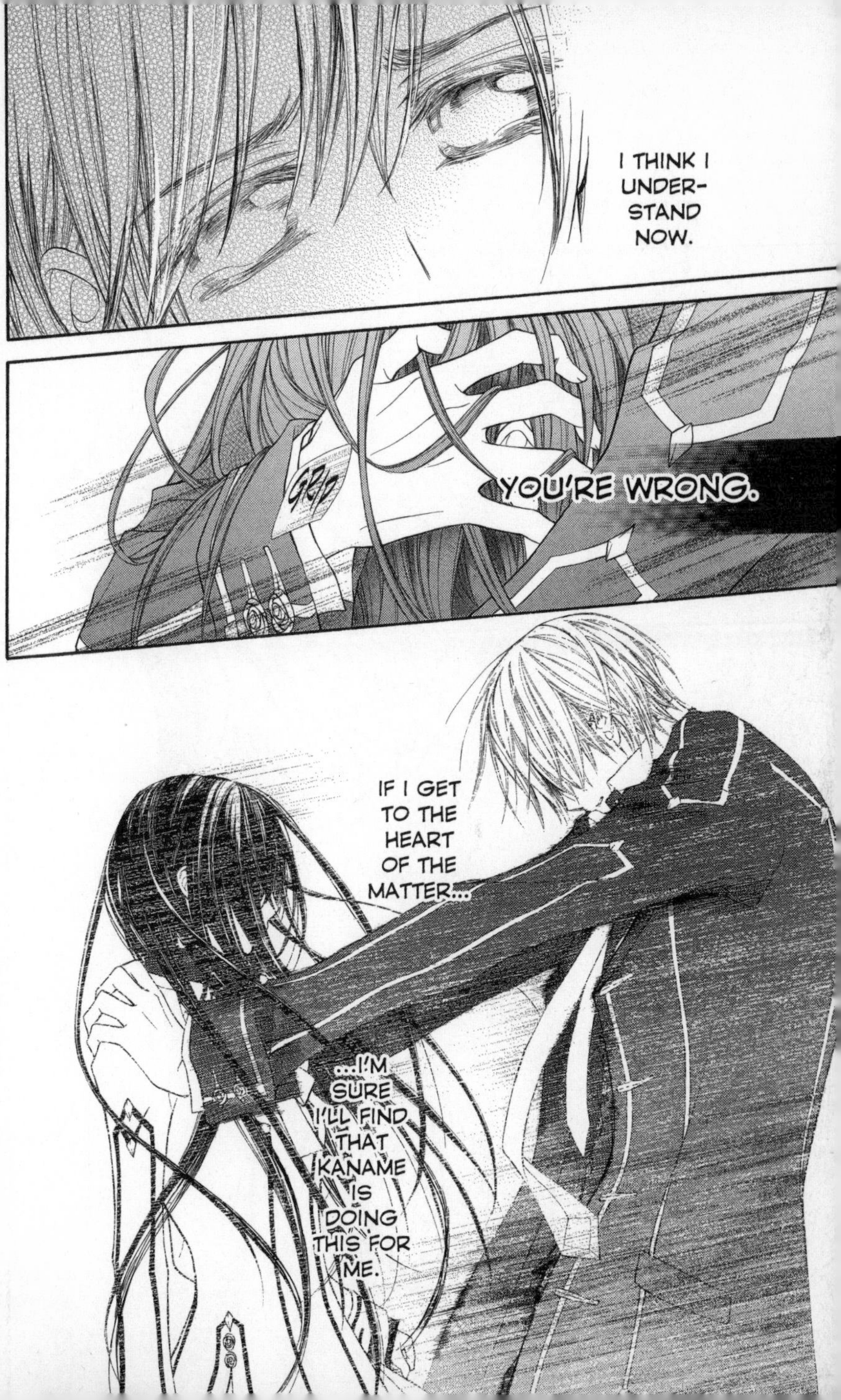
I THINK I UNDERSTAND NOW.
YOU'RE WRONG.
IF I GET TO THE HEART OF THE MATTER...
...I'M SURE I'LL FIND THAT KANAME IS DOING THIS FOR ME.

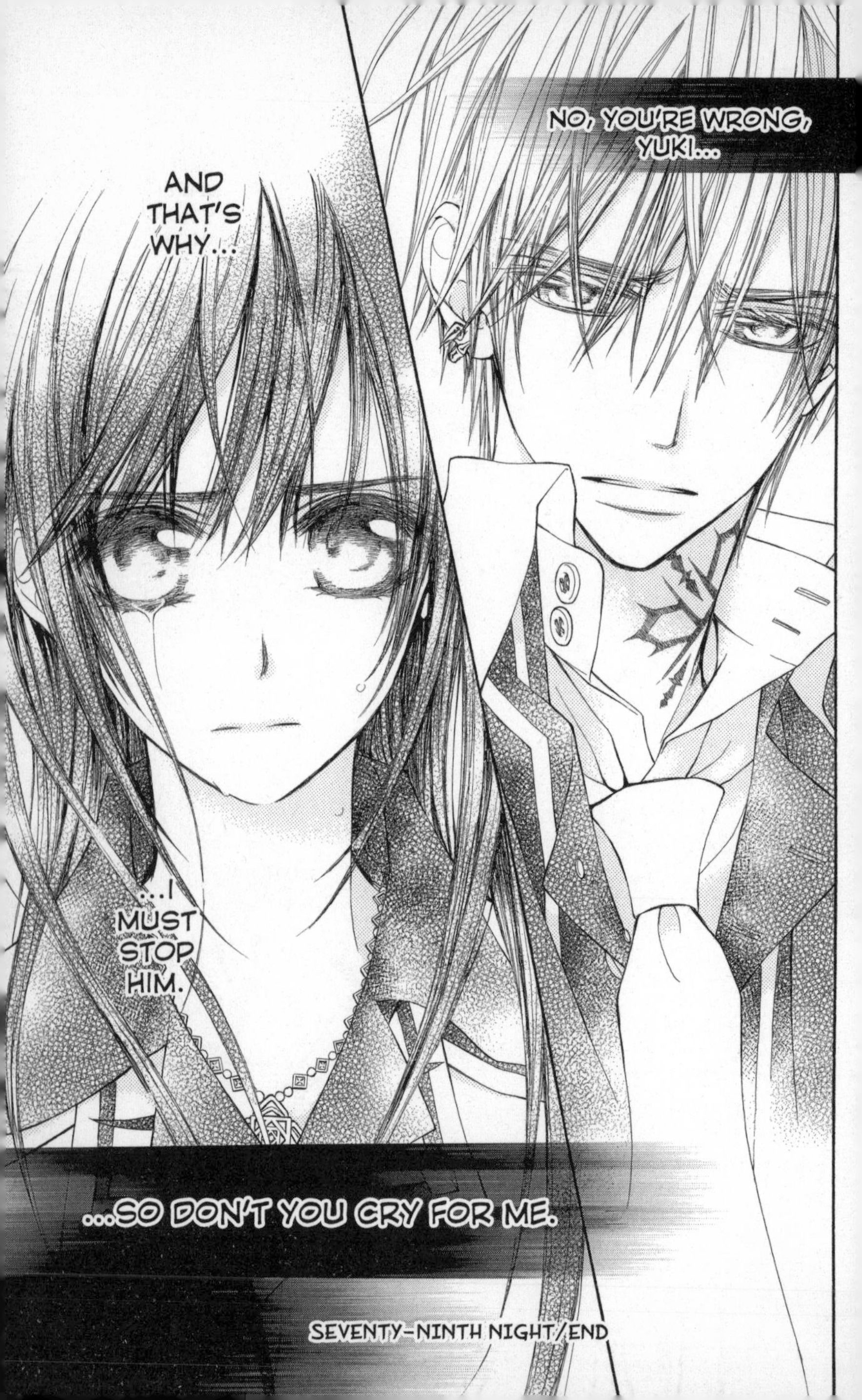
NO, YOU'RE WRONG, YUKI...
AND THAT'S WHY...
...I MUST STOP HIM.
...SO DON'T YOU CRY FOR ME.
SEVENTY-NINTH NIGHT/END

FLUT

I'VE
ALWAYS
WANTED
TO CATCH
ONE. ♡

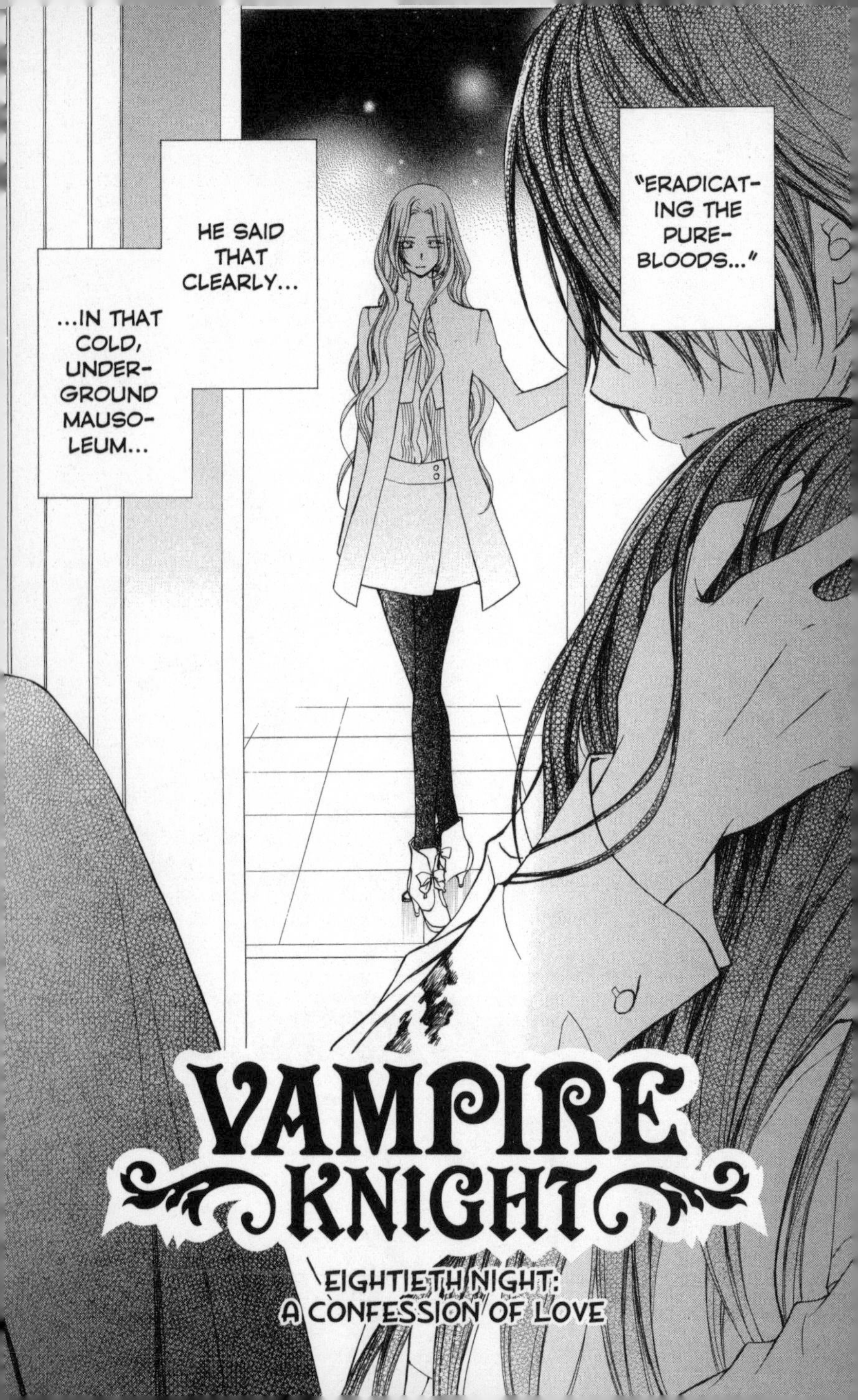
"ERADICATING THE PURE-BLOODS..."
HE SAID THAT CLEARLY...
...IN THAT COLD, UNDERGROUND MAUSOLEUM...
VAMPIRE KNIGHT
EIGHTIETH NIGHT: A CONFESSION OF LOVE

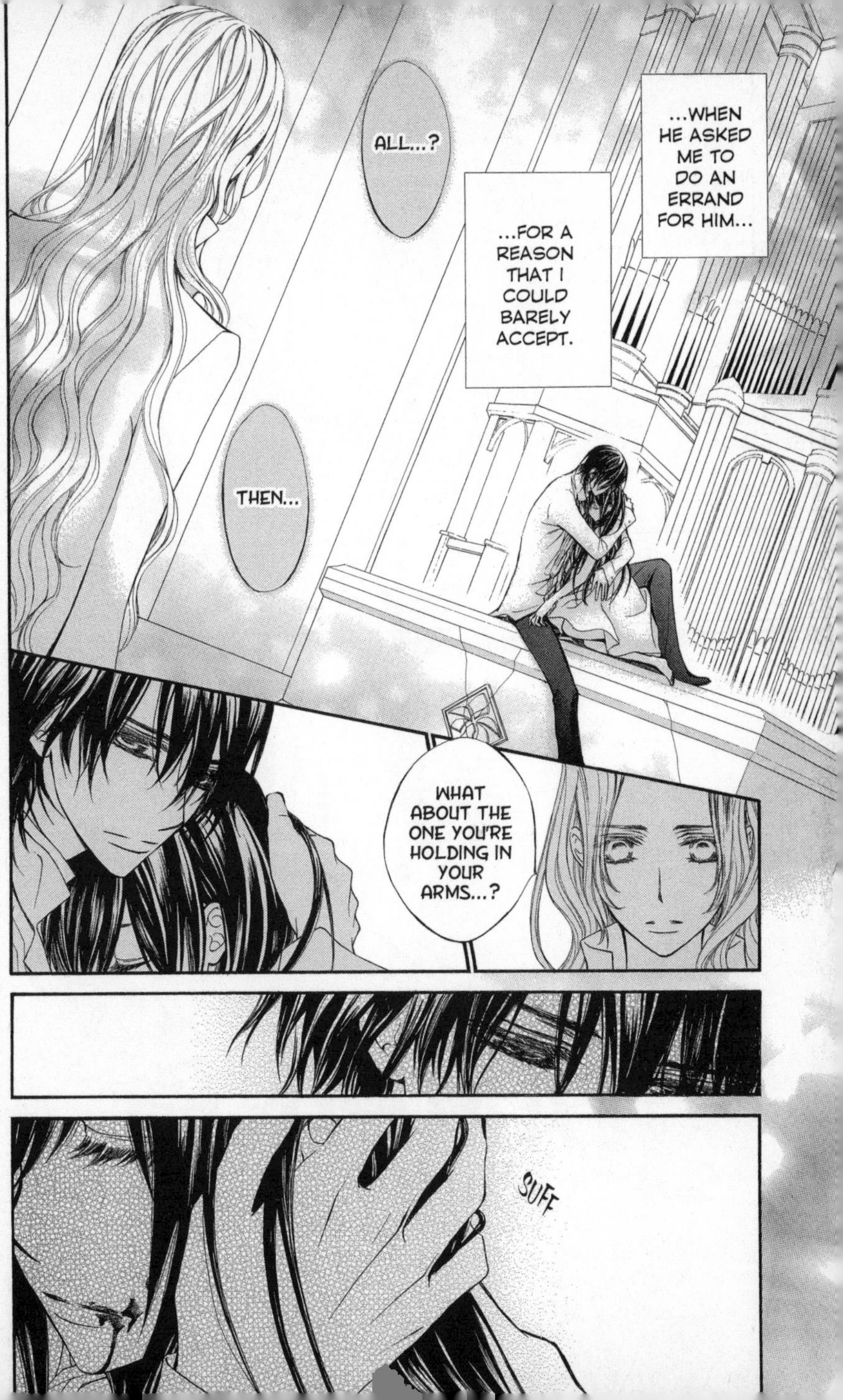
...WHEN HE ASKED ME TO DO AN ERRAND FOR HIM...
...FOR A REASON THAT I COULD BARELY ACCEPT.
ALL...?
THEN...
WHAT ABOUT THE ONE YOU'RE HOLDING IN YOUR ARMS...?
SUFF

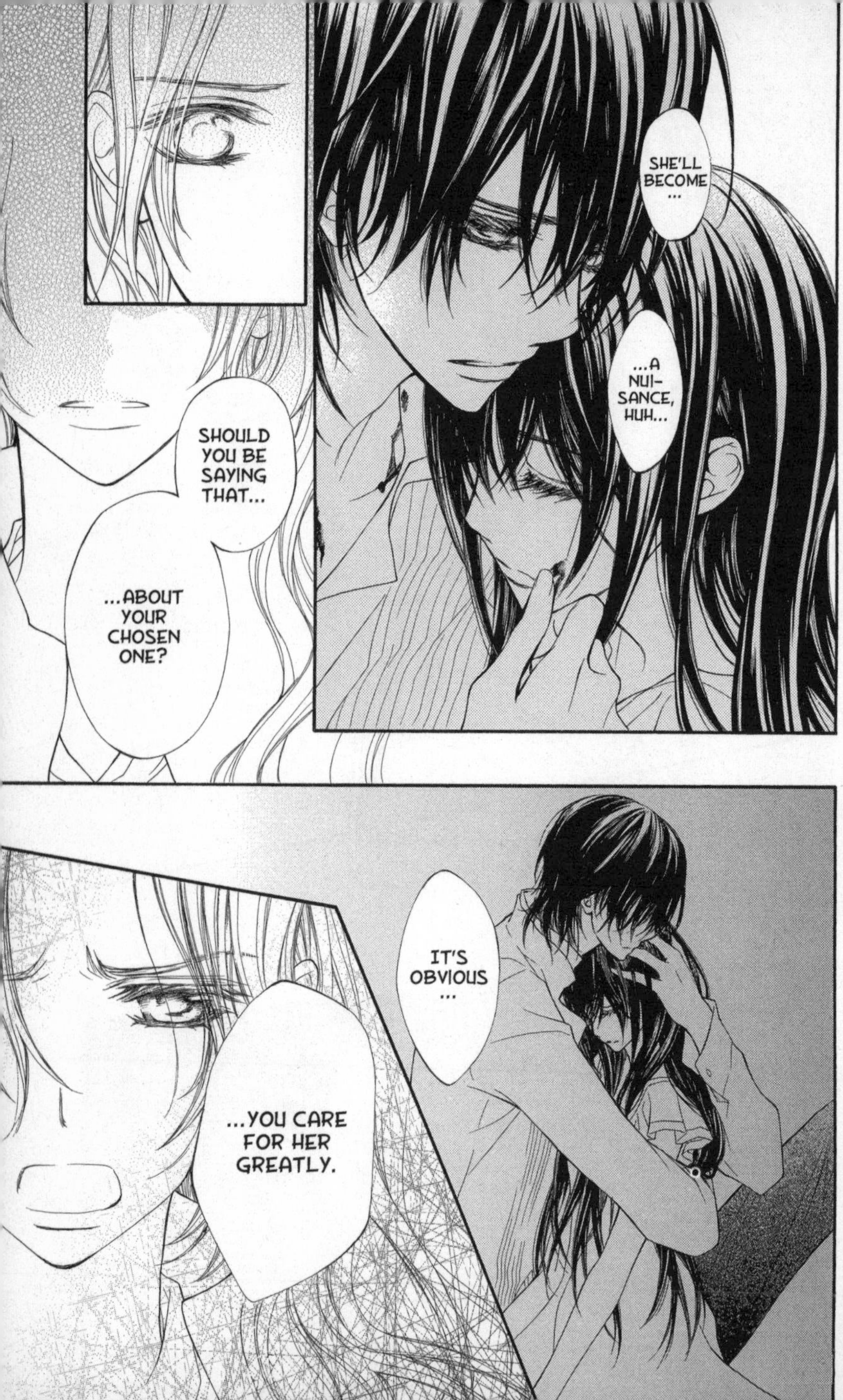
SHE'LL BECOME ...
...A NUI-SANCE, HUH...
SHOULD YOU BE SAYING THAT...
...ABOUT YOUR CHOSEN ONE?
IT'S OBVIOUS ...
...YOU CARE FOR HER GREATLY.

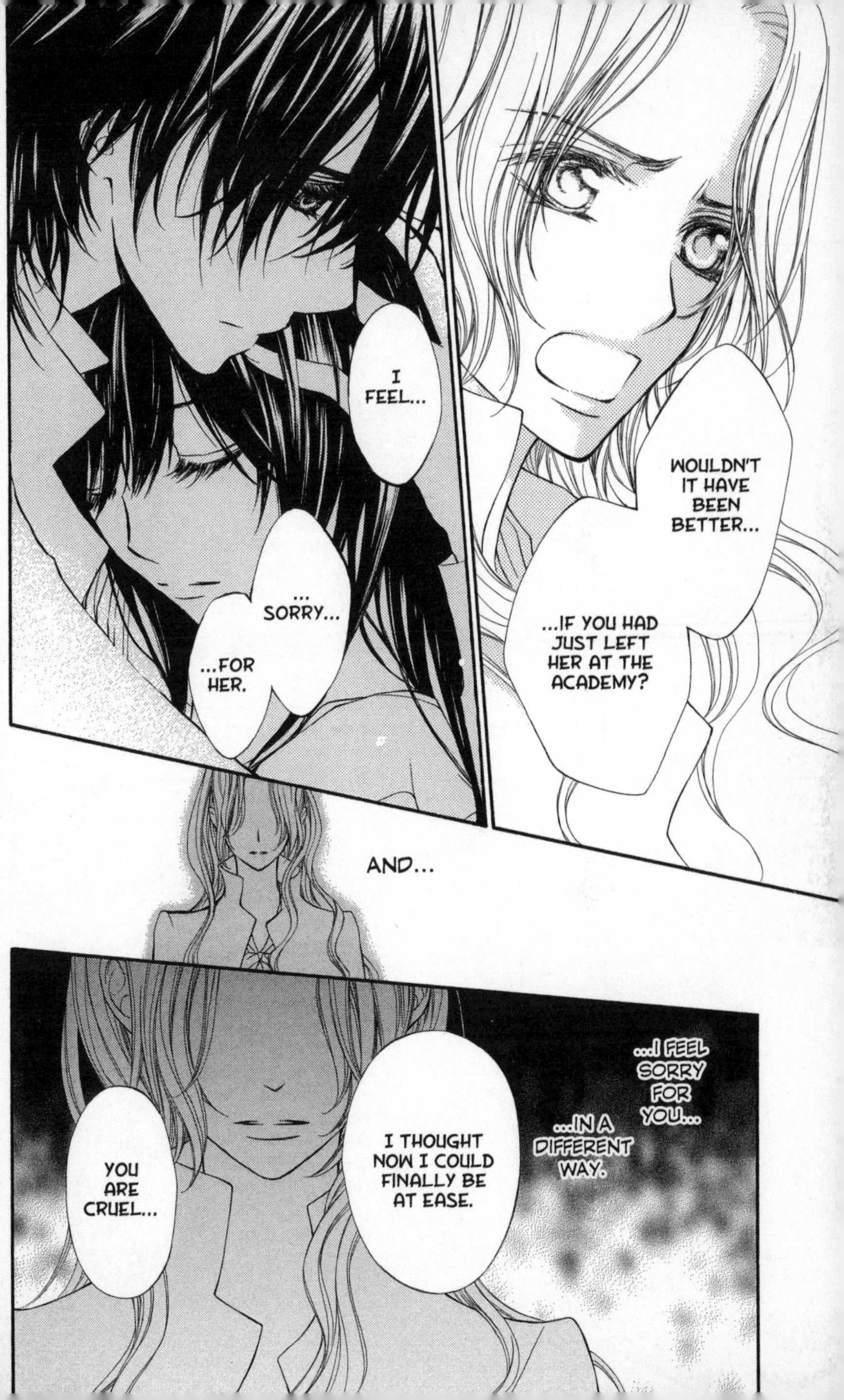
WOULDN'T IT HAVE BEEN BETTER...
...IF YOU HAD JUST LEFT HER AT THE ACADEMY?
I FEEL...
... SORRY...
...FOR HER.
AND...
...I FEEL SORRY FOR YOU...
...IN A DIFFERENT WAY.
I THOUGHT NOW I COULD FINALLY BE AT EASE.
YOU ARE CRUEL...

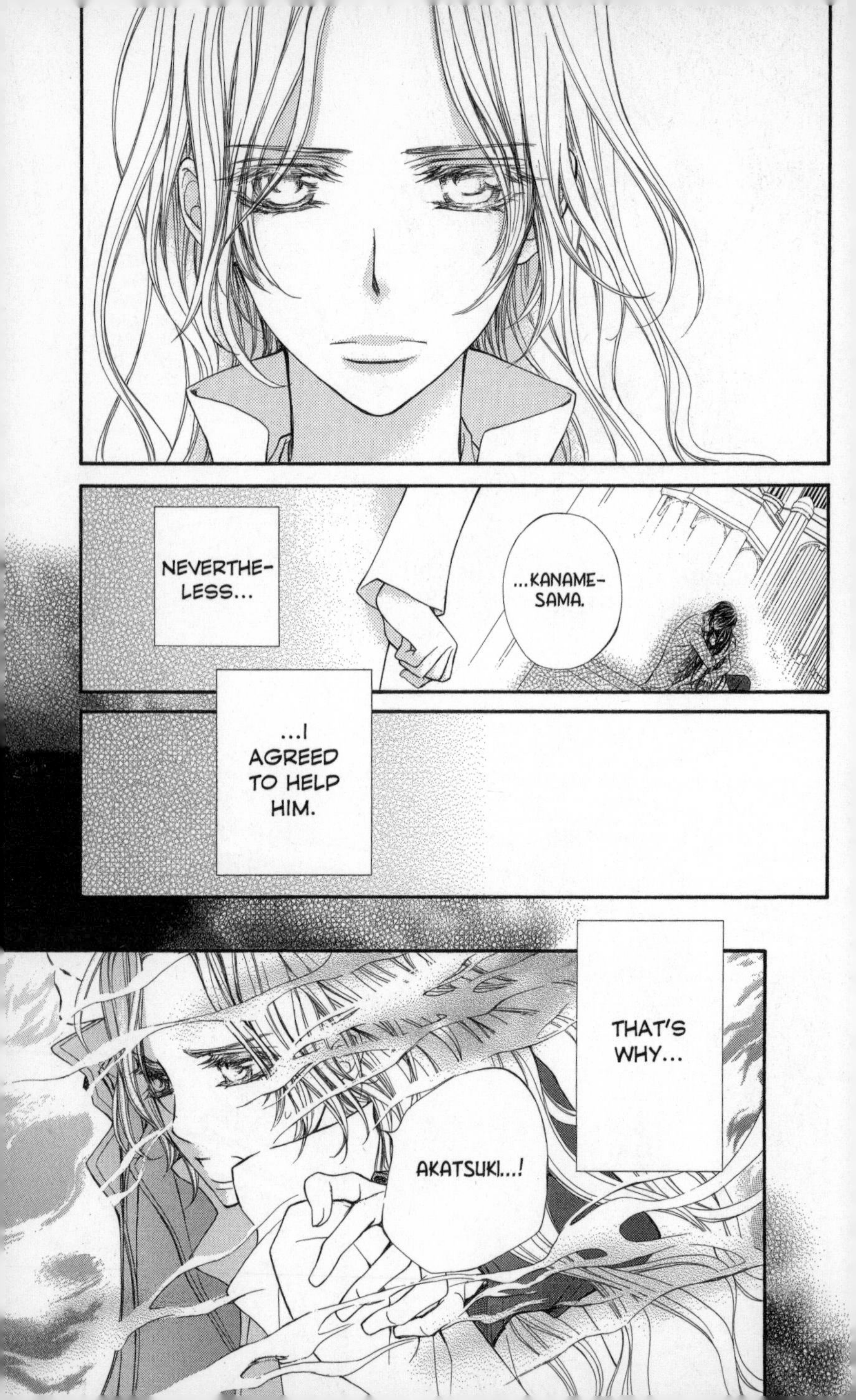
...KANAME-SAMA.
NEVERTHE-LESS...
...I AGREED TO HELP HIM.
THAT'S WHY...
AKATSUKI...!

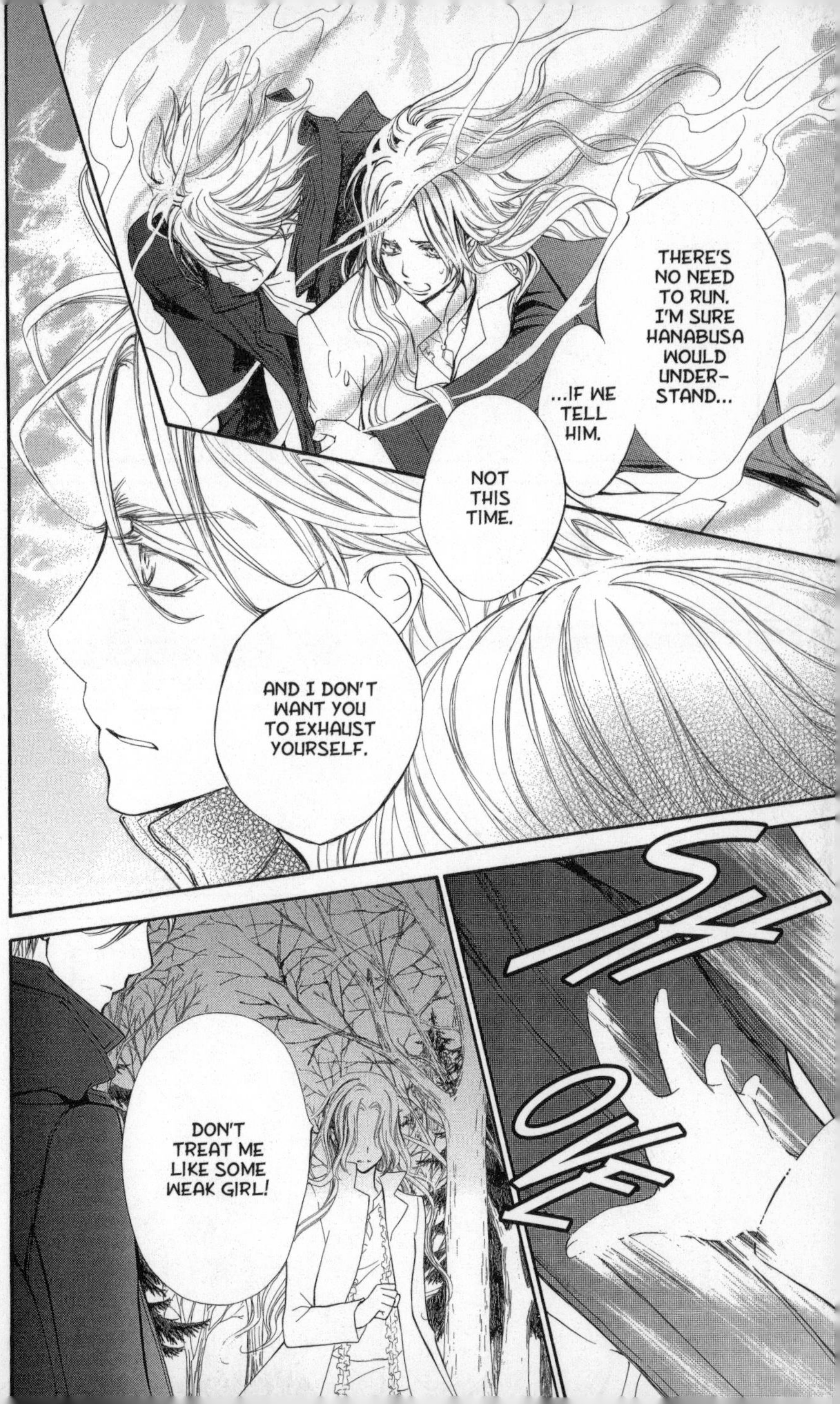
THERE'S NO NEED TO RUN. I'M SURE HANABUSA WOULD UNDER-STAND...
...IF WE TELL HIM.
NOT THIS TIME.
AND I DON'T WANT YOU TO EXHAUST YOURSELF.
SHOOF
DON'T TREAT ME LIKE SOME WEAK GIRL!

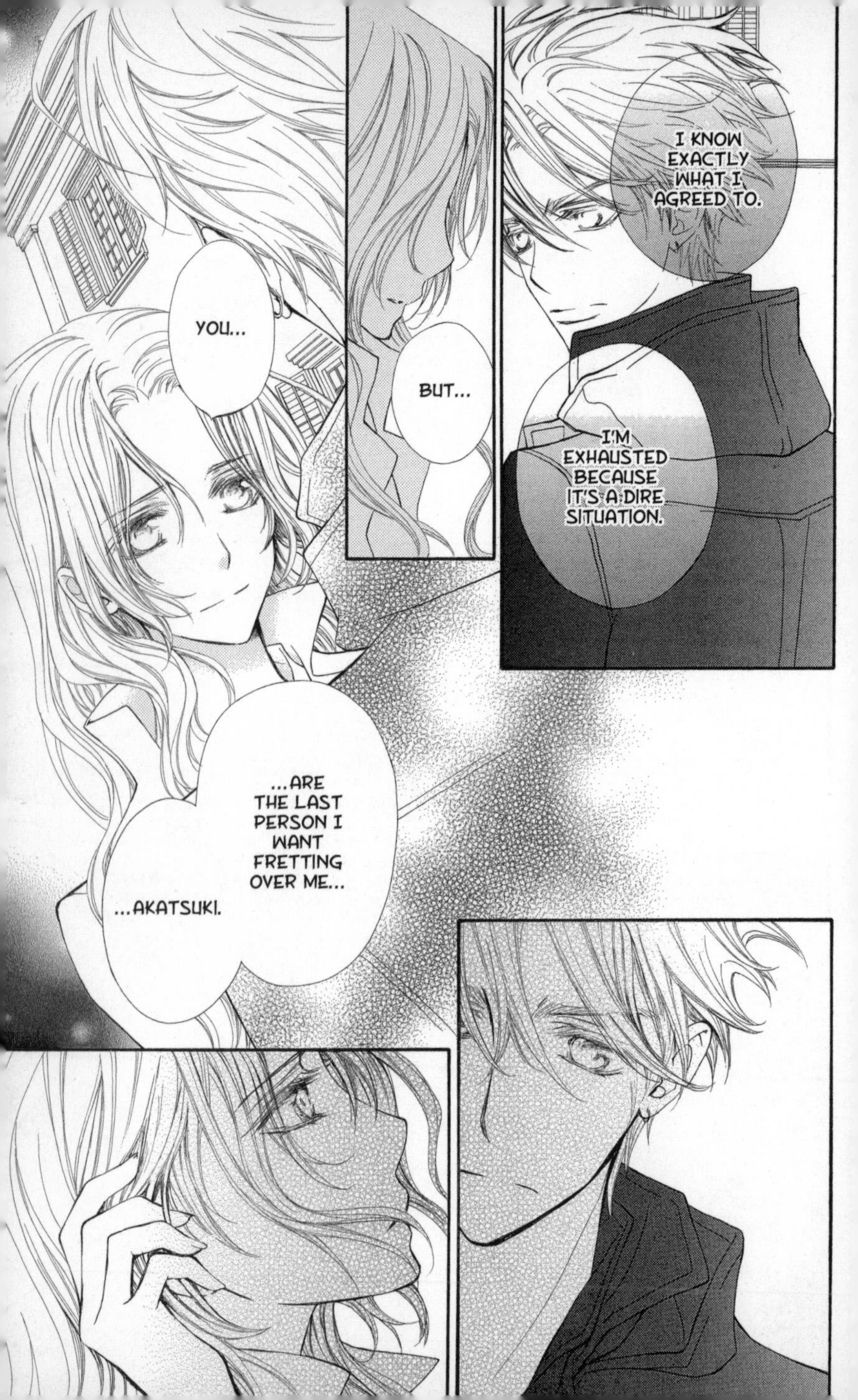
I KNOW EXACTLY WHAT I AGREED TO.
I'M EXHAUSTED BECAUSE IT'S A DIRE SITUATION.
BUT...
YOU...
...ARE THE LAST PERSON I WANT FRETTING OVER ME...
...AKATSUKI.

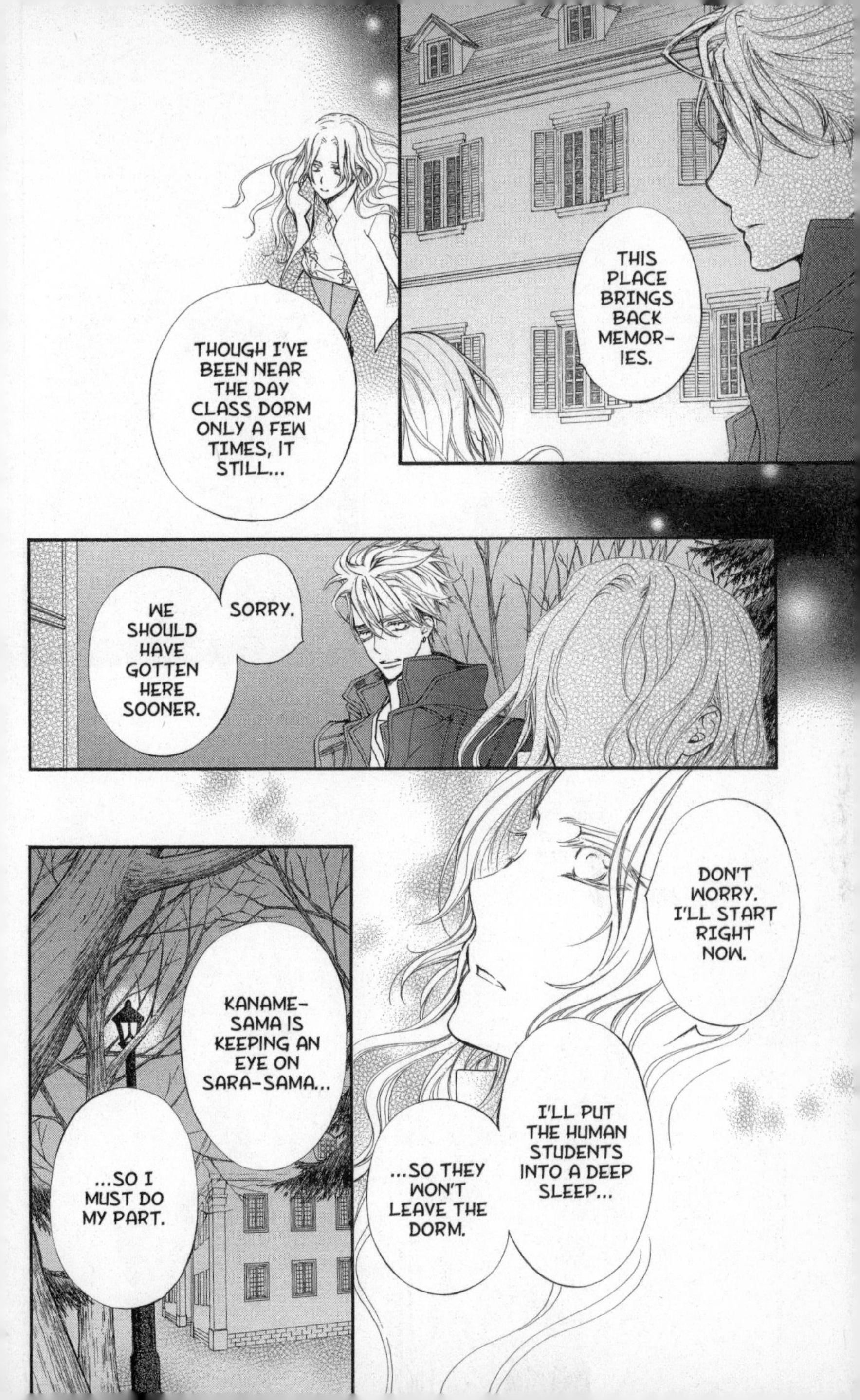
THIS PLACE BRINGS BACK MEMORIES.
THOUGH I'VE BEEN NEAR THE DAY CLASS DORM ONLY A FEW TIMES, IT STILL...
SORRY.
WE SHOULD HAVE GOTTEN HERE SOONER.
DON'T WORRY. I'LL START RIGHT NOW.
I'LL PUT THE HUMAN STUDENTS INTO A DEEP SLEEP...
...SO THEY WON'T LEAVE THE DORM.
KANAME-SAMA IS KEEPING AN EYE ON SARA-SAMA...
...SO I MUST DO MY PART.

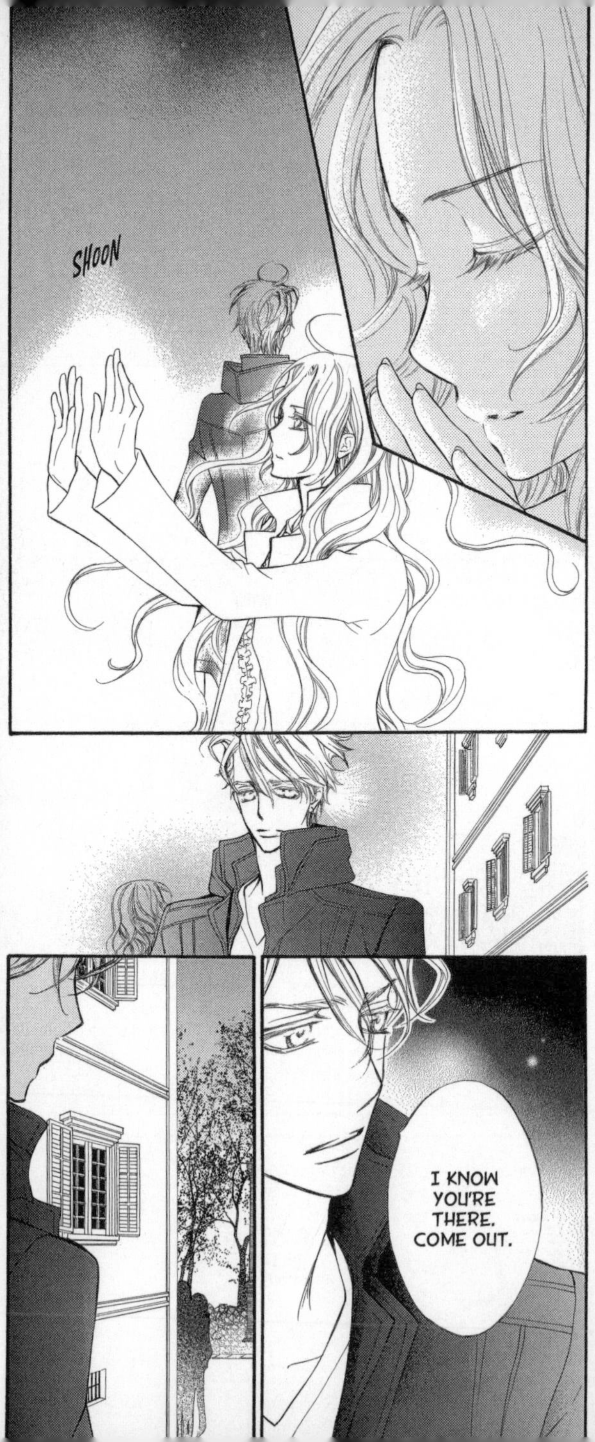
SHOON
I KNOW YOU'RE THERE. COME OUT.

II

I included a 12-page one-shot I wrote while working on *Vampire Knight* instead. It's a very different type of manga. It forced me to realize how inadequate my skills are... I was happy the one-shot received very good reviews. I hope you will enjoy it.

The cover illustration for this volume is of Kaname and Ichijo. I had always wanted to do a color illustration of "The Night Class President and Vice President," but I kept missing the chance to do it. Given that there aren't many volumes left, I decided to draw them for the cover of volume 17, though the illustration doesn't have much to do with its contents. I had already decided on the covers for volumes 18 and 19, so this was the only one left... There are other illustrations that I still want to draw, so I'm thinking of a way to present all of them.

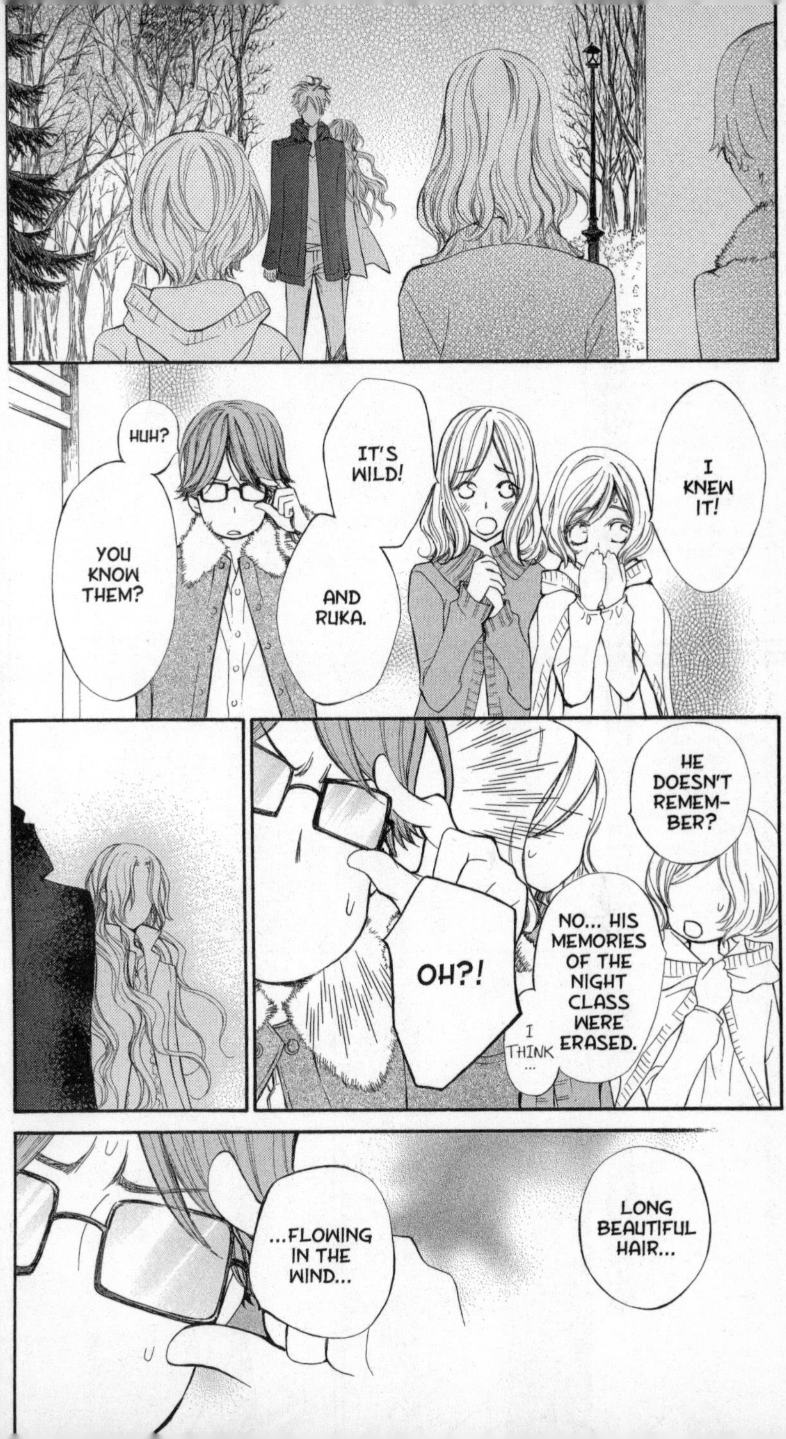
I KNEW IT!
IT'S WILD!
AND RUKA.
HUH?
YOU KNOW THEM?
HE DOESN'T REMEMBER?
NO... HIS MEMORIES OF THE NIGHT CLASS WERE ERASED.
I THINK...
OH?!
LONG BEAUTIFUL HAIR...
...FLOWING IN THE WIND...

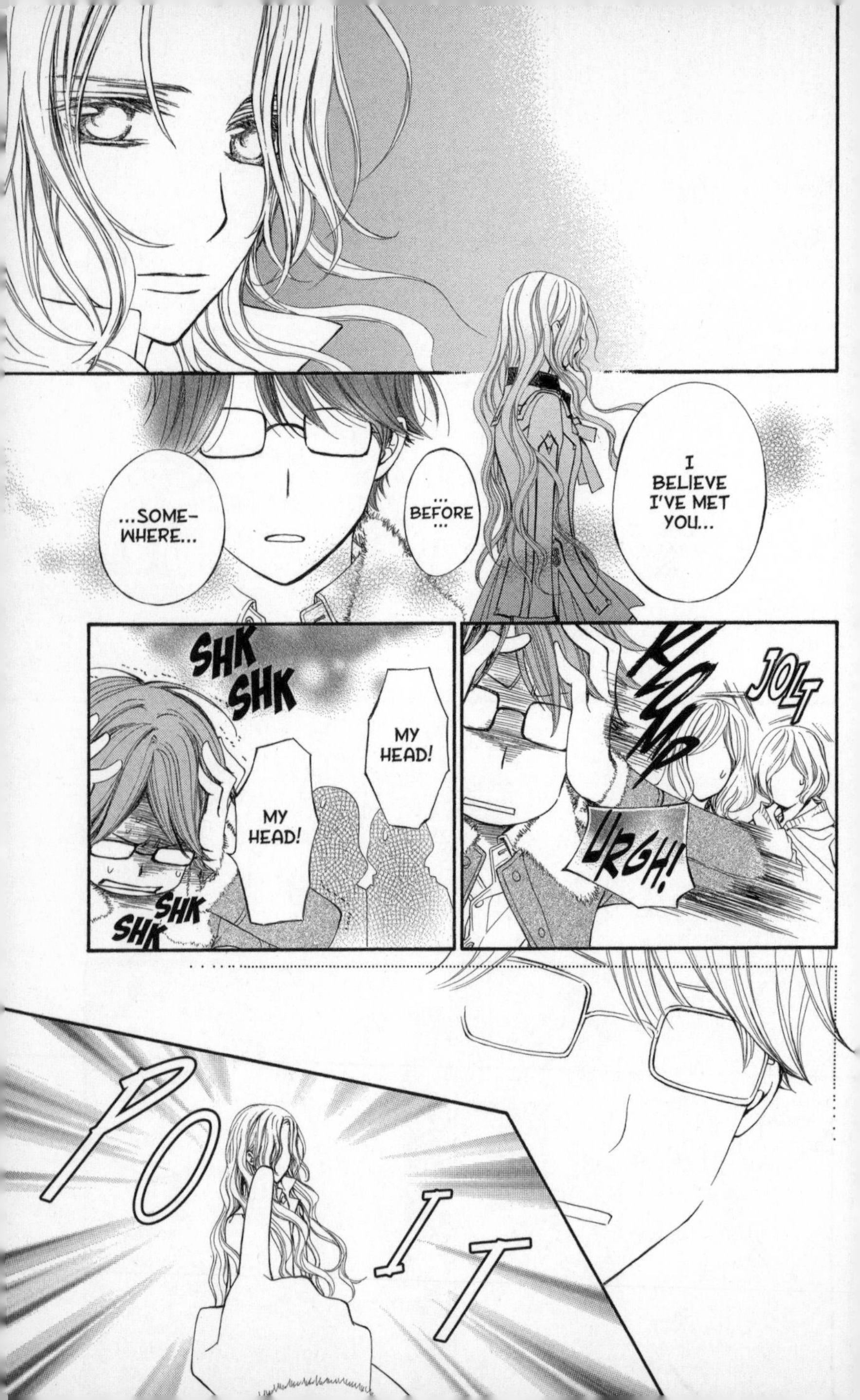
I BELIEVE I'VE MET YOU...
...BEFORE...
...SOME-WHERE...
WHOMP
JOLT
URGH!
SHK SHK
MY HEAD!
MY HEAD!
SHK SHK
POIT

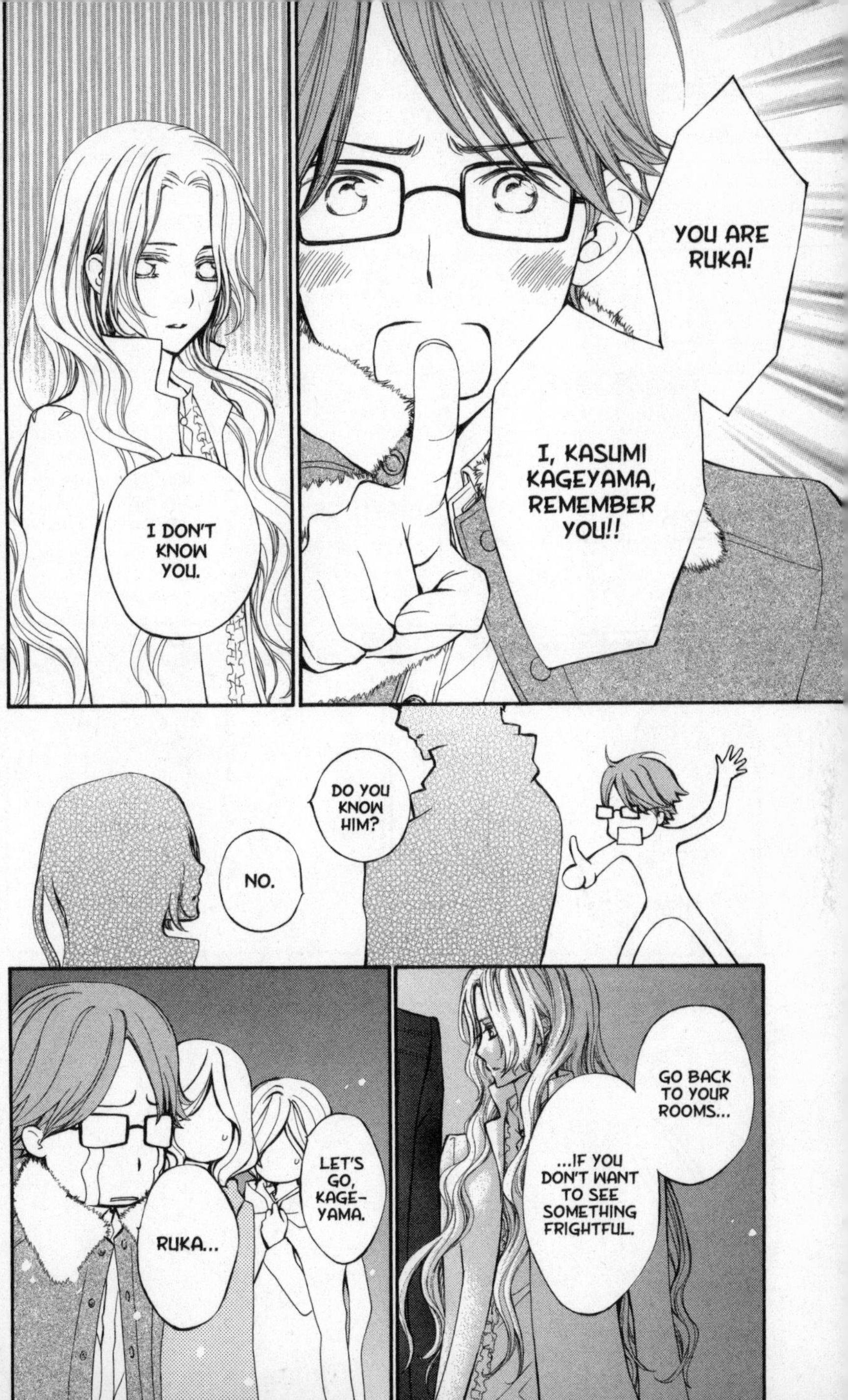
YOU ARE RUKA!
I, KASUMI KAGEYAMA, REMEMBER YOU!!
I DON'T KNOW YOU.
DO YOU KNOW HIM?
NO.
GO BACK TO YOUR ROOMS...
...IF YOU DON'T WANT TO SEE SOMETHING FRIGHTFUL.
LET'S GO, KAGE-YAMA.
RUKA...

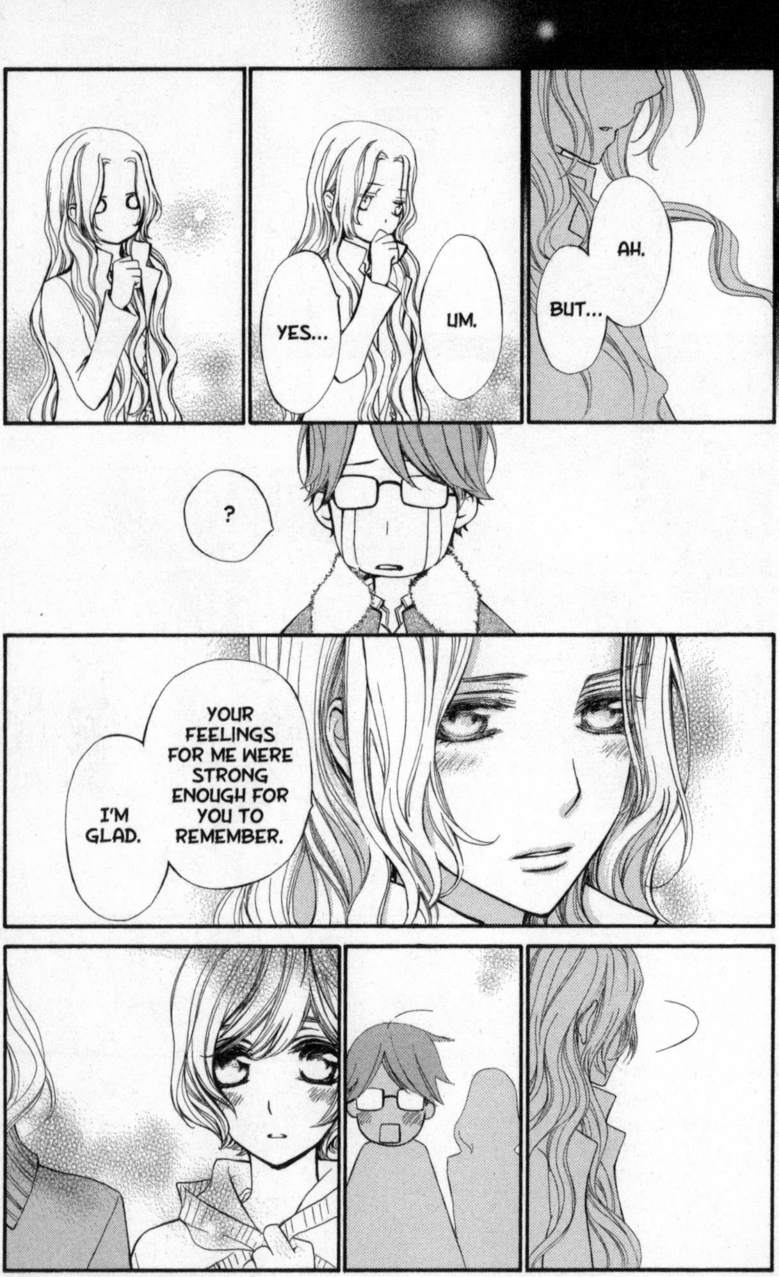
AH.
BUT...
UM.
YES...
?
YOUR FEELINGS FOR ME WERE STRONG ENOUGH FOR YOU TO REMEMBER.
I'M GLAD.

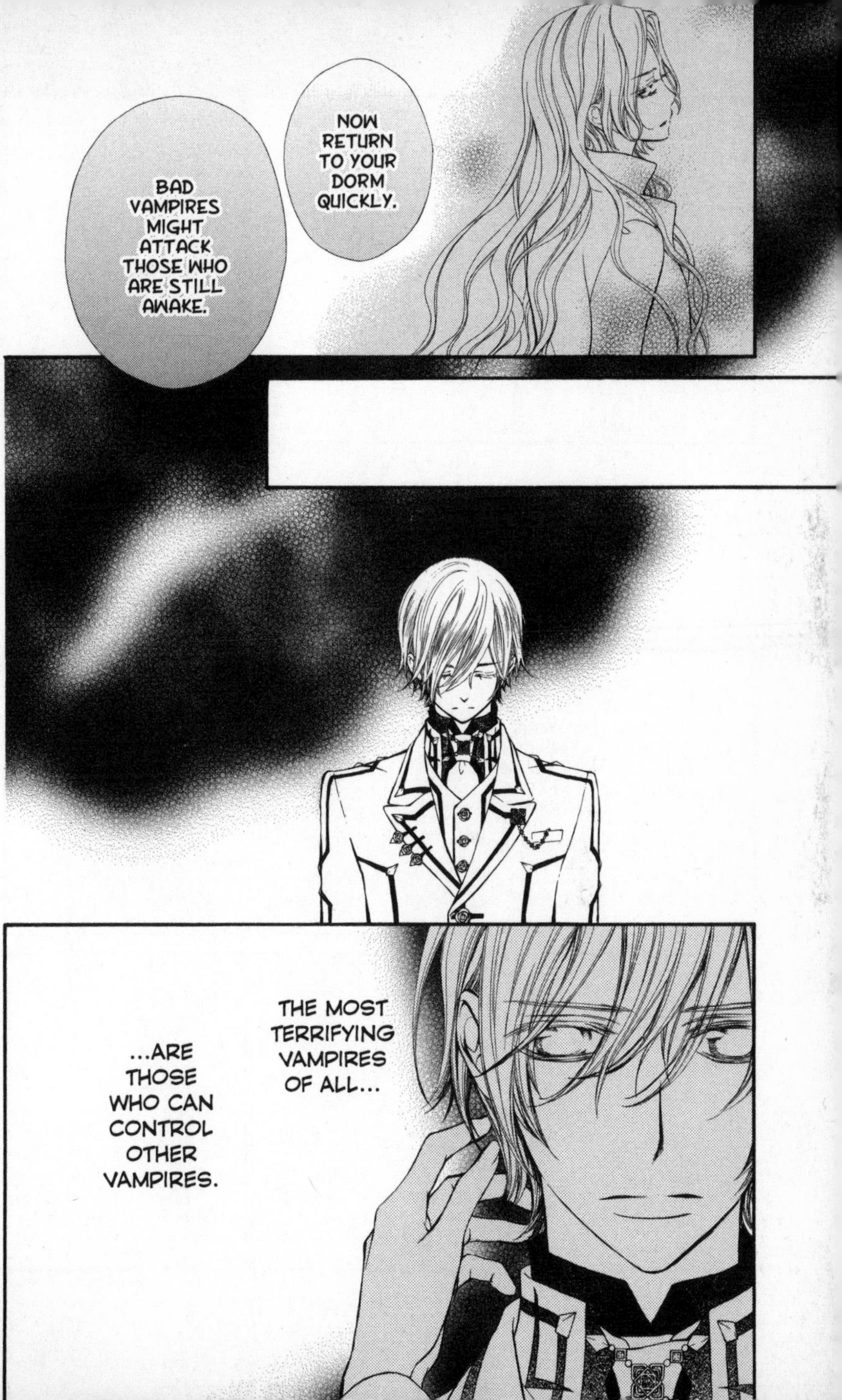
NOW RETURN TO YOUR DORM QUICKLY.
BAD VAMPIRES MIGHT ATTACK THOSE WHO ARE STILL AWAKE.
THE MOST TERRIFYING VAMPIRES OF ALL...
...ARE THOSE WHO CAN CONTROL OTHER VAMPIRES.

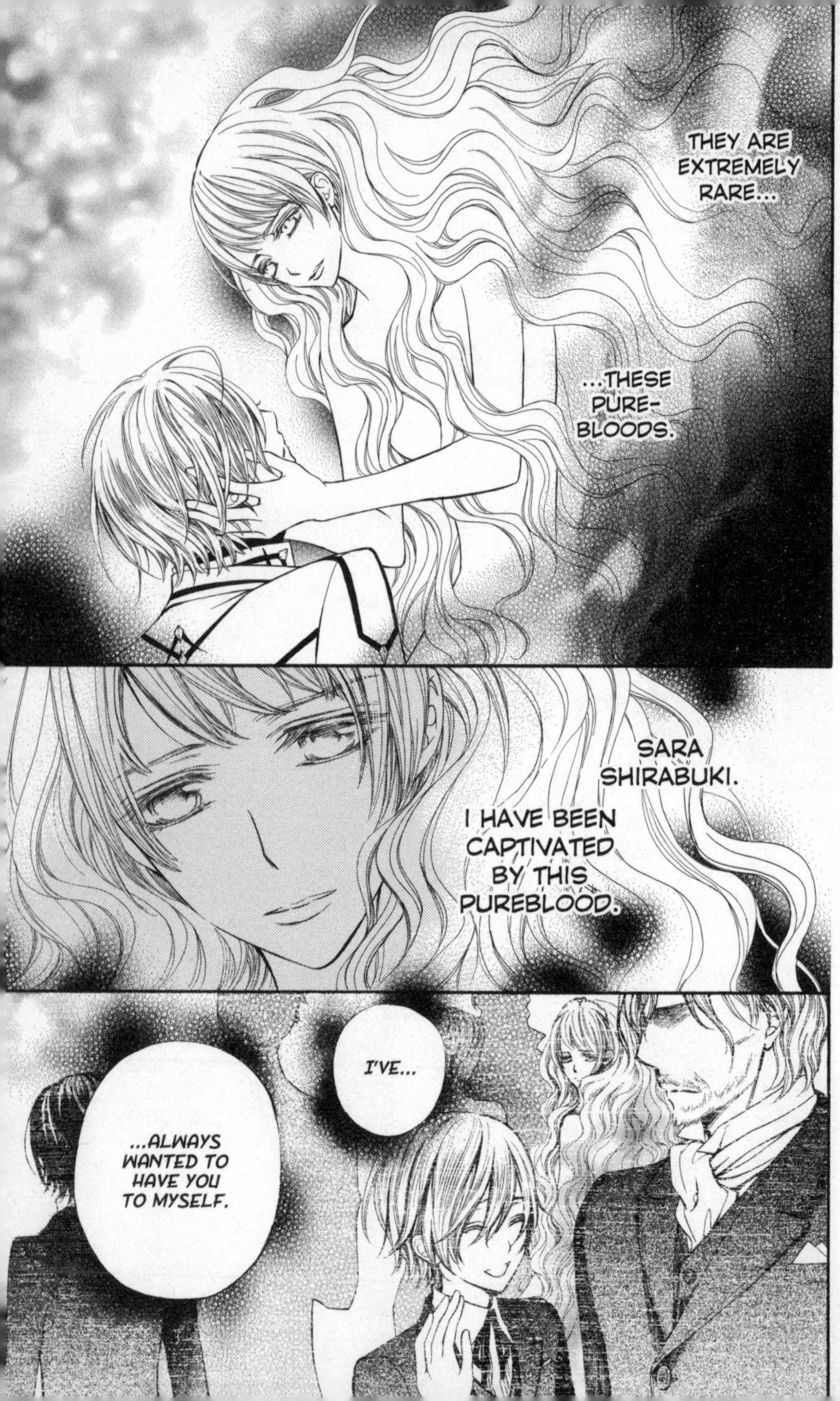
THEY ARE EXTREMELY RARE...
...THESE PURE-BLOODS.
SARA SHIRABUKI.
I HAVE BEEN CAPTIVATED BY THIS PUREBLOOD.
I'VE...
...ALWAYS WANTED TO HAVE YOU TO MYSELF.

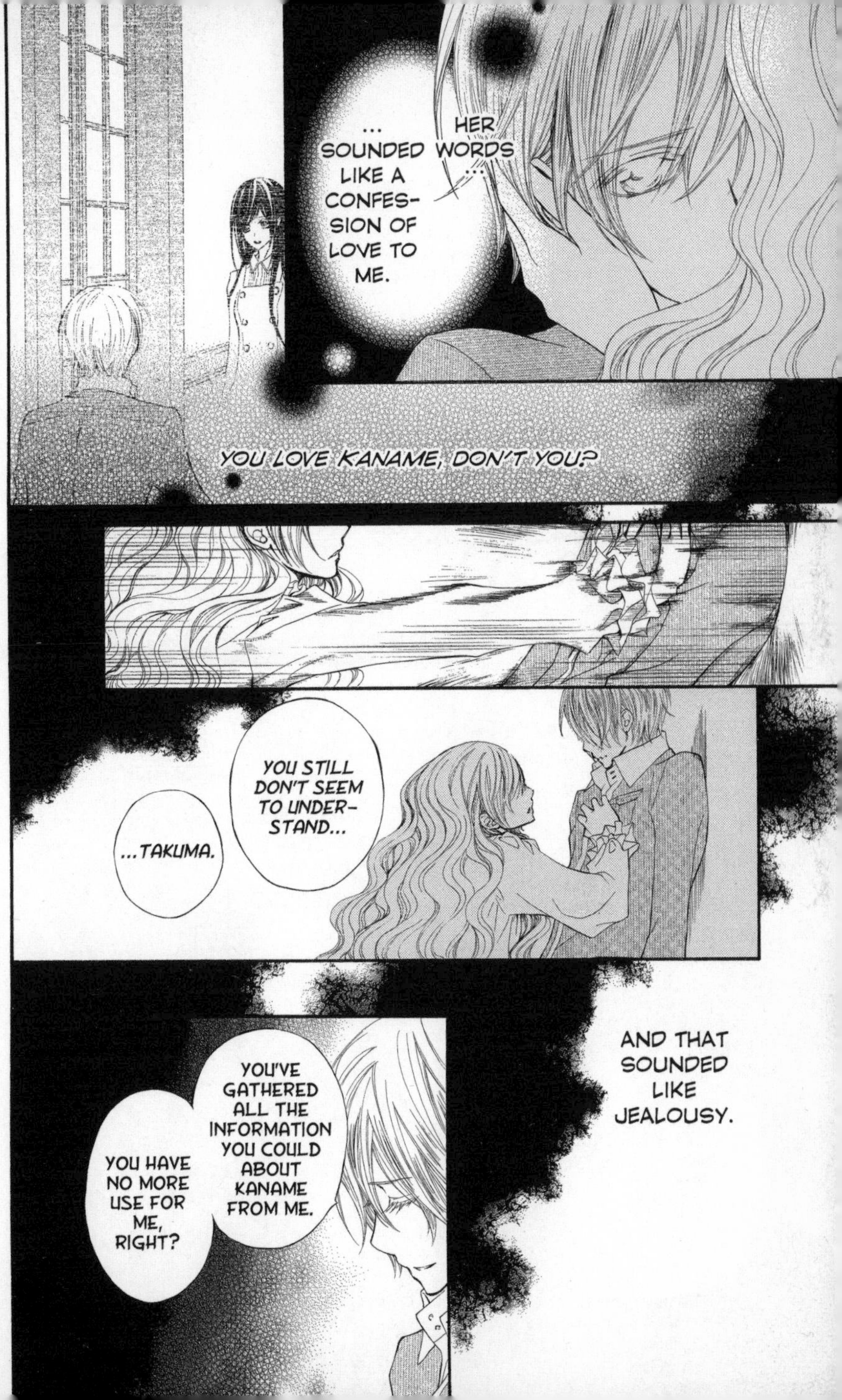
HER WORDS...
...SOUNDED LIKE A CONFESSION OF LOVE TO ME.
YOU LOVE KANAME, DON'T YOU?
YOU STILL DON'T SEEM TO UNDERSTAND...
...TAKUMA.
AND THAT SOUNDED LIKE JEALOUSY.
YOU'VE GATHERED ALL THE INFORMATION YOU COULD ABOUT KANAME FROM ME.
YOU HAVE NO MORE USE FOR ME, RIGHT?

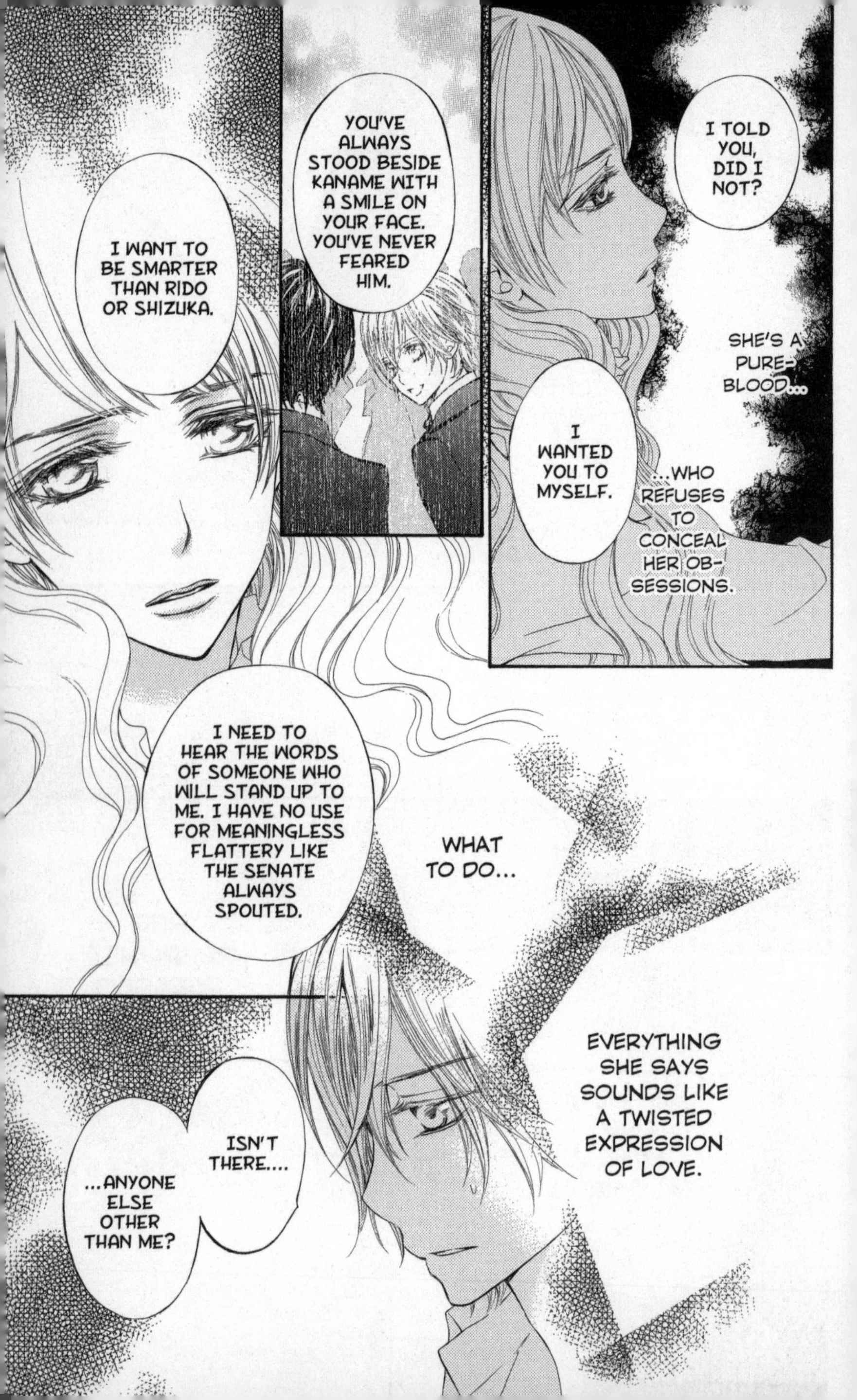
I TOLD YOU, DID I NOT?
SHE'S A PURE-BLOOD...
I WANTED YOU TO MYSELF.
...WHO REFUSES TO CONCEAL HER OB-SESSIONS.
YOU'VE ALWAYS STOOD BESIDE KANAME WITH A SMILE ON YOUR FACE. YOU'VE NEVER FEARED HIM.
I WANT TO BE SMARTER THAN RIDO OR SHIZUKA.
I NEED TO HEAR THE WORDS OF SOMEONE WHO WILL STAND UP TO ME. I HAVE NO USE FOR MEANINGLESS FLATTERY LIKE THE SENATE ALWAYS SPOUTED.
WHAT TO DO...
EVERYTHING SHE SAYS SOUNDS LIKE A TWISTED EXPRESSION OF LOVE.
ISN'T THERE....
...ANYONE ELSE OTHER THAN ME?

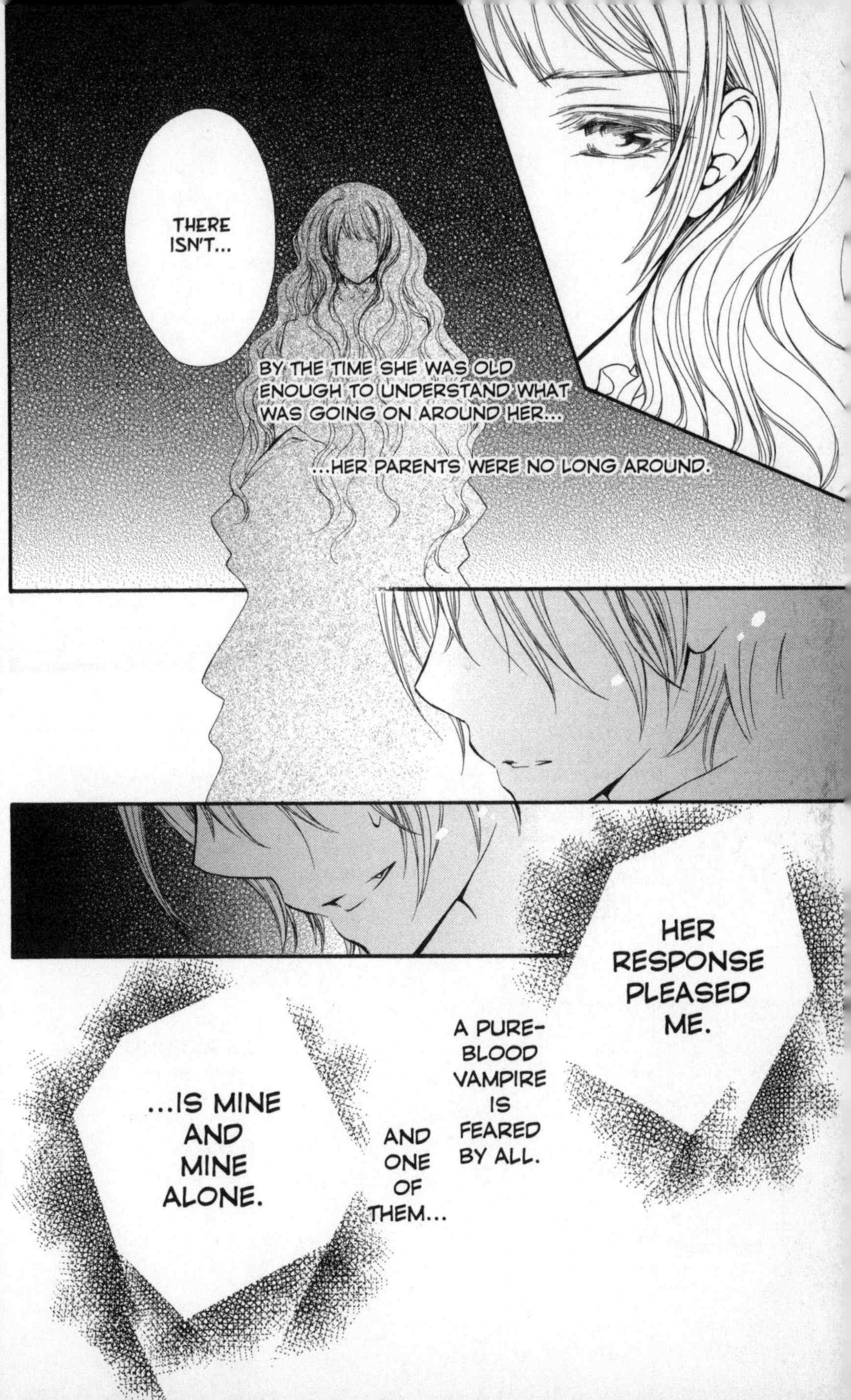
THERE ISN'T...
BY THE TIME SHE WAS OLD ENOUGH TO UNDERSTAND WHAT WAS GOING ON AROUND HER...
...HER PARENTS WERE NO LONG AROUND.
HER RESPONSE PLEASED ME.
A PURE-BLOOD VAMPIRE IS FEARED BY ALL.
AND ONE OF THEM...
...IS MINE AND MINE ALONE.

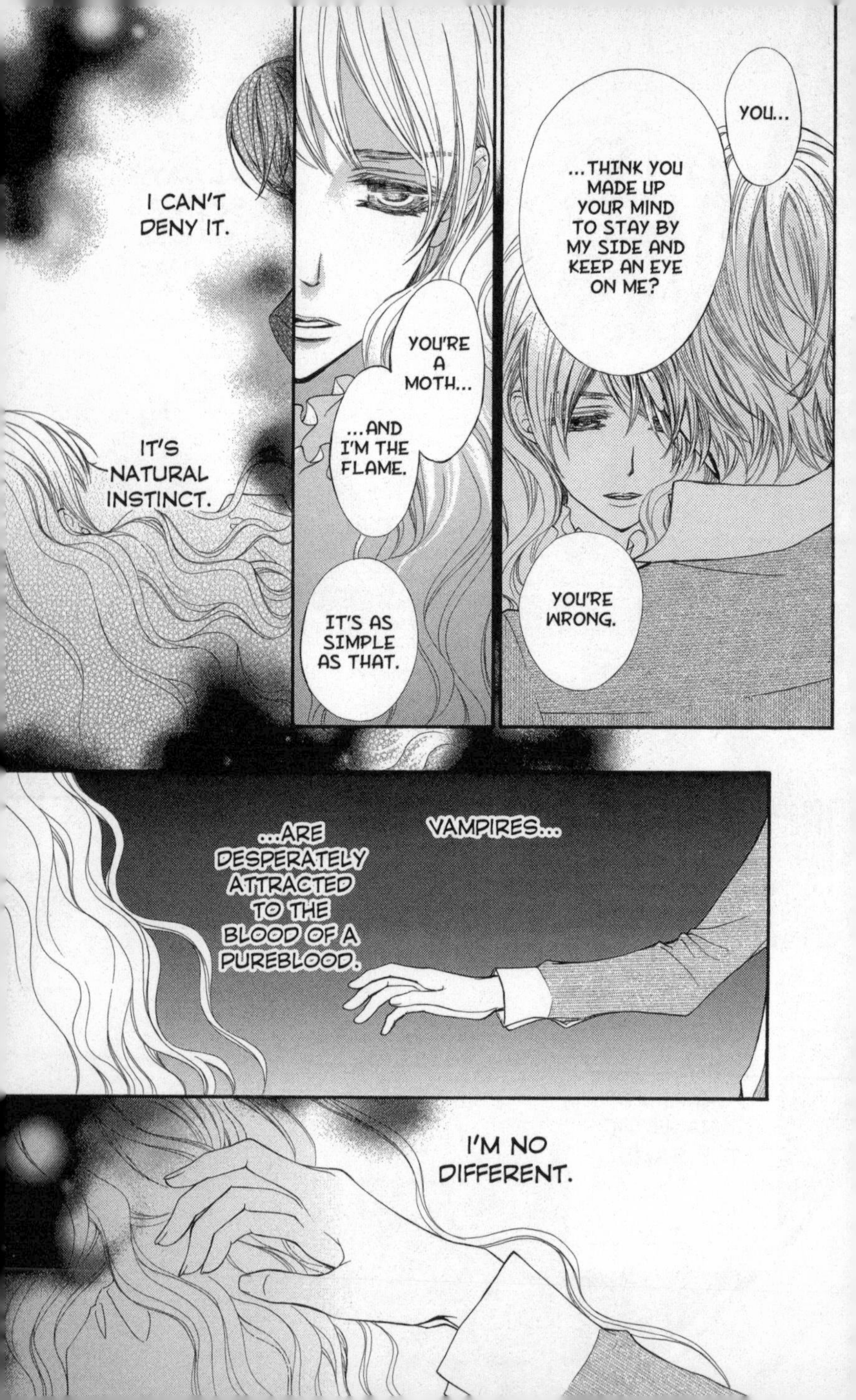
YOU...
...THINK YOU MADE UP YOUR MIND TO STAY BY MY SIDE AND KEEP AN EYE ON ME?
YOU'RE WRONG.
YOU'RE A MOTH...
...AND I'M THE FLAME.
IT'S AS SIMPLE AS THAT.
I CAN'T DENY IT.
IT'S NATURAL INSTINCT.
VAMPIRES...
...ARE DESPERATELY ATTRACTED TO THE BLOOD OF A PUREBLOOD.
I'M NO DIFFERENT.

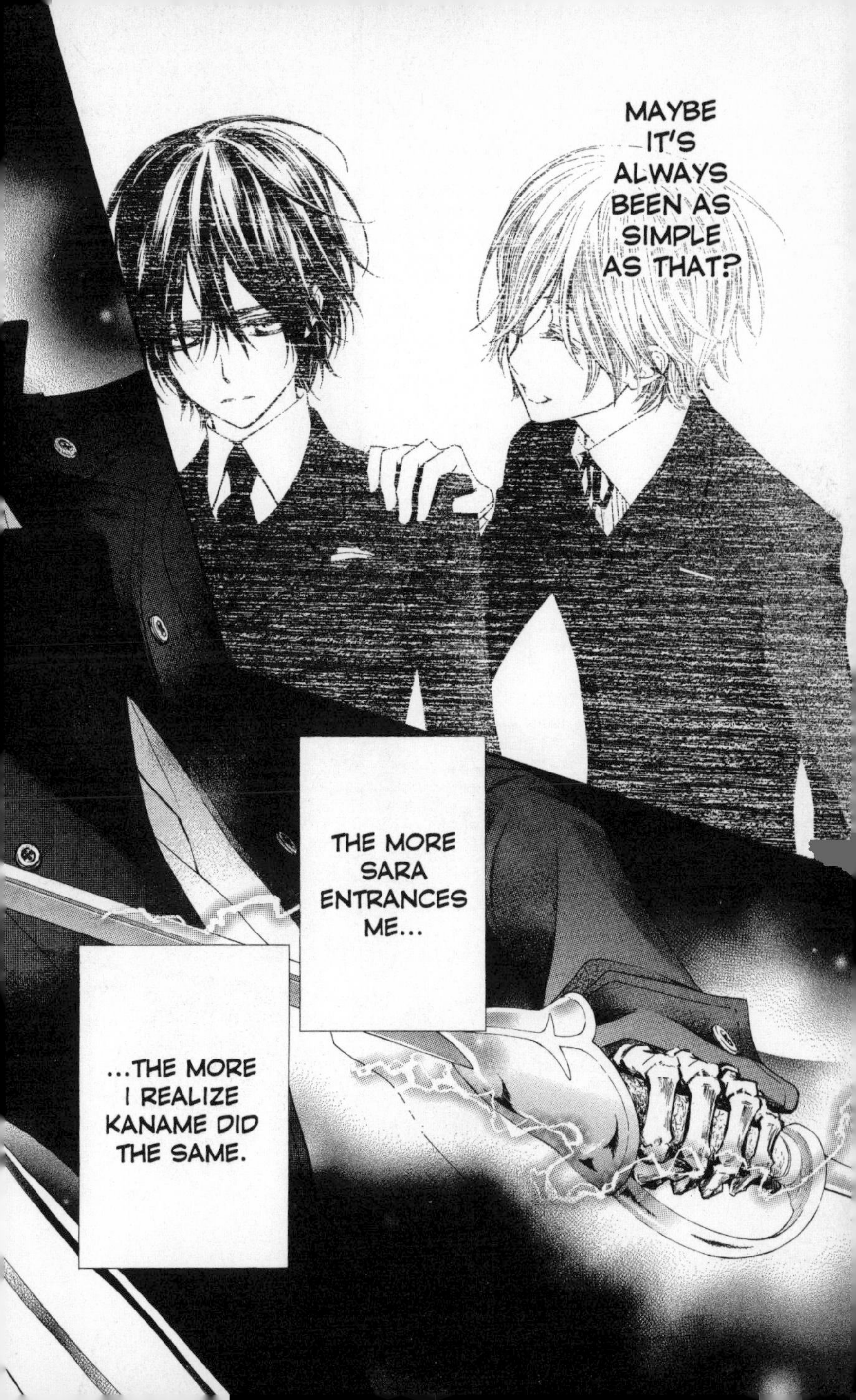
MAYBE IT'S ALWAYS BEEN AS SIMPLE AS THAT?
THE MORE SARA ENTRANCES ME...
...THE MORE I REALIZE KANAME DID THE SAME.

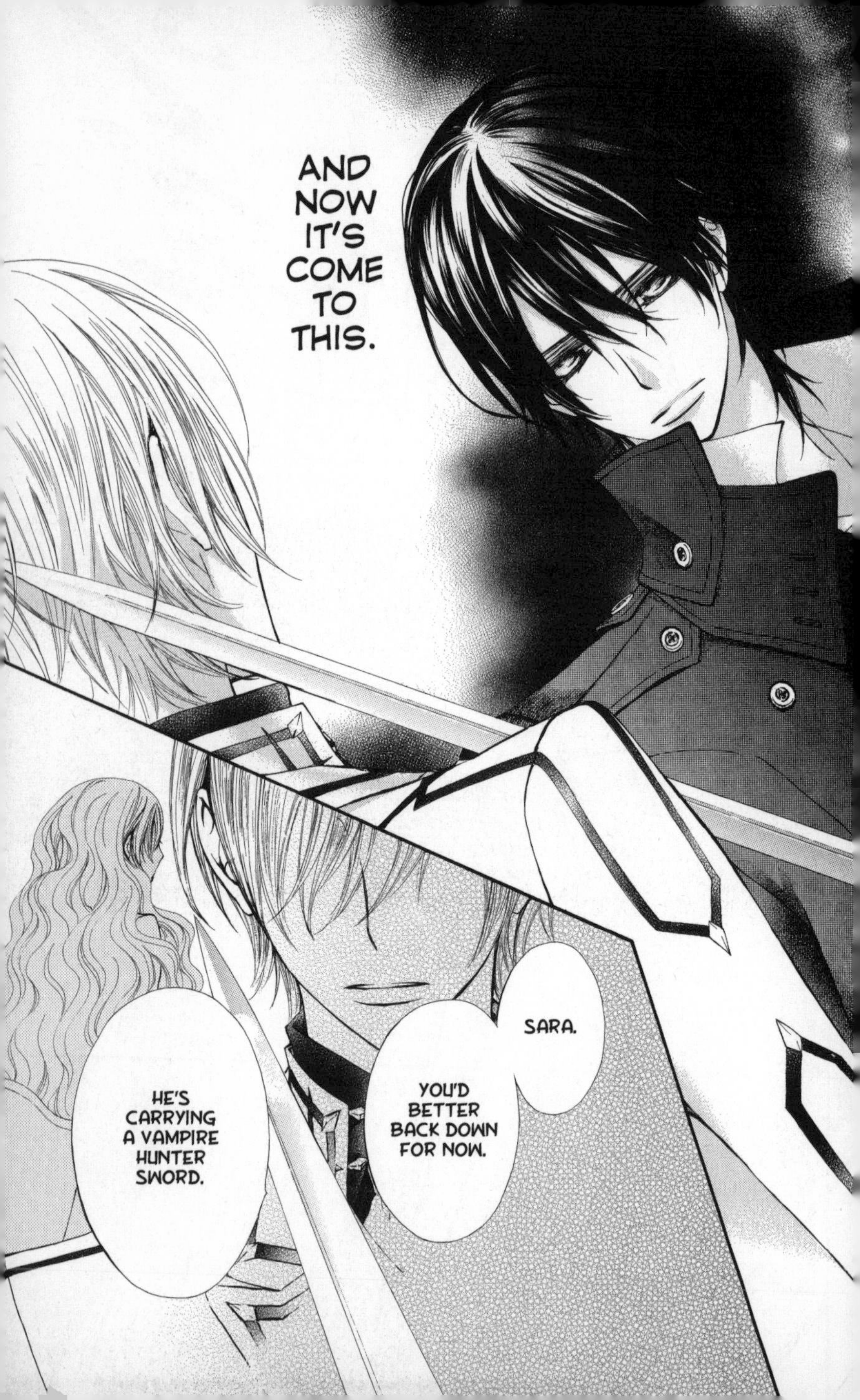
AND NOW IT'S COME TO THIS.
SARA.
YOU'D BETTER BACK DOWN FOR NOW.
HE'S CARRYING A VAMPIRE HUNTER SWORD.

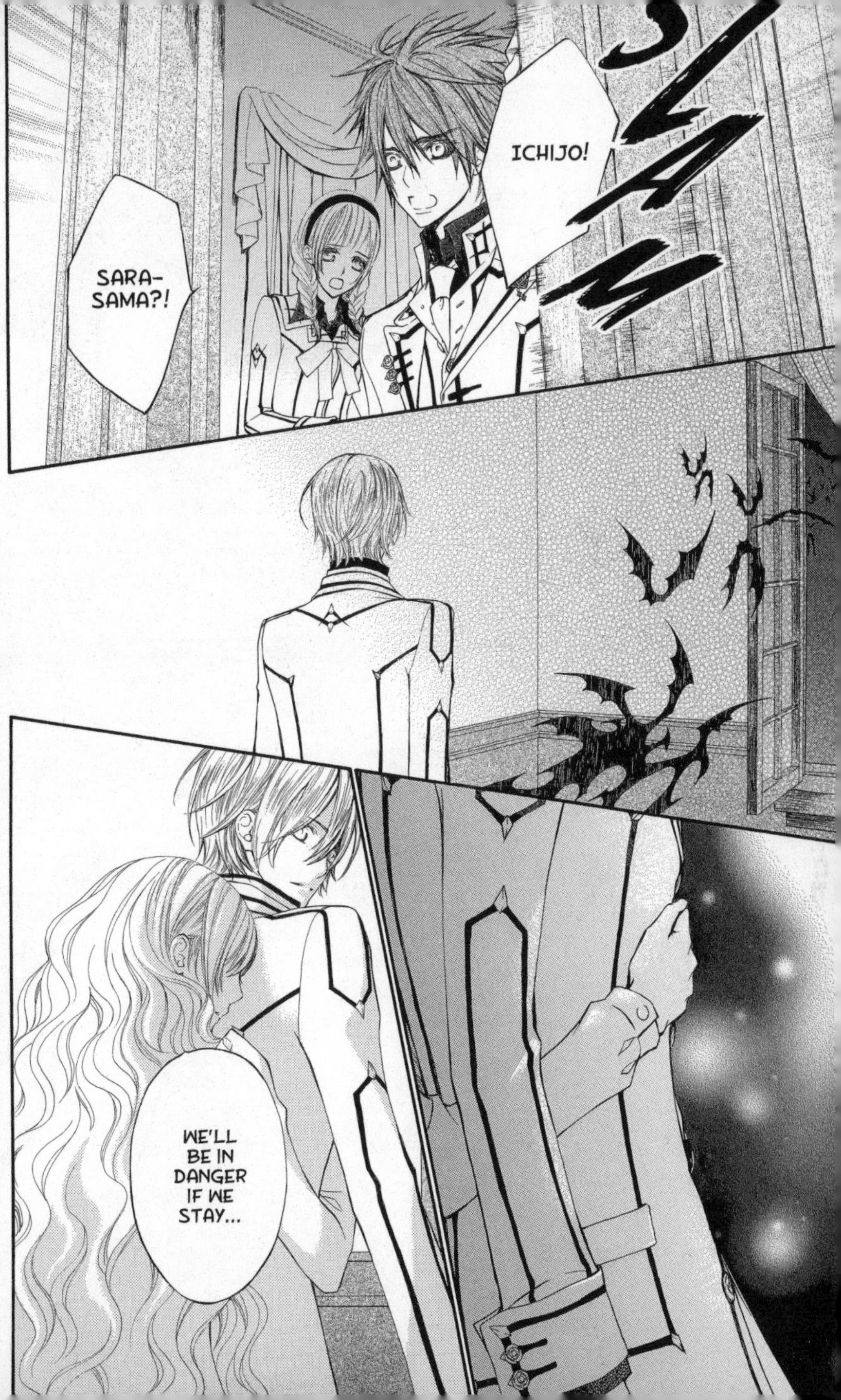
SLAM
ICHIJO!
SARA-SAMA?!
WE'LL BE IN DANGER IF WE STAY...

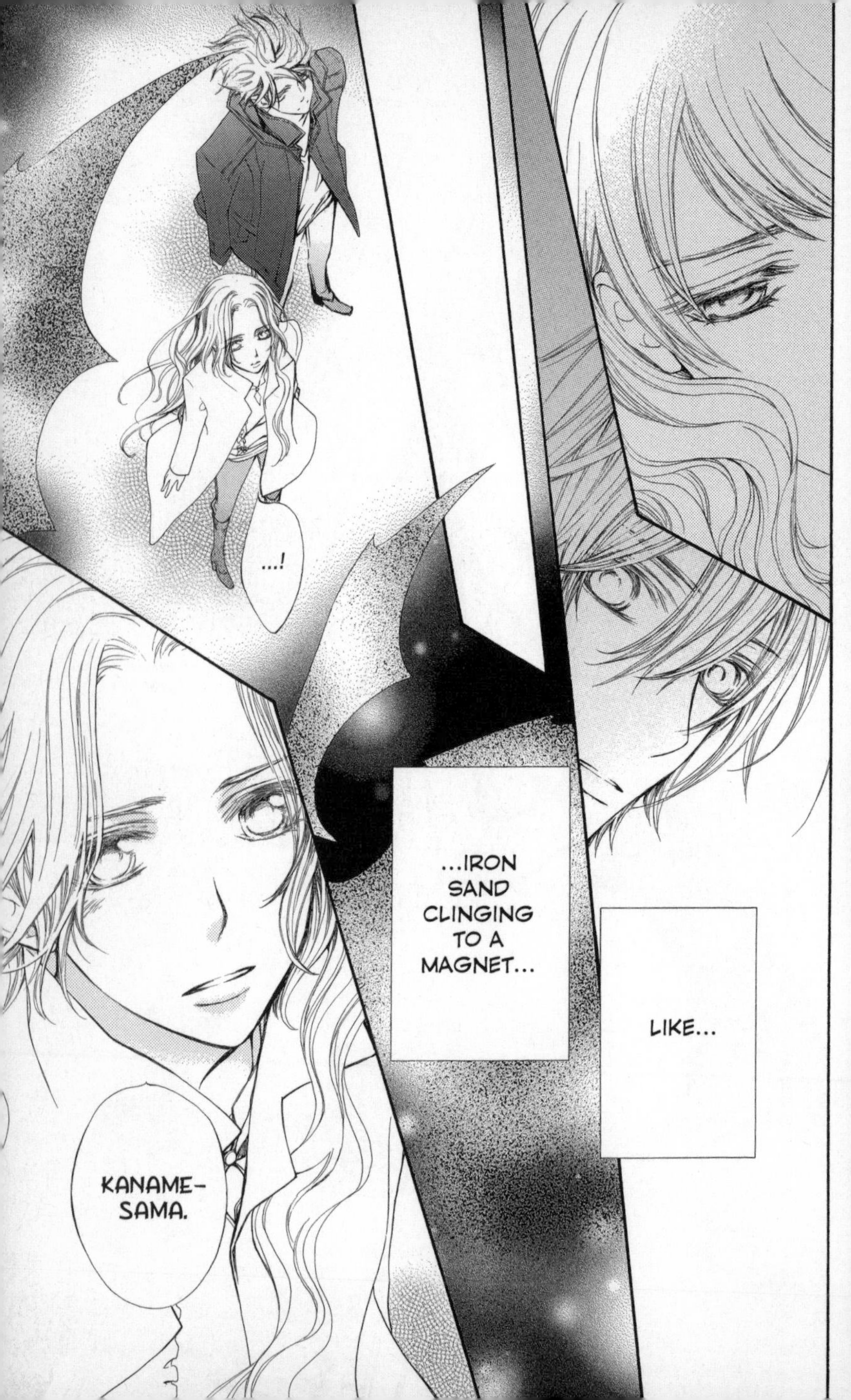
LIKE...
...IRON SAND CLINGING TO A MAGNET...
...!
KANAME-SAMA.

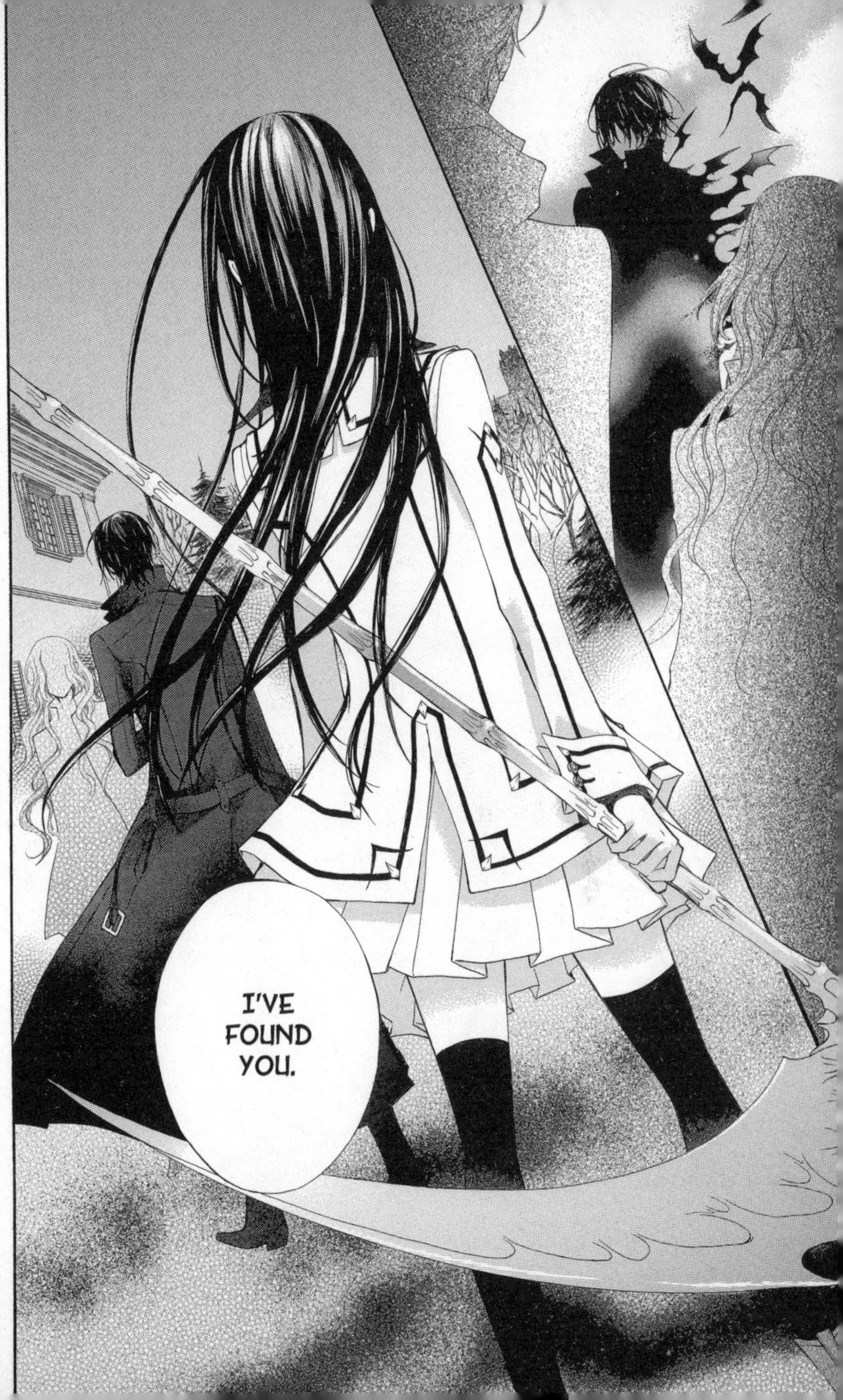
I'VE FOUND YOU.

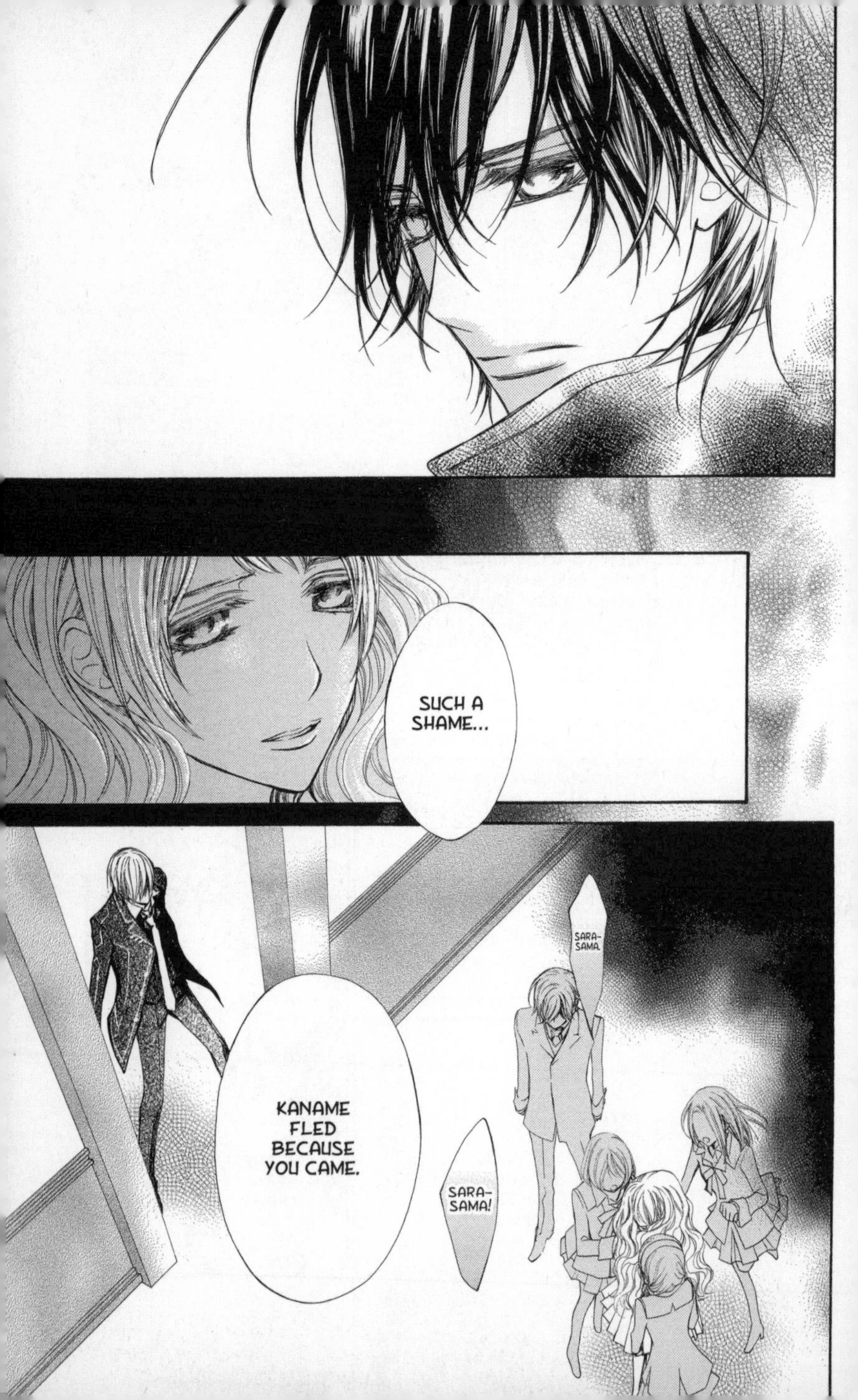
SUCH A SHAME...
SARA-SAMA
SARA-SAMA!
KANAME FLED BECAUSE YOU CAME.

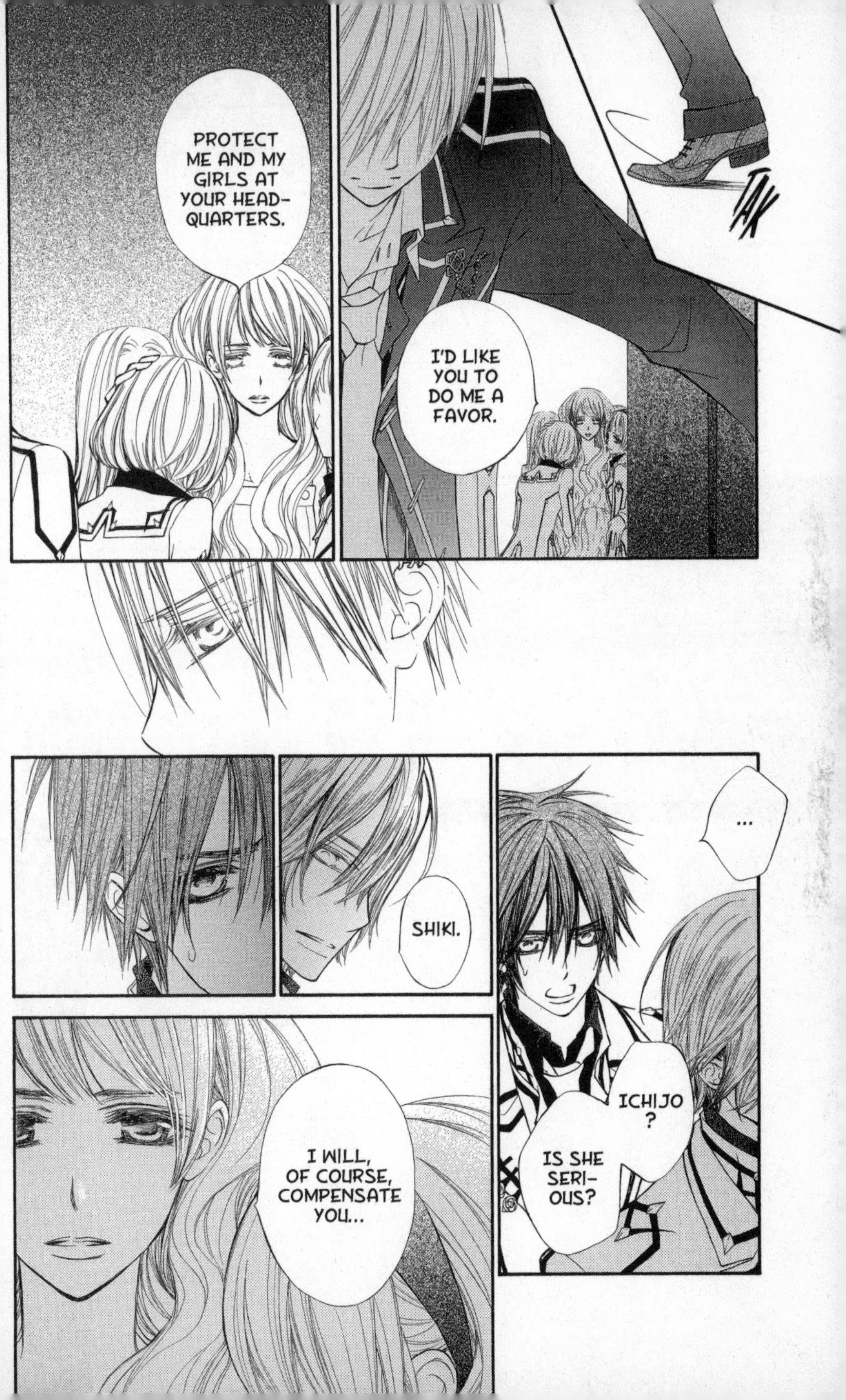
TAK
I'D LIKE YOU TO DO ME A FAVOR.
PROTECT ME AND MY GIRLS AT YOUR HEAD-QUARTERS.
...
ICHIJO?
IS SHE SERI-OUS?
SHIKI.
I WILL, OF COURSE, COMPENSATE YOU...

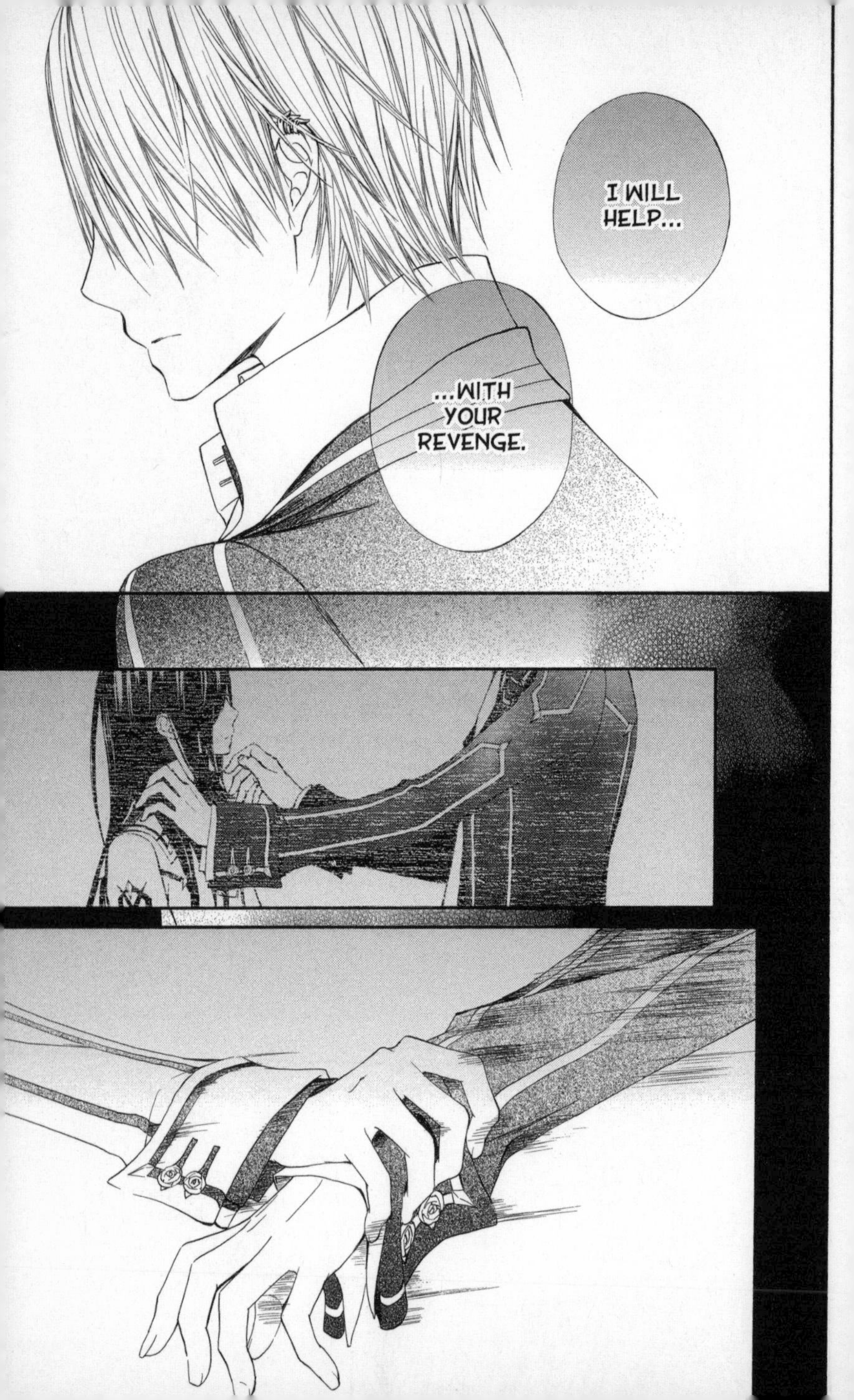
I WILL HELP...
...WITH YOUR REVENGE.

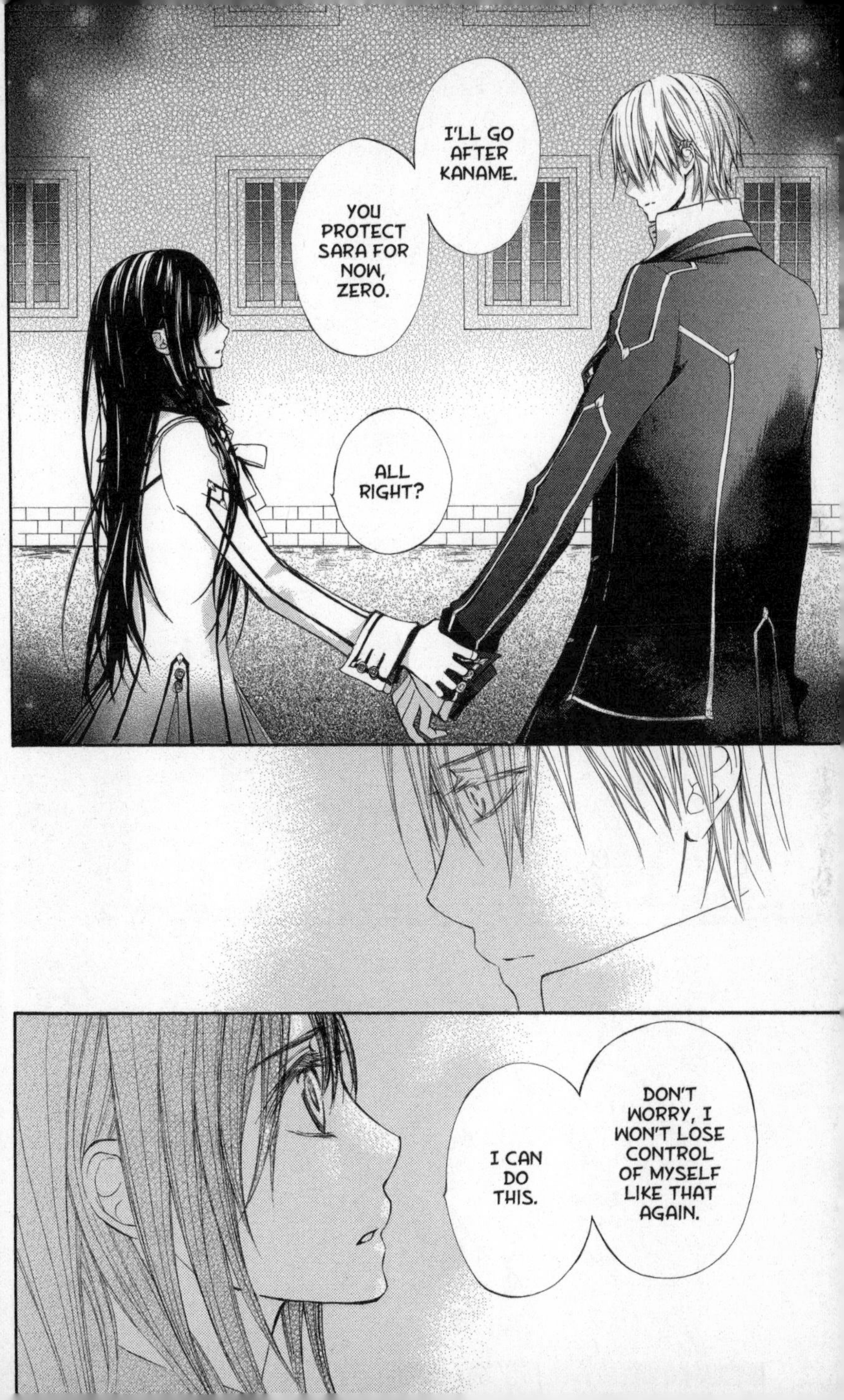
I'LL GO AFTER KANAME.
YOU PROTECT SARA FOR NOW, ZERO.
ALL RIGHT?
DON'T WORRY, I WON'T LOSE CONTROL OF MYSELF LIKE THAT AGAIN.
I CAN DO THIS.

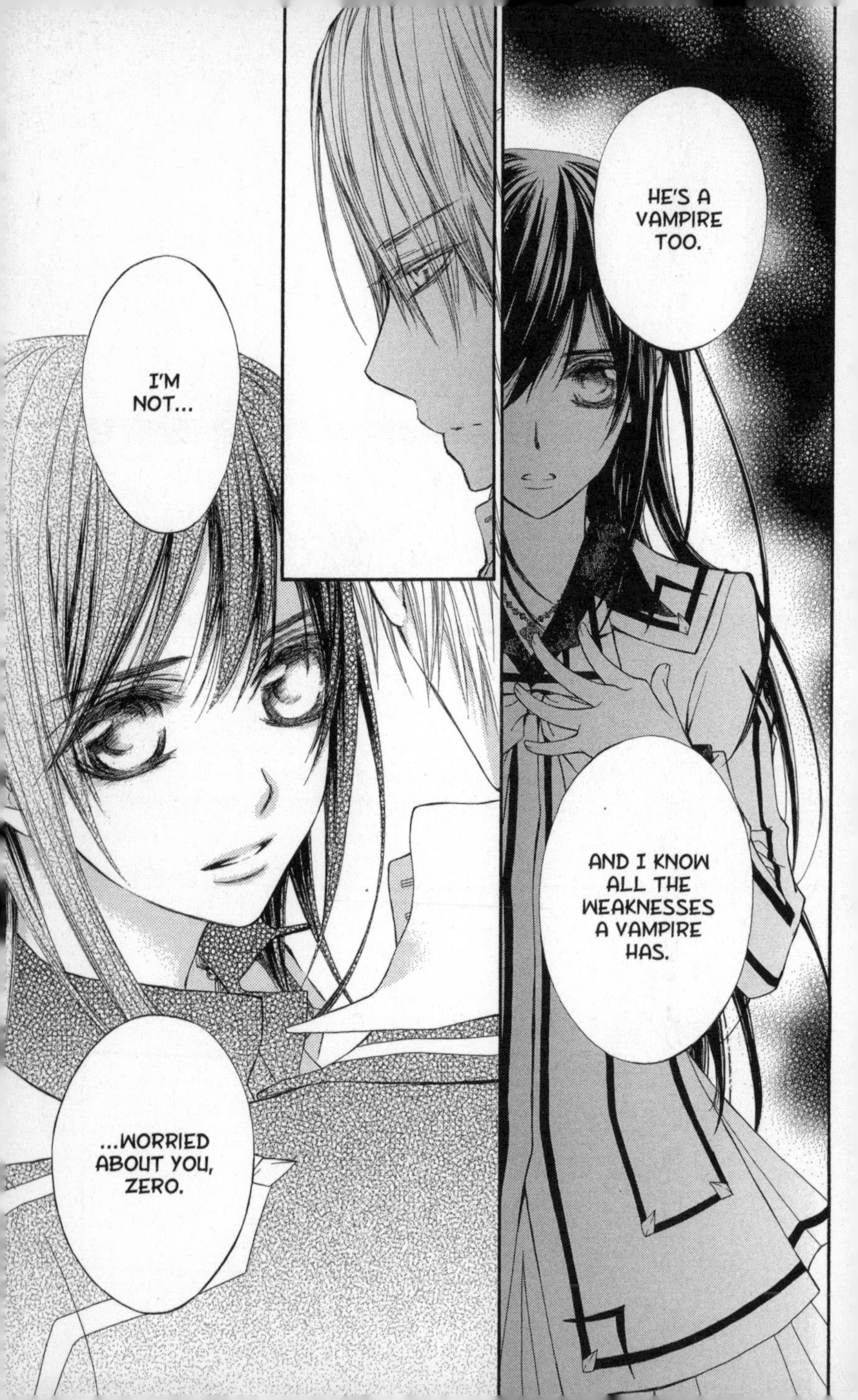
HE'S A VAMPIRE TOO.
AND I KNOW ALL THE WEAKNESSES A VAMPIRE HAS.
I'M NOT...
...WORRIED ABOUT YOU, ZERO.

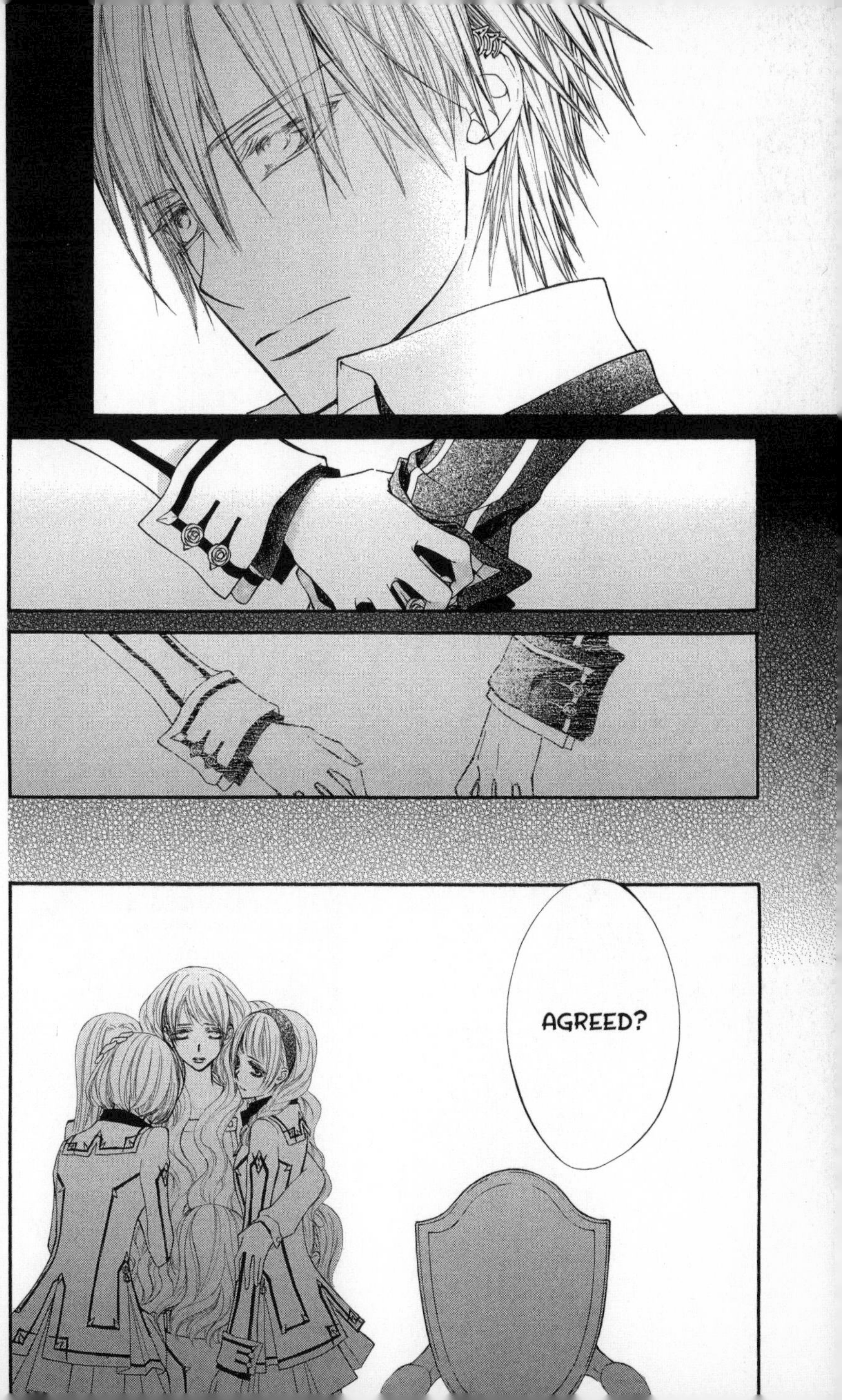
AGREED?

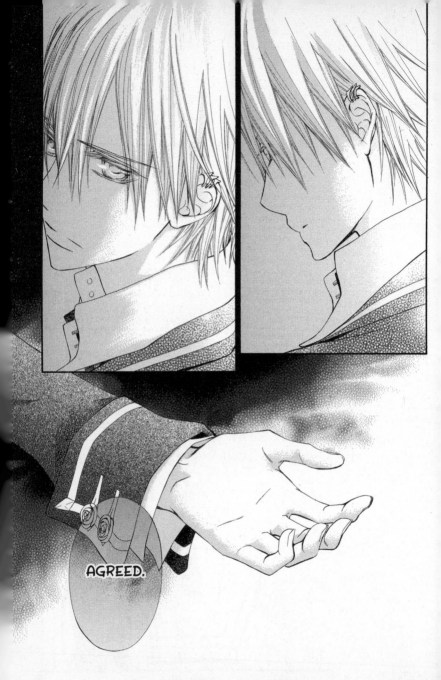

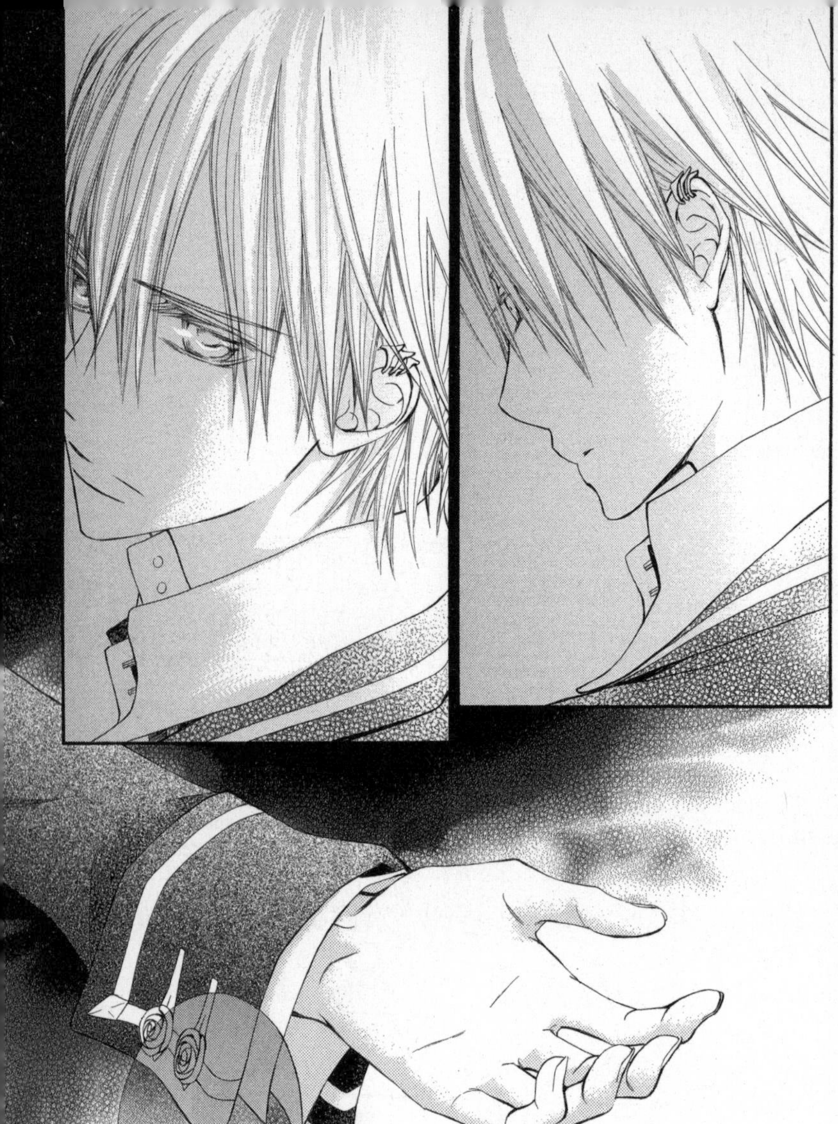
AGREED.

EIGHTIETH NIGHT/END

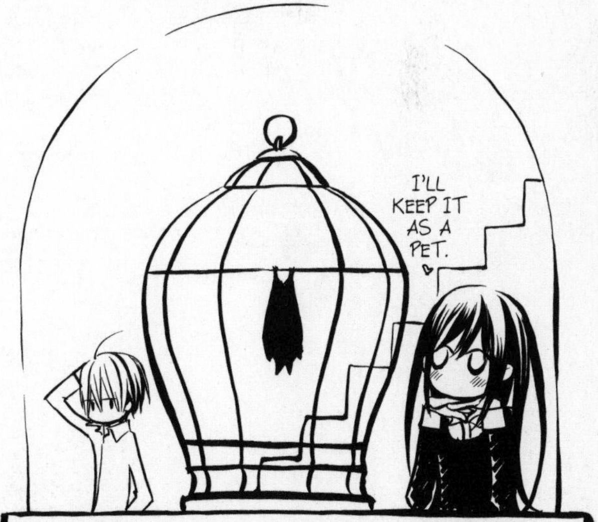
I'LL KEEP IT AS A PET.

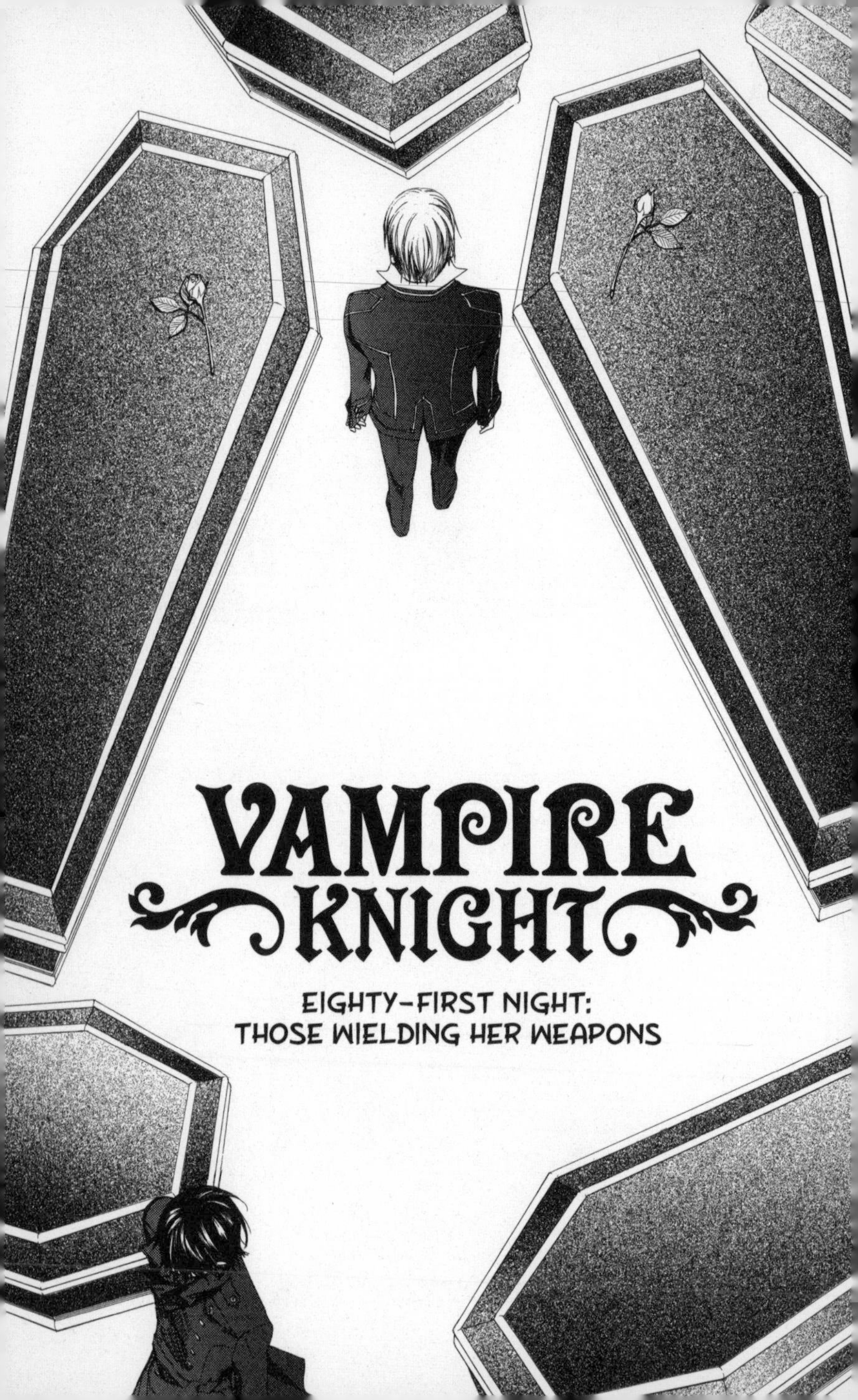
VAMPIRE KNIGHT
EIGHTY-FIRST NIGHT:
THOSE WIELDING HER WEAPONS

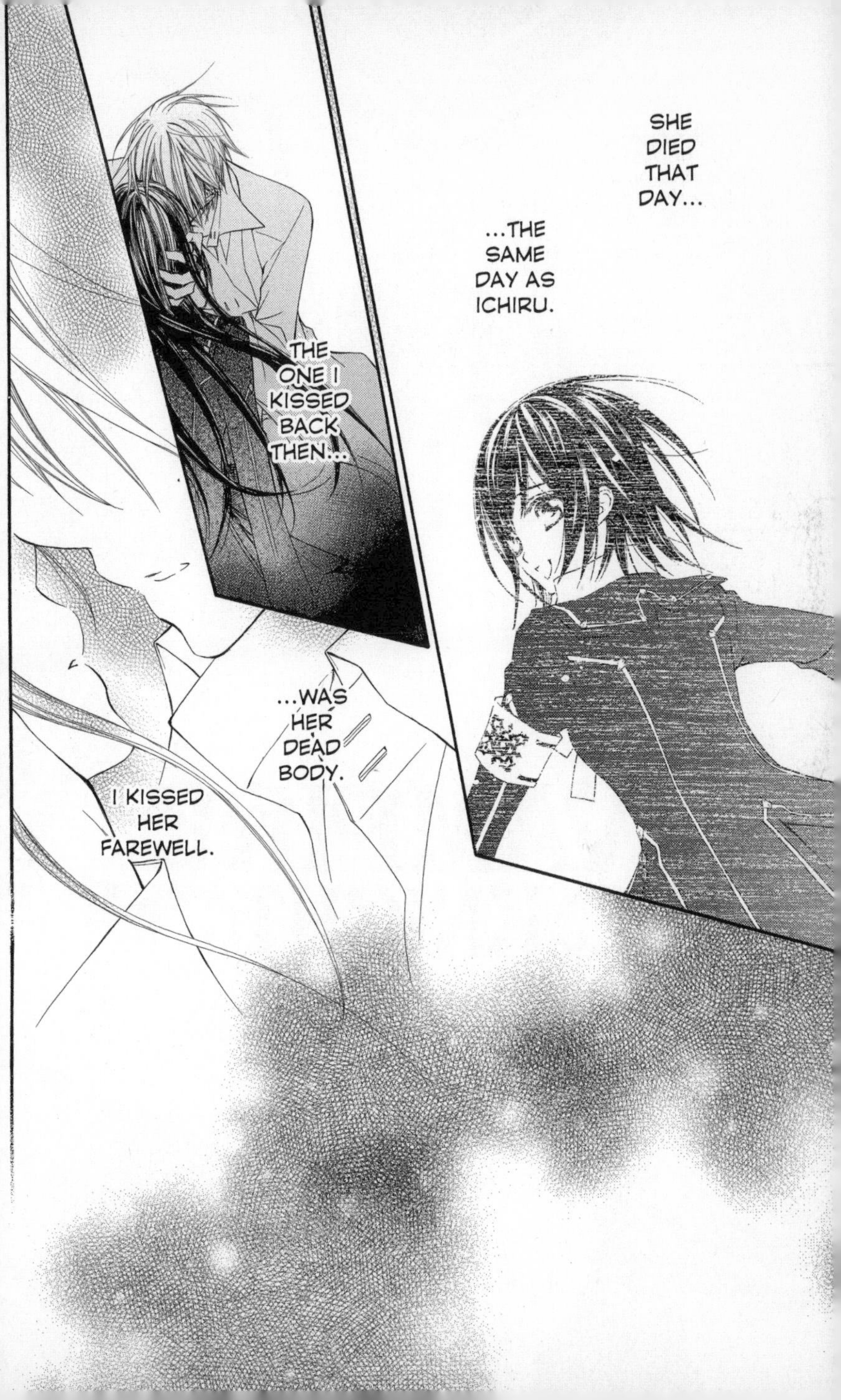
SHE DIED THAT DAY...
...THE SAME DAY AS ICHIRU.
THE ONE I KISSED BACK THEN...
...WAS HER DEAD BODY.
I KISSED HER FAREWELL.

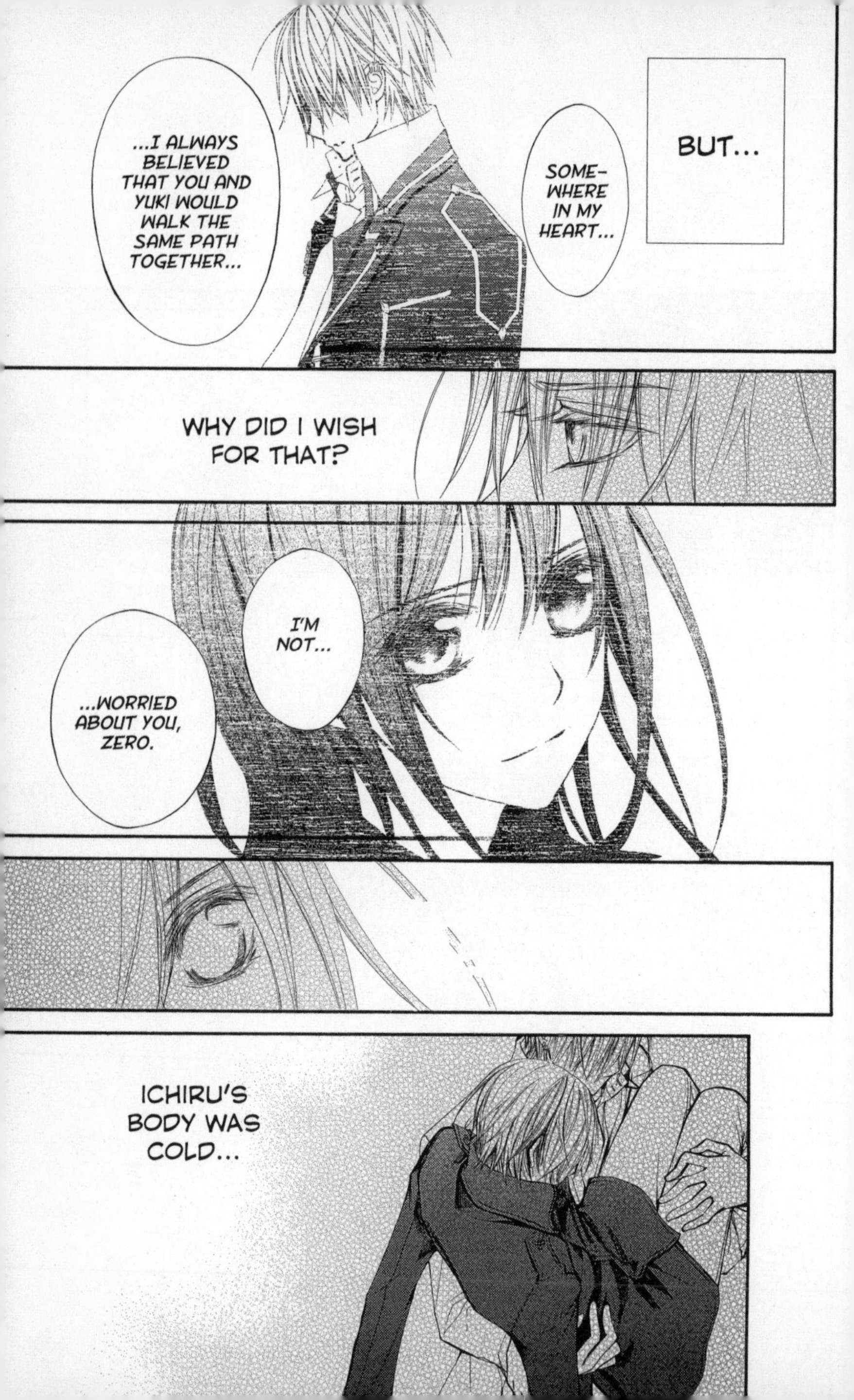
BUT...
SOME-WHERE IN MY HEART...
...I ALWAYS BELIEVED THAT YOU AND YUKI WOULD WALK THE SAME PATH TOGETHER...
WHY DID I WISH FOR THAT?
I'M NOT...
...WORRIED ABOUT YOU, ZERO.
ICHIRU'S BODY WAS COLD...

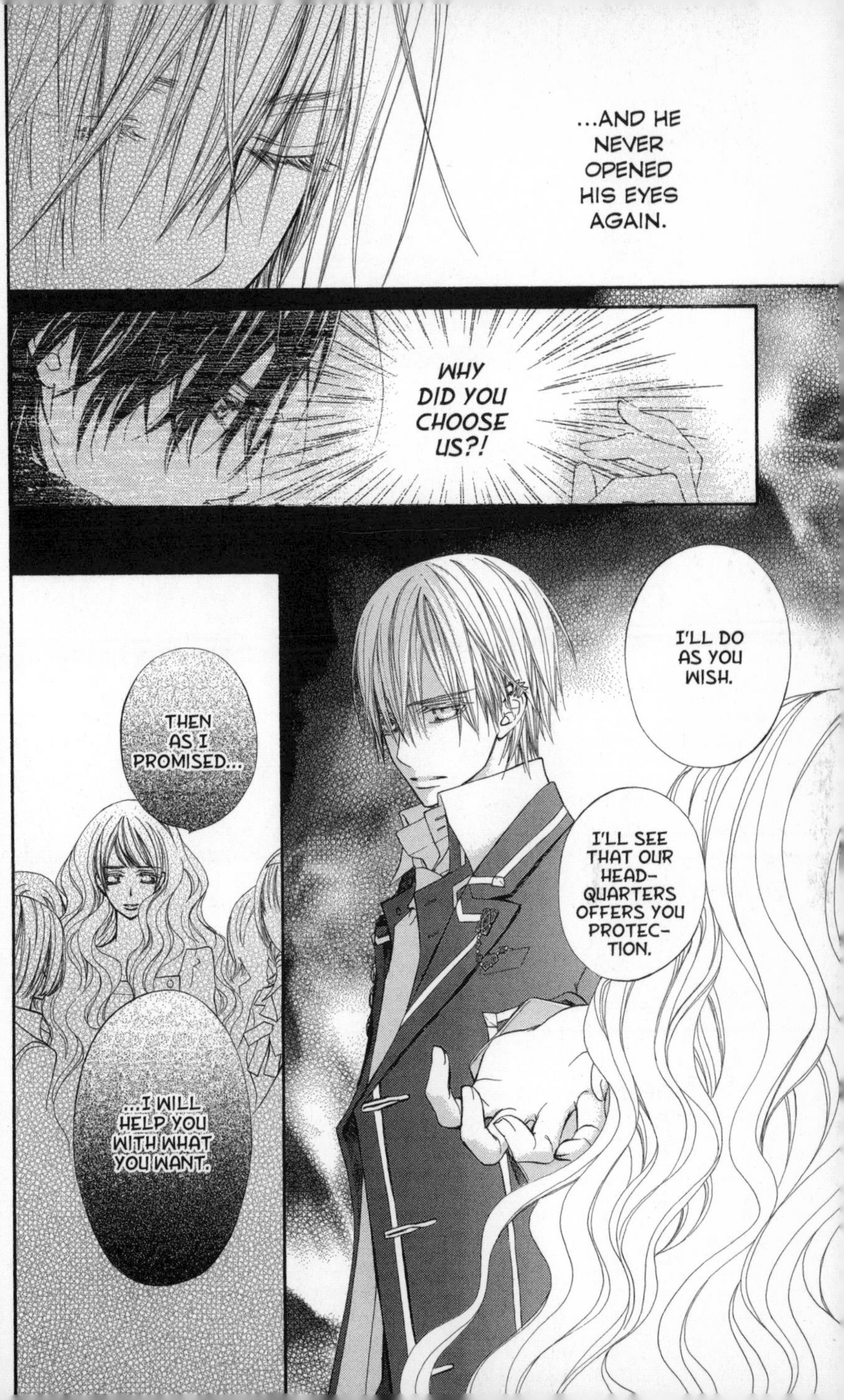
...AND HE NEVER OPENED HIS EYES AGAIN.
WHY DID YOU CHOOSE US?!
I'LL DO AS YOU WISH.
I'LL SEE THAT OUR HEAD-QUARTERS OFFERS YOU PROTECTION.
THEN AS I PROMISED...
...I WILL HELP YOU WITH WHAT YOU WANT.

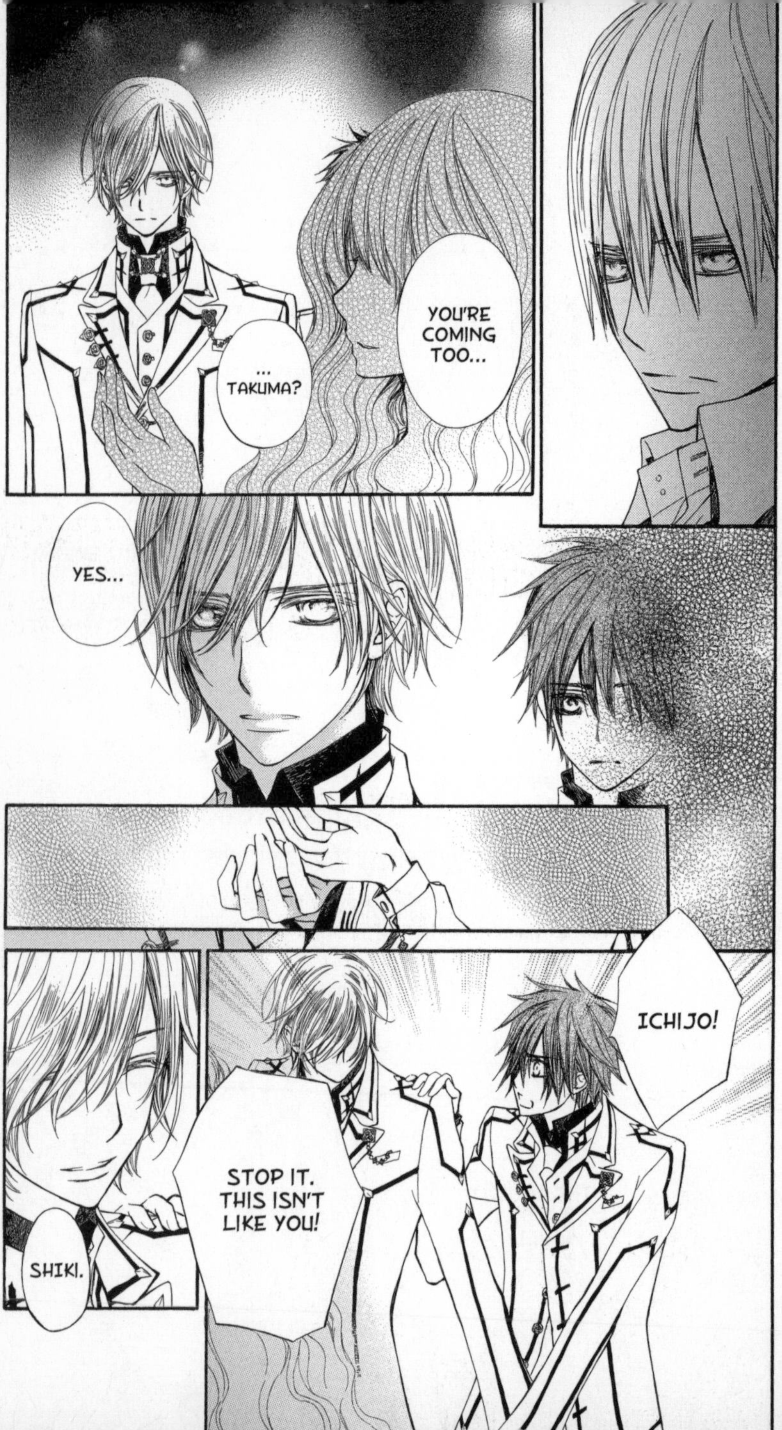
YOU'RE COMING TOO...
...TAKUMA?
YES...
ICHIJO!
STOP IT. THIS ISN'T LIKE YOU!
SHIKI.

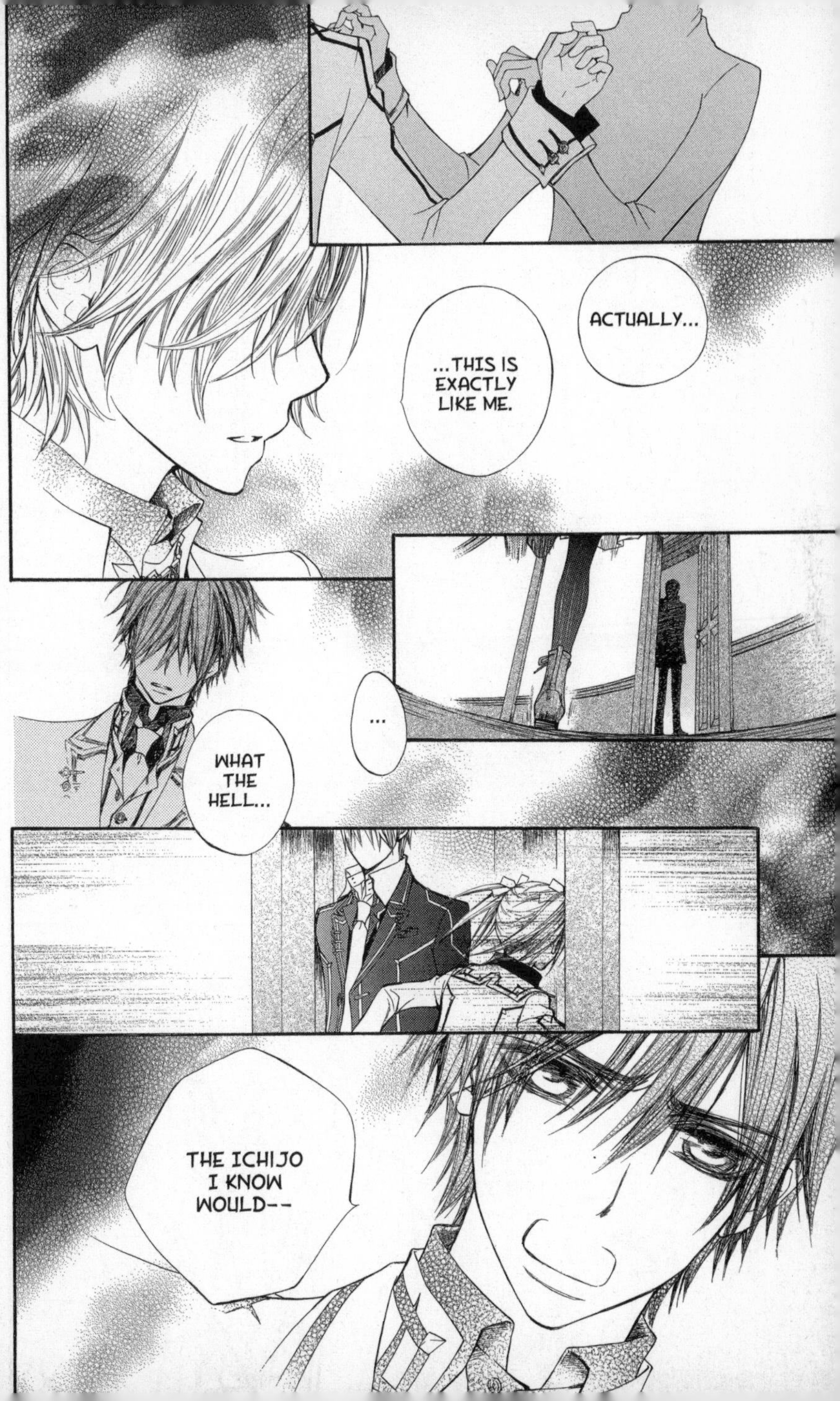
ACTUALLY...
...THIS IS EXACTLY LIKE ME.
...
WHAT THE HELL...
THE ICHIJO I KNOW WOULD--

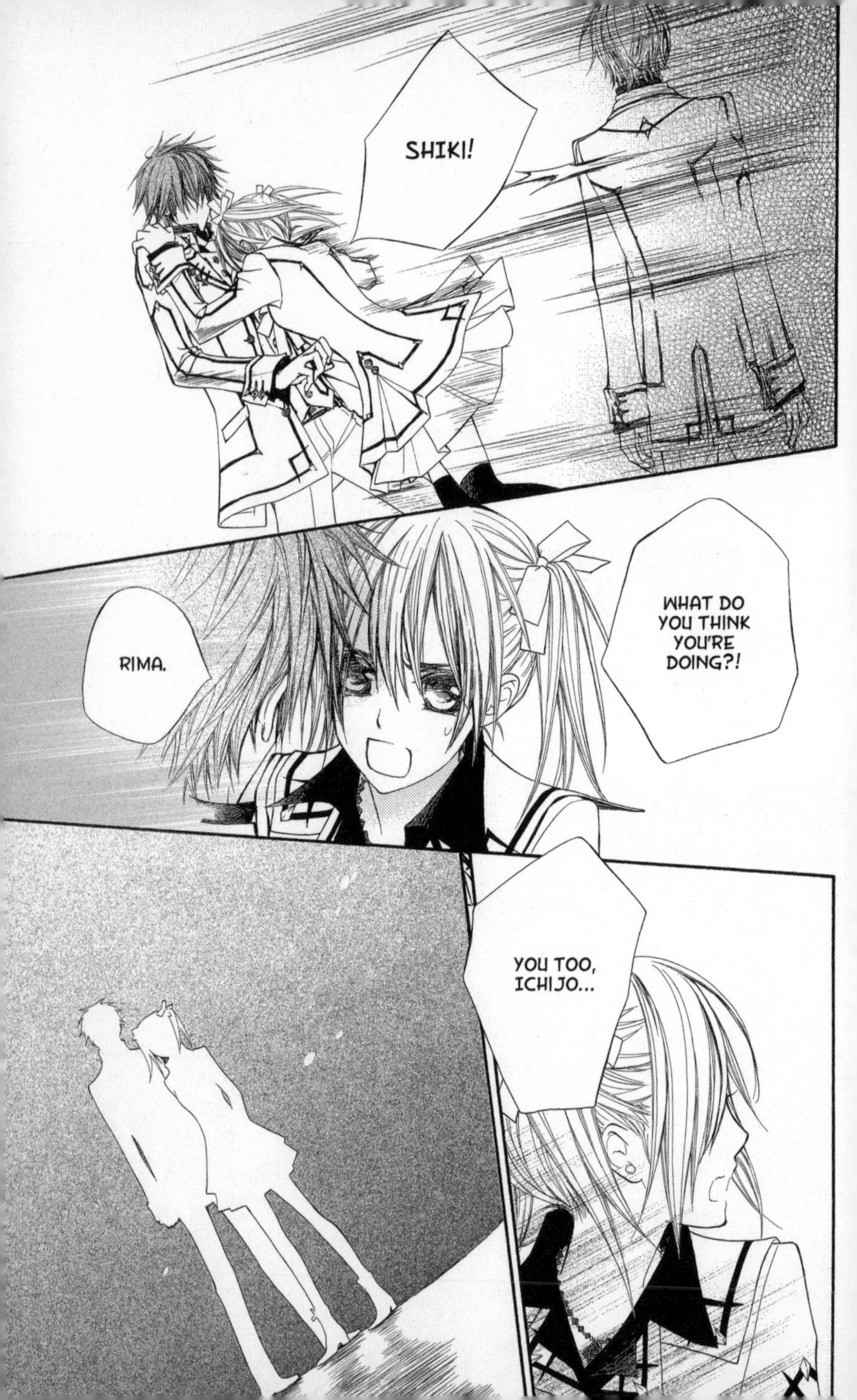
SHIKI!
WHAT DO YOU THINK YOU'RE DOING?!
RIMA.
YOU TOO, ICHIJO...

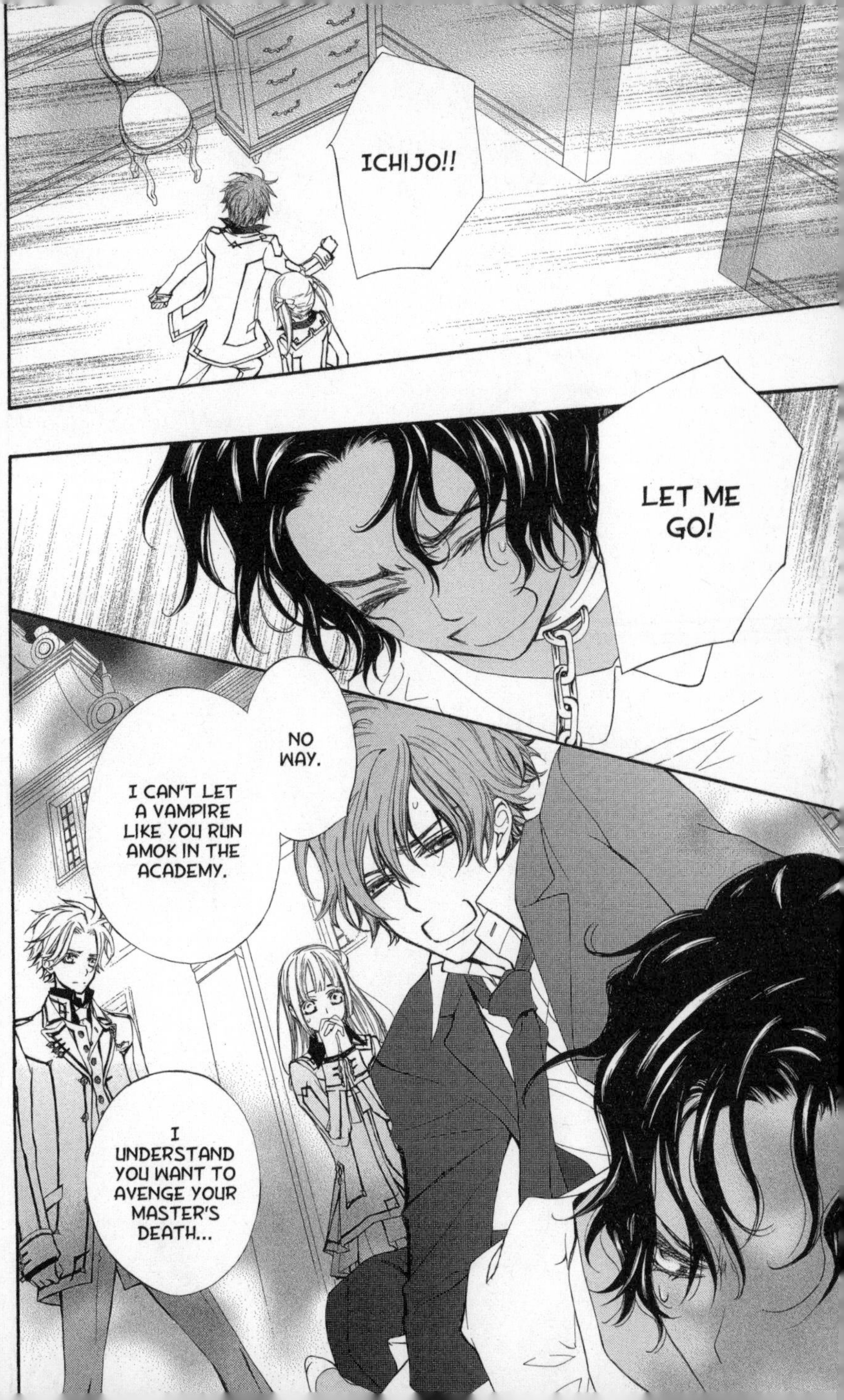
ICHIJO!!
LET ME GO!
NO WAY.
I CAN'T LET A VAMPIRE LIKE YOU RUN AMOK IN THE ACADEMY.
I UNDERSTAND YOU WANT TO AVENGE YOUR MASTER'S DEATH...

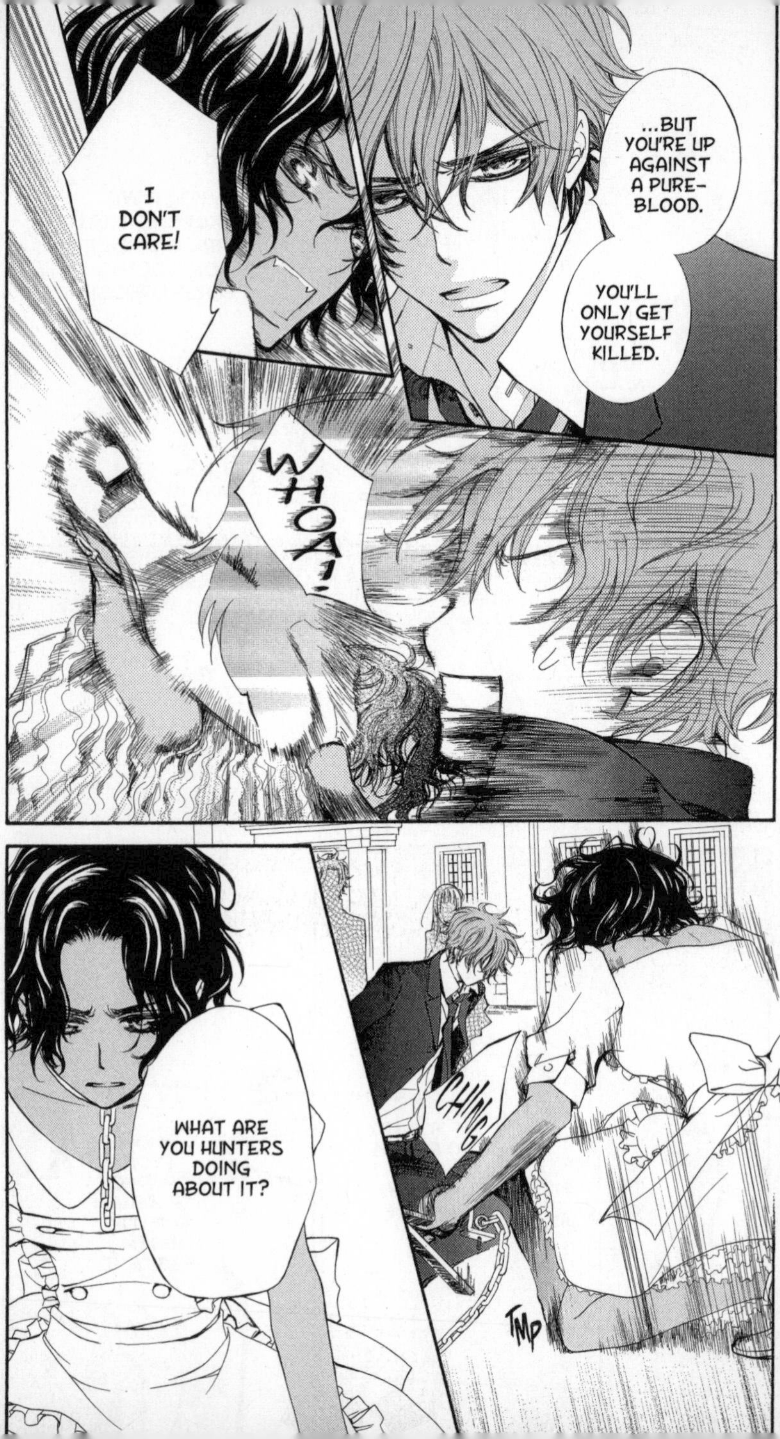
...BUT YOU'RE UP AGAINST A PURE-BLOOD.
YOU'LL ONLY GET YOURSELF KILLED.
I DON'T CARE!
WHOA!
CHING
TMP
WHAT ARE YOU HUNTERS DOING ABOUT IT?

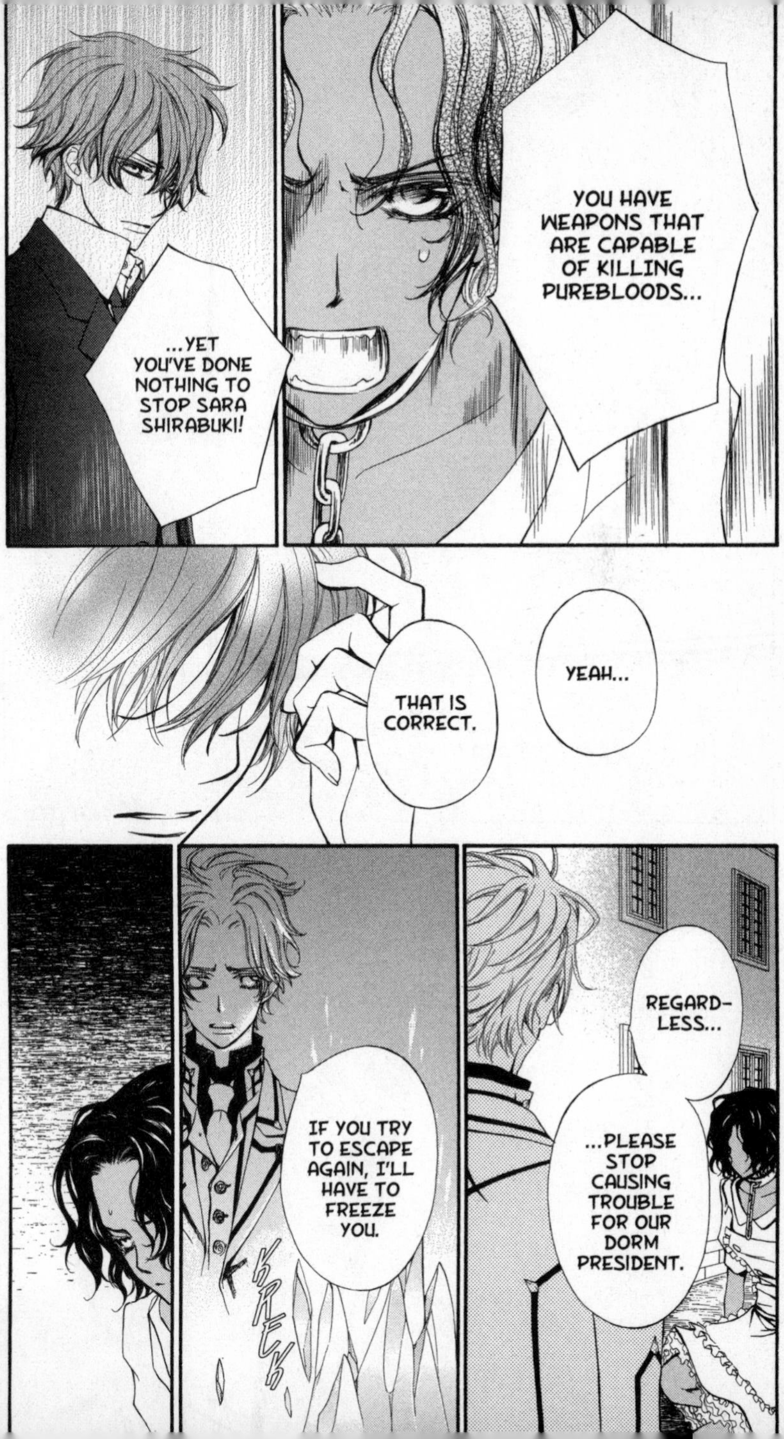
YOU HAVE WEAPONS THAT ARE CAPABLE OF KILLING PUREBLOODS...
...YET YOU'VE DONE NOTHING TO STOP SARA SHIRABUKI!
YEAH...
THAT IS CORRECT.
REGARD-LESS...
...PLEASE STOP CAUSING TROUBLE FOR OUR DORM PRESIDENT.
IF YOU TRY TO ESCAPE AGAIN, I'LL HAVE TO FREEZE YOU.
KREK

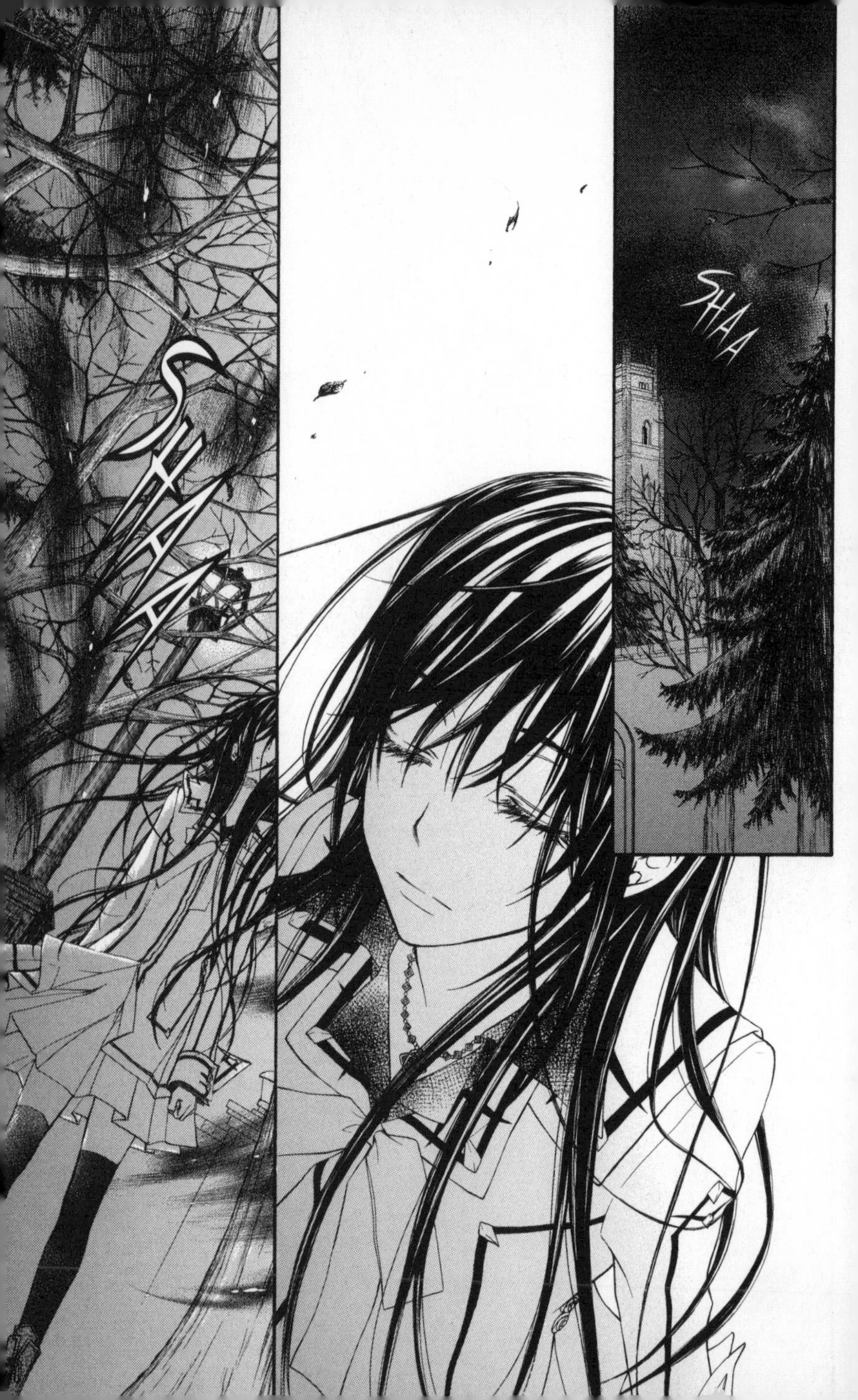
SHAA
SHAAAA

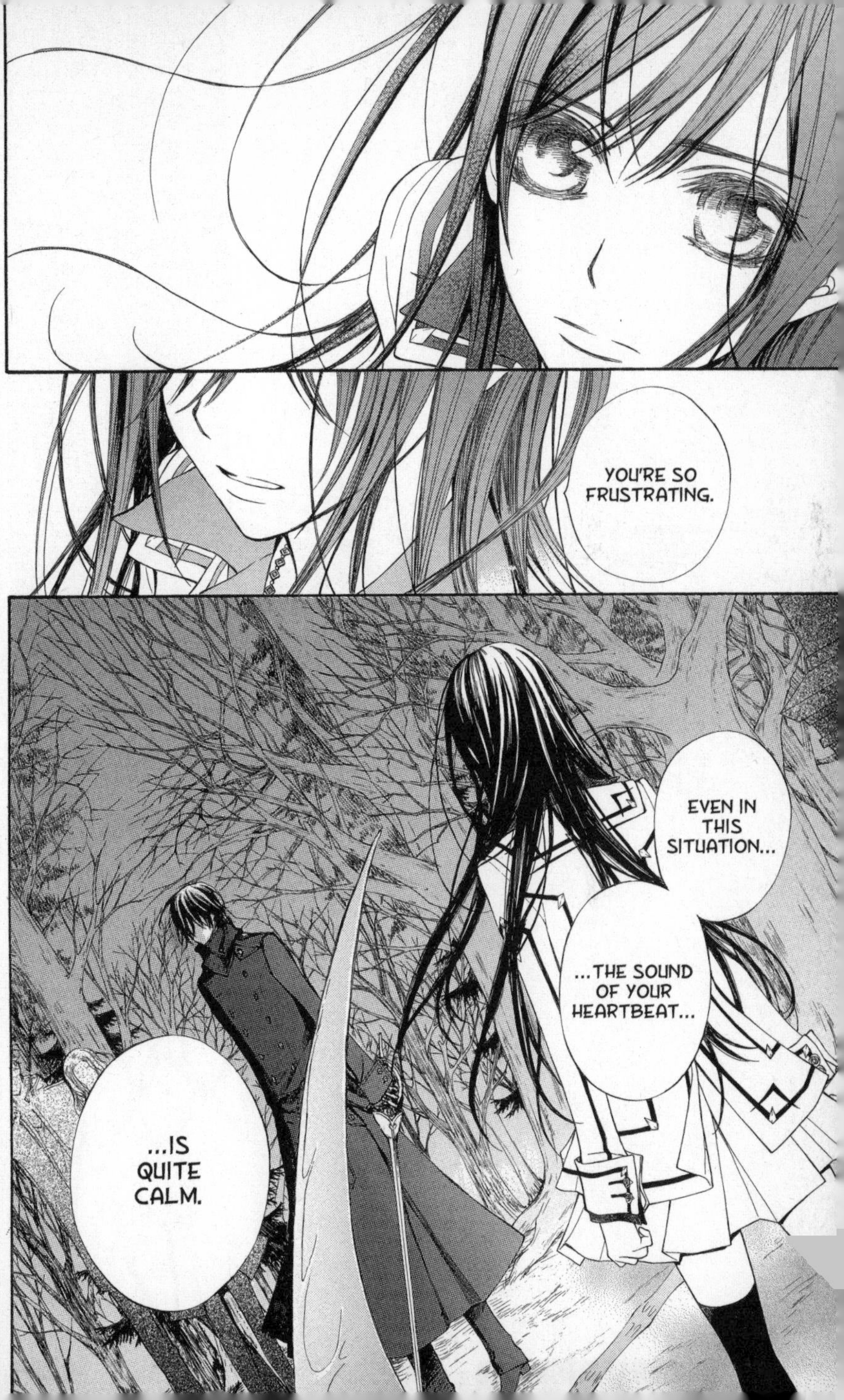
YOU'RE SO FRUSTRATING.
EVEN IN THIS SITUATION...
...THE SOUND OF YOUR HEARTBEAT...
...IS QUITE CALM.

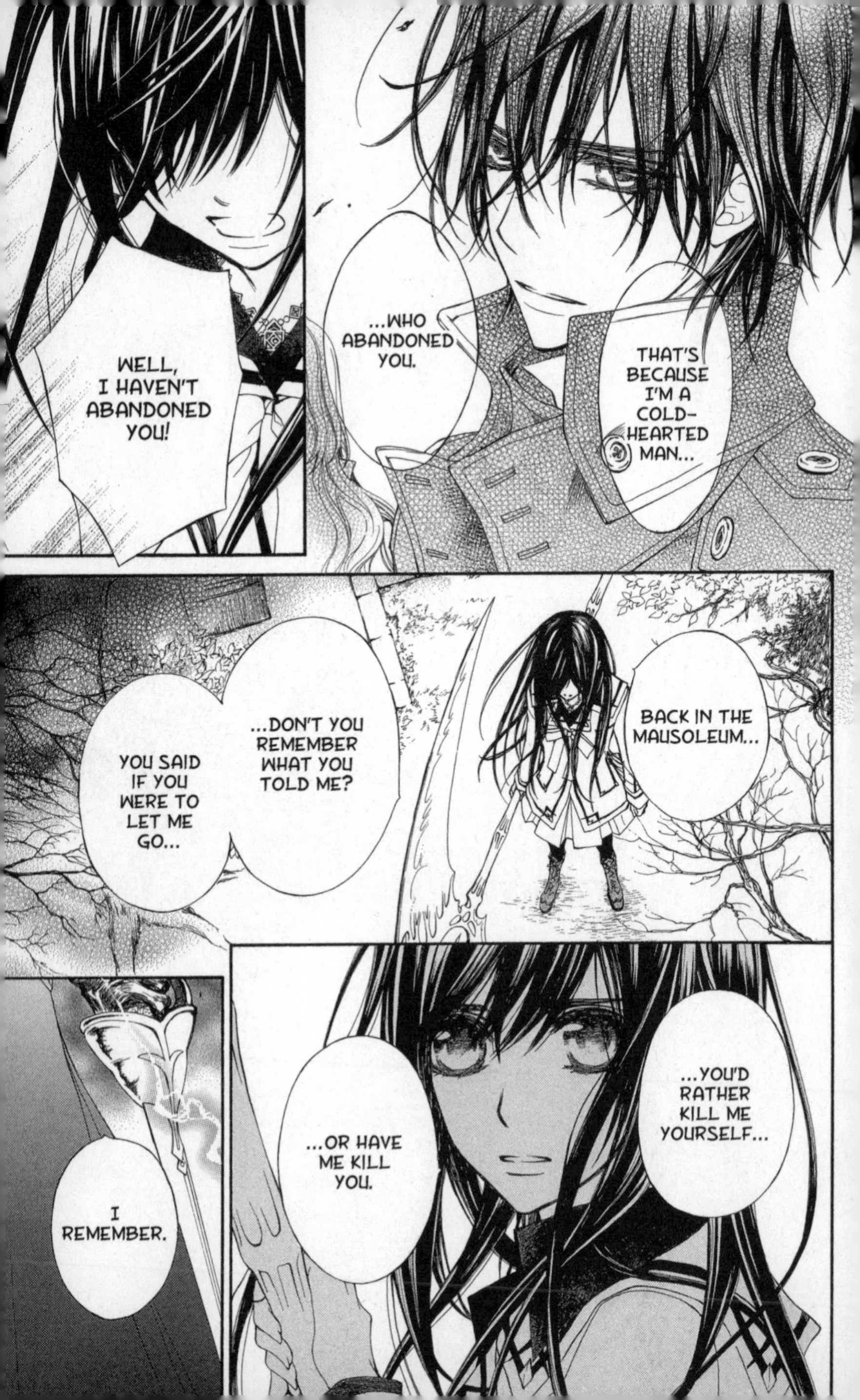
THAT'S BECAUSE I'M A COLD-HEARTED MAN...
...WHO ABANDONED YOU.
WELL, I HAVEN'T ABANDONED YOU!
BACK IN THE MAUSOLEUM...
...DON'T YOU REMEMBER WHAT YOU TOLD ME?
YOU SAID IF YOU WERE TO LET ME GO...
...YOU'D RATHER KILL ME YOURSELF...
...OR HAVE ME KILL YOU.
I REMEMBER.

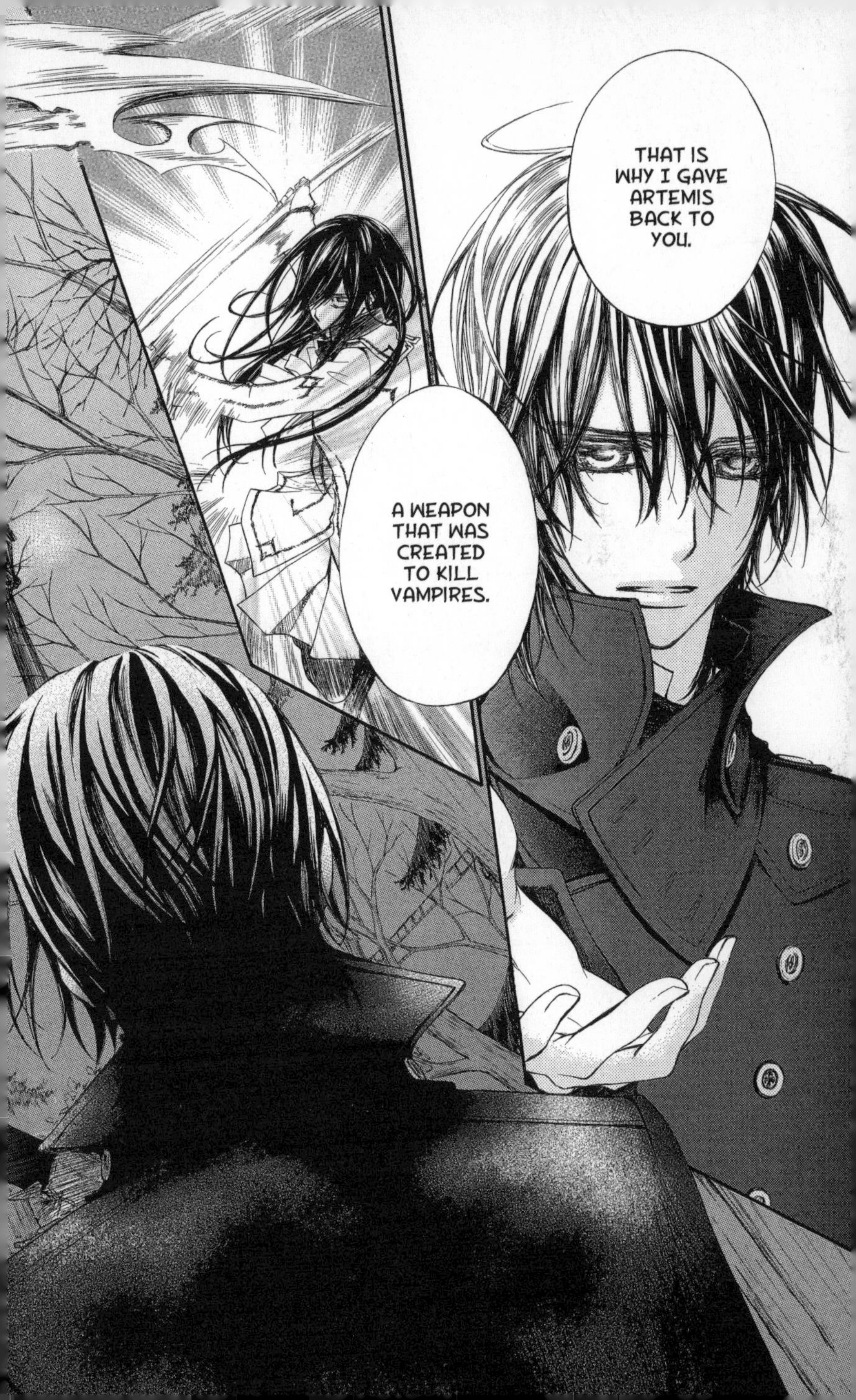
THAT IS WHY I GAVE ARTEMIS BACK TO YOU.
A WEAPON THAT WAS CREATED TO KILL VAMPIRES.

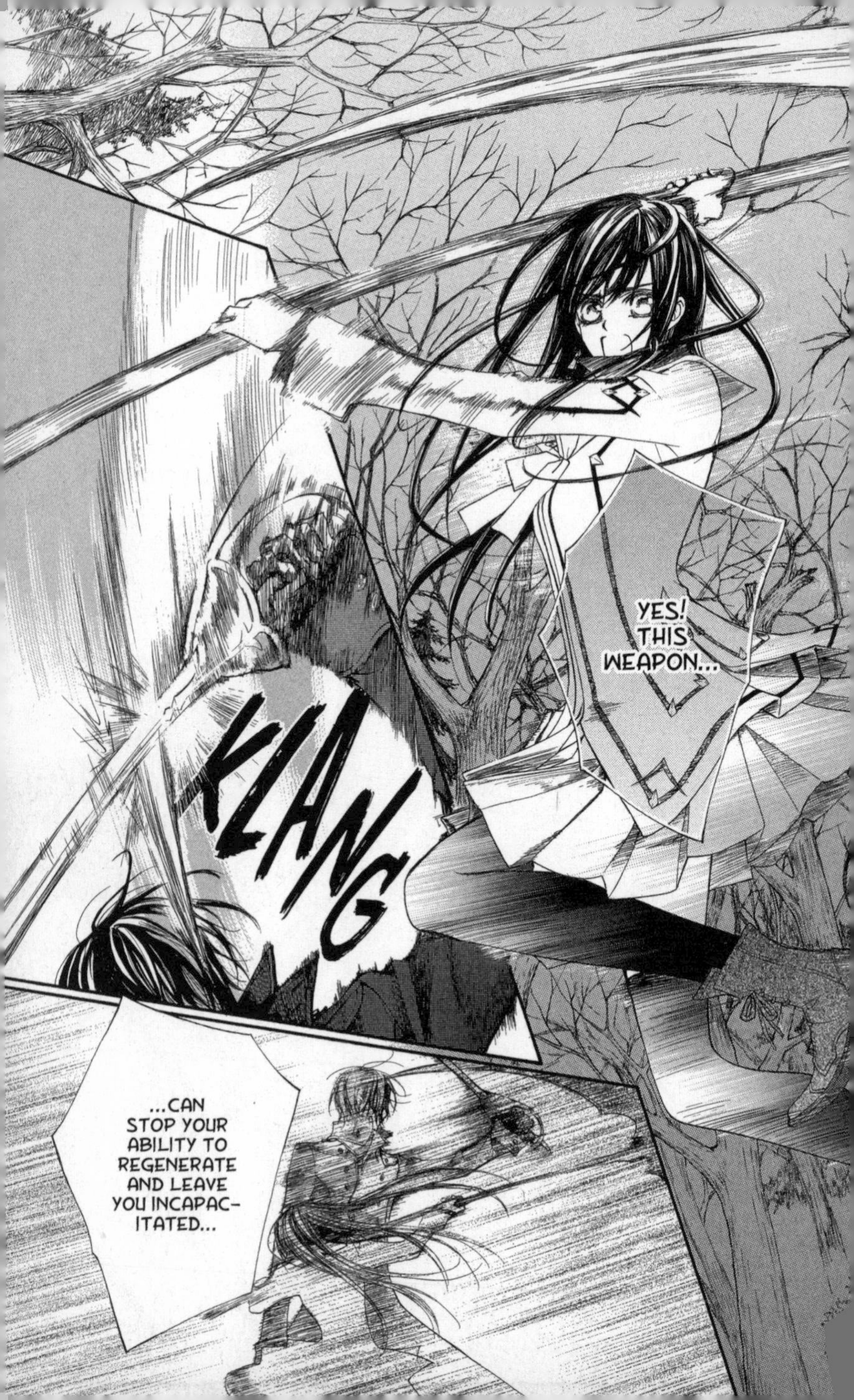
YES! THIS WEAPON...
KLANG
...CAN STOP YOUR ABILITY TO REGENERATE AND LEAVE YOU INCAPACITATED...

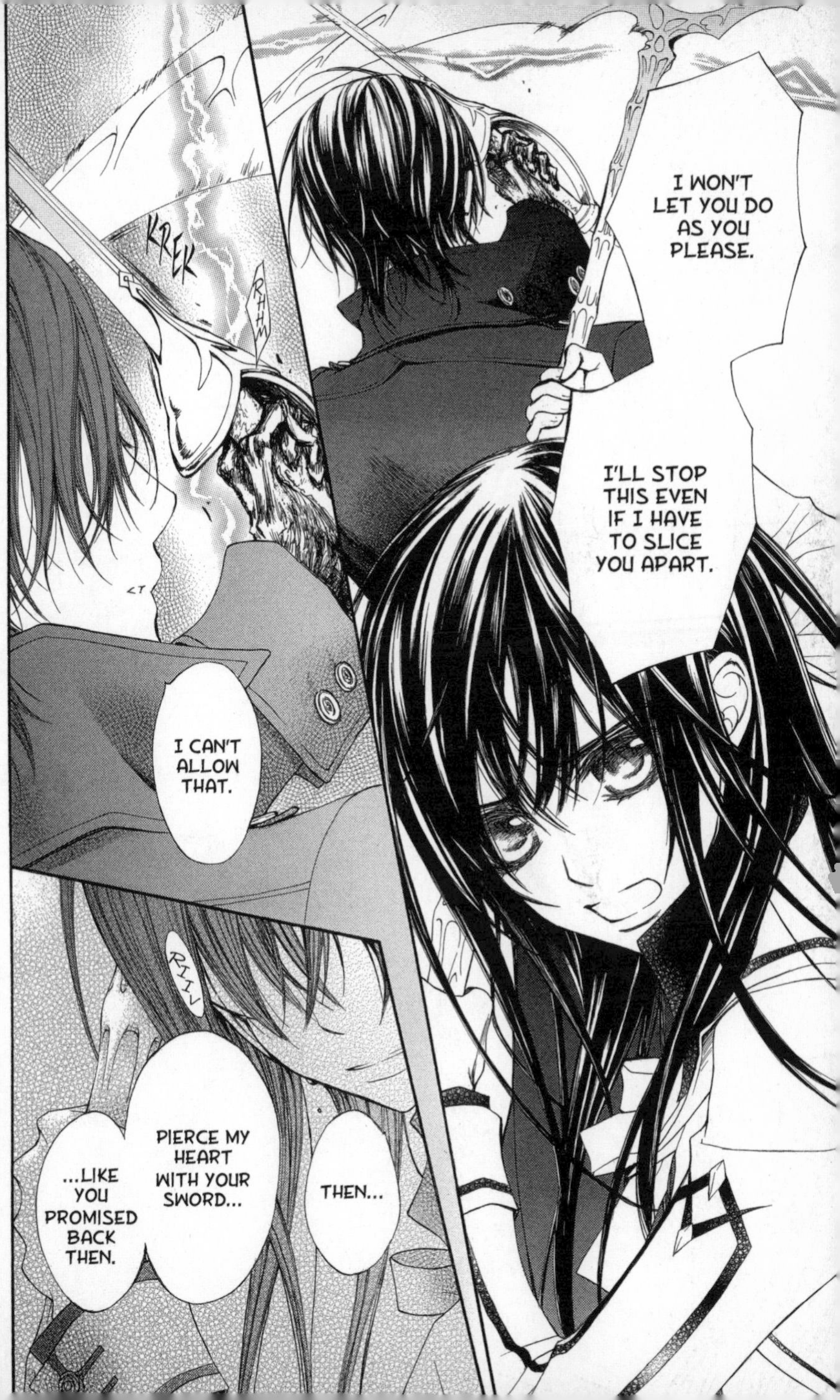
I WON'T LET YOU DO AS YOU PLEASE.
I'LL STOP THIS EVEN IF I HAVE TO SLICE YOU APART.
KREK
RHHM
I CAN'T ALLOW THAT.
RIIN
THEN...
PIERCE MY HEART WITH YOUR SWORD...
...LIKE YOU PROMISED BACK THEN.

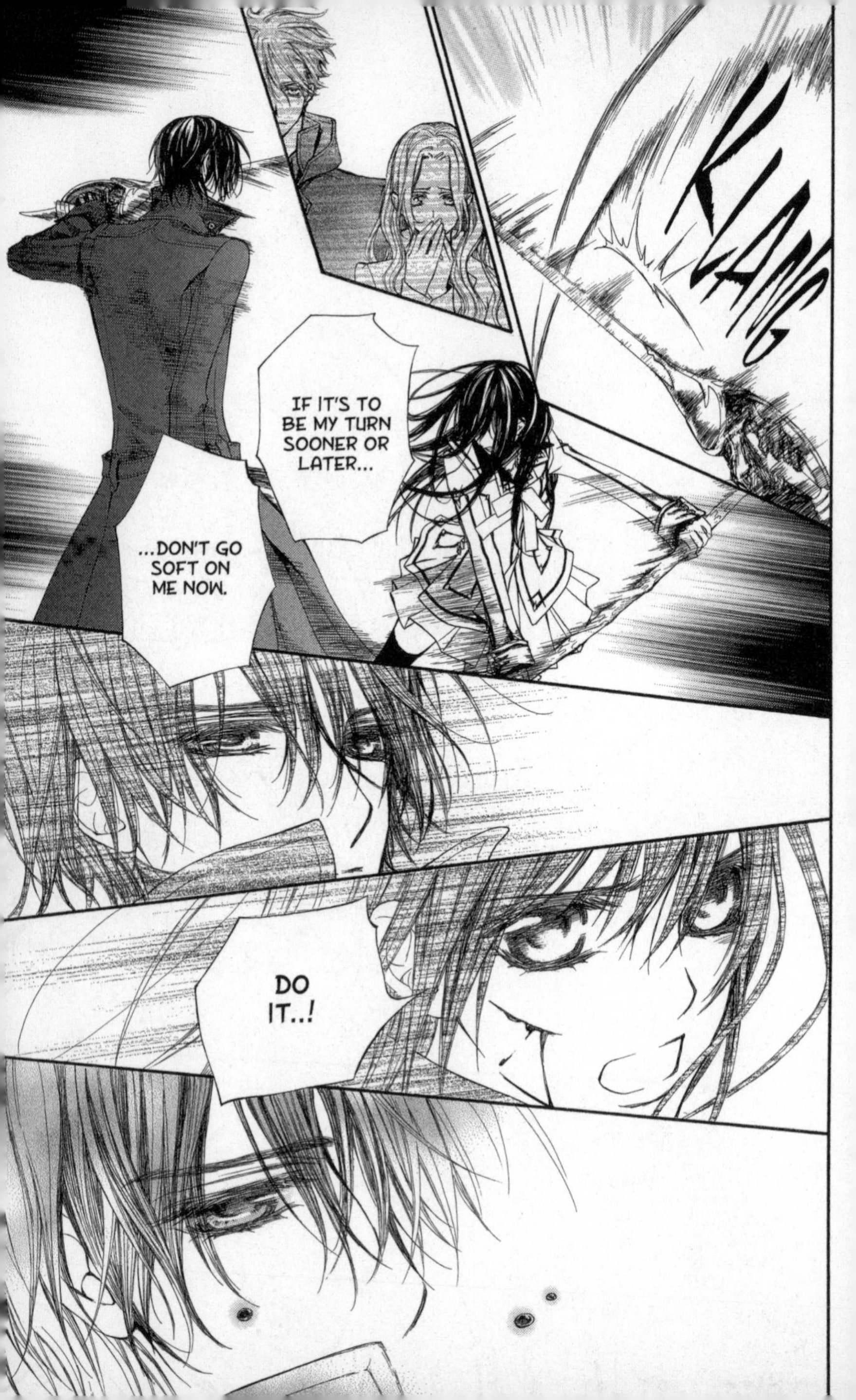
KLANG
IF IT'S TO BE MY TURN SOONER OR LATER...
...DON'T GO SOFT ON ME NOW.
DO IT...!

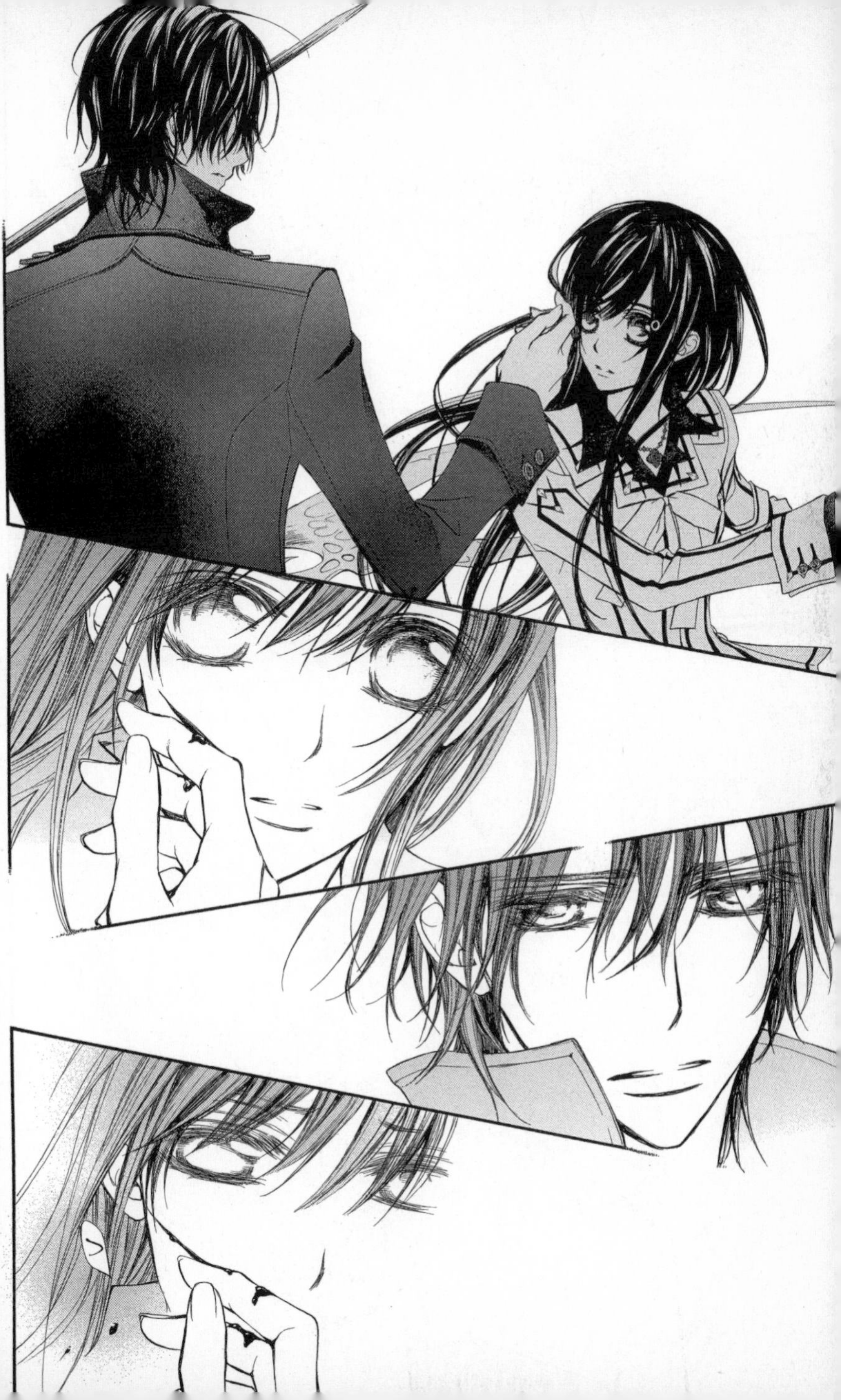

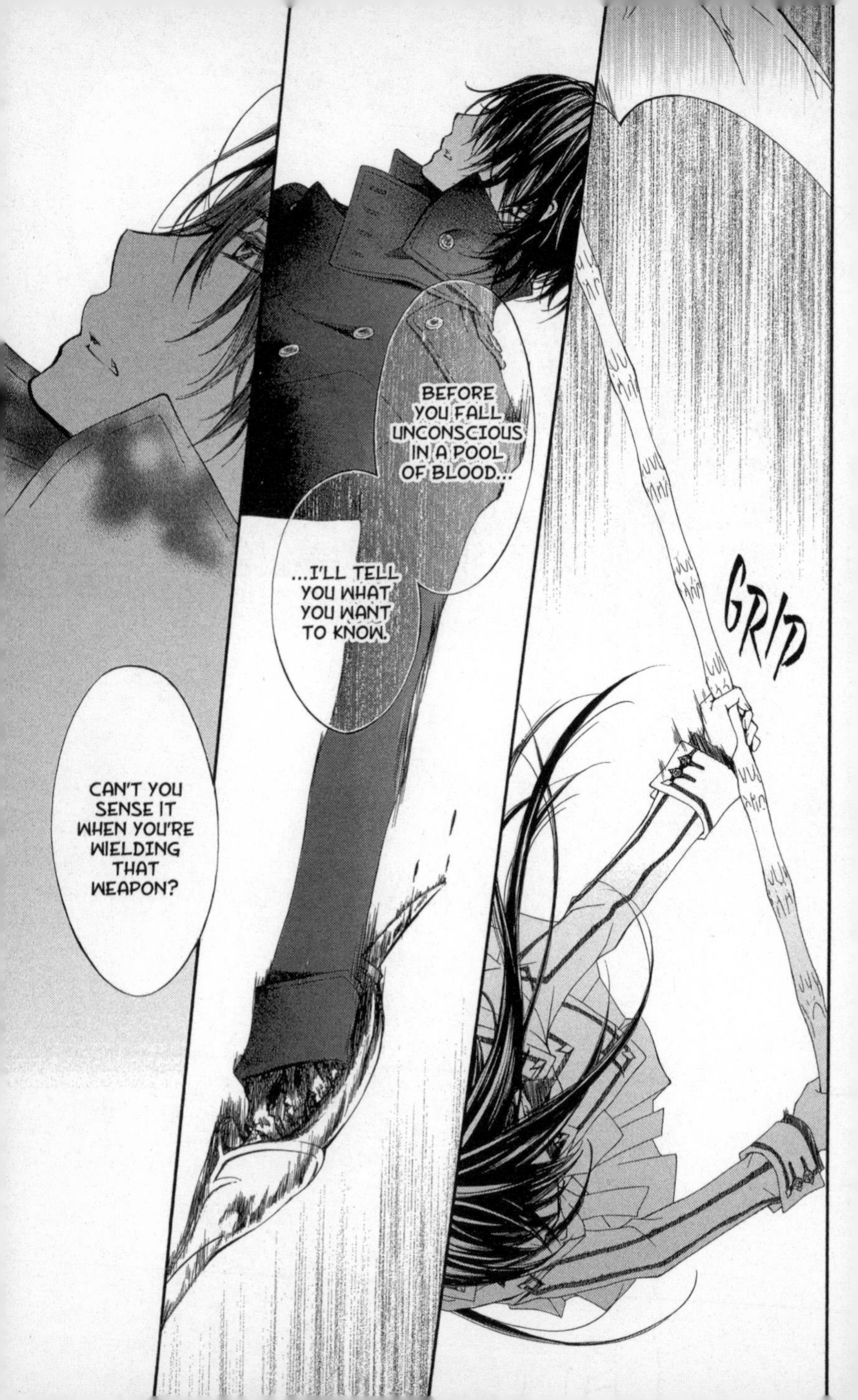
GRIP
BEFORE YOU FALL UNCONSCIOUS IN A POOL OF BLOOD...
...I'LL TELL YOU WHAT YOU WANT TO KNOW.
CAN'T YOU SENSE IT WHEN YOU'RE WIELDING THAT WEAPON?

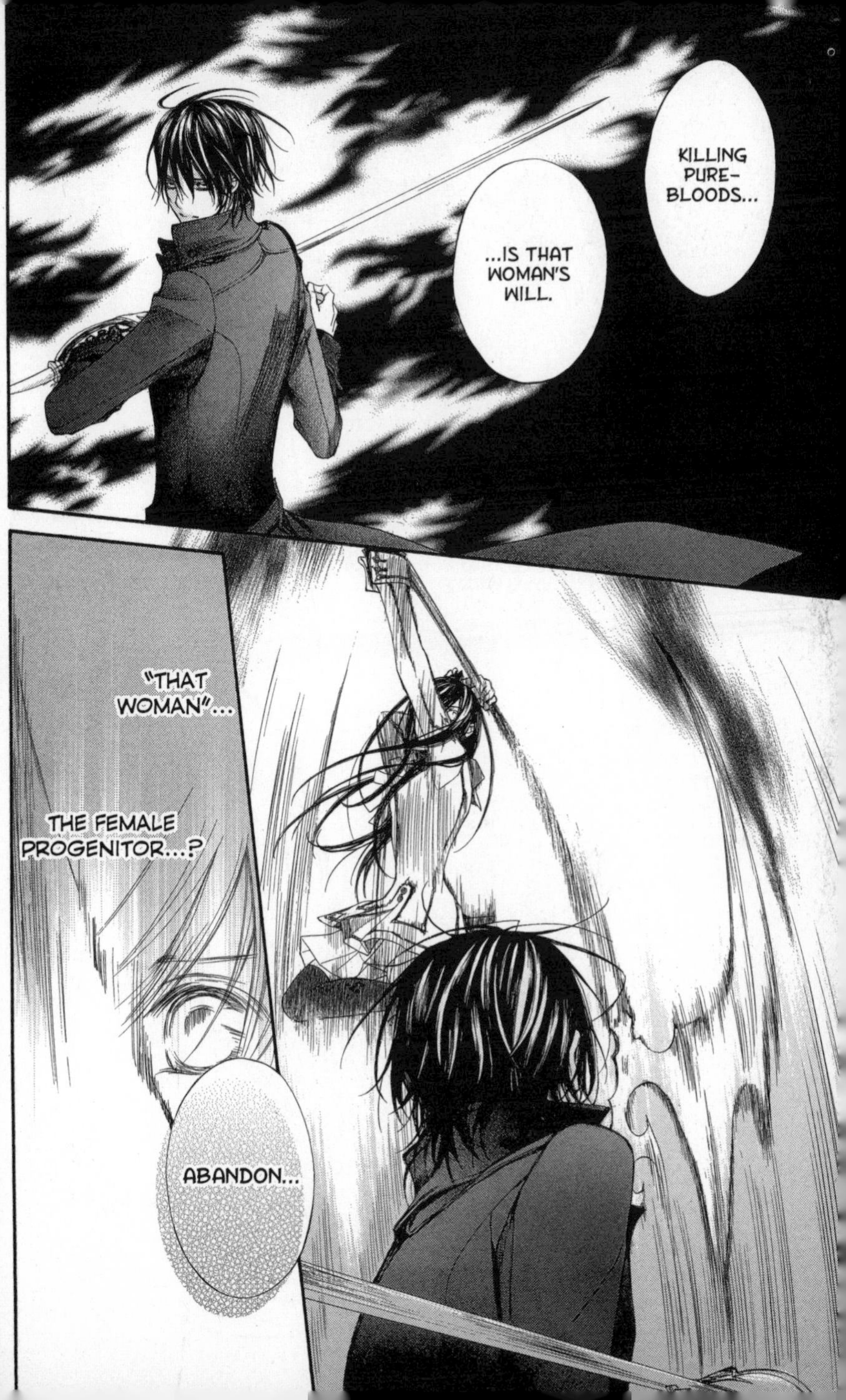
KILLING PURE-BLOODS...
...IS THAT WOMAN'S WILL.
"THAT WOMAN"...
THE FEMALE PROGENITOR...?
ABANDON...

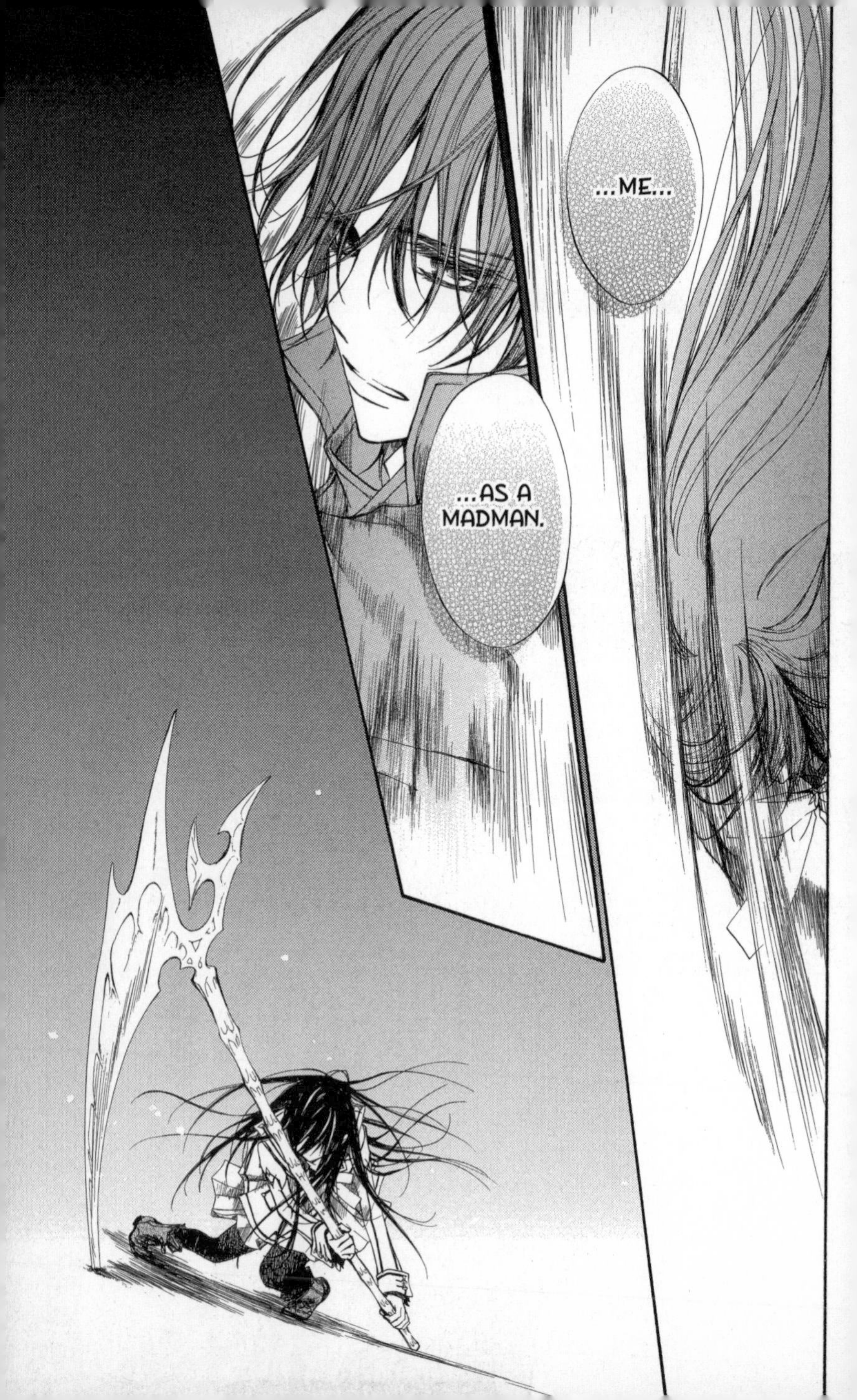
...ME...
...AS A MADMAN.

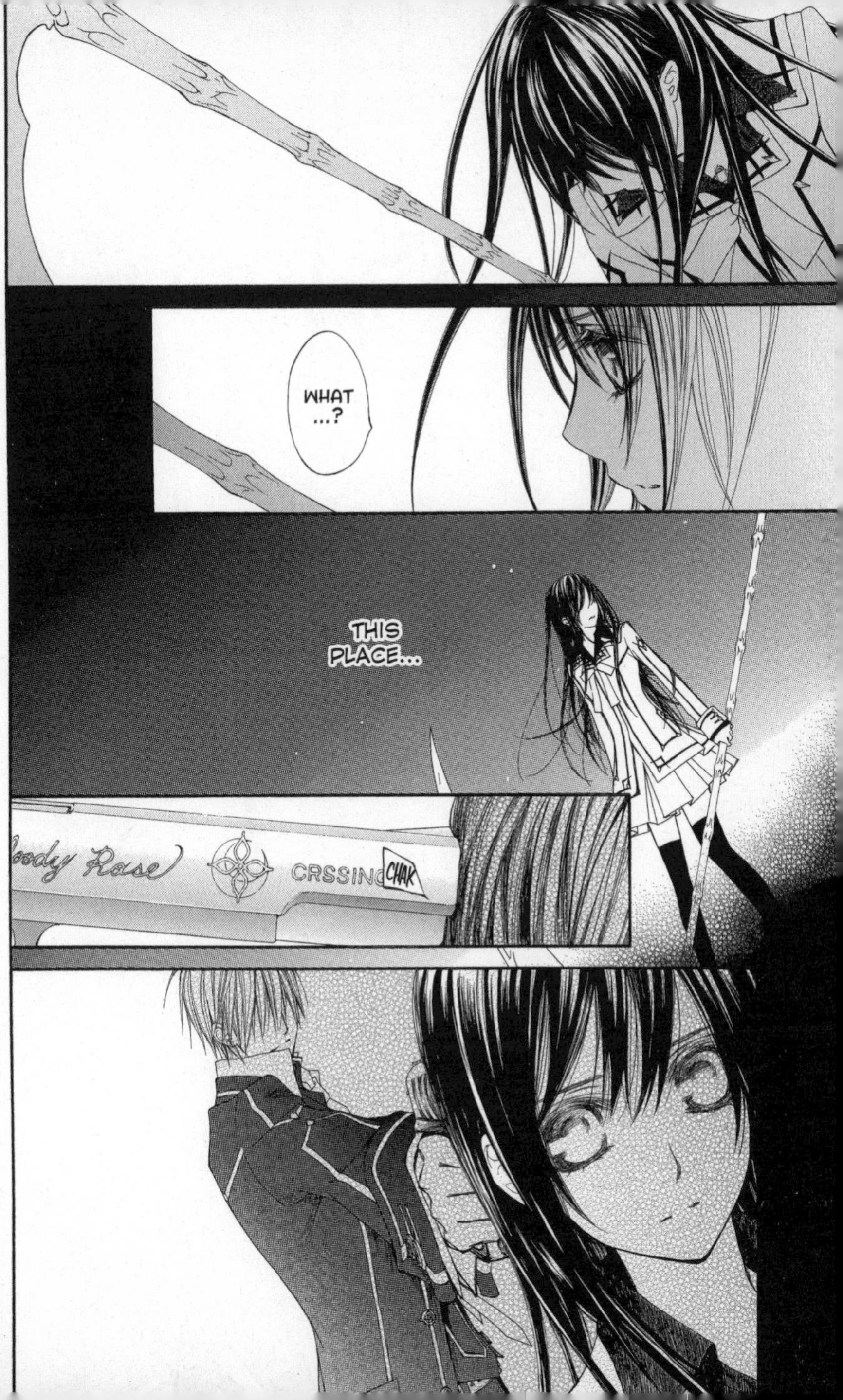
WHAT ...?
THIS PLACE...
CHAK

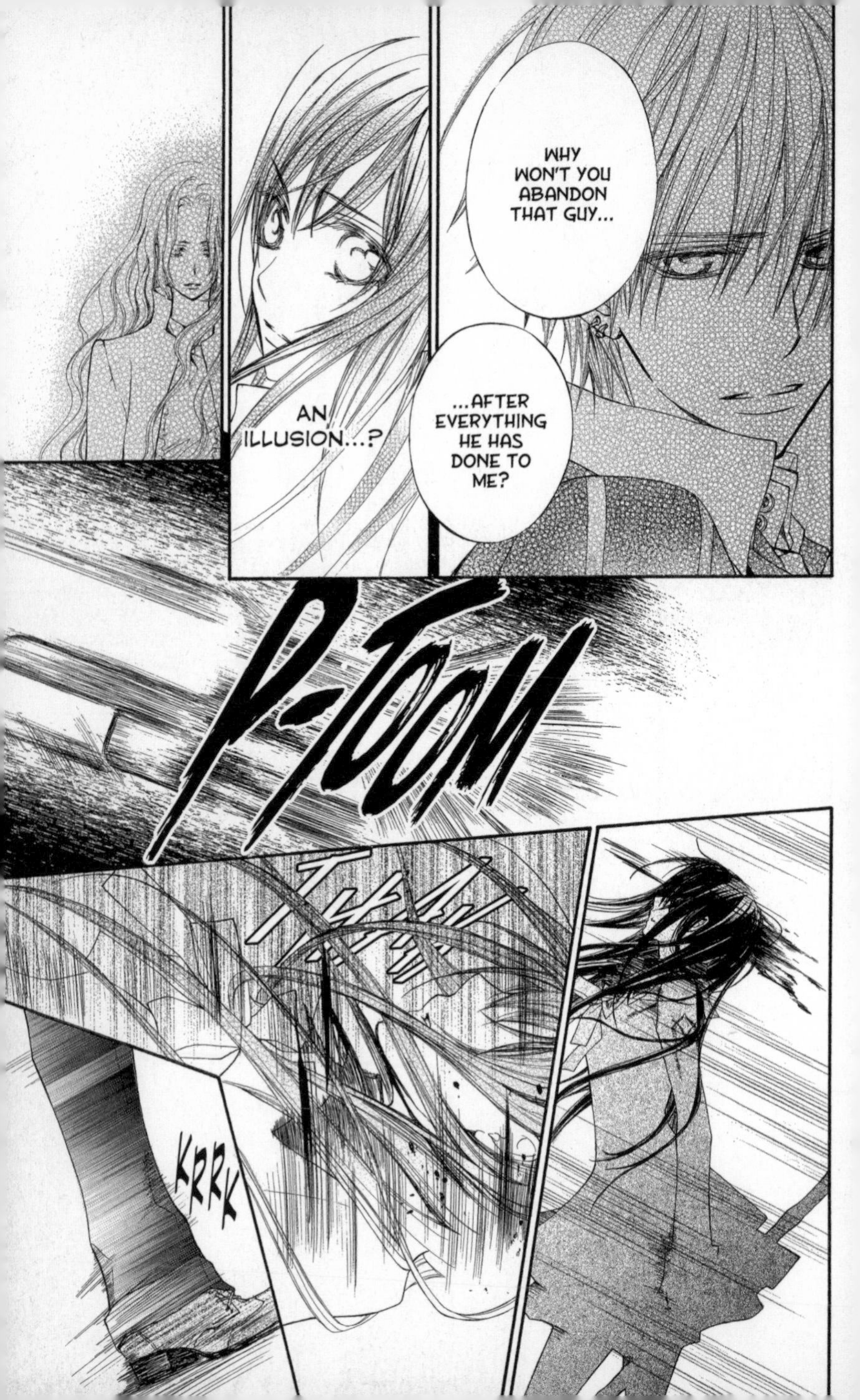
WHY WON'T YOU ABANDON THAT GUY...
...AFTER EVERYTHING HE HAS DONE TO ME?
AN ILLUSION...?
P-TOOM
KRRK

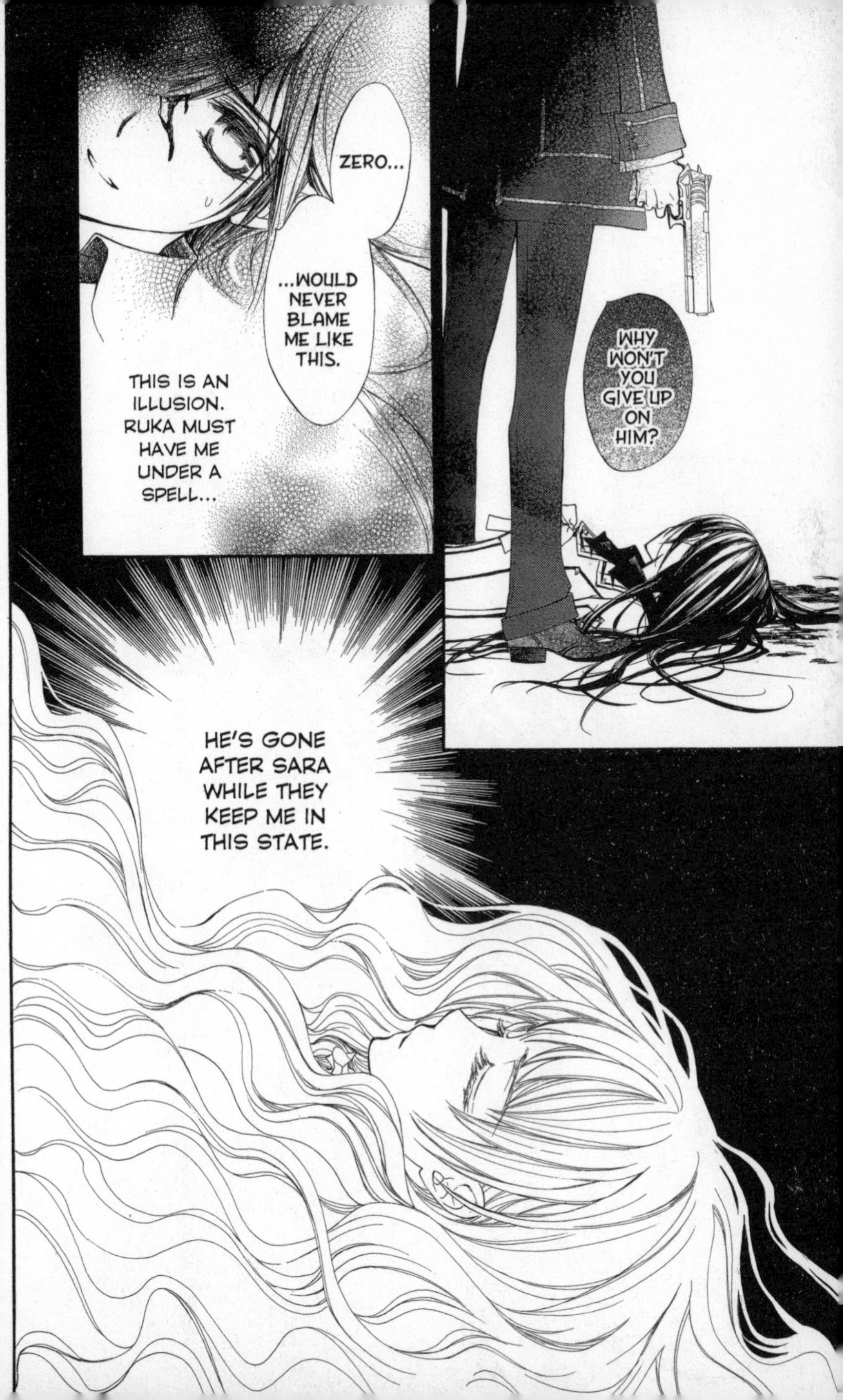
WHY WON'T YOU GIVE UP ON HIM?
ZERO...
...WOULD NEVER BLAME ME LIKE THIS.
THIS IS AN ILLUSION. RUKA MUST HAVE ME UNDER A SPELL...
HE'S GONE AFTER SARA WHILE THEY KEEP ME IN THIS STATE.

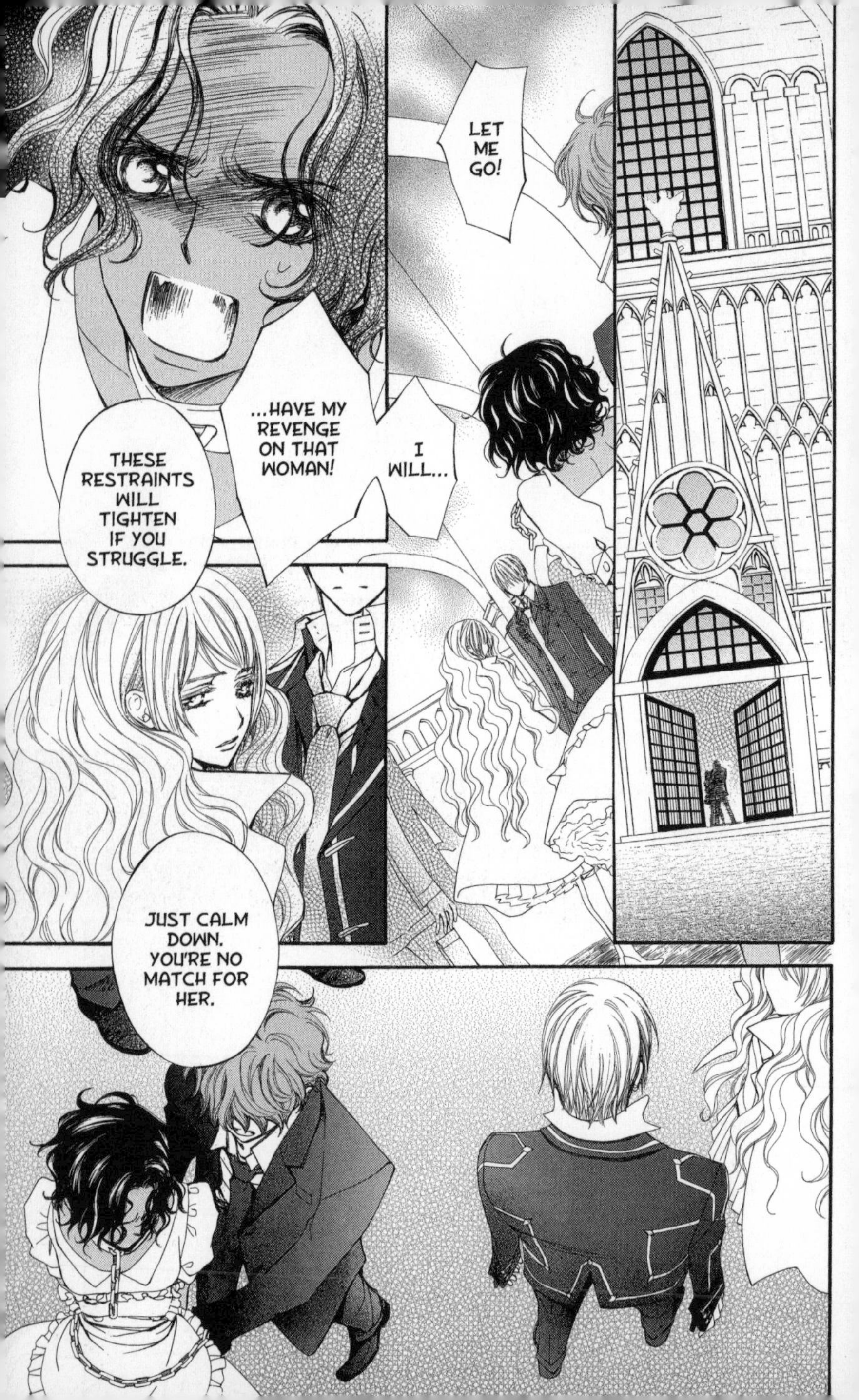
LET ME GO!
I WILL...
...HAVE MY REVENGE ON THAT WOMAN!
THESE RESTRAINTS WILL TIGHTEN IF YOU STRUGGLE.
JUST CALM DOWN. YOU'RE NO MATCH FOR HER.

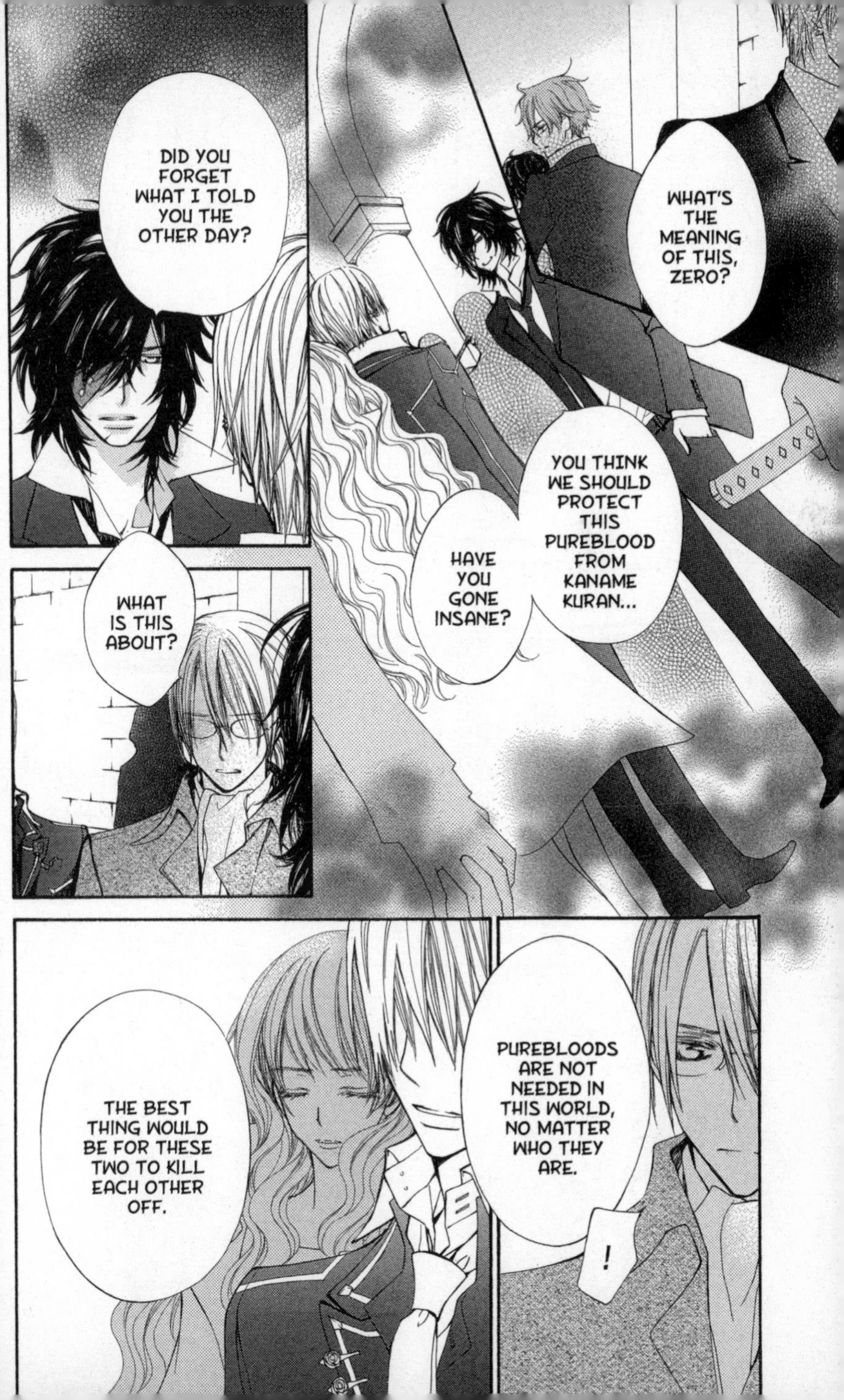
WHAT'S THE MEANING OF THIS, ZERO?
YOU THINK WE SHOULD PROTECT THIS PUREBLOOD FROM KANAME KURAN...
HAVE YOU GONE INSANE?
DID YOU FORGET WHAT I TOLD YOU THE OTHER DAY?
WHAT IS THIS ABOUT?
PUREBLOODS ARE NOT NEEDED IN THIS WORLD, NO MATTER WHO THEY ARE.
!
THE BEST THING WOULD BE FOR THESE TWO TO KILL EACH OTHER OFF.

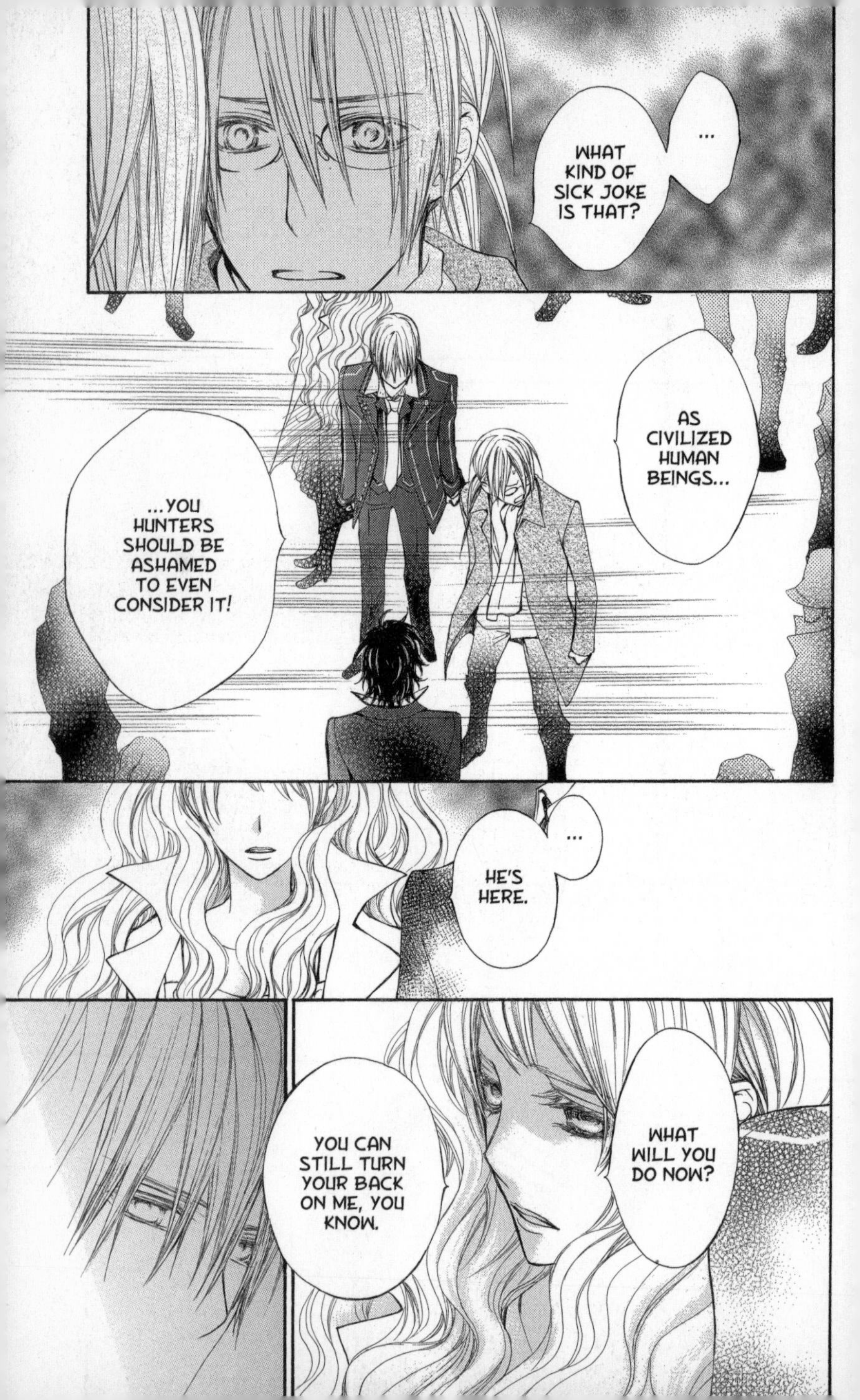
...
WHAT KIND OF SICK JOKE IS THAT?
AS CIVILIZED HUMAN BEINGS...
...YOU HUNTERS SHOULD BE ASHAMED TO EVEN CONSIDER IT!
...
HE'S HERE.
WHAT WILL YOU DO NOW?
YOU CAN STILL TURN YOUR BACK ON ME, YOU KNOW.

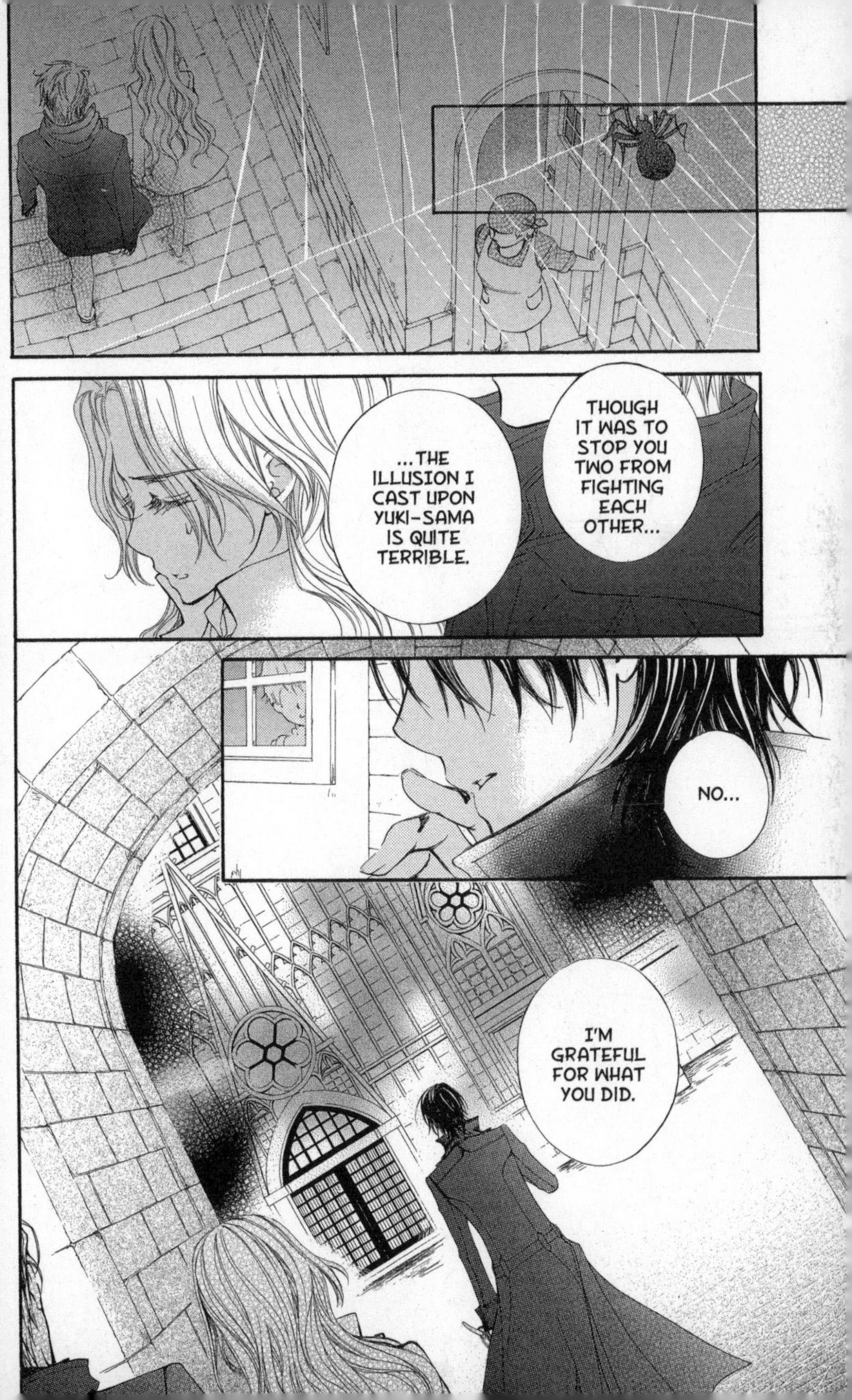
THOUGH IT WAS TO STOP YOU TWO FROM FIGHTING EACH OTHER...
...THE ILLUSION I CAST UPON YUKI-SAMA IS QUITE TERRIBLE.
NO...
I'M GRATEFUL FOR WHAT YOU DID.

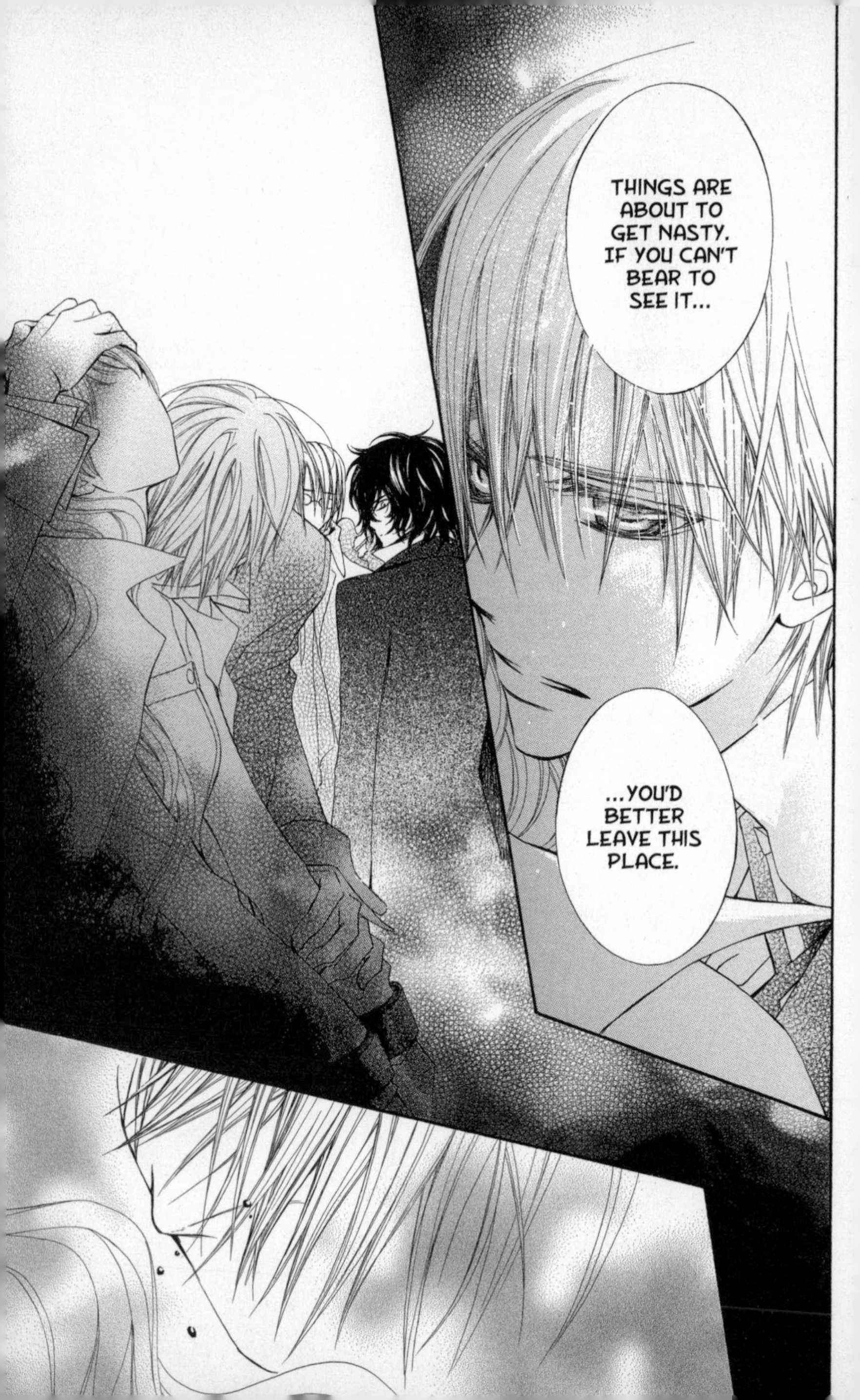
THINGS ARE ABOUT TO GET NASTY. IF YOU CAN'T BEAR TO SEE IT...
...YOU'D BETTER LEAVE THIS PLACE.

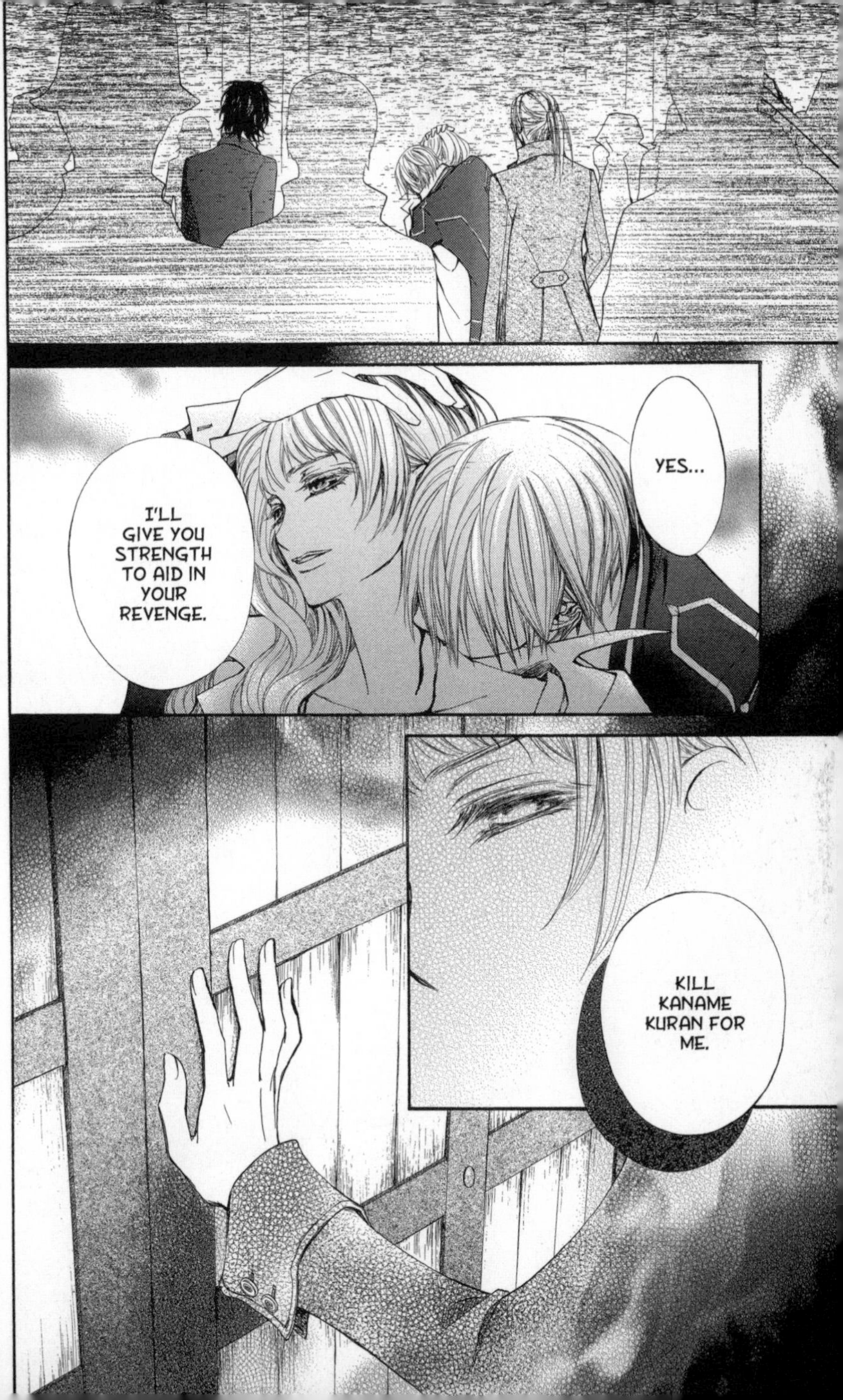
YES...
I'LL GIVE YOU STRENGTH TO AID IN YOUR REVENGE.
KILL KANAME KURAN FOR ME.

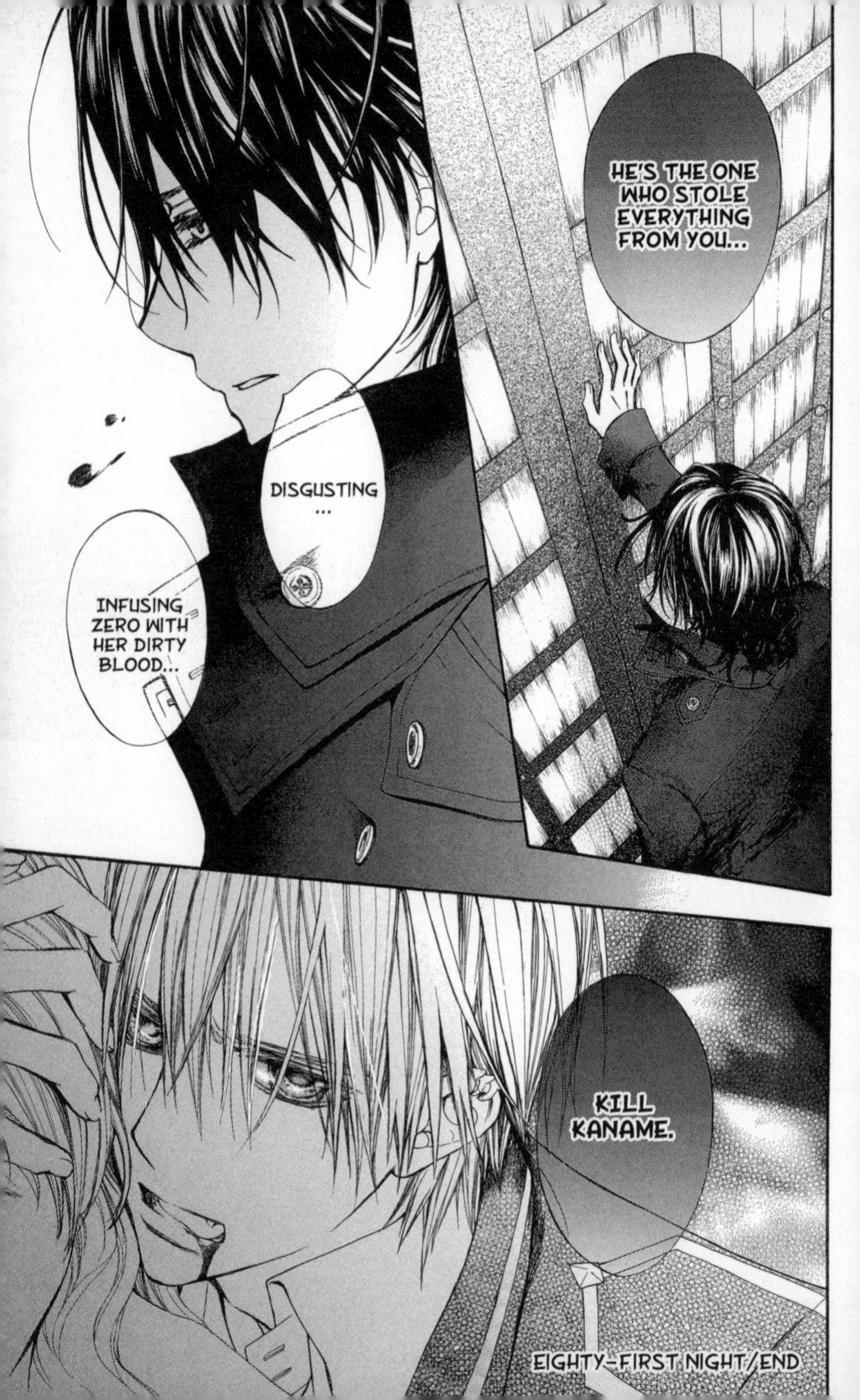
HE'S THE ONE WHO STOLE EVERYTHING FROM YOU...
DISGUSTING...
INFUSING ZERO WITH HER DIRTY BLOOD...
KILL KANAME.
EIGHTY-FIRST NIGHT/END

SHE
LIKES
ANIMALS,
I GUESS...

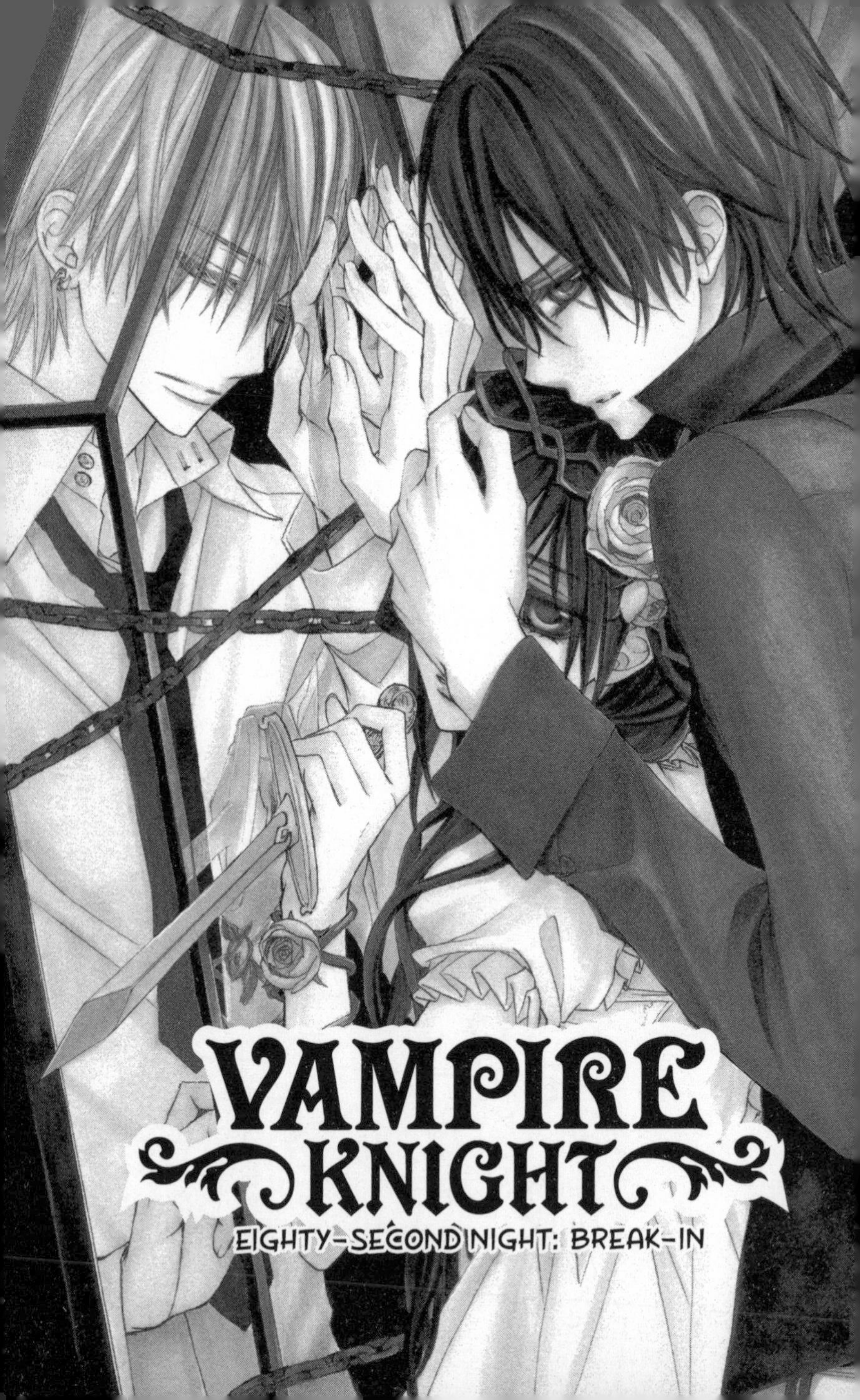
VAMPIRE
KNIGHT
EIGHTY-SECOND NIGHT: BREAK-IN

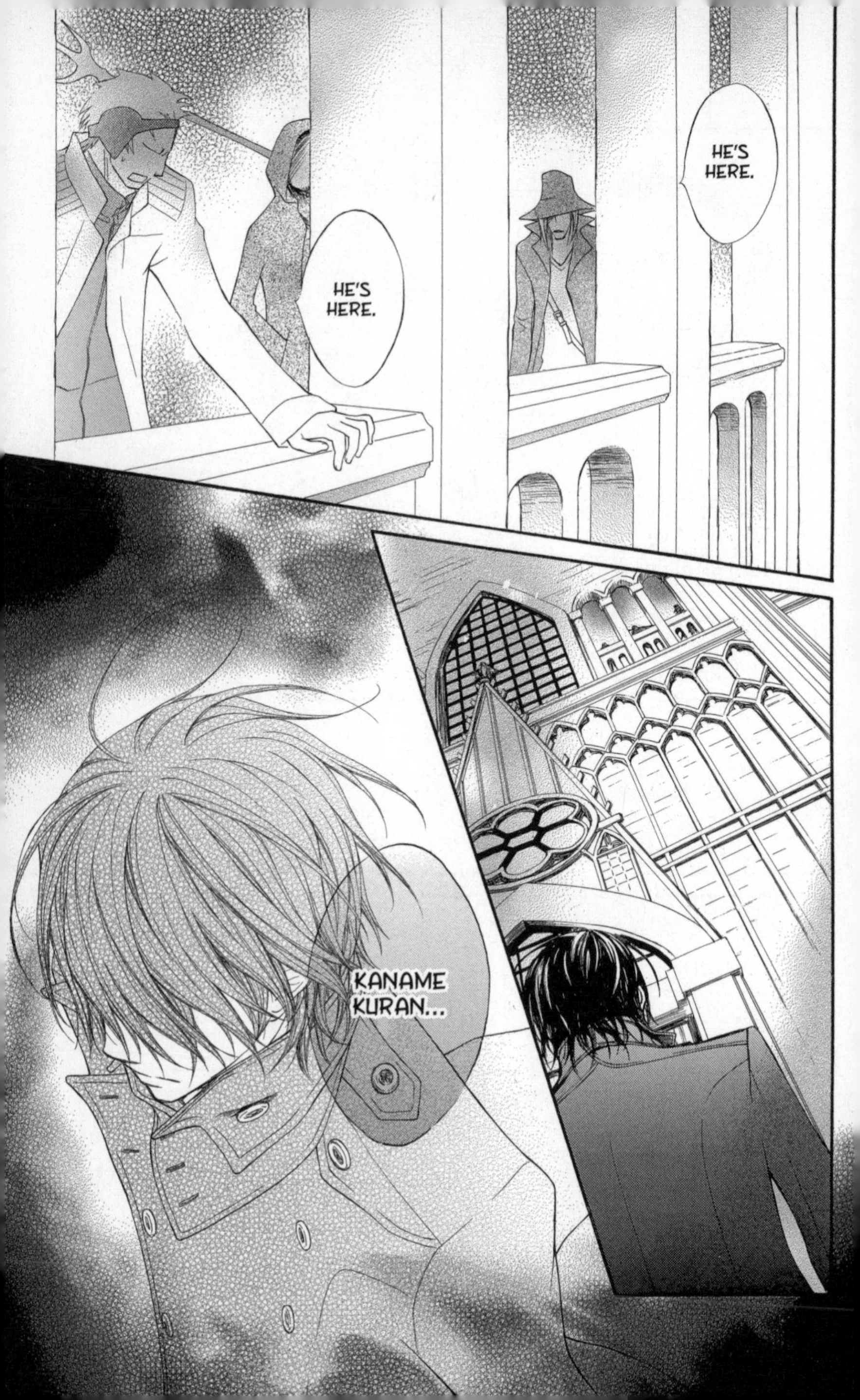
HE'S HERE.
HE'S HERE.
KANAME KURAN...

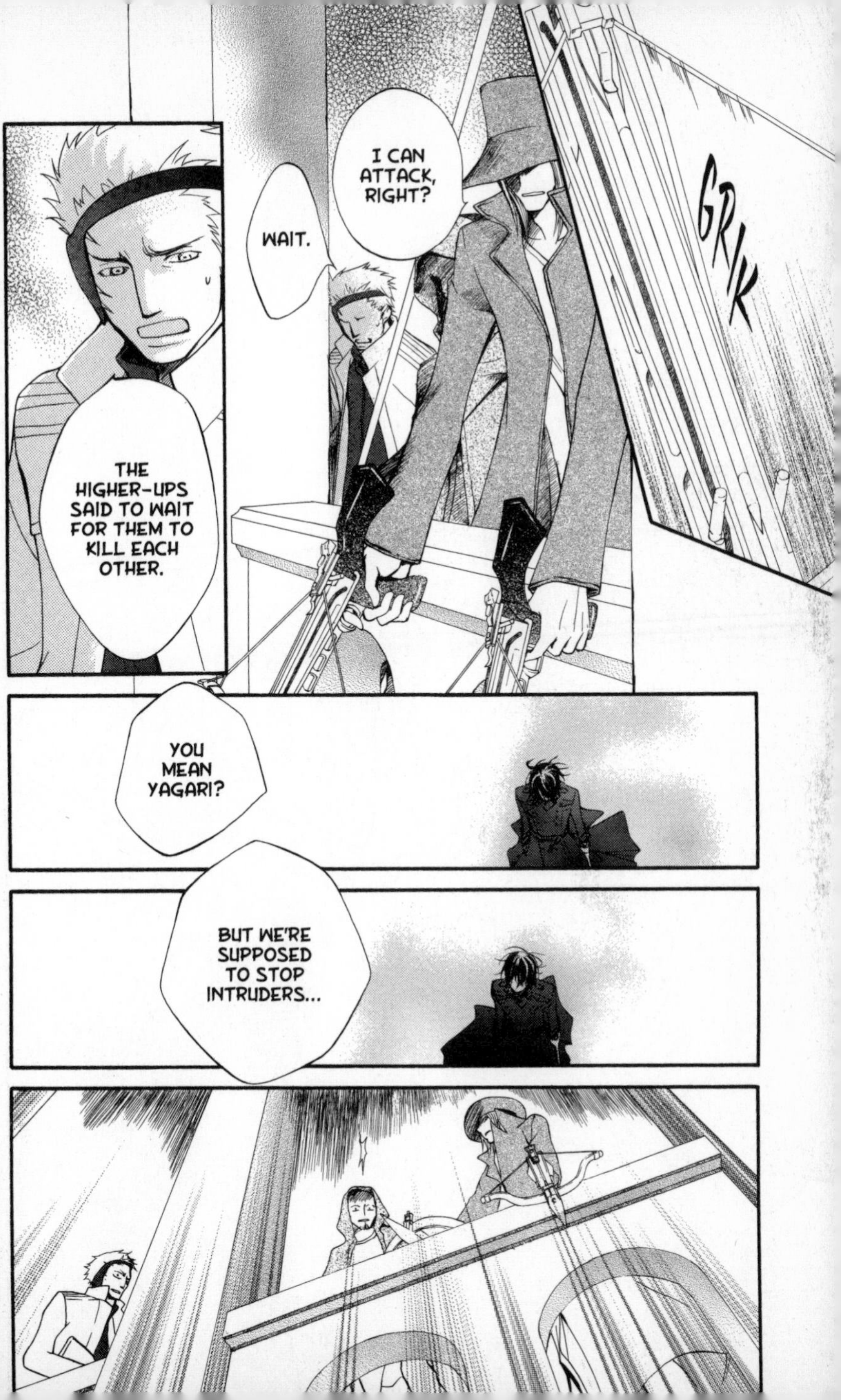
GRIK
I CAN ATTACK, RIGHT?
WAIT.
THE HIGHER-UPS SAID TO WAIT FOR THEM TO KILL EACH OTHER.
YOU MEAN YAGARI?
BUT WE'RE SUPPOSED TO STOP INTRUDERS...

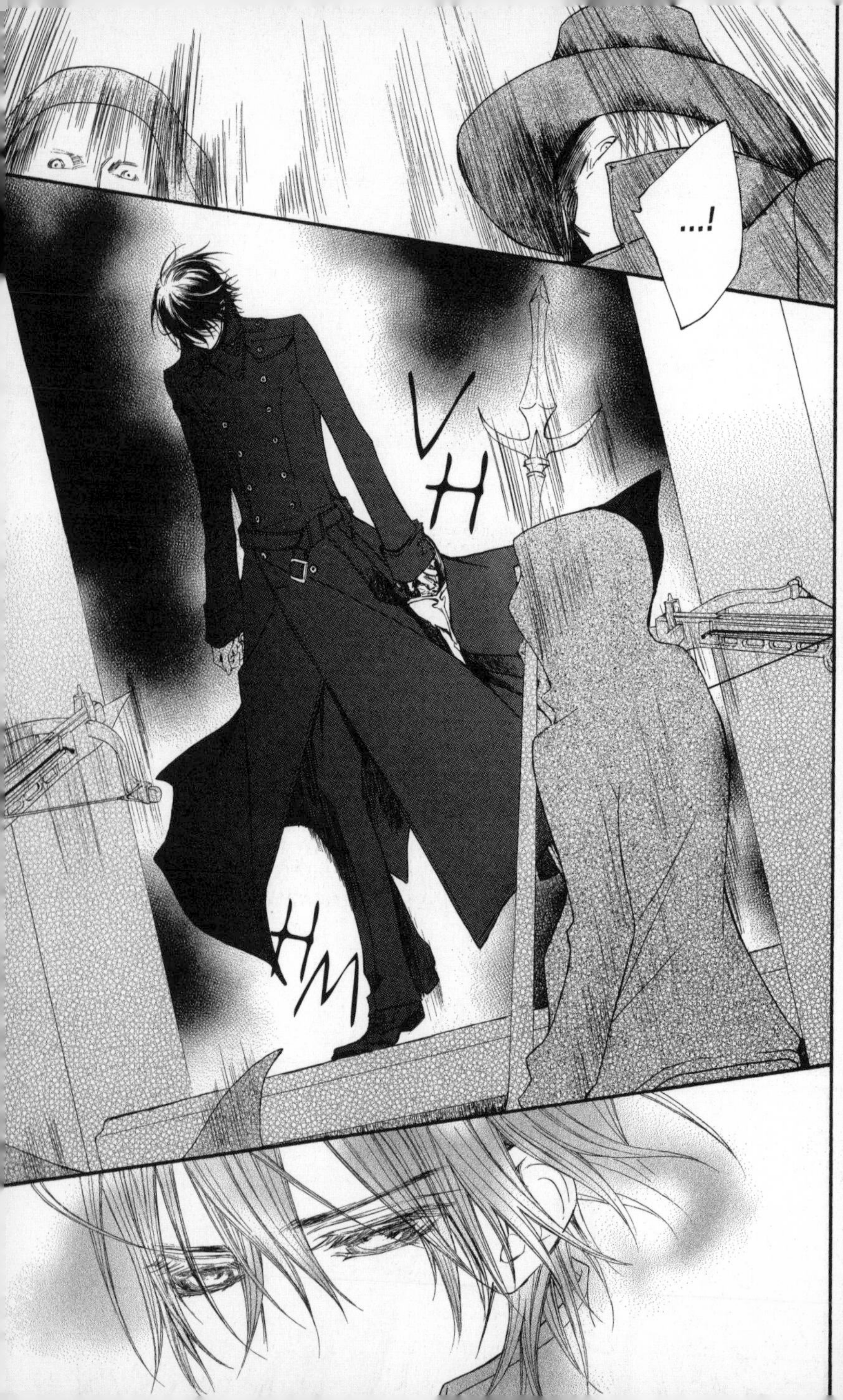
...!
VH
HM

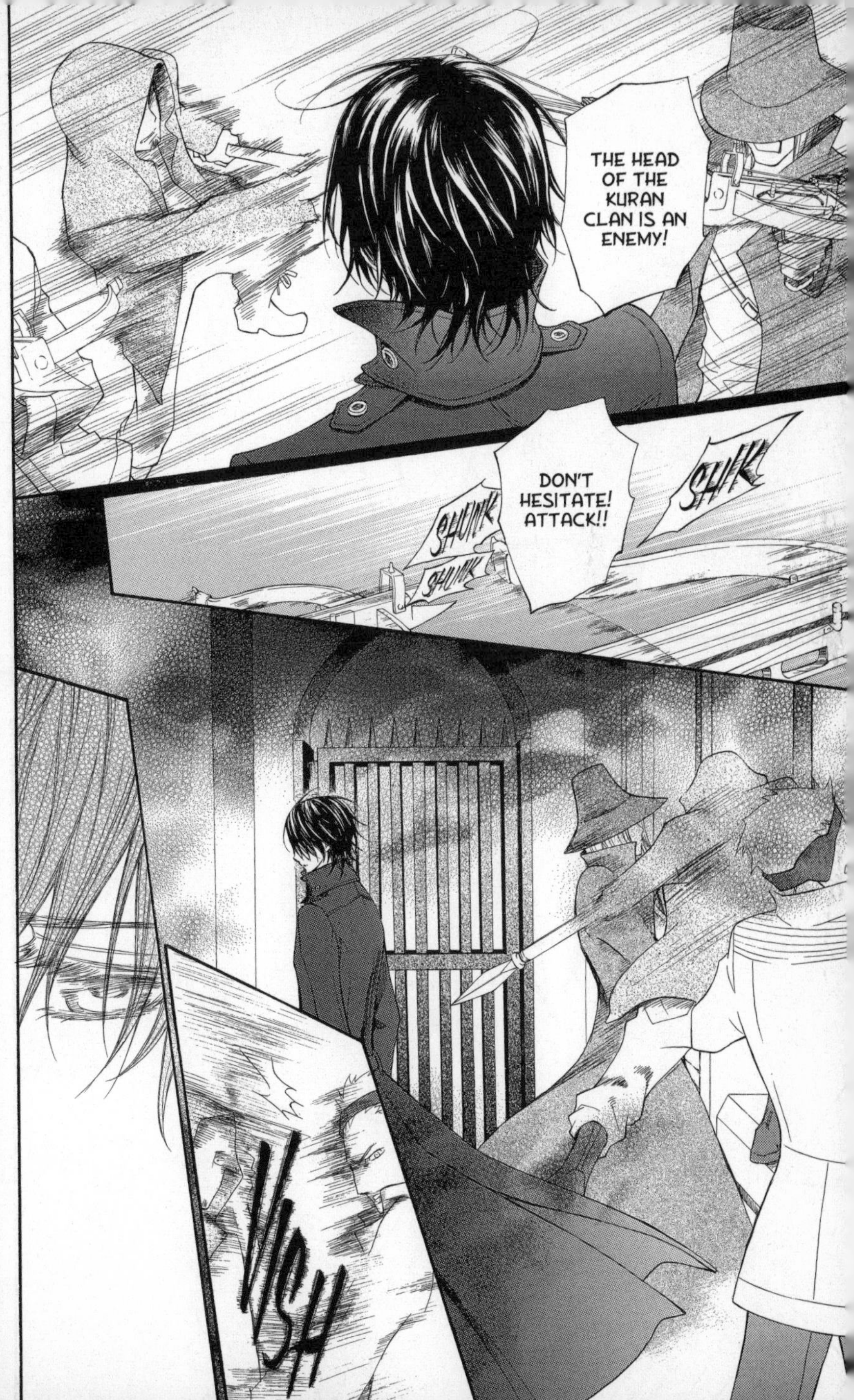
THE HEAD OF THE KURAN CLAN IS AN ENEMY!
SHIK
DON'T HESITATE! ATTACK!!
SHUNK
SHUNK
VISH

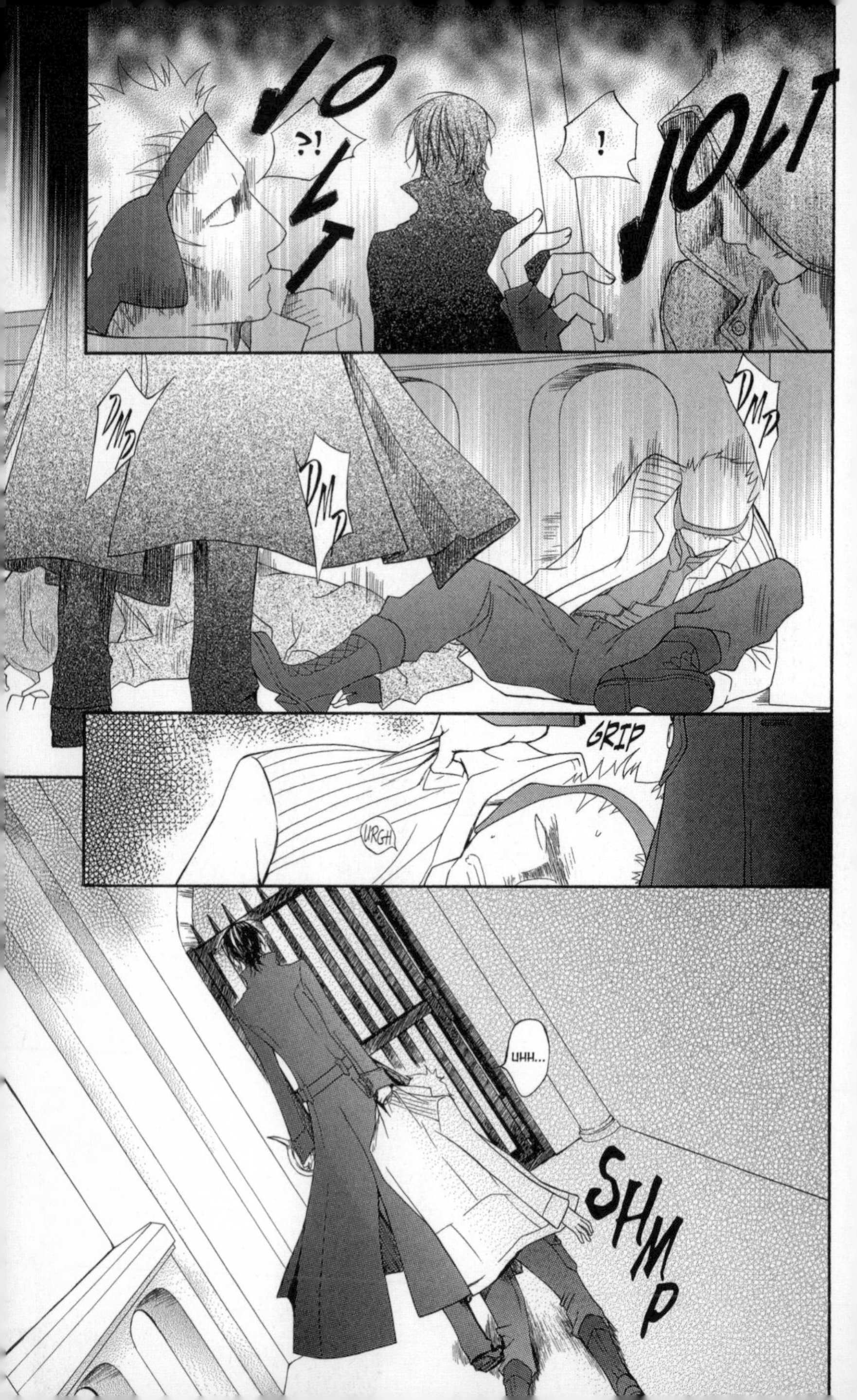
JOLT
!
JOLT
?!
DMP
DMP
DMP
GRIP
URGH
UHH...
SHMP

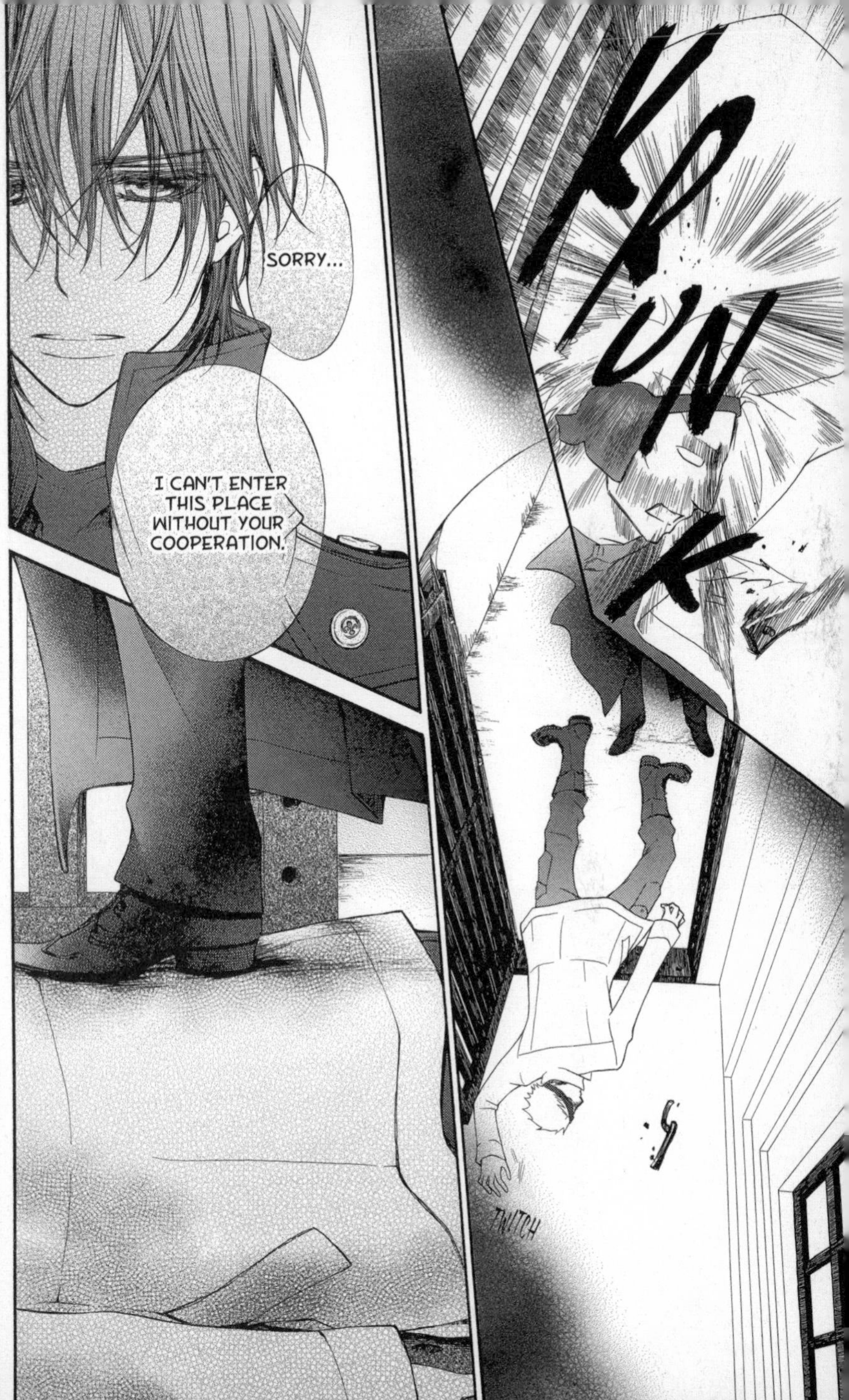
KRUNK
TWITCH
SORRY...
I CAN'T ENTER THIS PLACE WITHOUT YOUR COOPERATION.

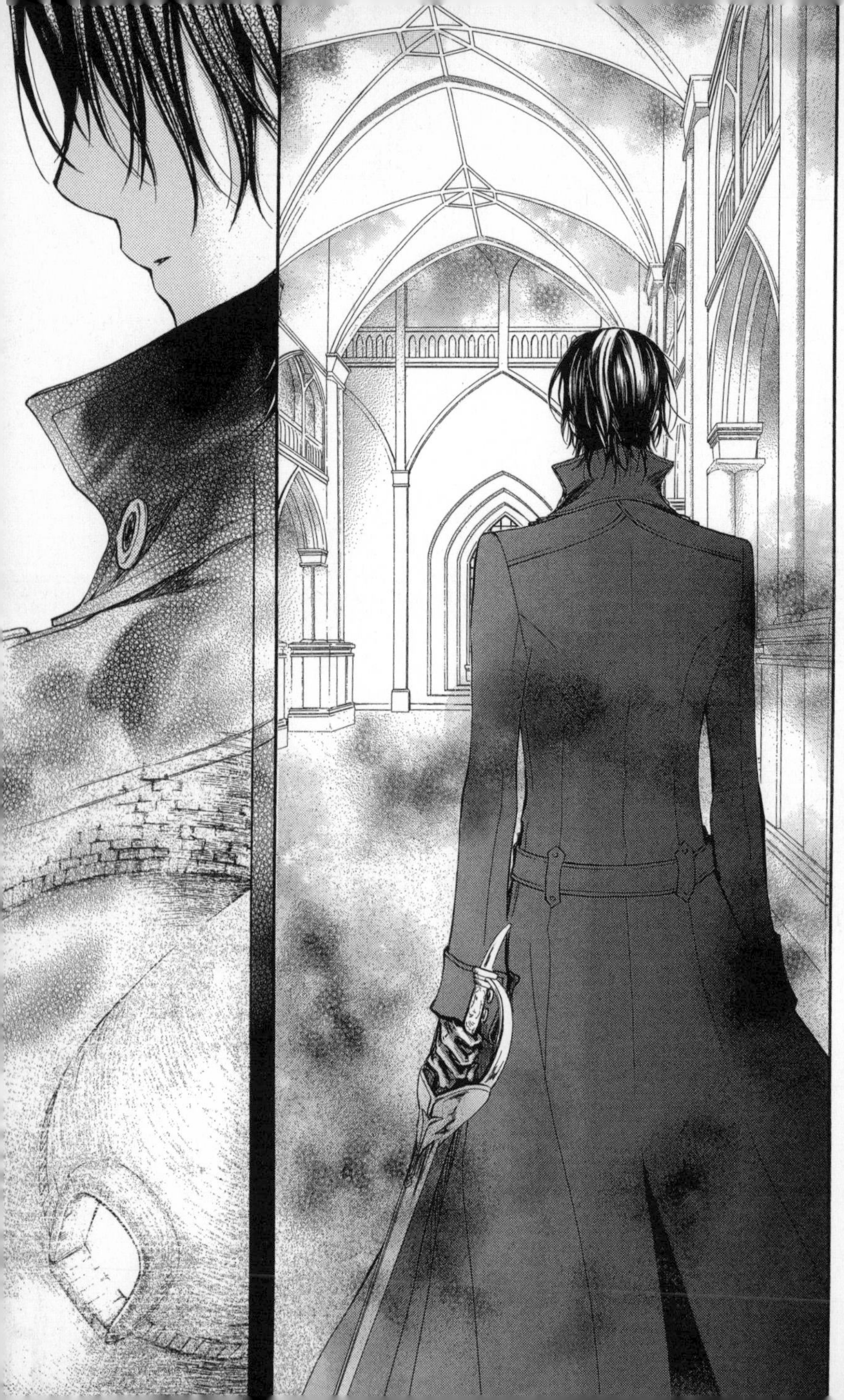

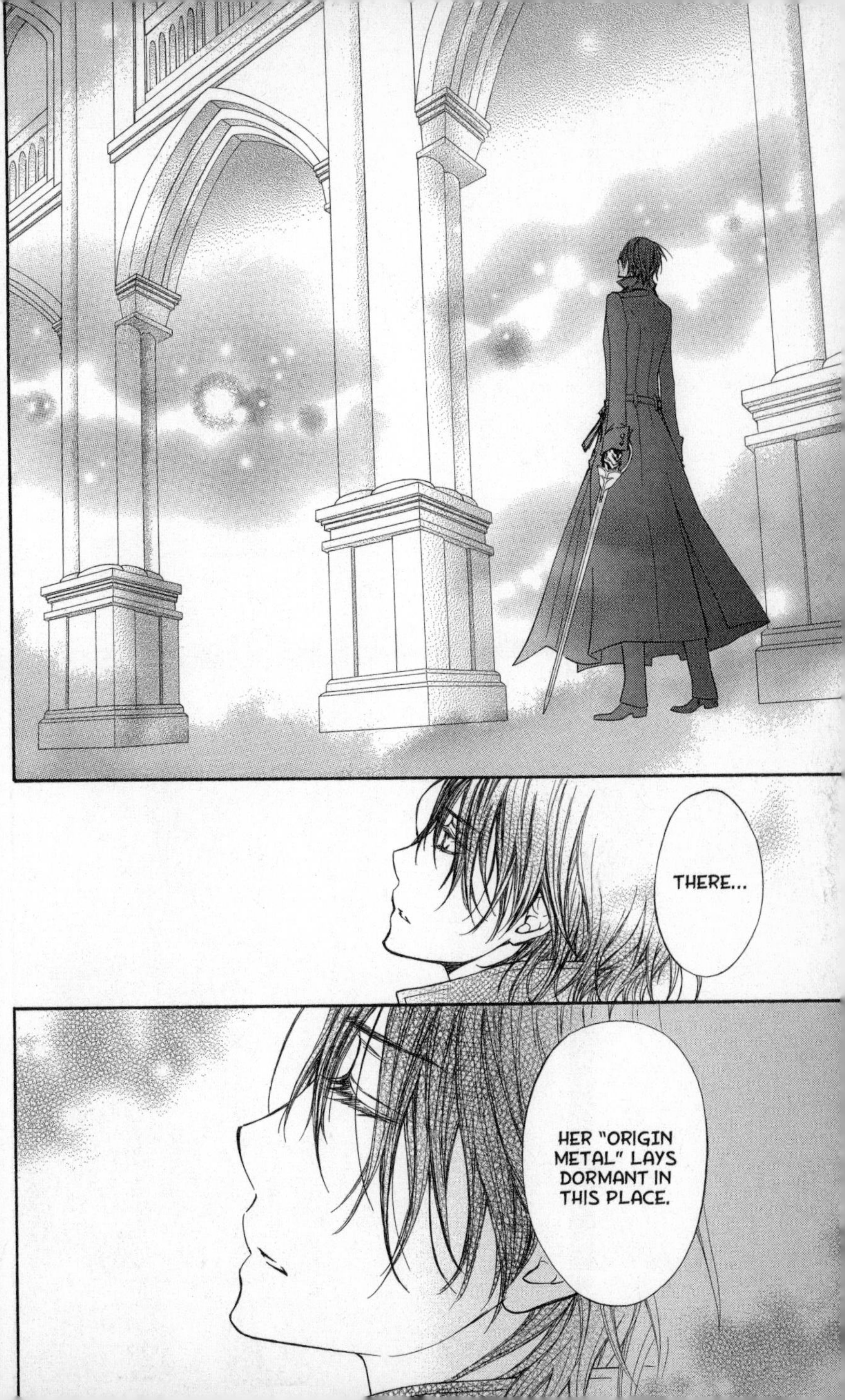
THERE...
HER "ORIGIN METAL" LAYS DORMANT IN THIS PLACE.

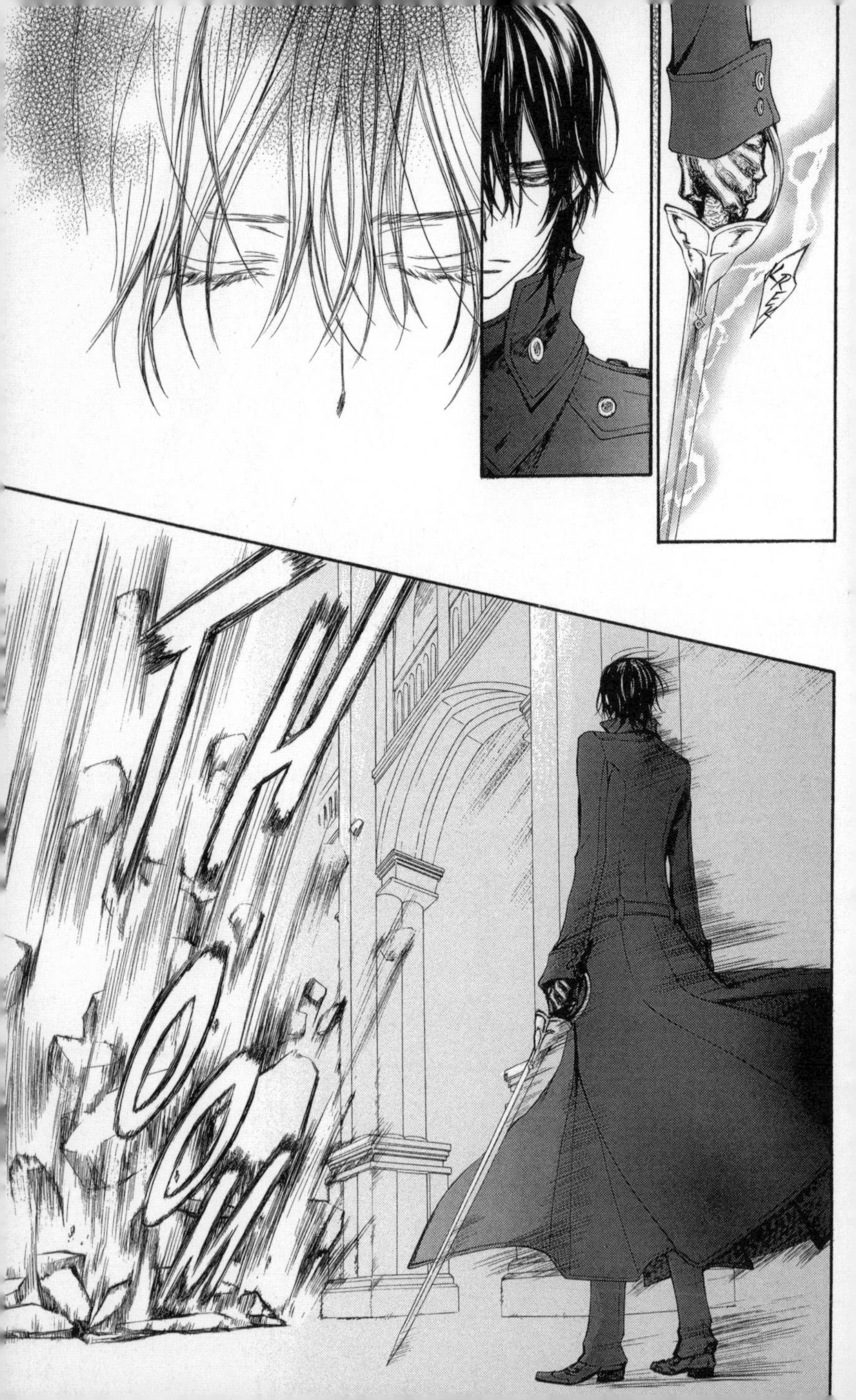
KREE
WHOOM

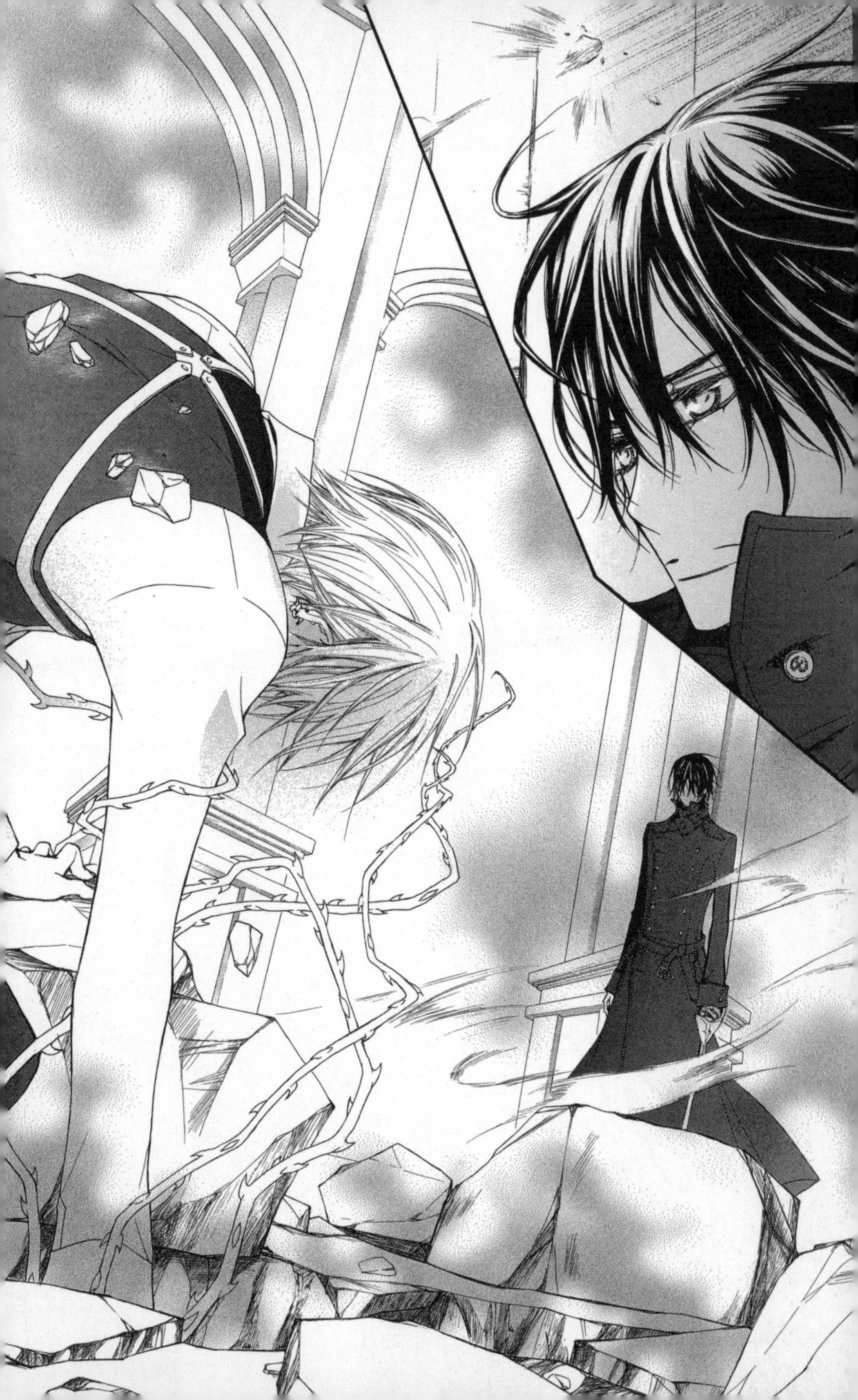

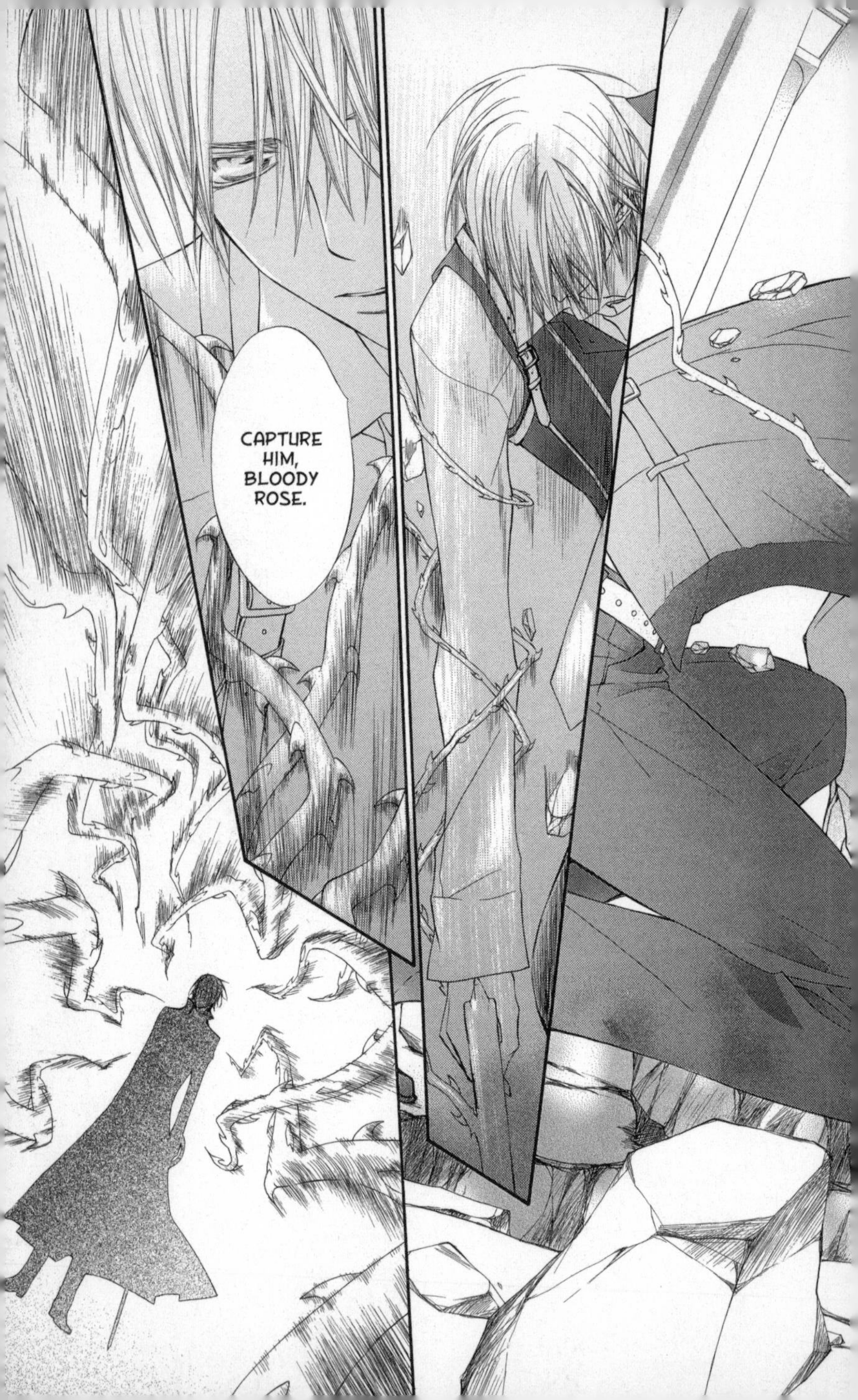
CAPTURE HIM, BLOODY ROSE.

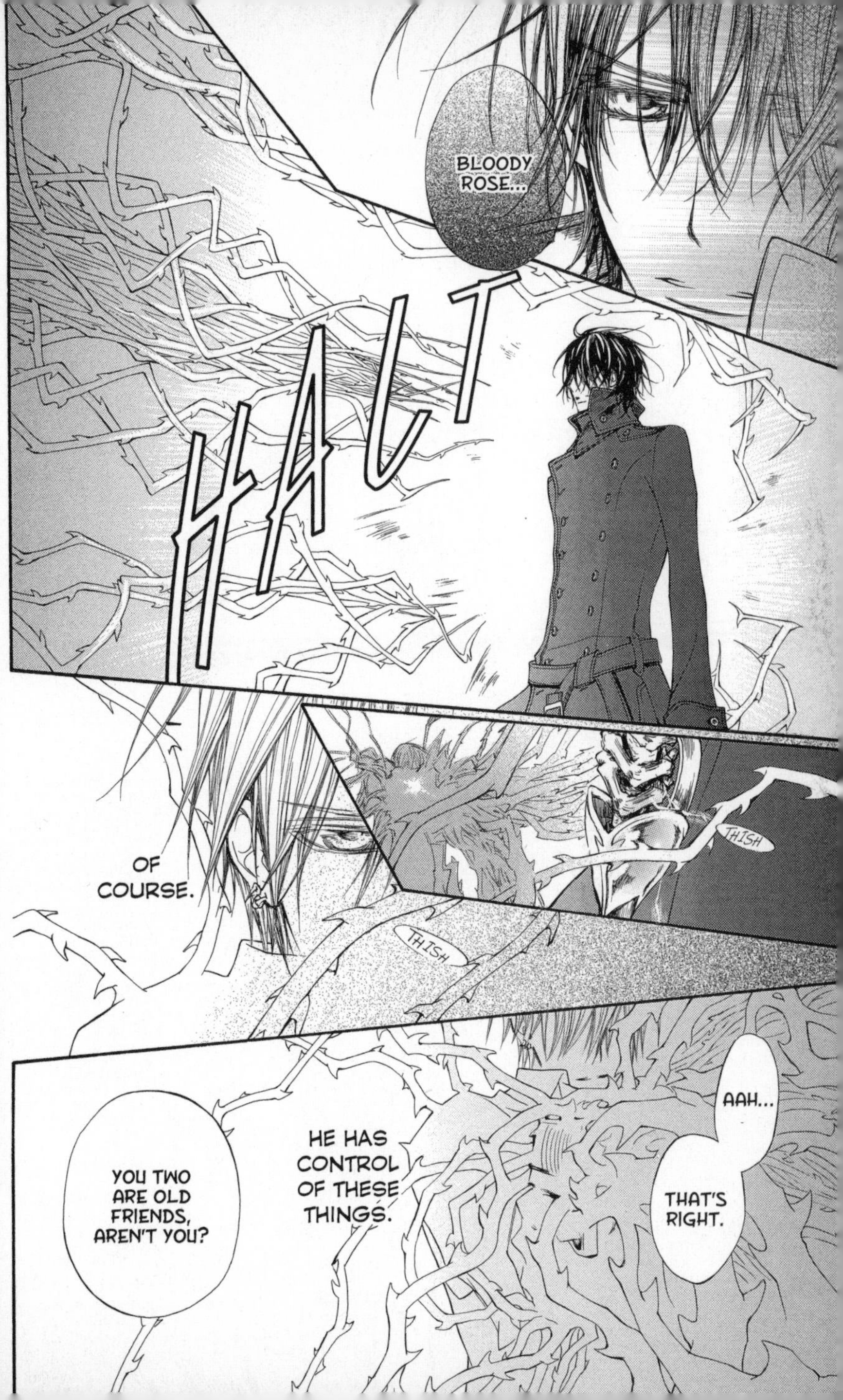
BLOODY ROSE...
HALT
THISH
OF COURSE.
THISH
AAH...
THAT'S RIGHT.
HE HAS CONTROL OF THESE THINGS.
YOU TWO ARE OLD FRIENDS, AREN'T YOU?

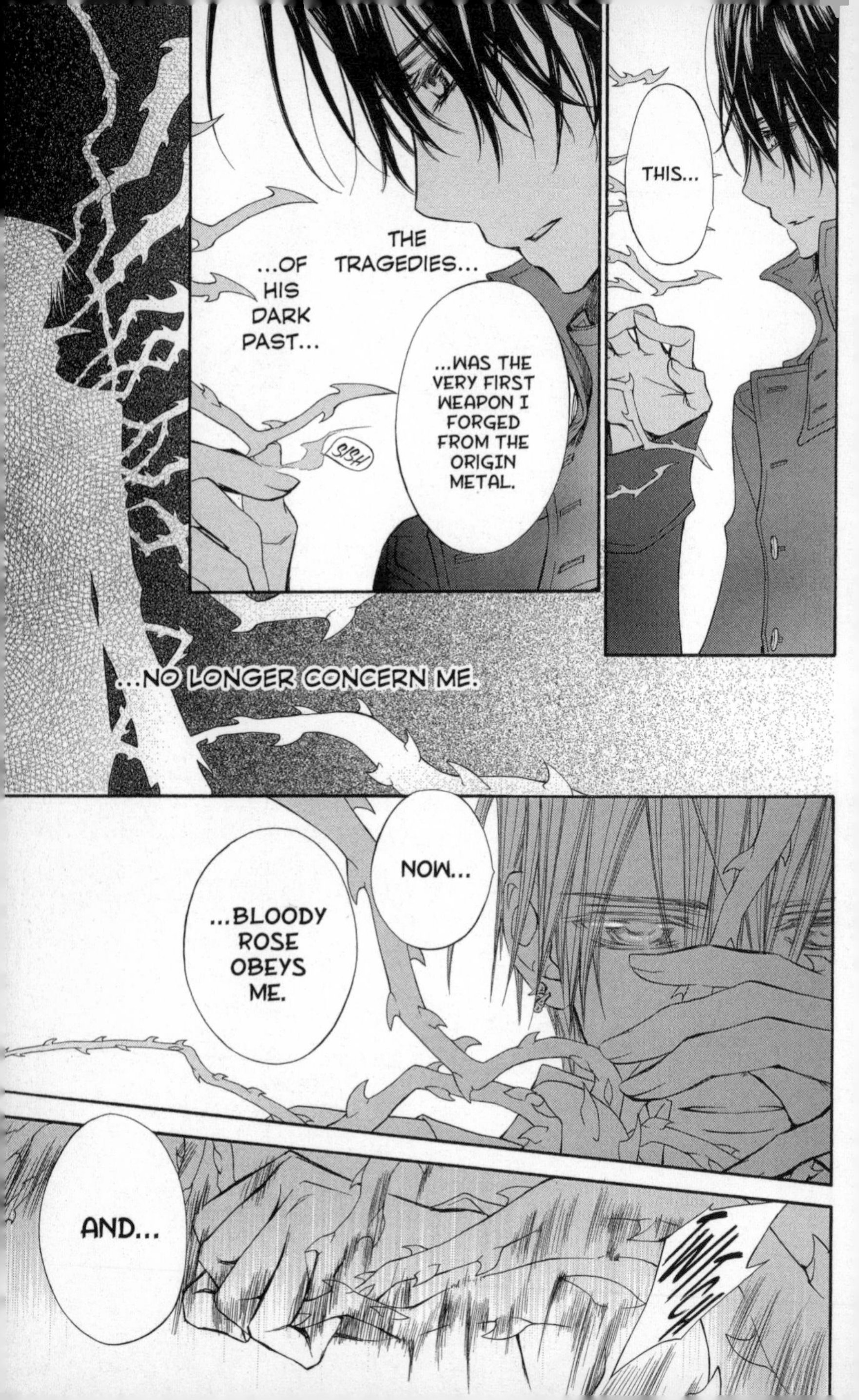
THIS...
THE TRAGEDIES...
...OF HIS DARK PAST...
...WAS THE VERY FIRST WEAPON I FORGED FROM THE ORIGIN METAL.
SISH
...NO LONGER CONCERN ME.
NOW...
...BLOODY ROSE OBEYS ME.
AND...

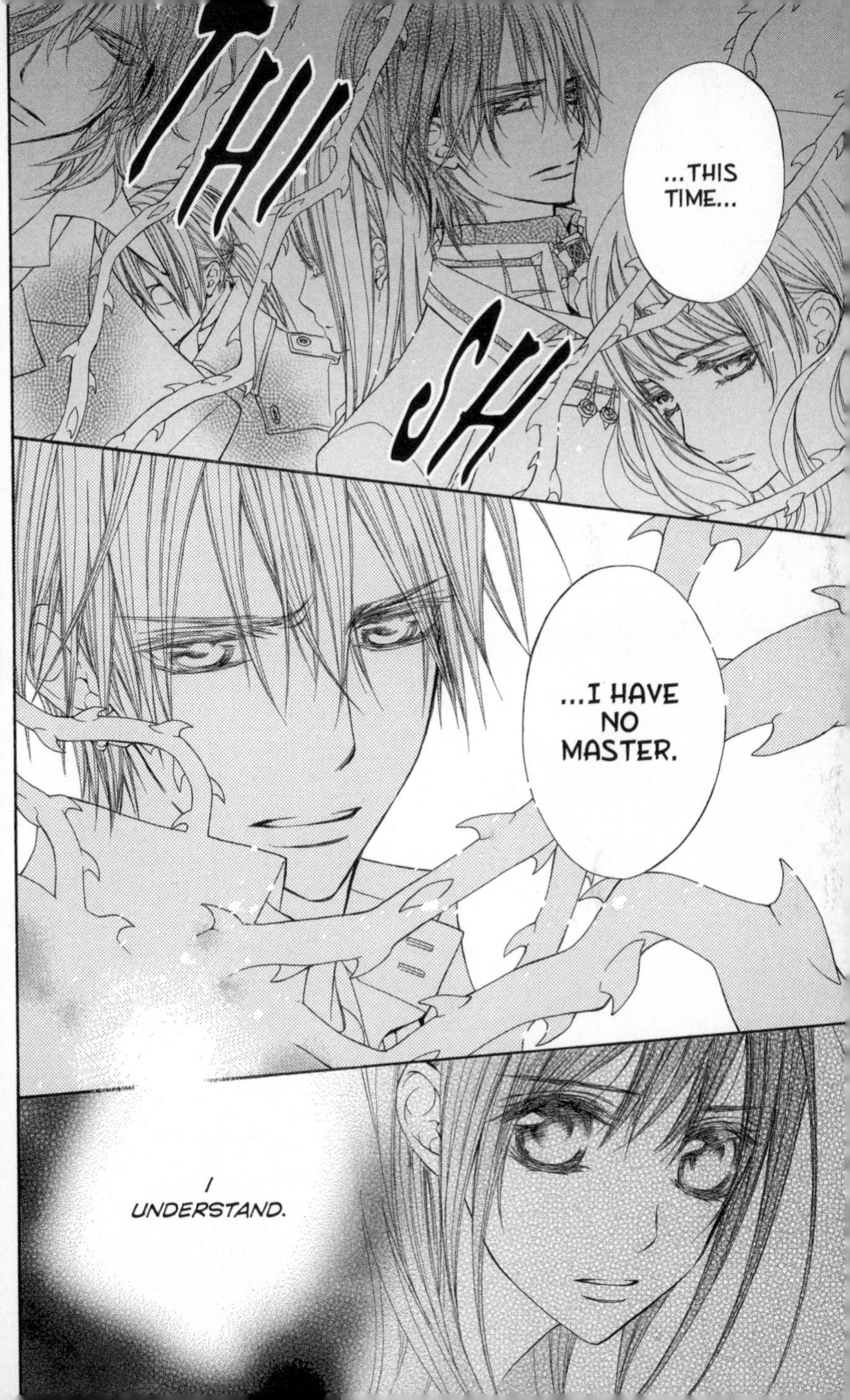
...THIS TIME...
THISH
...I HAVE NO MASTER.
I UNDERSTAND.

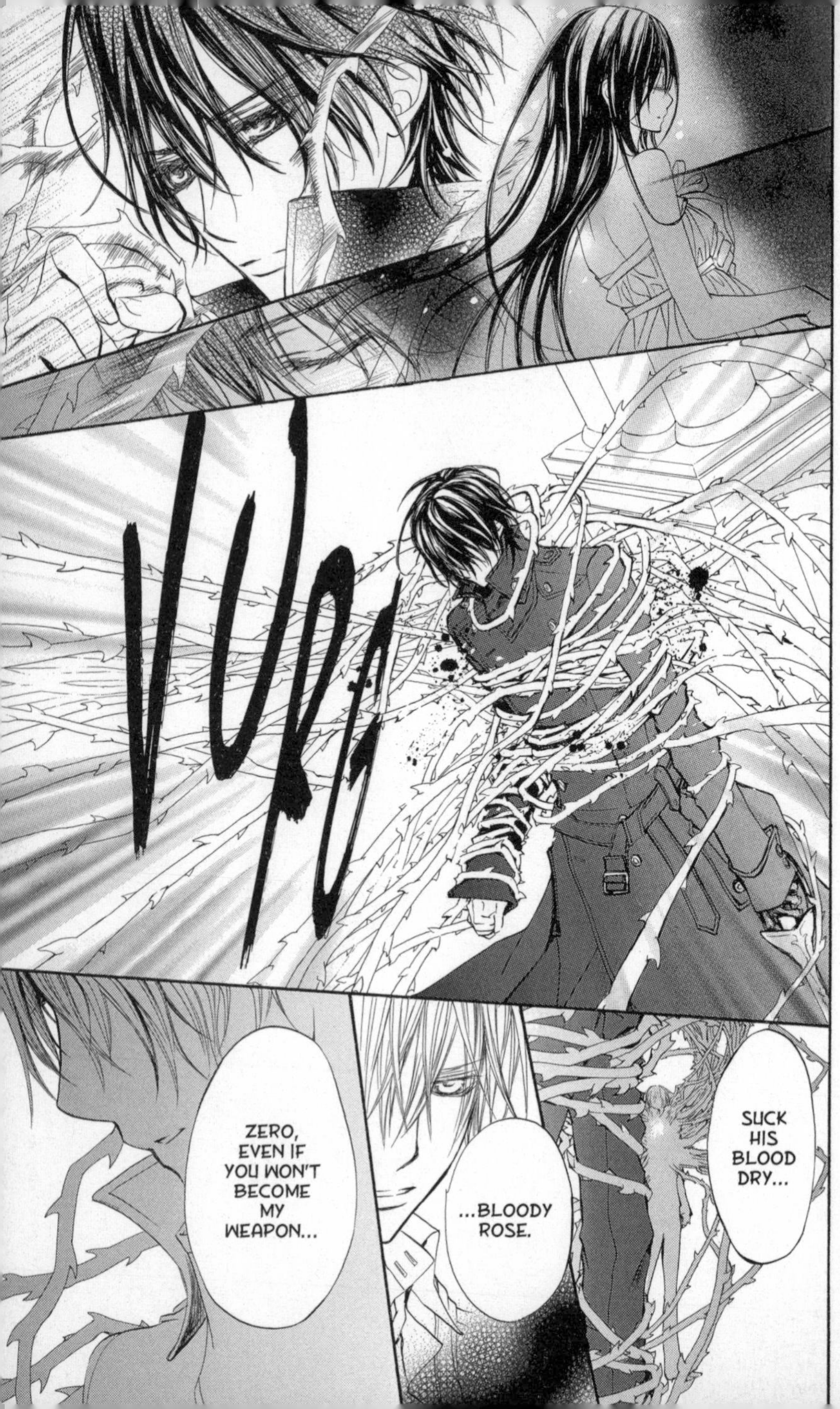
SUCK HIS BLOOD DRY...
...BLOODY ROSE.
ZERO, EVEN IF YOU WON'T BECOME MY WEAPON...

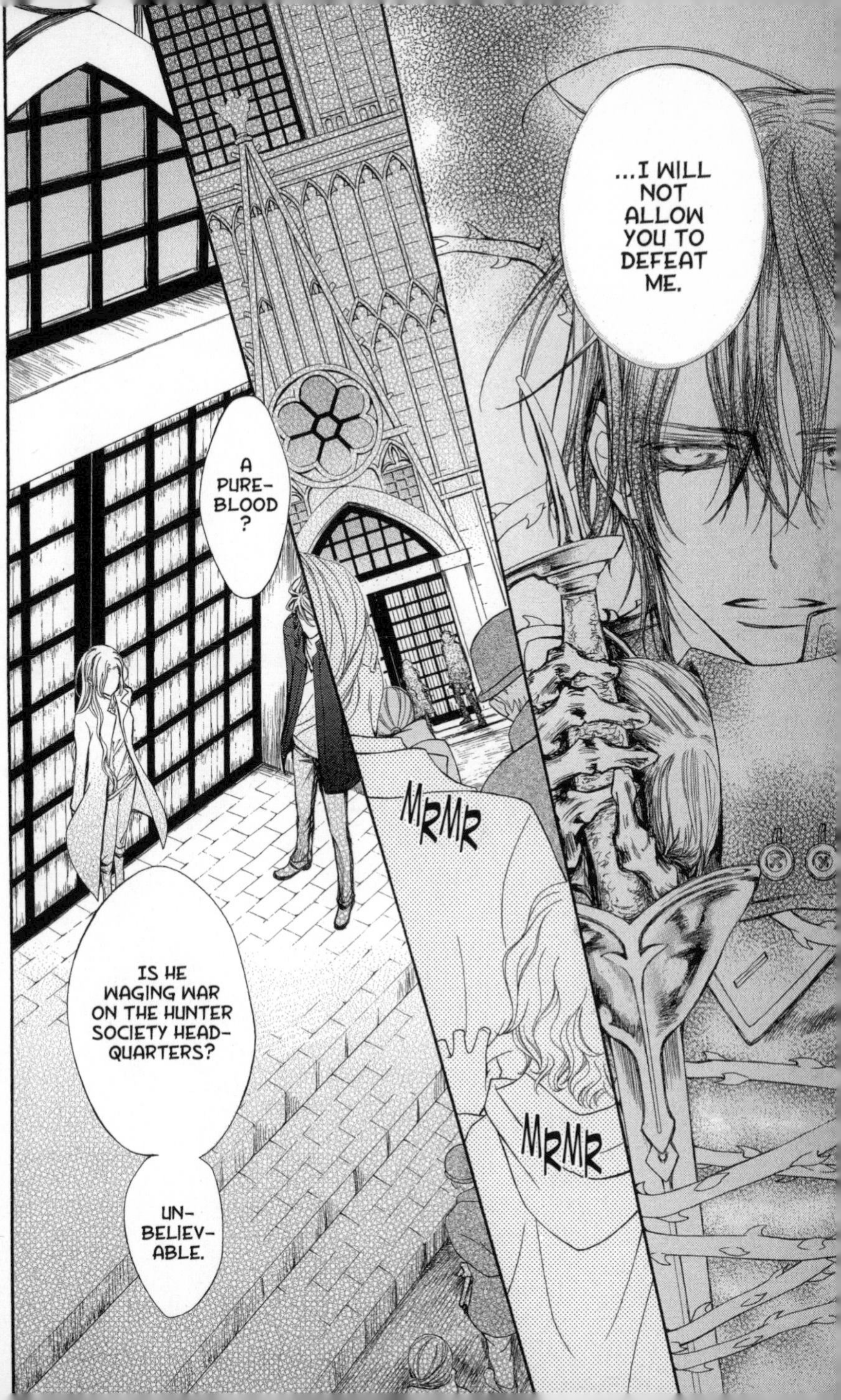
...I WILL NOT ALLOW YOU TO DEFEAT ME.
MRMR
MRMR
A PURE-BLOOD?
IS HE WAGING WAR ON THE HUNTER SOCIETY HEAD-QUARTERS?
UN-BELIEV-ABLE.

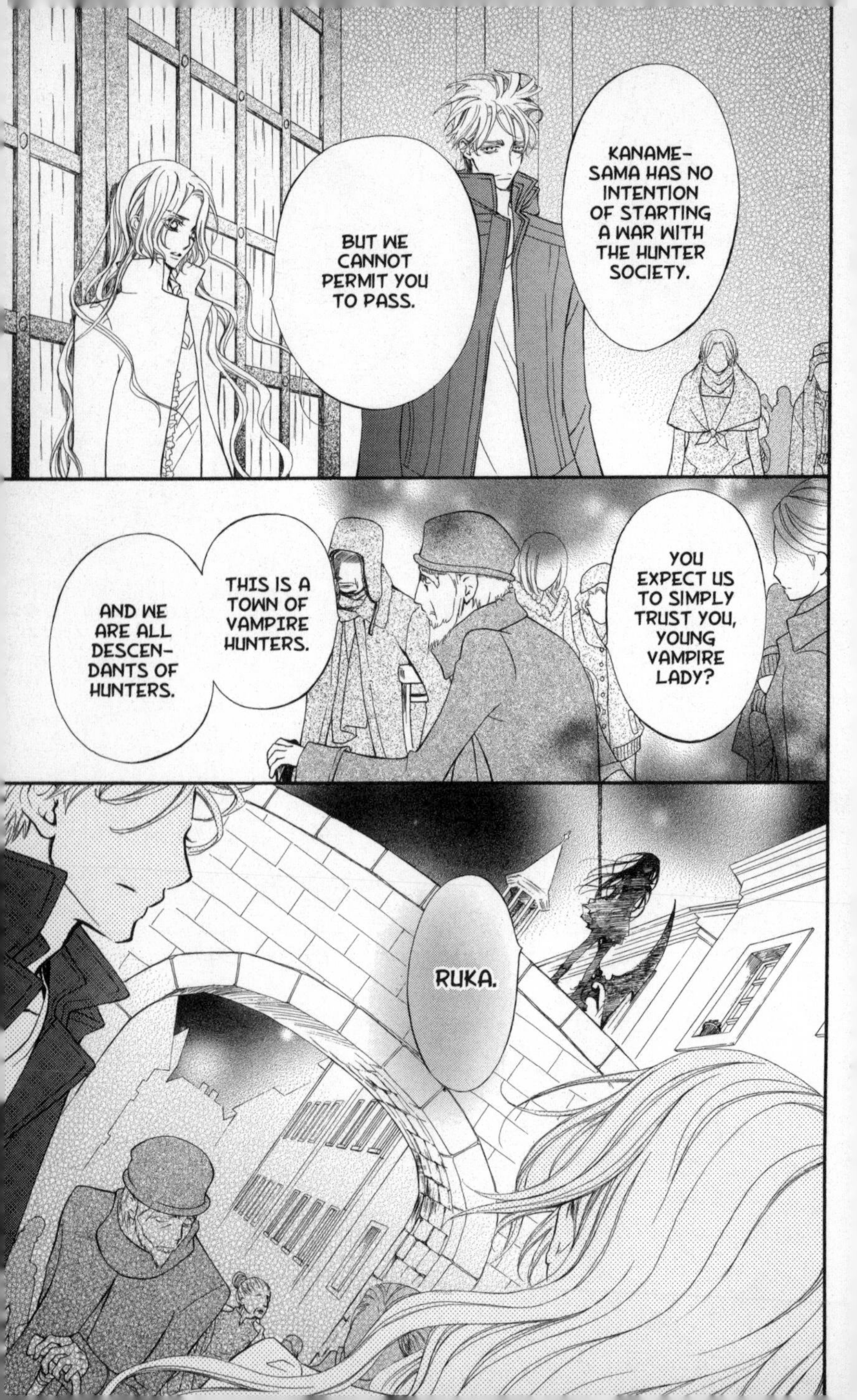
KANAME-SAMA HAS NO INTENTION OF STARTING A WAR WITH THE HUNTER SOCIETY.
BUT WE CANNOT PERMIT YOU TO PASS.
YOU EXPECT US TO SIMPLY TRUST YOU, YOUNG VAMPIRE LADY?
THIS IS A TOWN OF VAMPIRE HUNTERS.
AND WE ARE ALL DESCEN-DANTS OF HUNTERS.
RUKA.

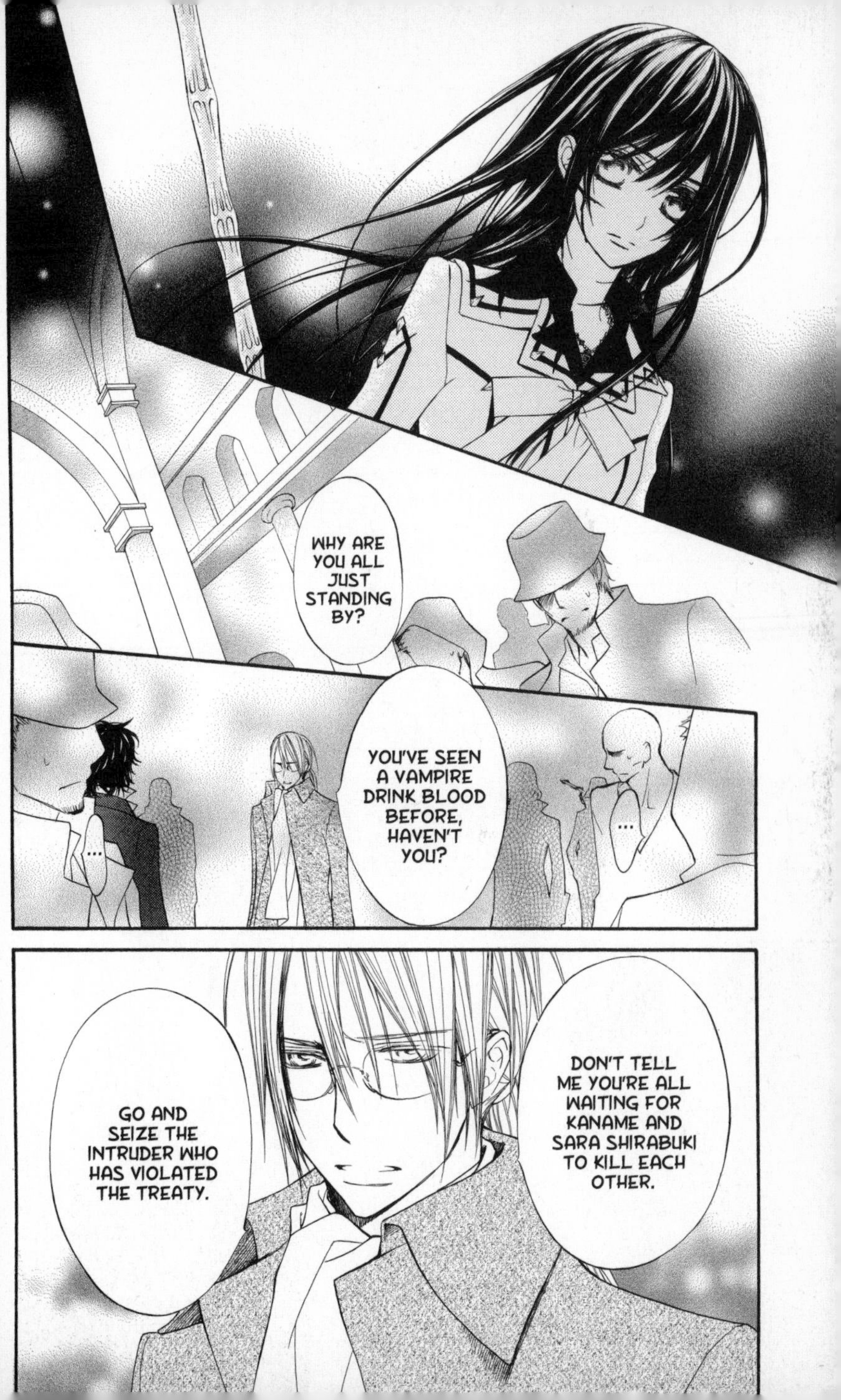
WHY ARE YOU ALL JUST STANDING BY?
YOU'VE SEEN A VAMPIRE DRINK BLOOD BEFORE, HAVEN'T YOU?
...
...
DON'T TELL ME YOU'RE ALL WAITING FOR KANAME AND SARA SHIRABUKI TO KILL EACH OTHER.
GO AND SEIZE THE INTRUDER WHO HAS VIOLATED THE TREATY.

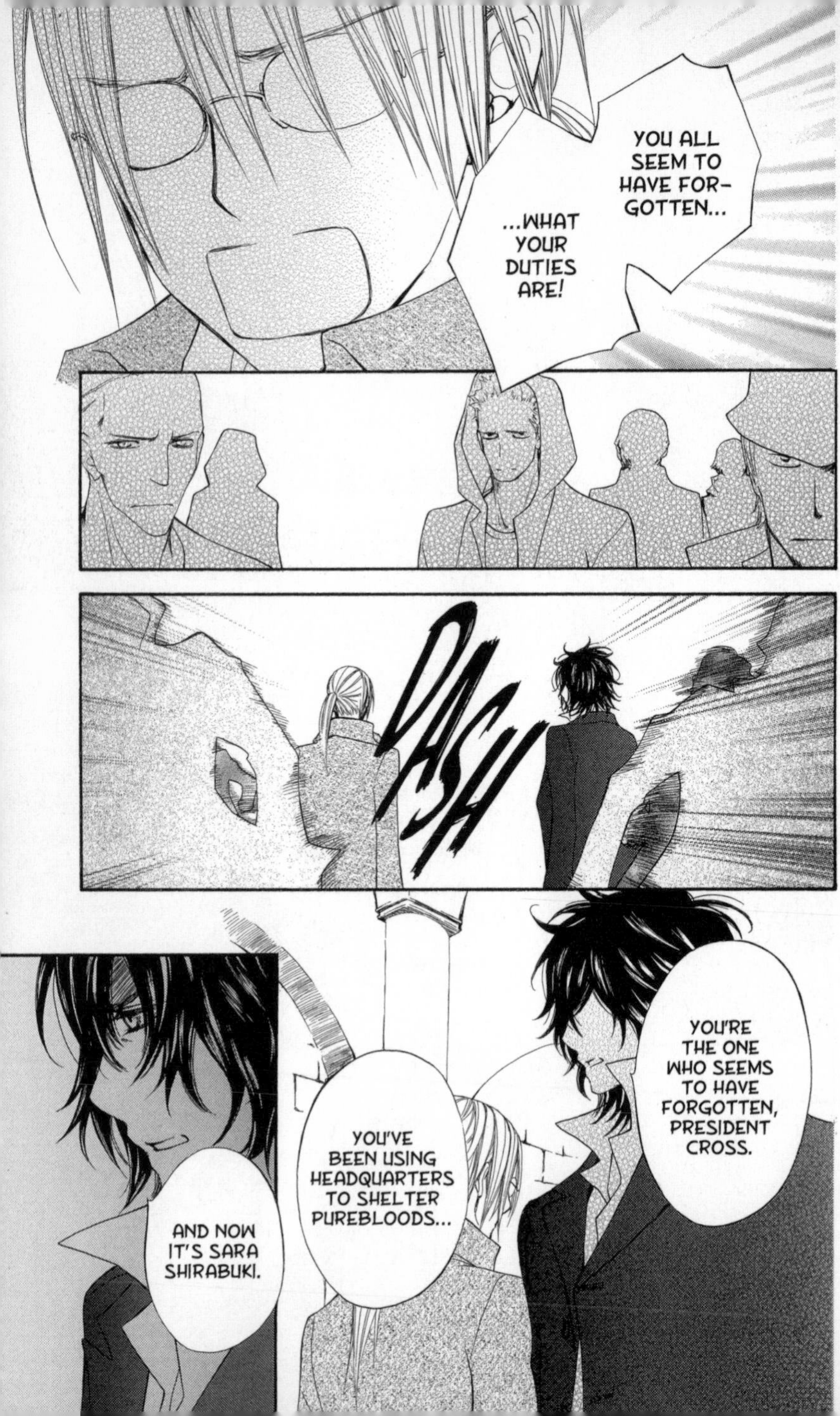
YOU ALL SEEM TO HAVE FOR-GOTTEN...
...WHAT YOUR DUTIES ARE!
DASH
YOU'RE THE ONE WHO SEEMS TO HAVE FORGOTTEN, PRESIDENT CROSS.
YOU'VE BEEN USING HEADQUARTERS TO SHELTER PUREBLOODS...
AND NOW IT'S SARA SHIRABUKI.

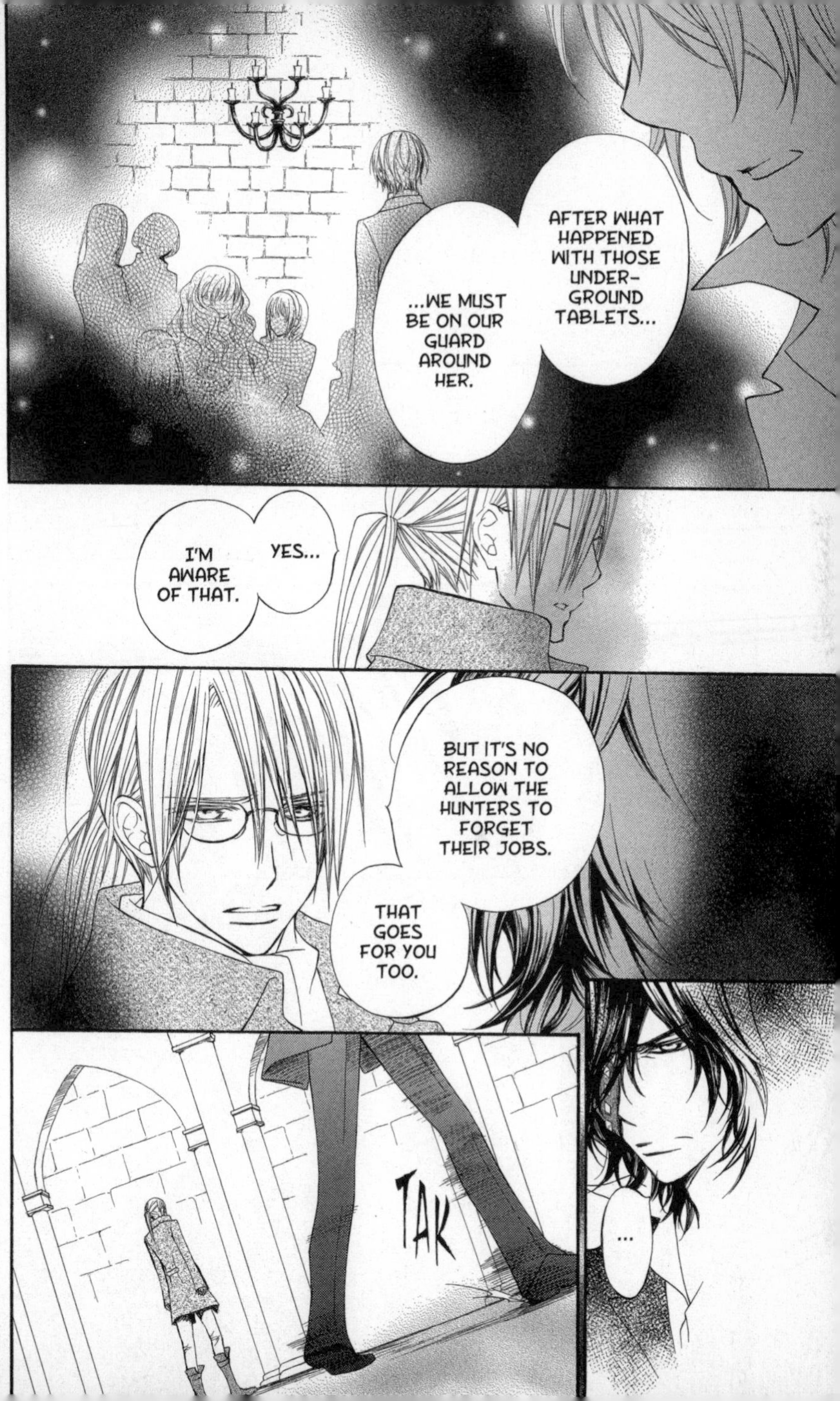
AFTER WHAT HAPPENED WITH THOSE UNDER-GROUND TABLETS...
...WE MUST BE ON OUR GUARD AROUND HER.
YES...
I'M AWARE OF THAT.
BUT IT'S NO REASON TO ALLOW THE HUNTERS TO FORGET THEIR JOBS.
THAT GOES FOR YOU TOO.
...
TAK

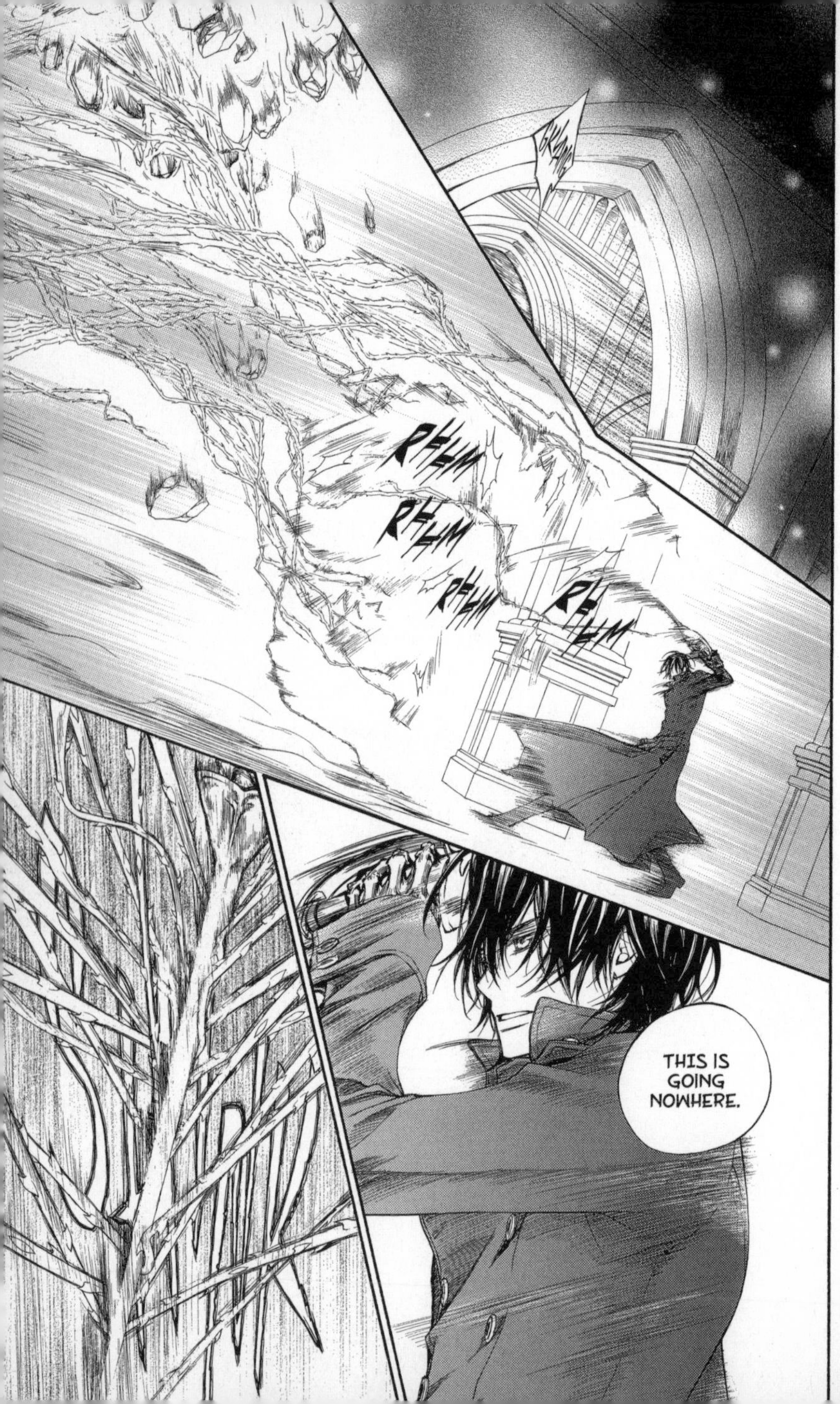
RRUM
RRUM
RRUM
RRUM
THIS IS GOING NOWHERE.

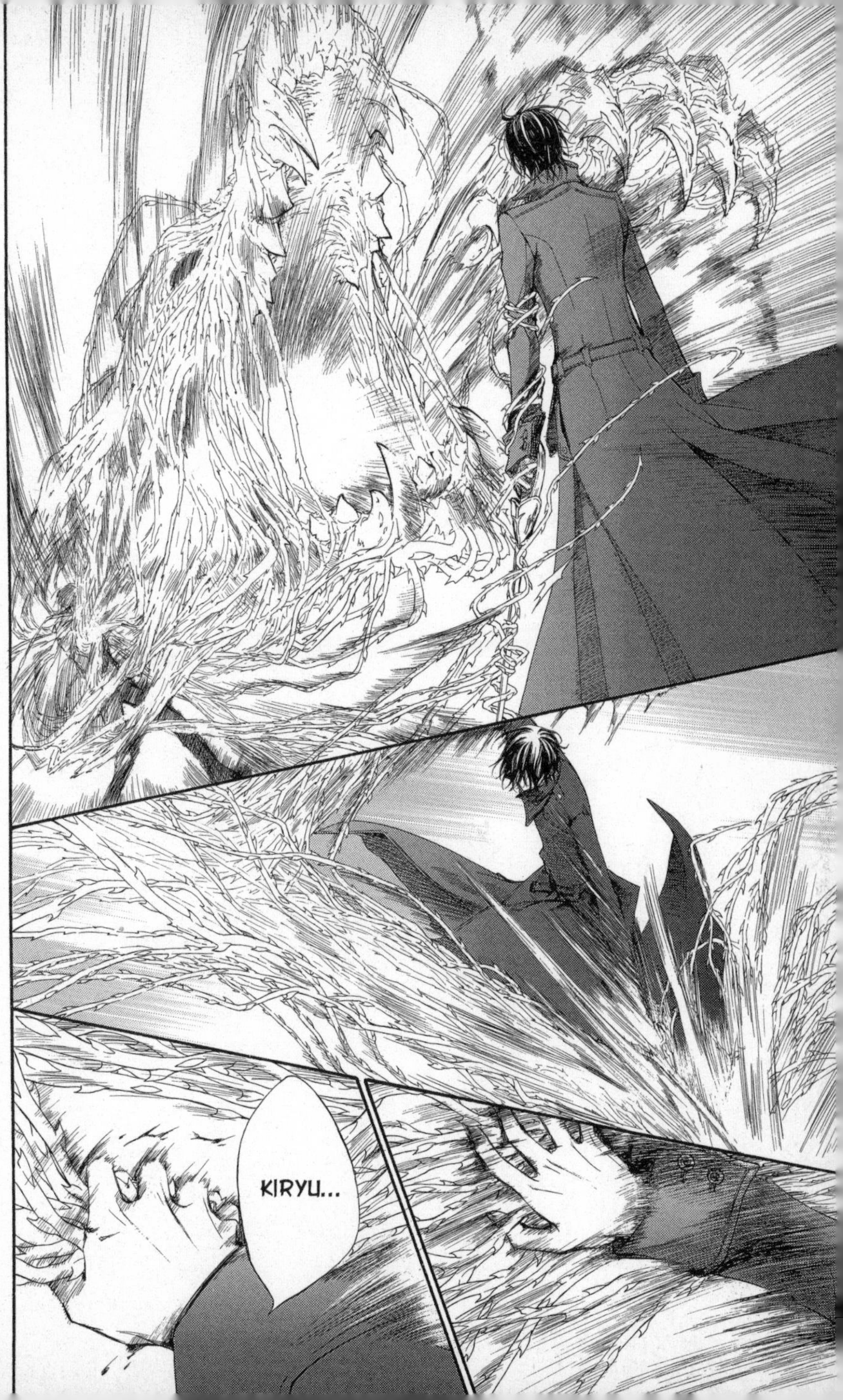
KIRYU...

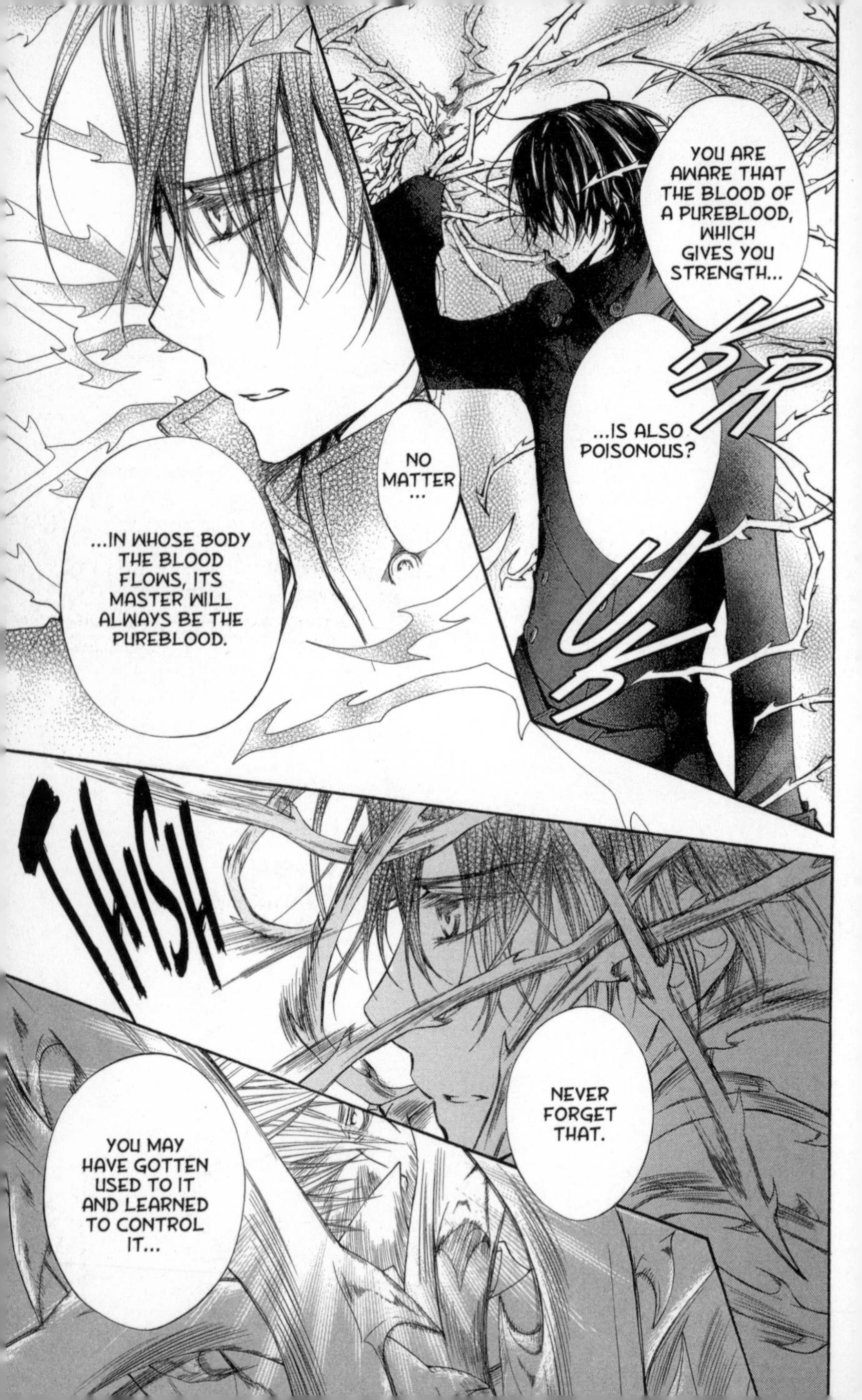
YOU ARE AWARE THAT THE BLOOD OF A PUREBLOOD, WHICH GIVES YOU STRENGTH...
...IS ALSO POISONOUS?
NO MATTER...
...IN WHOSE BODY THE BLOOD FLOWS, ITS MASTER WILL ALWAYS BE THE PUREBLOOD.
THISH
NEVER FORGET THAT.
YOU MAY HAVE GOTTEN USED TO IT AND LEARNED TO CONTROL IT...

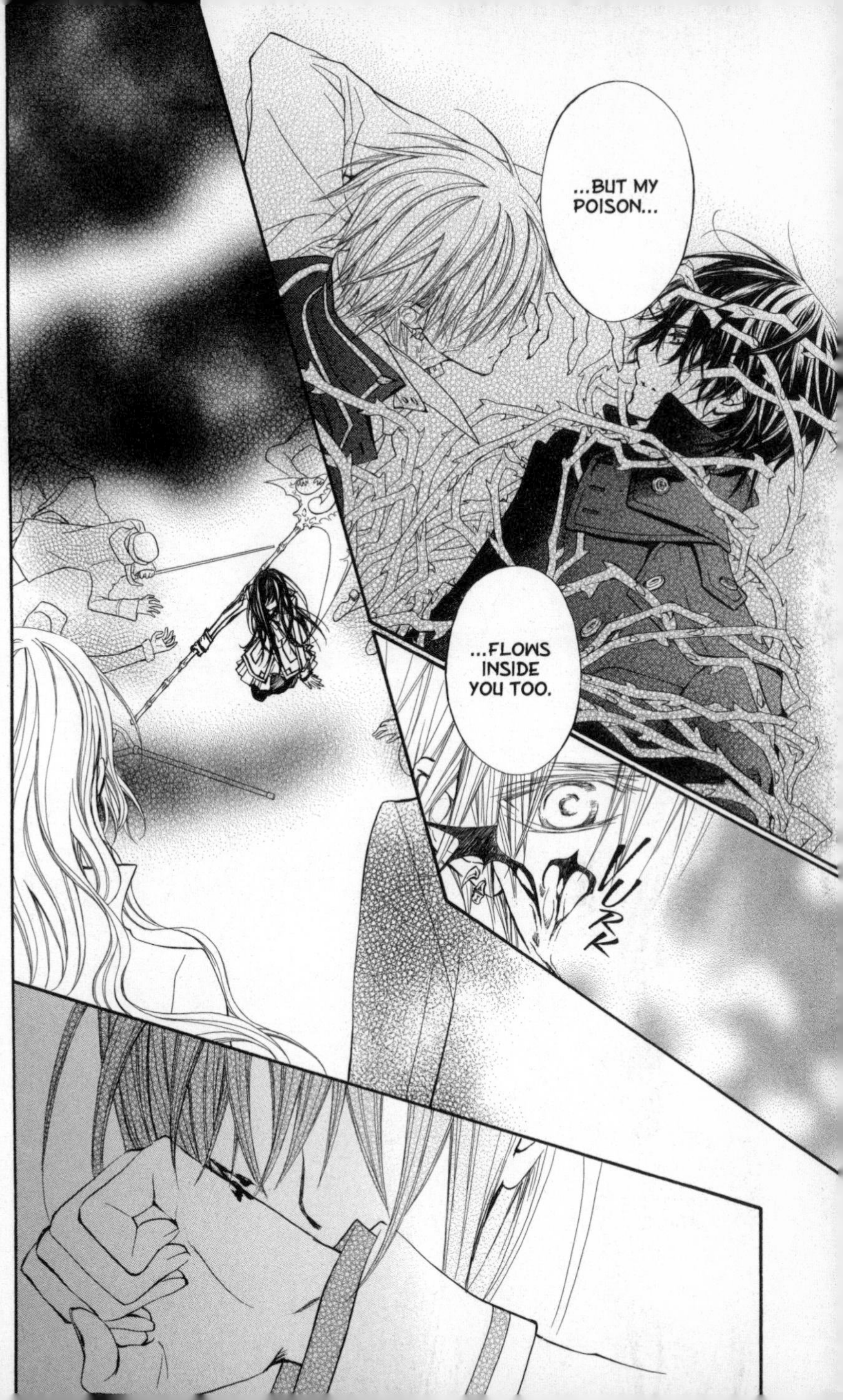
...BUT MY POISON...
...FLOWS INSIDE YOU TOO.
VURK

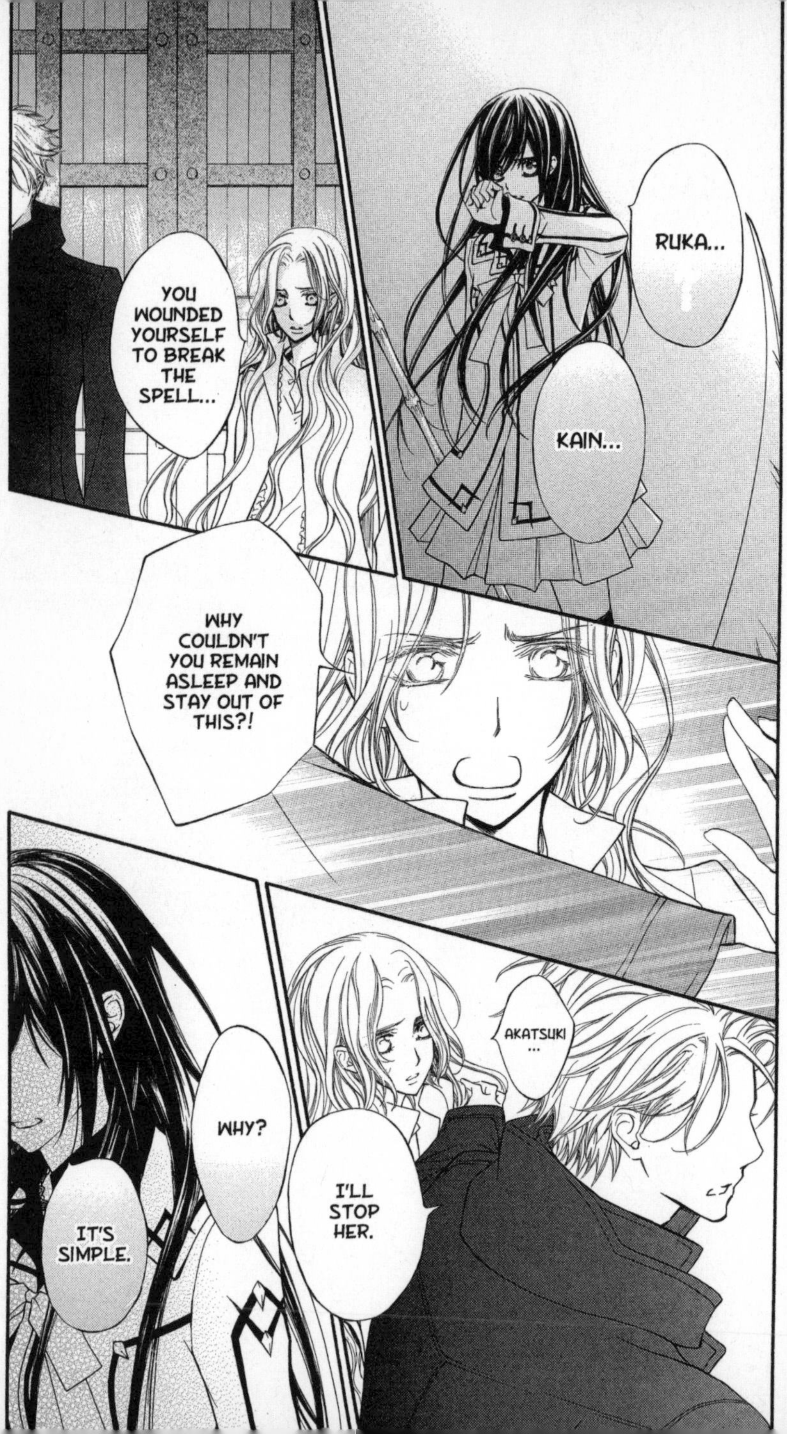
RUKA...
KAIN...
YOU WOUNDED YOURSELF TO BREAK THE SPELL...
WHY COULDN'T YOU REMAIN ASLEEP AND STAY OUT OF THIS?!
AKATSUKI ...
I'LL STOP HER.
WHY?
IT'S SIMPLE.

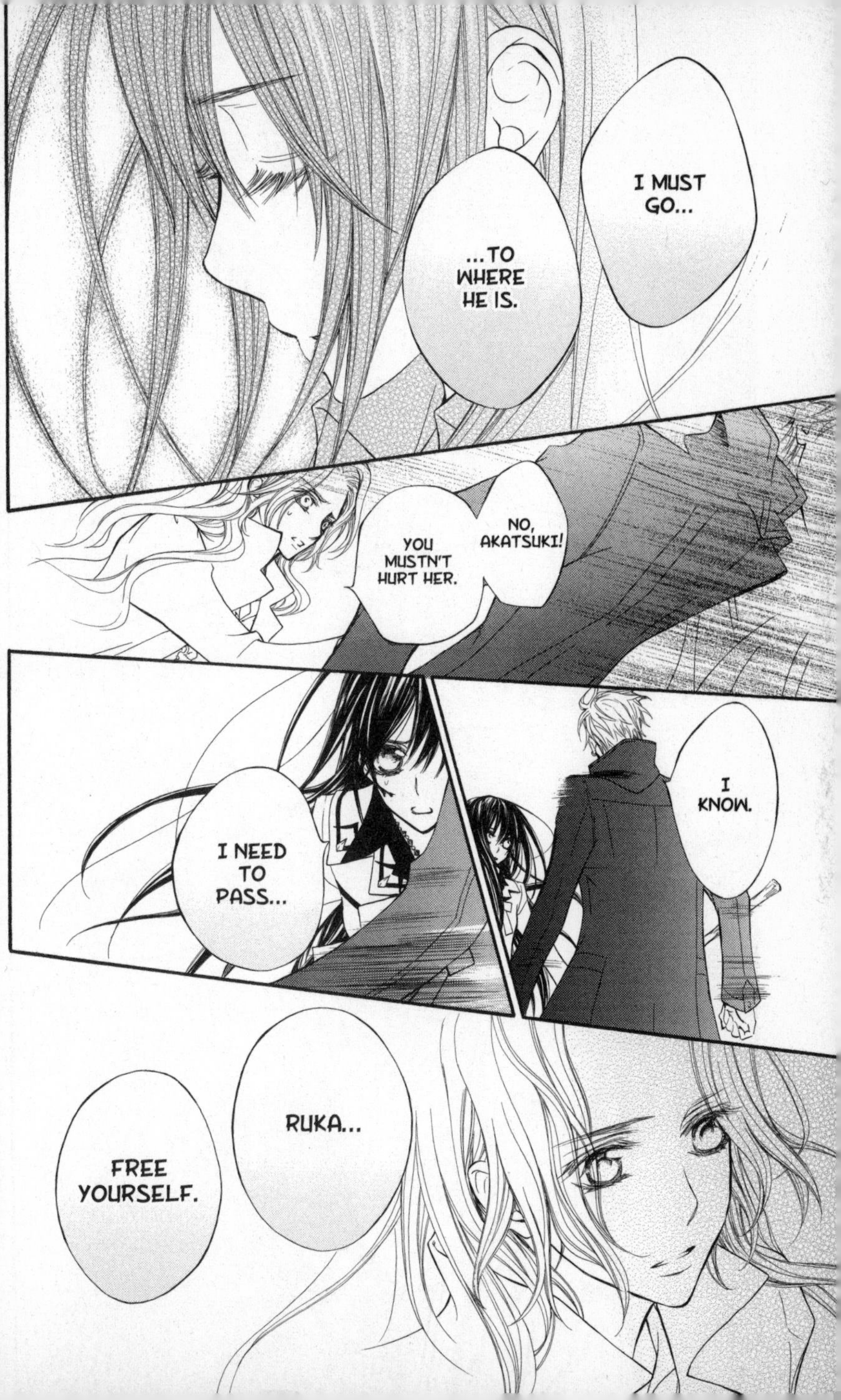
I MUST GO...
...TO WHERE HE IS.
NO, AKATSUKI!
YOU MUSTN'T HURT HER.
I KNOW.
I NEED TO PASS...
RUKA...
FREE YOURSELF.

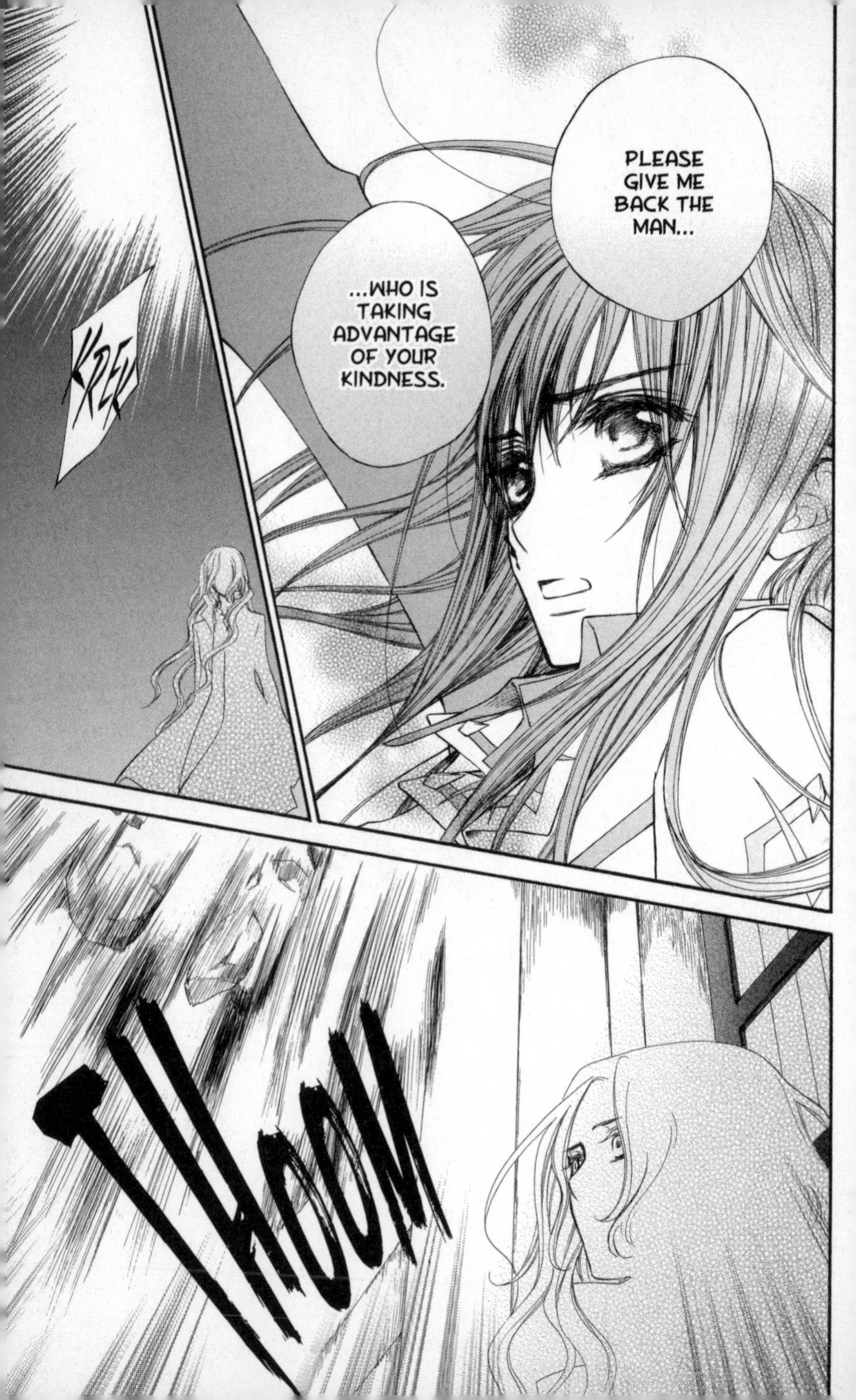
PLEASE GIVE ME BACK THE MAN...
...WHO IS TAKING ADVANTAGE OF YOUR KINDNESS.
KREK
THOOM

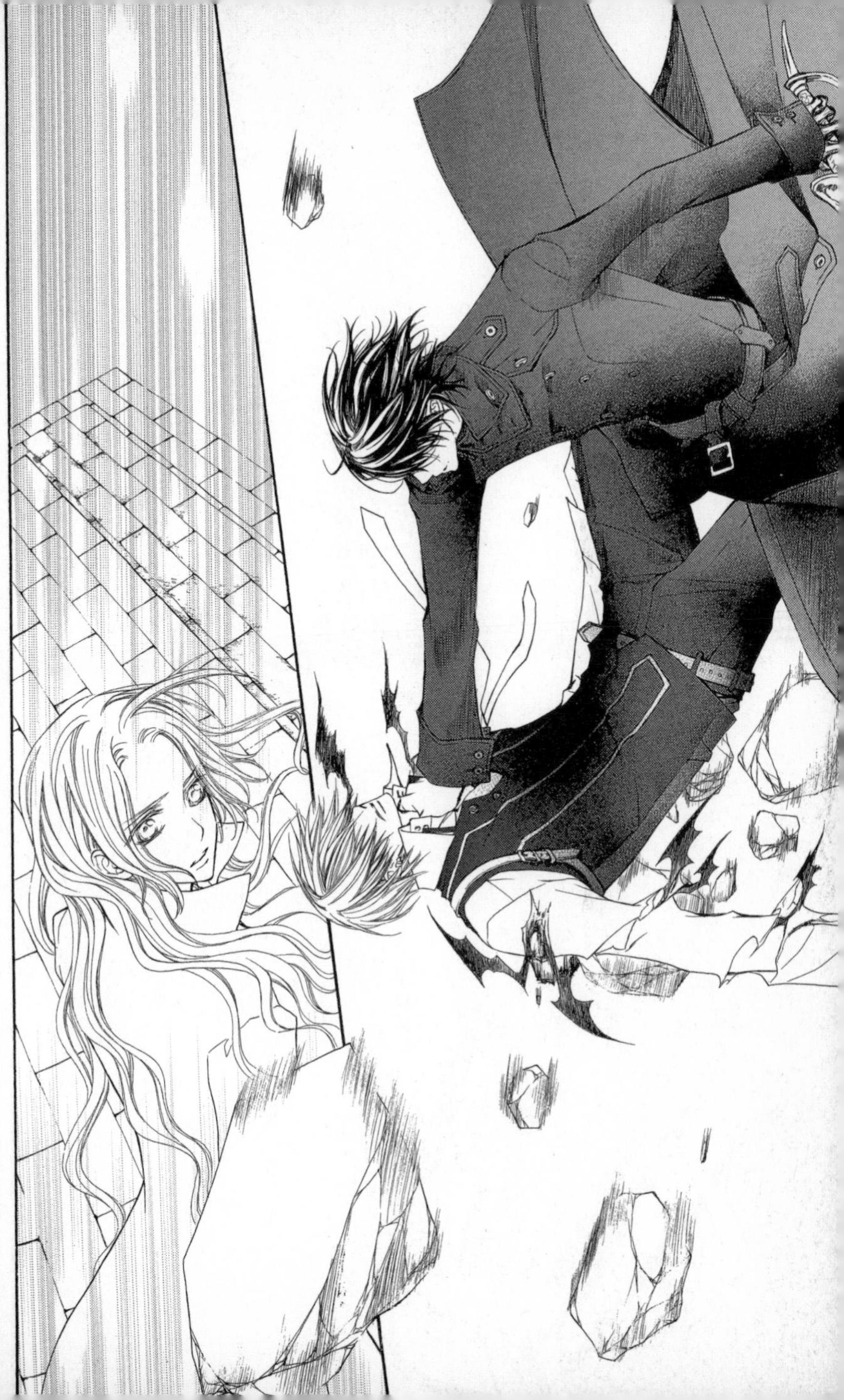

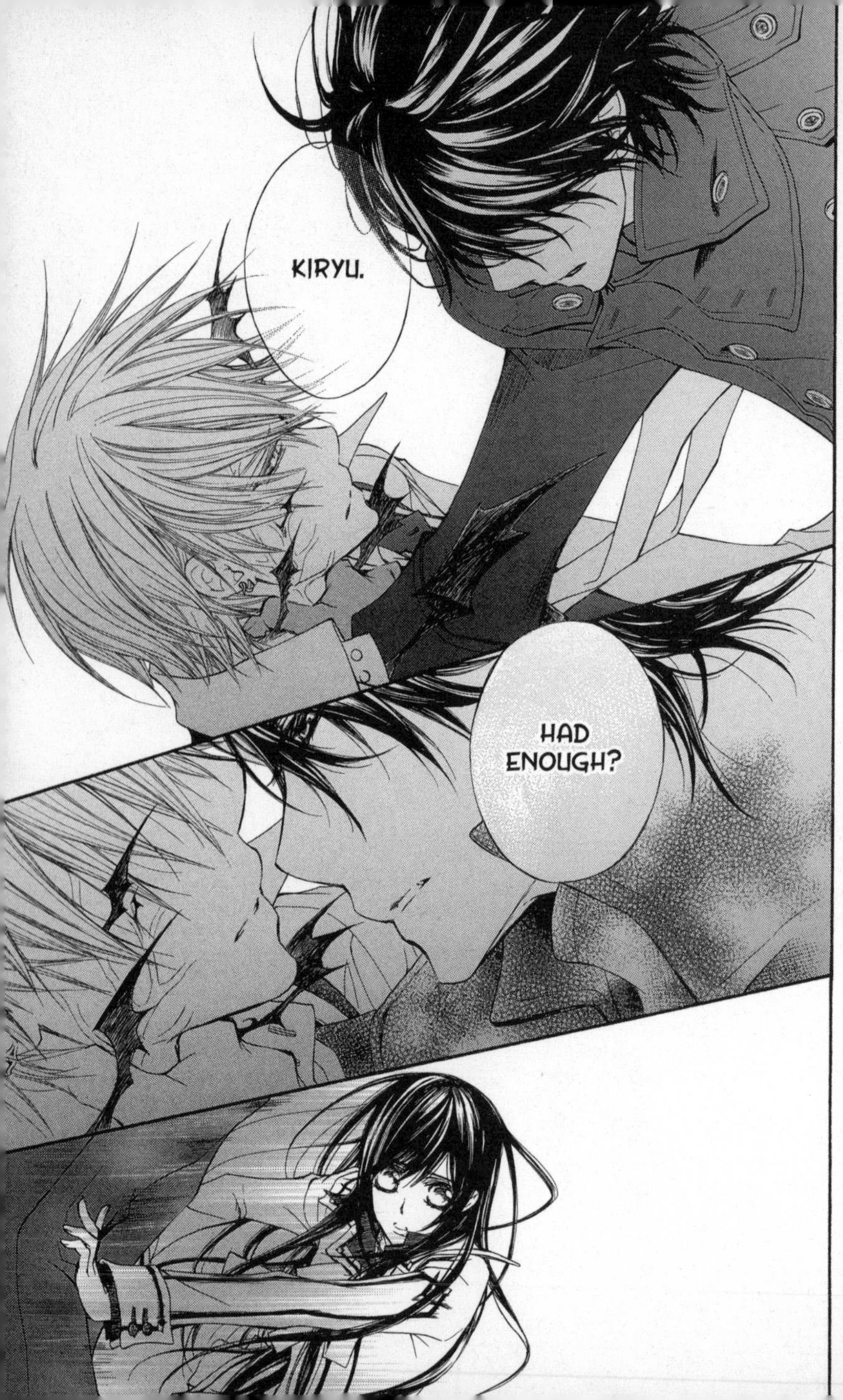
KIRYU.
HAD ENOUGH?

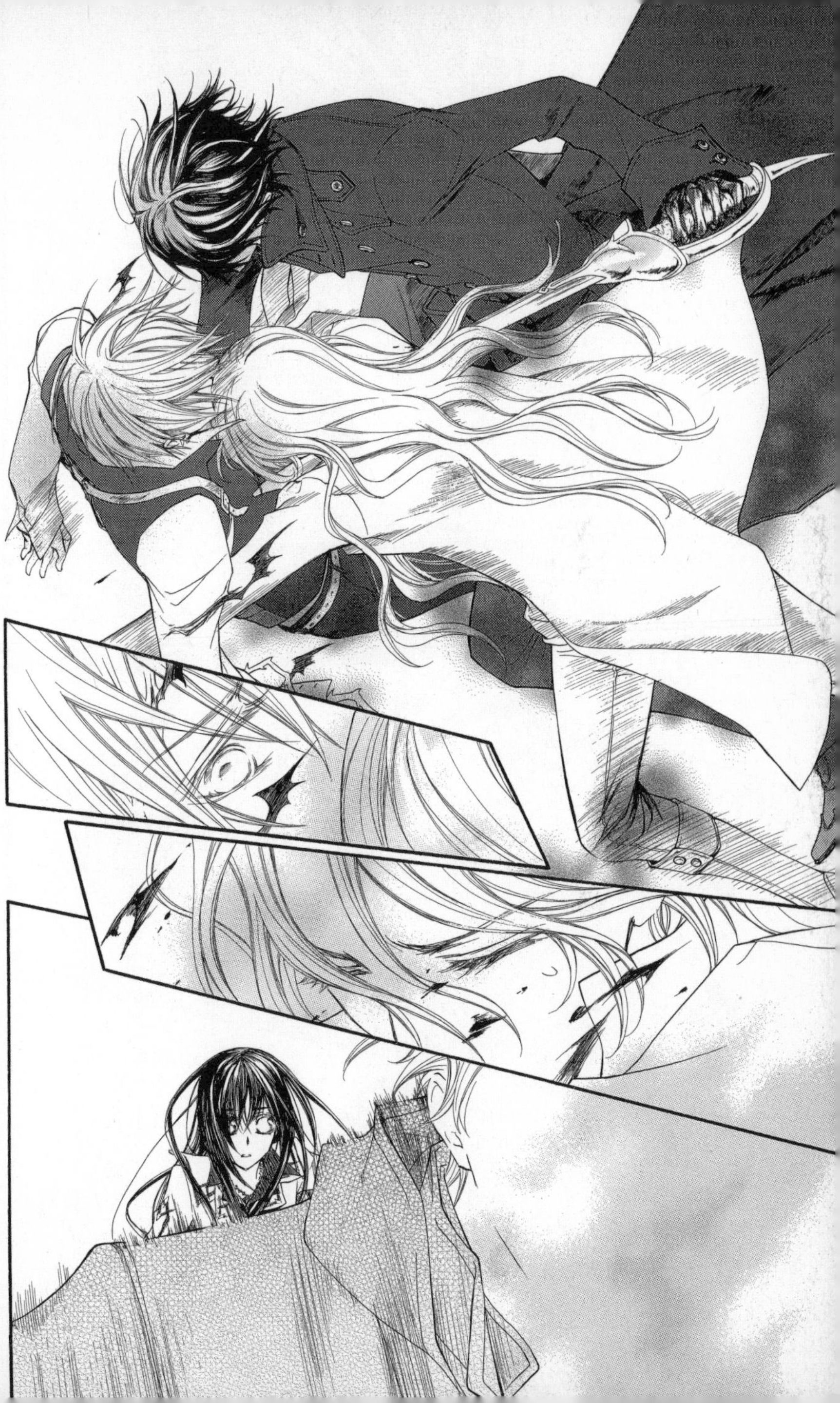

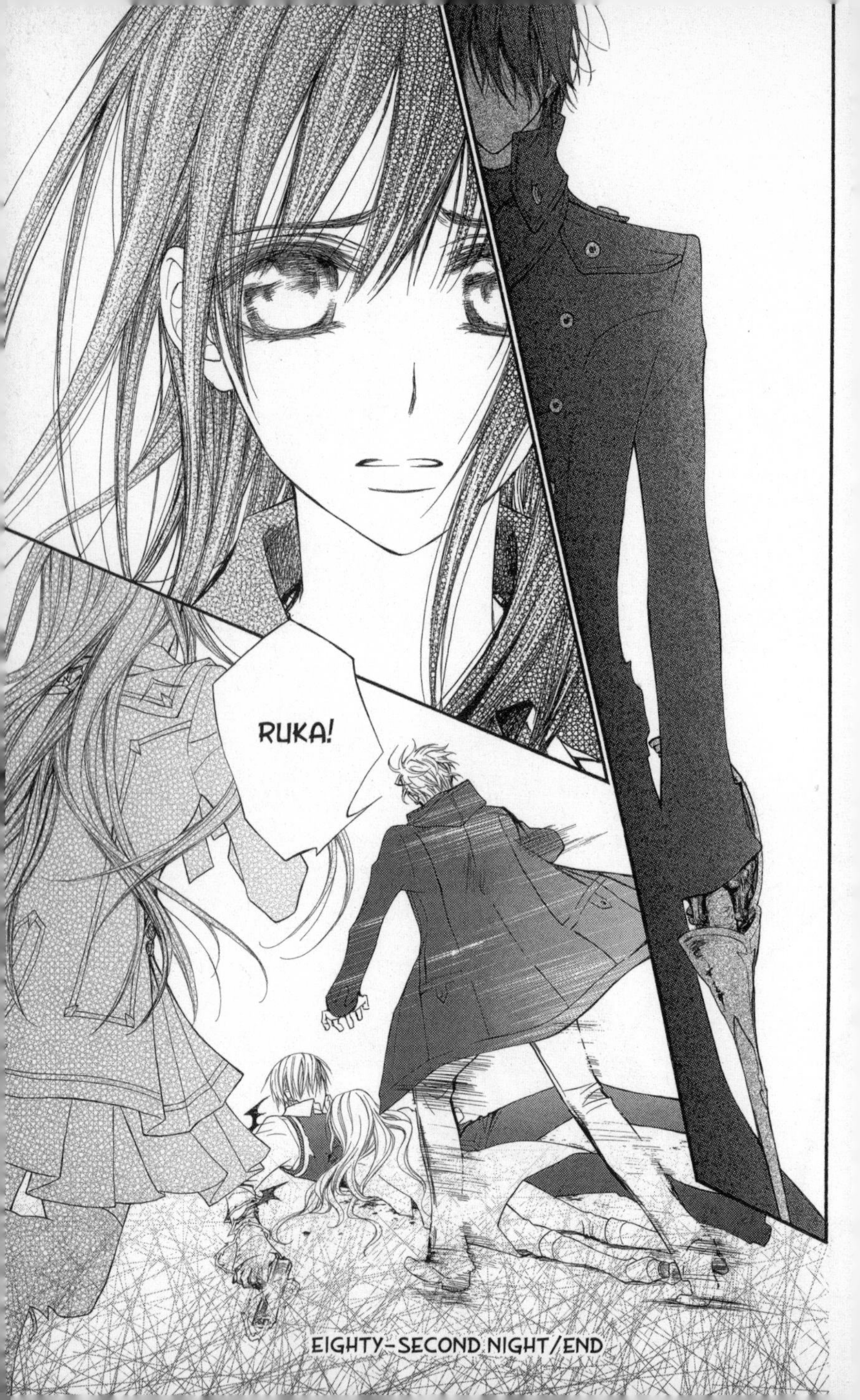

RUKA!
EIGHTY-SECOND NIGHT/END

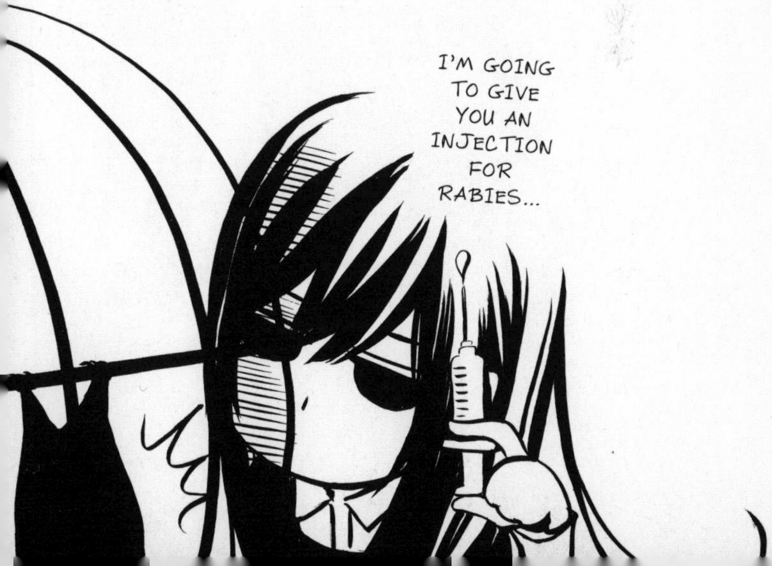
I'M GOING TO GIVE YOU AN INJECTION FOR RABIES...

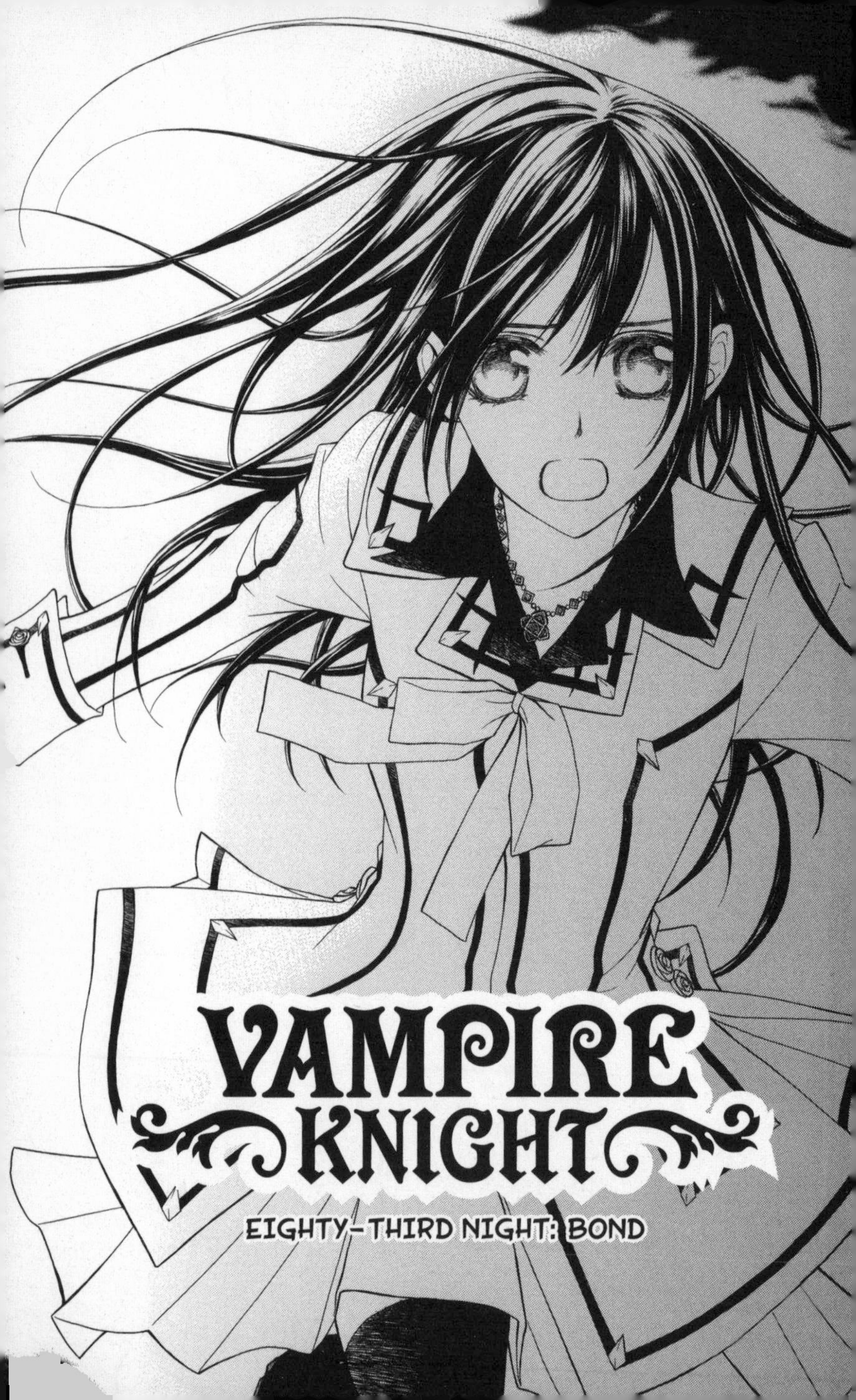
VAMPIRE
KNIGHT
EIGHTY-THIRD NIGHT: BOND

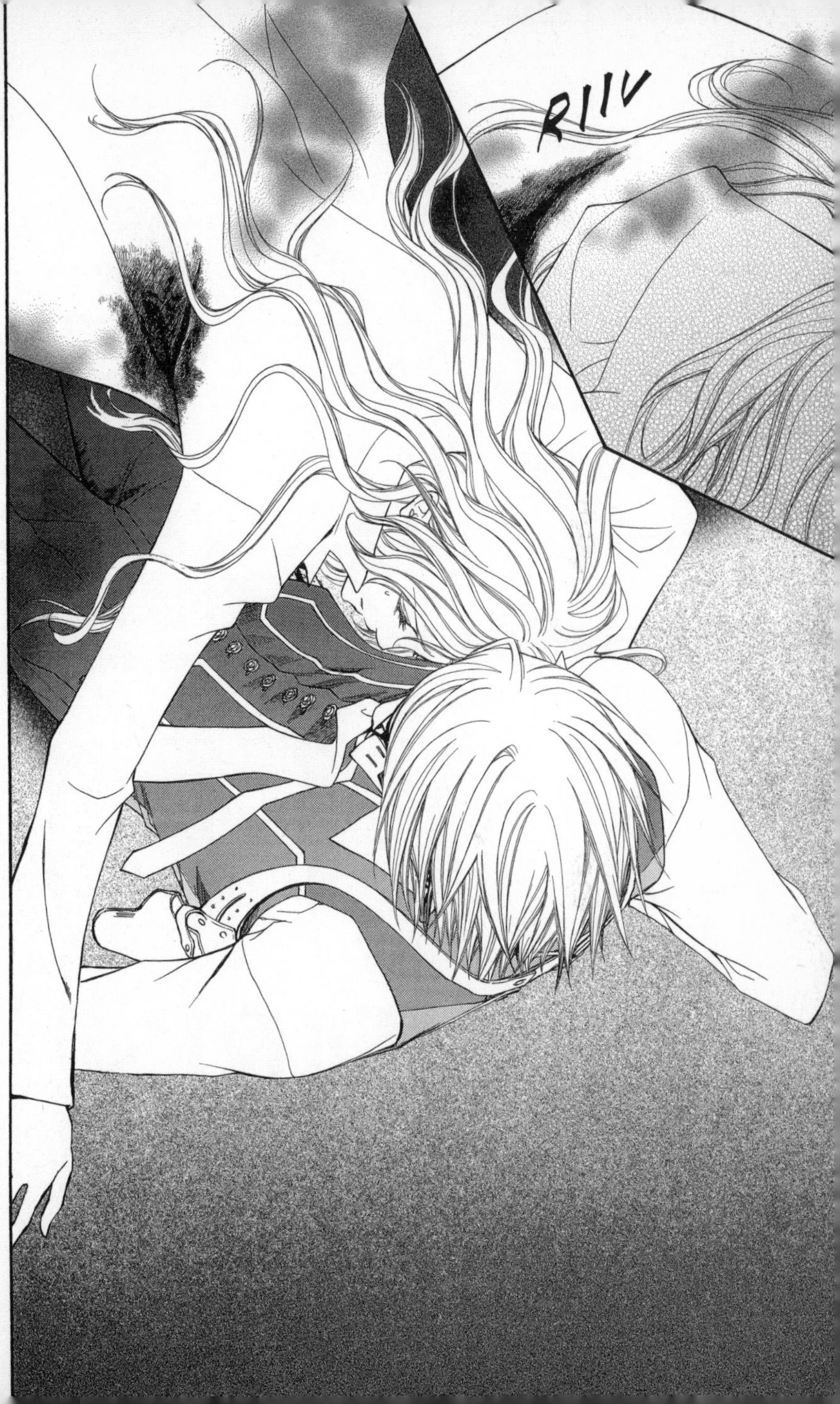
RIIV

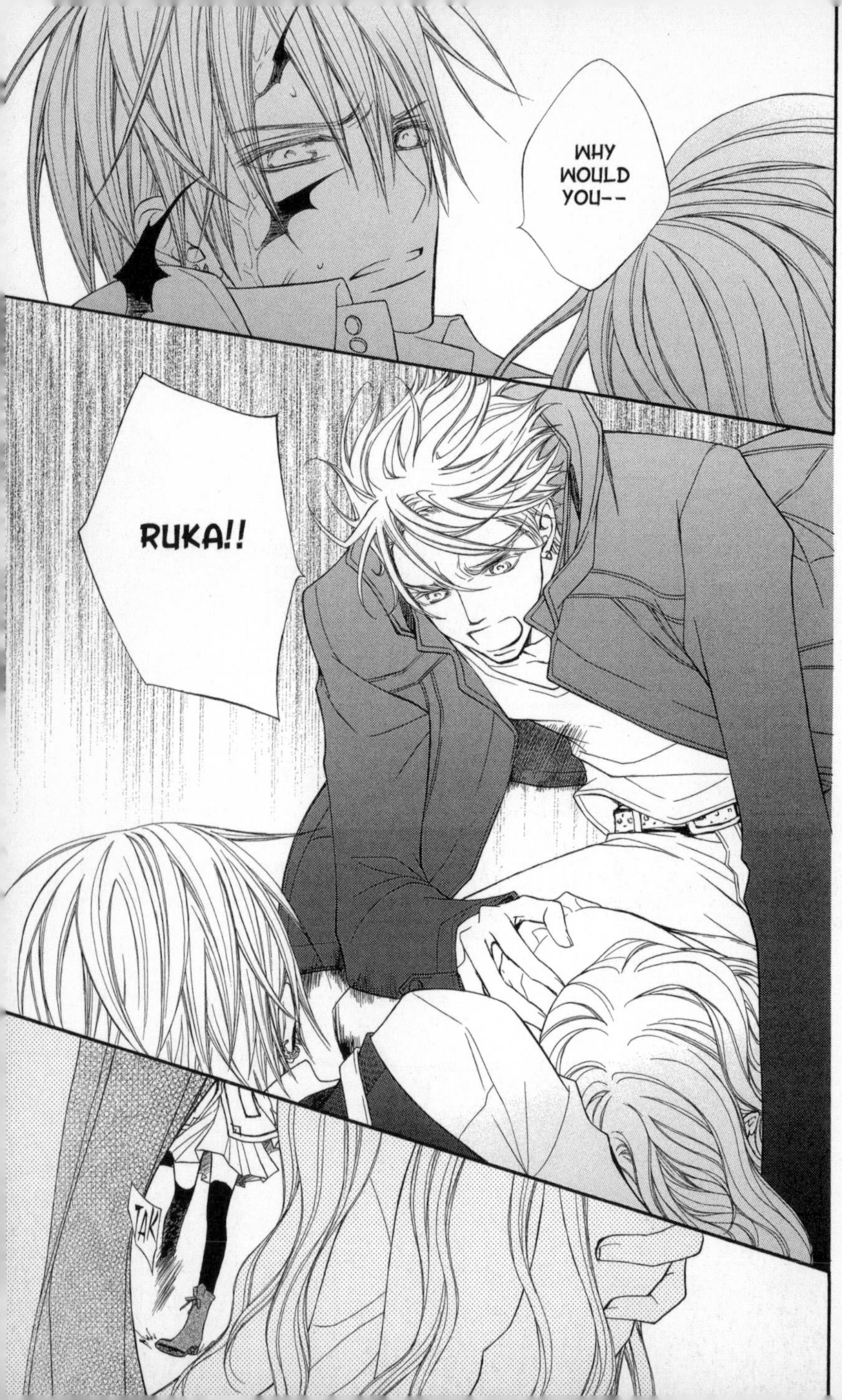
WHY WOULD YOU--
RUKA!!
TAK!

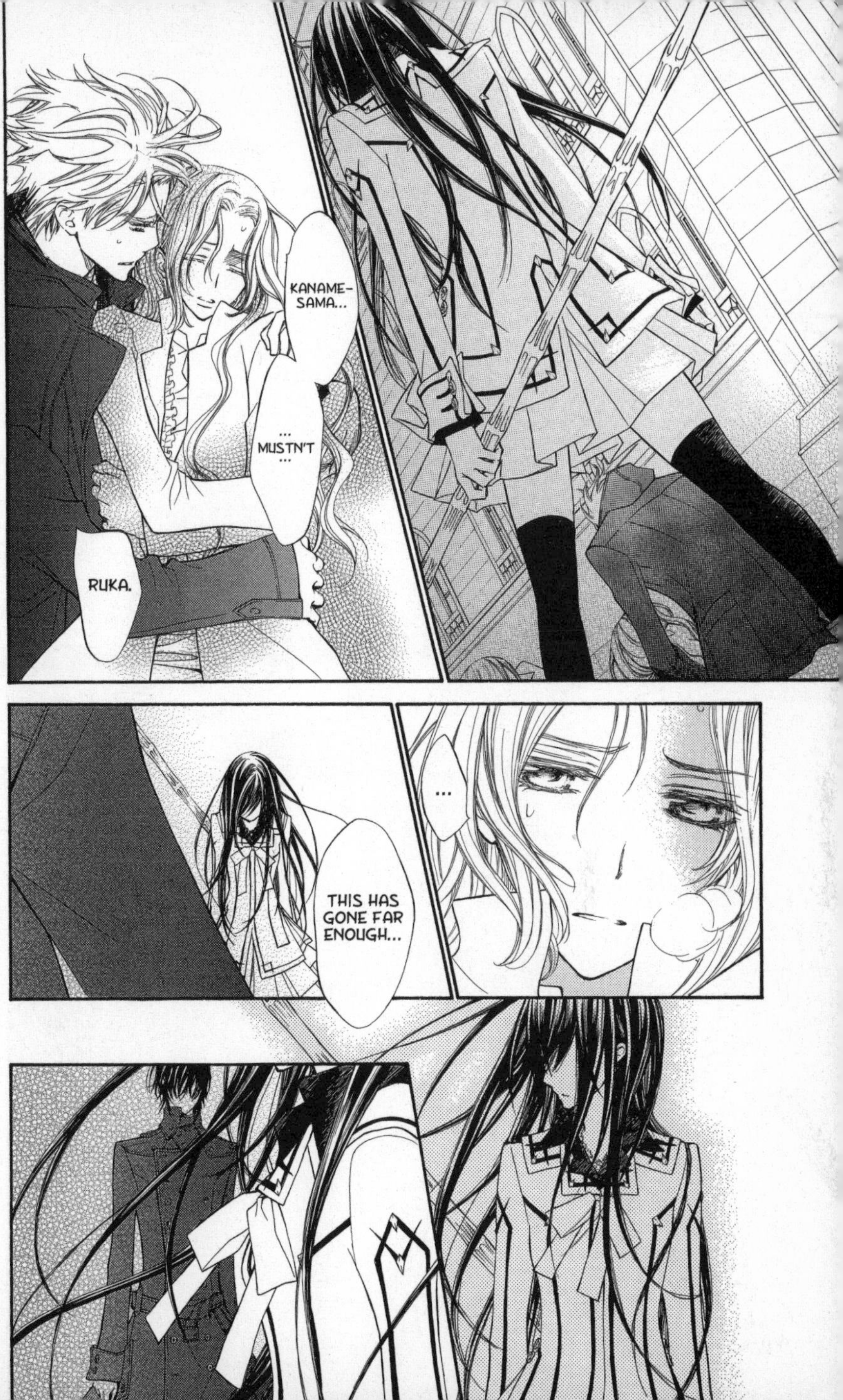
KANAME-SAMA...
... MUSTN'T ...
RUKA.
...
THIS HAS GONE FAR ENOUGH...

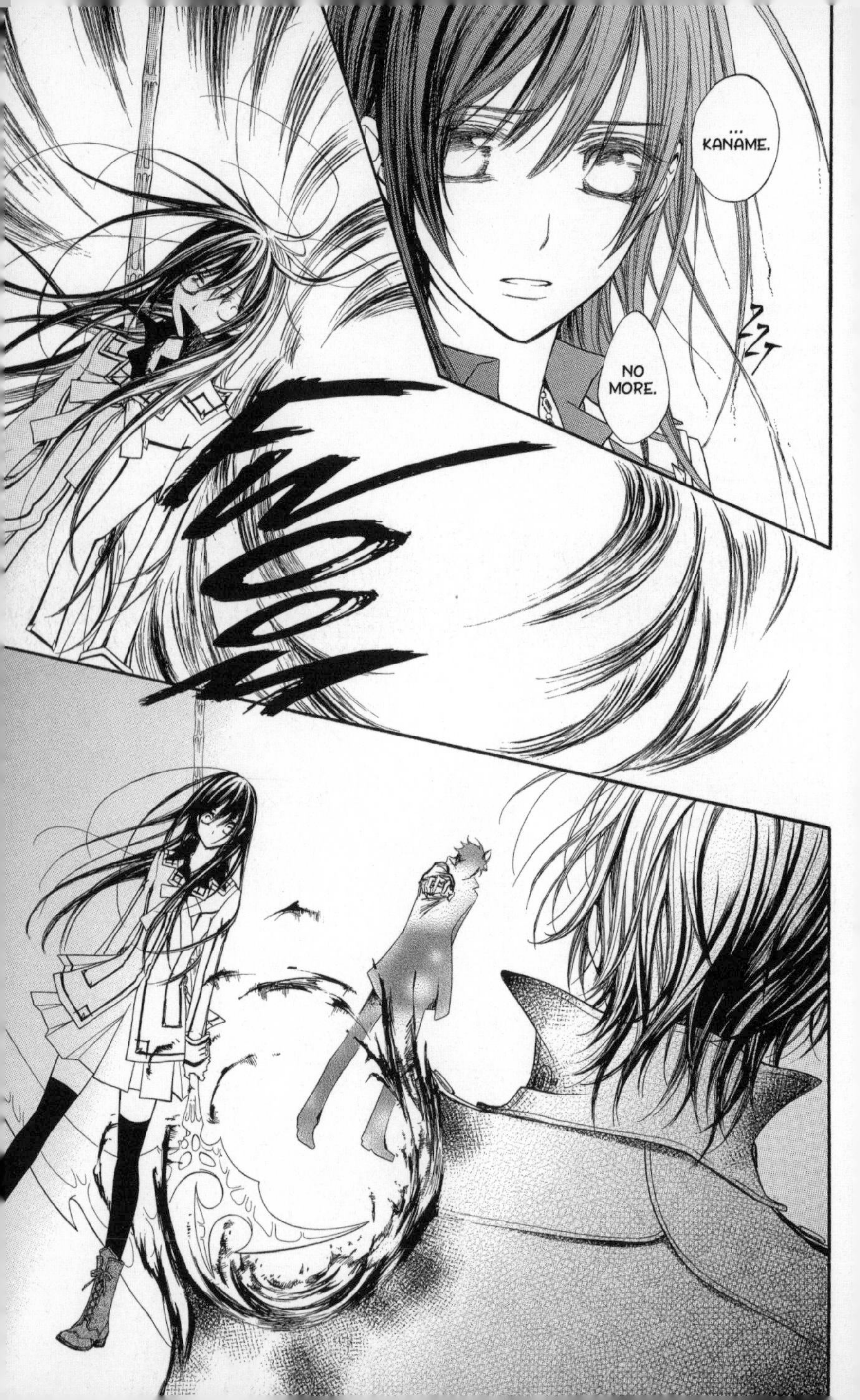
...KANAME.
NO MORE.

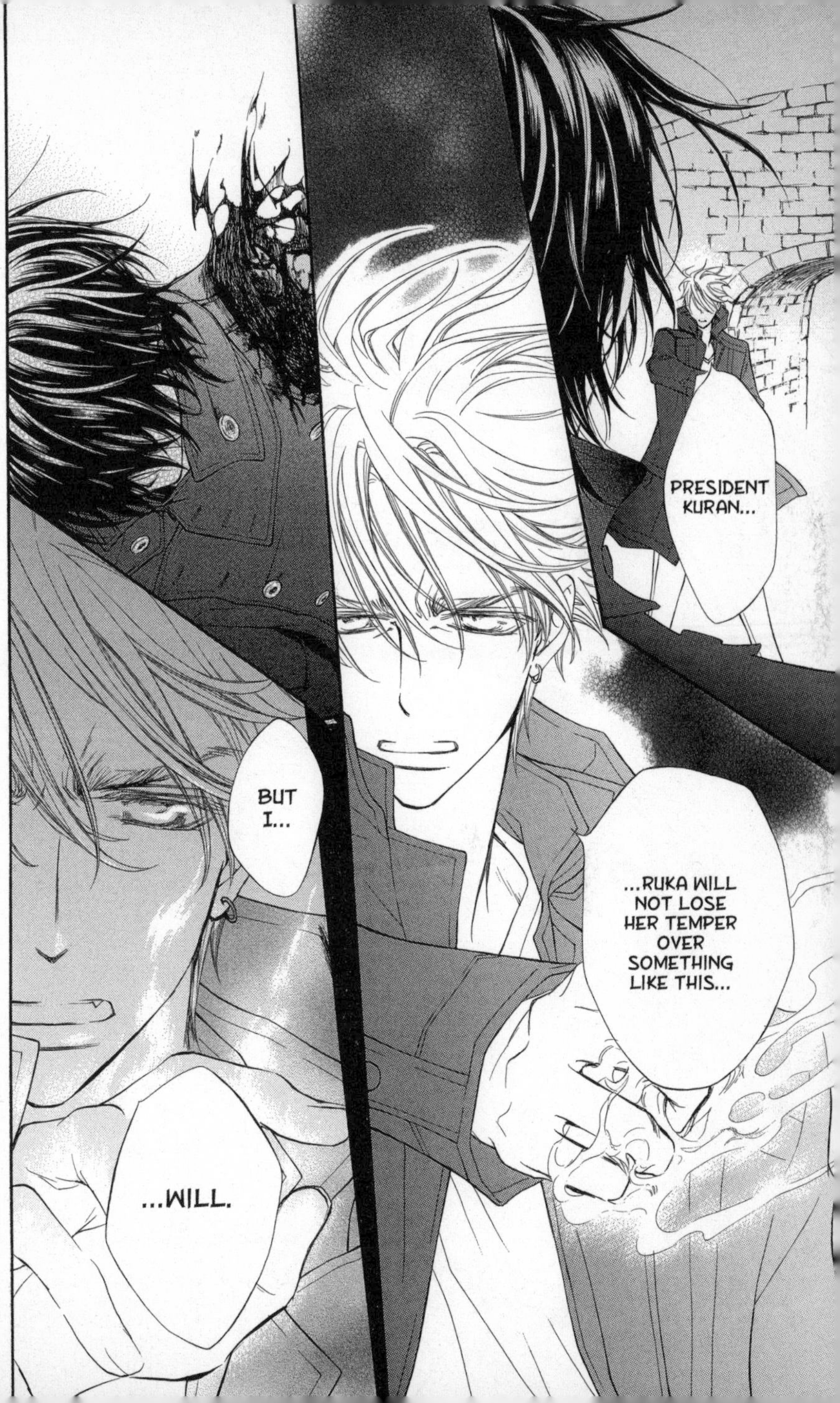
PRESIDENT KURAN...
...RUKA WILL NOT LOSE HER TEMPER OVER SOMETHING LIKE THIS...
BUT I...
...WILL.

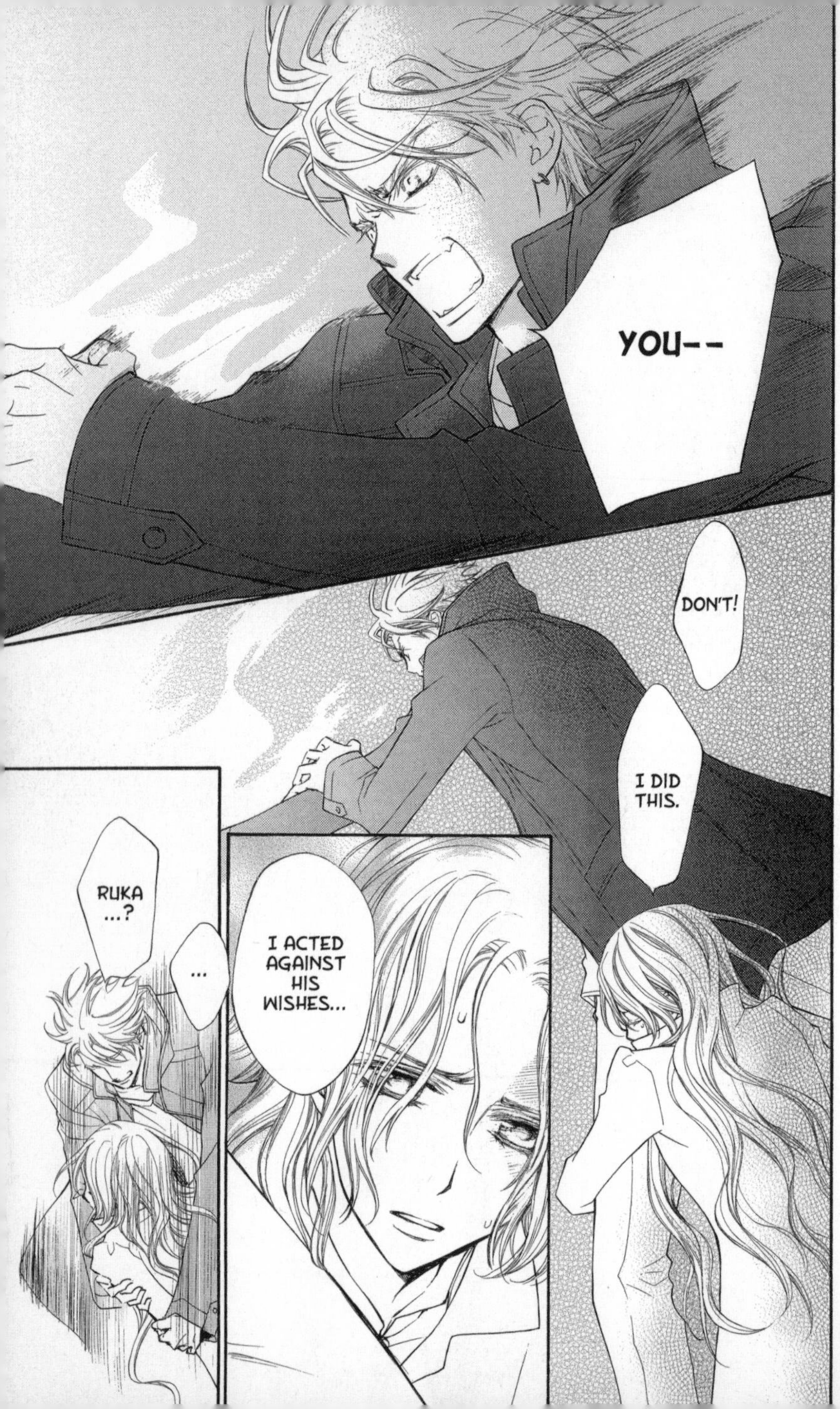
YOU--
DON'T!
I DID THIS.
I ACTED AGAINST HIS WISHES...
RUKA ...?
...

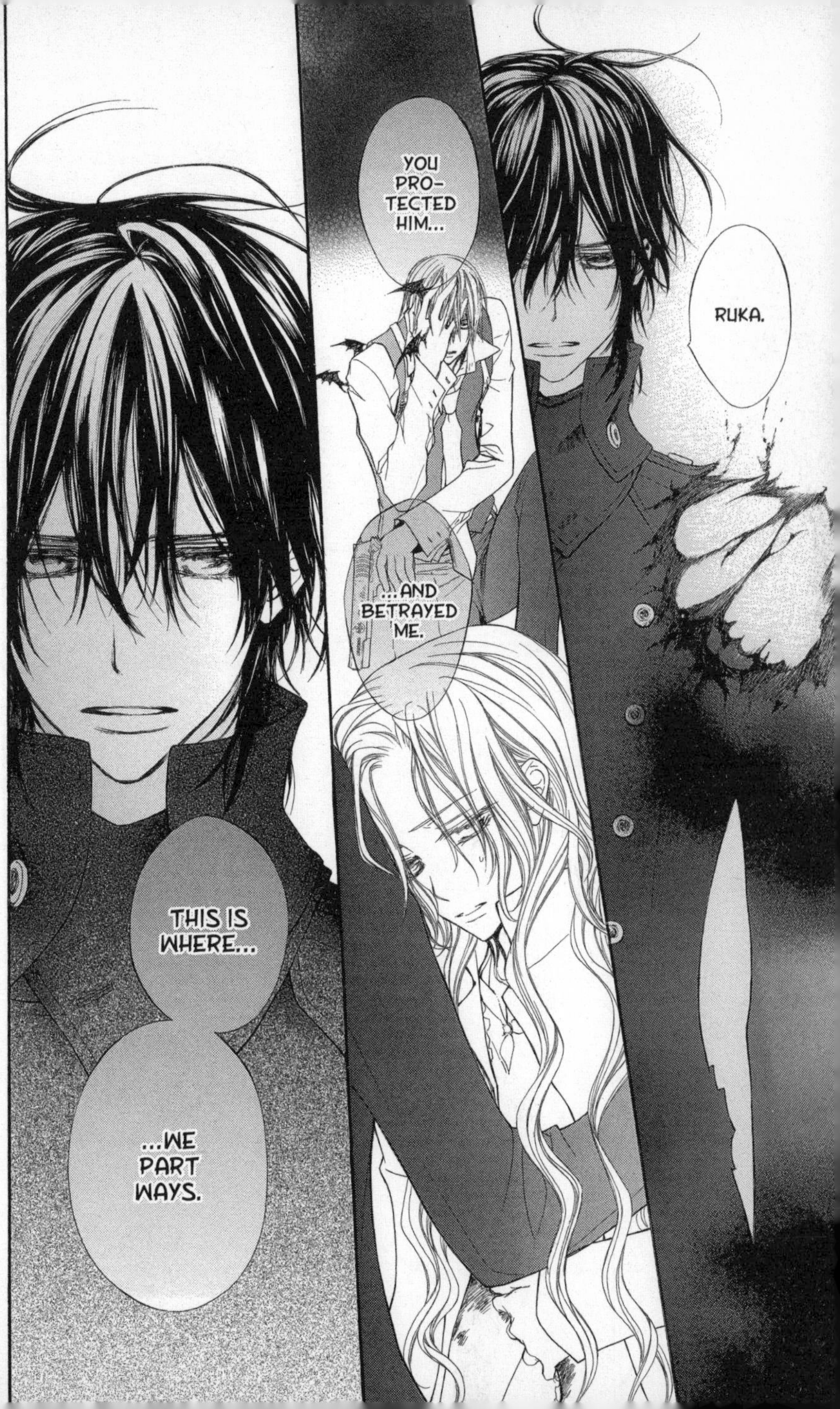
RUKA.
YOU PROTECTED HIM...
...AND BETRAYED ME.
THIS IS WHERE...
...WE PART WAYS.

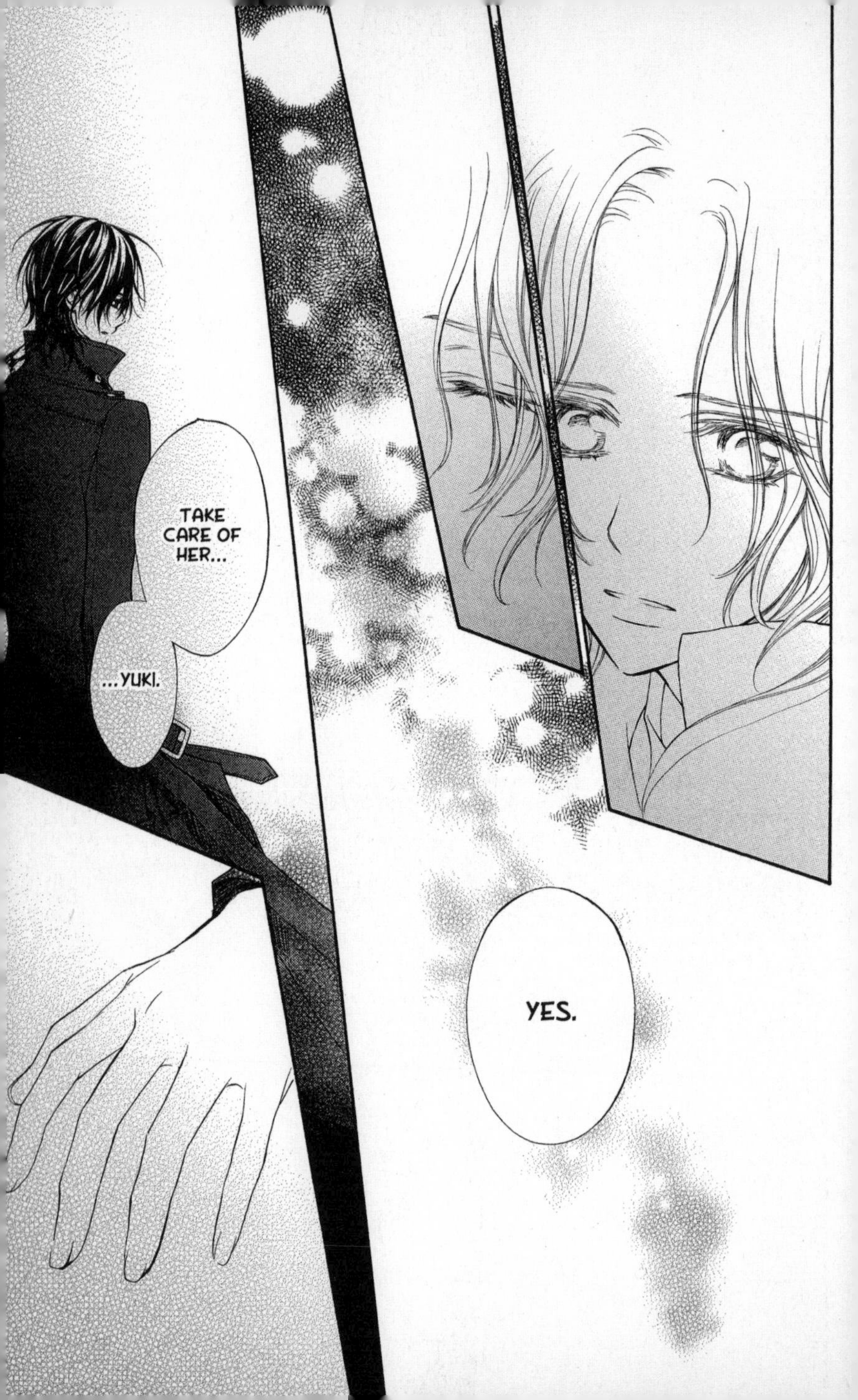
TAKE CARE OF HER...
...YUKI.
YES.

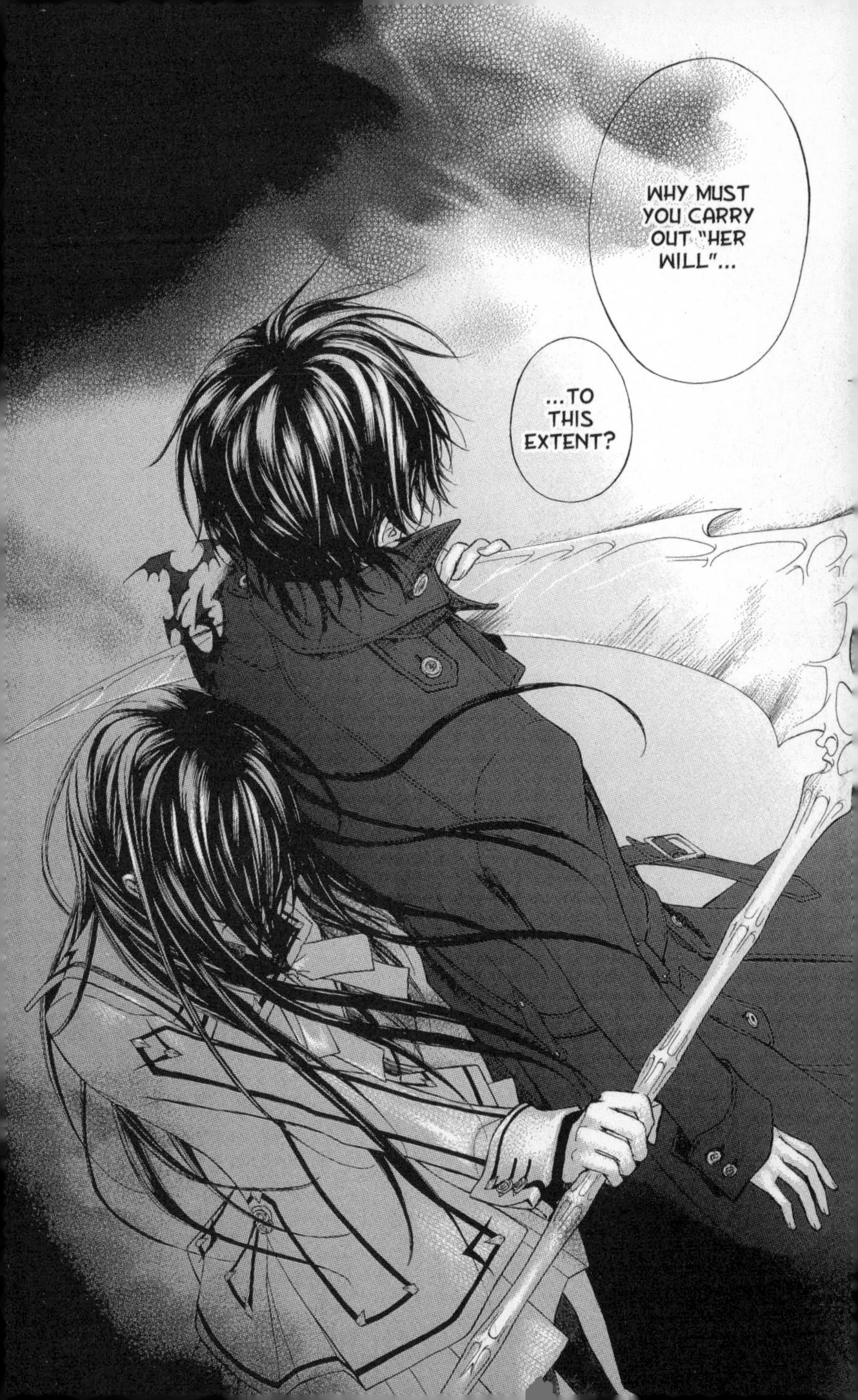
WHY MUST YOU CARRY OUT "HER WILL"...
...TO THIS EXTENT?

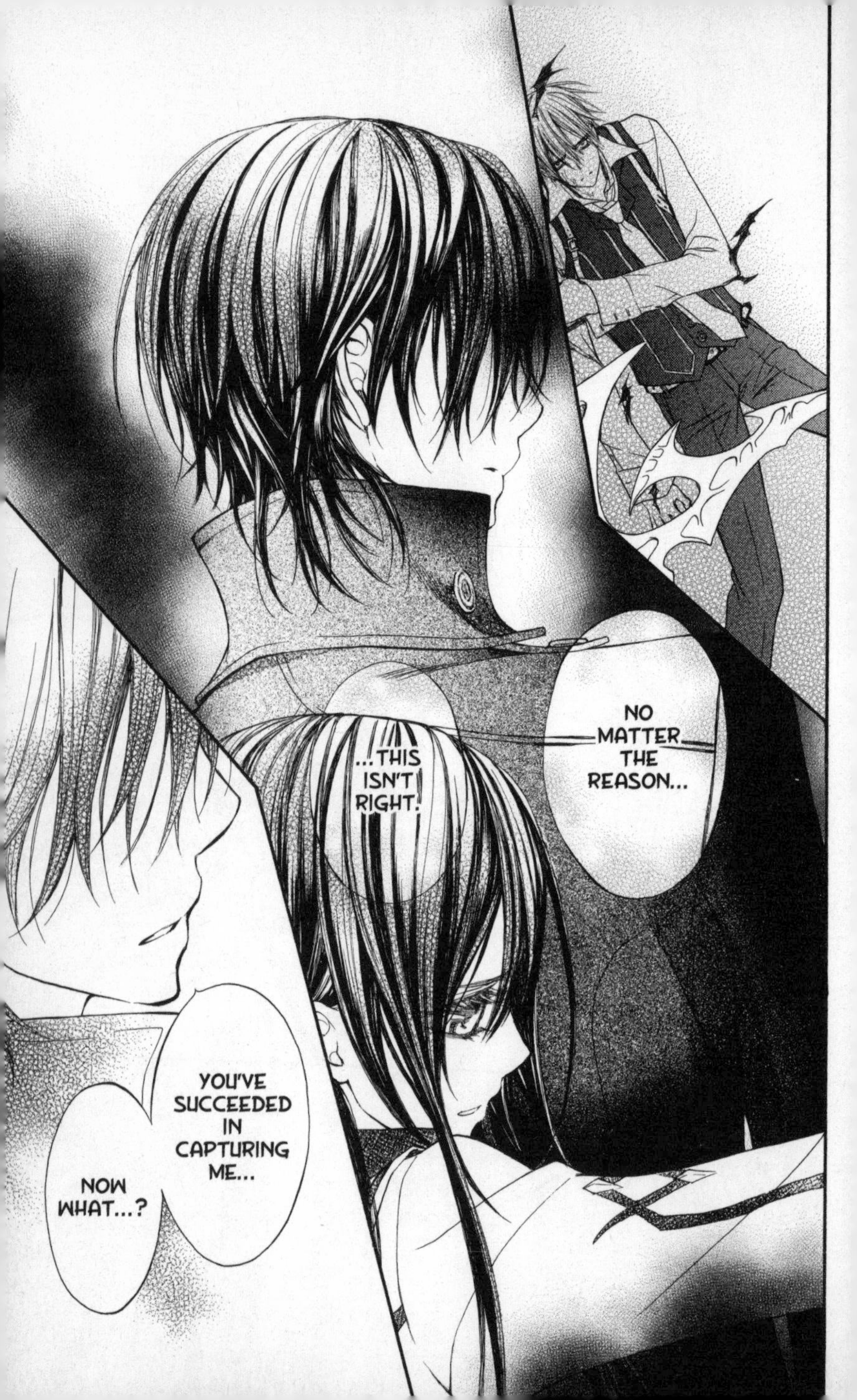
NO MATTER THE REASON...
...THIS ISN'T RIGHT.
YOU'VE SUCCEEDED IN CAPTURING ME...
NOW WHAT...?

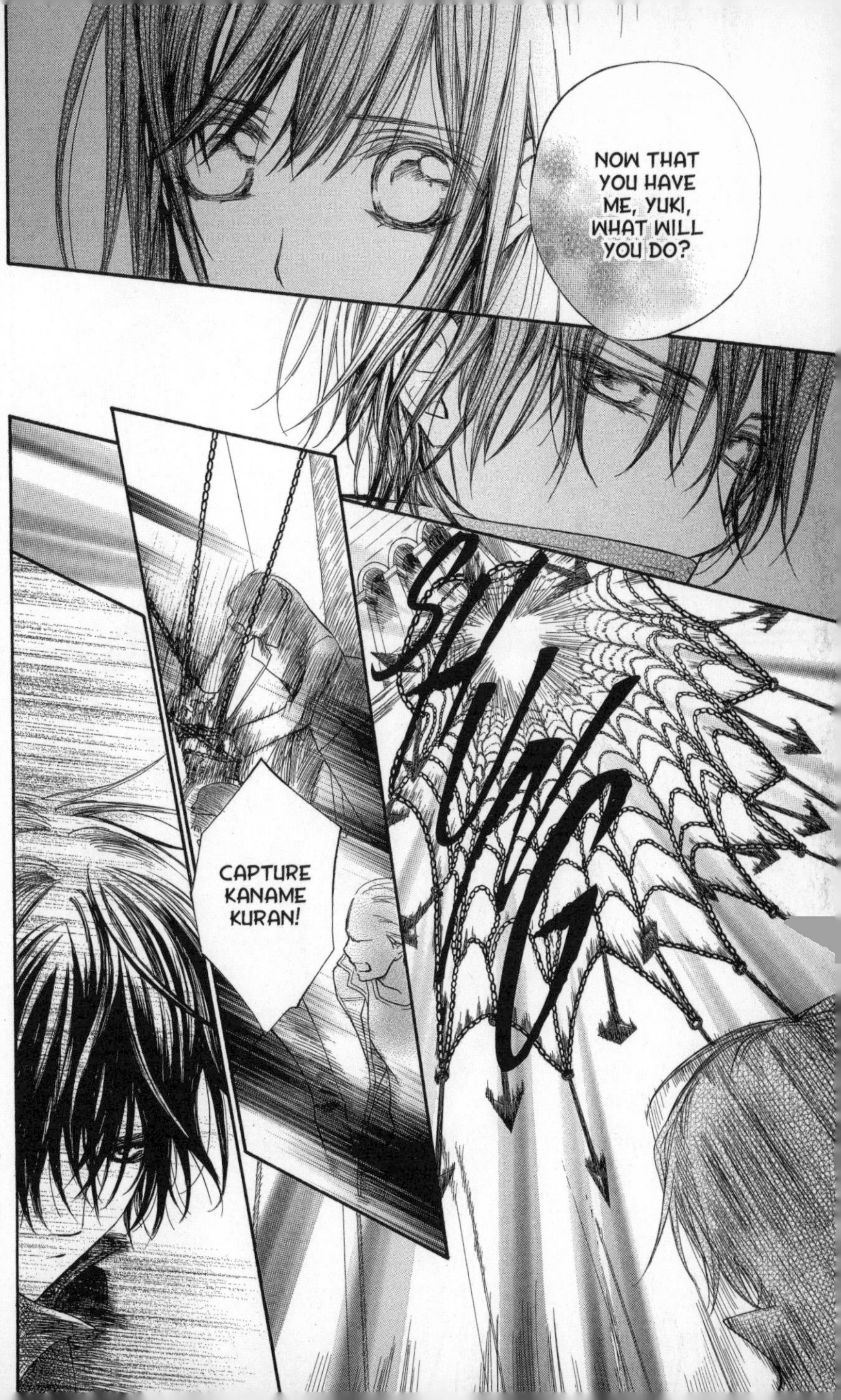
NOW THAT YOU HAVE ME, YUKI, WHAT WILL YOU DO?
CAPTURE KANAME KURAN!
SHING

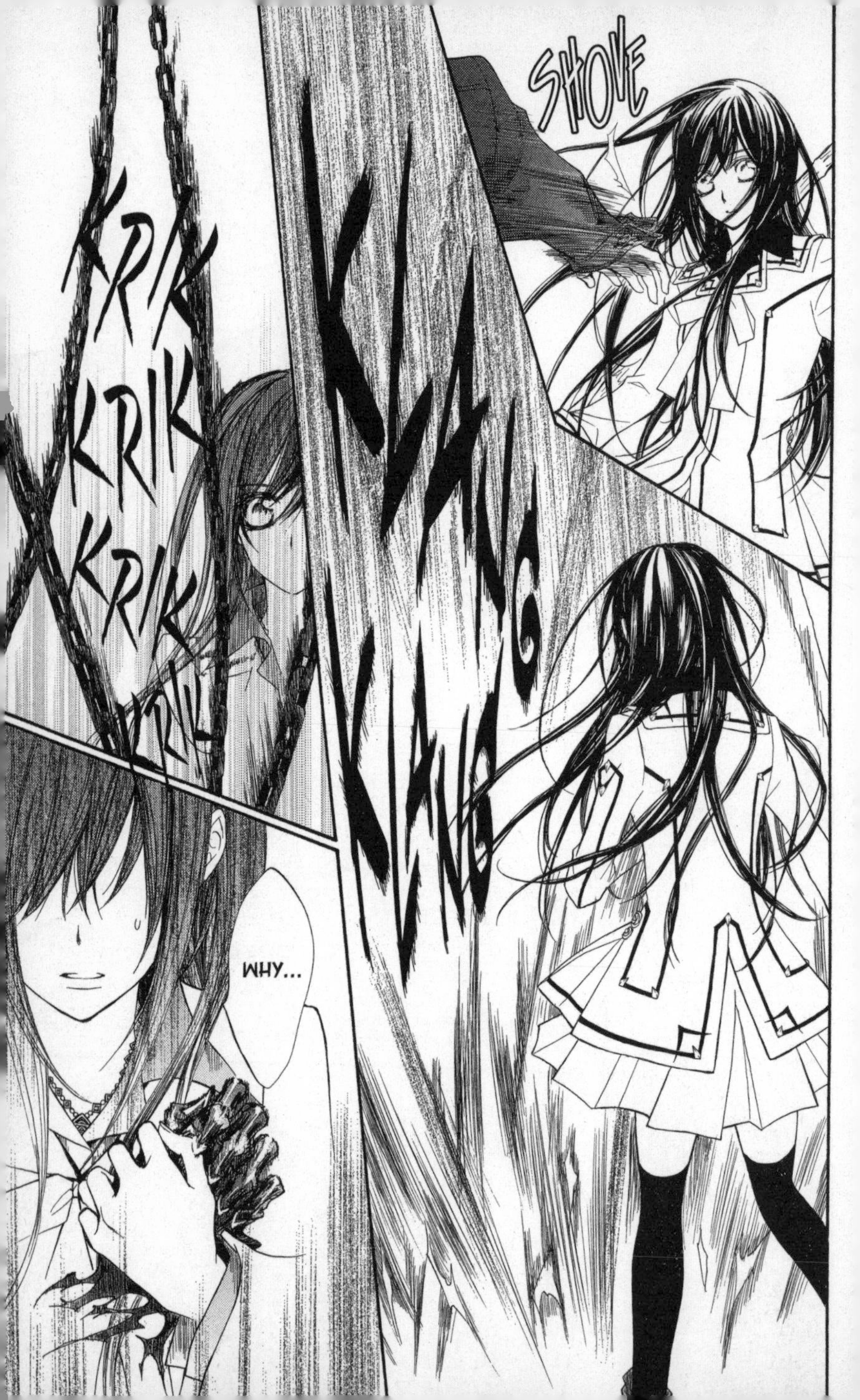
SHOVE
KLANG
KLANG
KRIK
KRIK
KRIK
WHY...

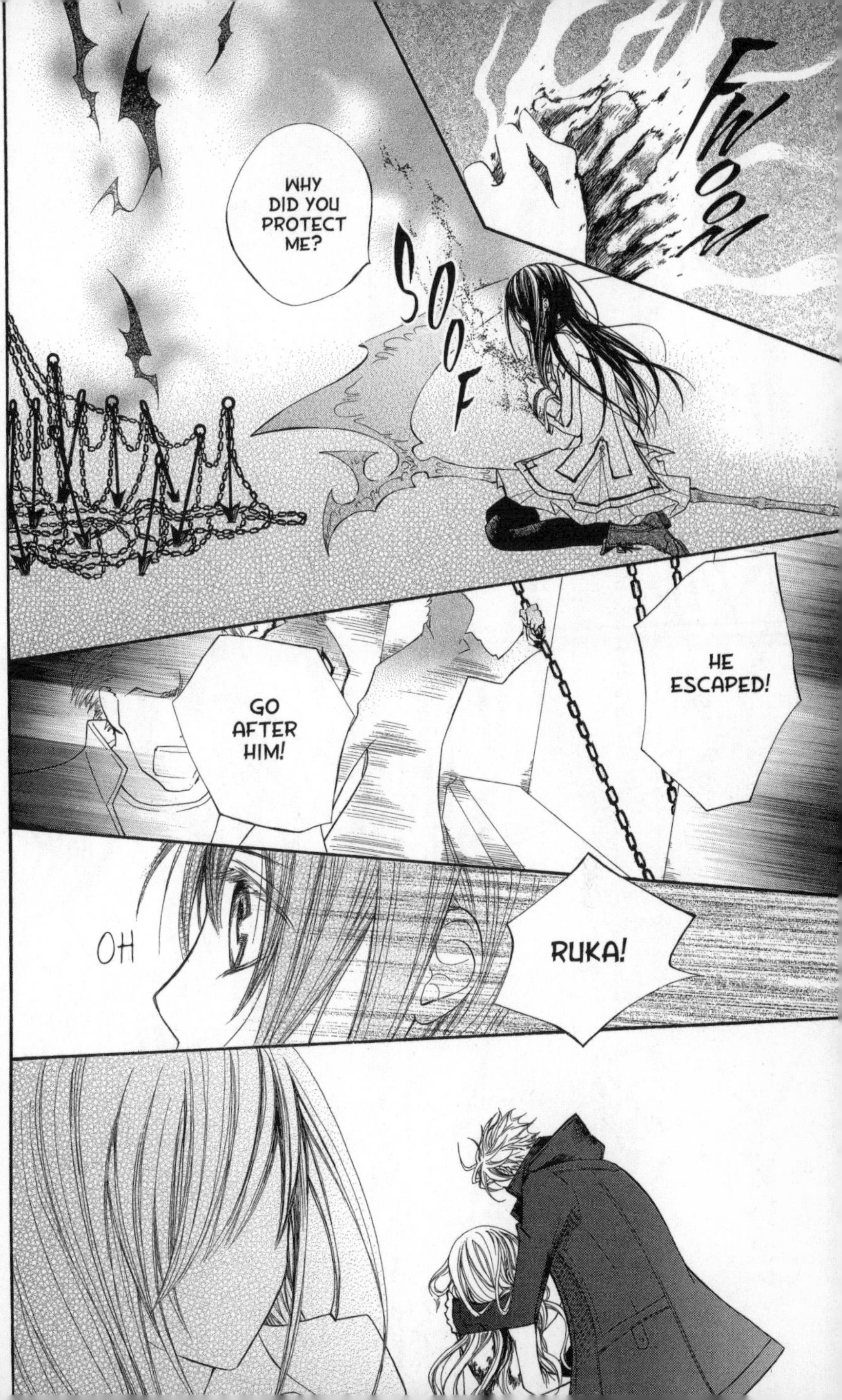
FWOOOM
SOOOF
WHY DID YOU PROTECT ME?
HE ESCAPED!
GO AFTER HIM!
RUKA!
OH

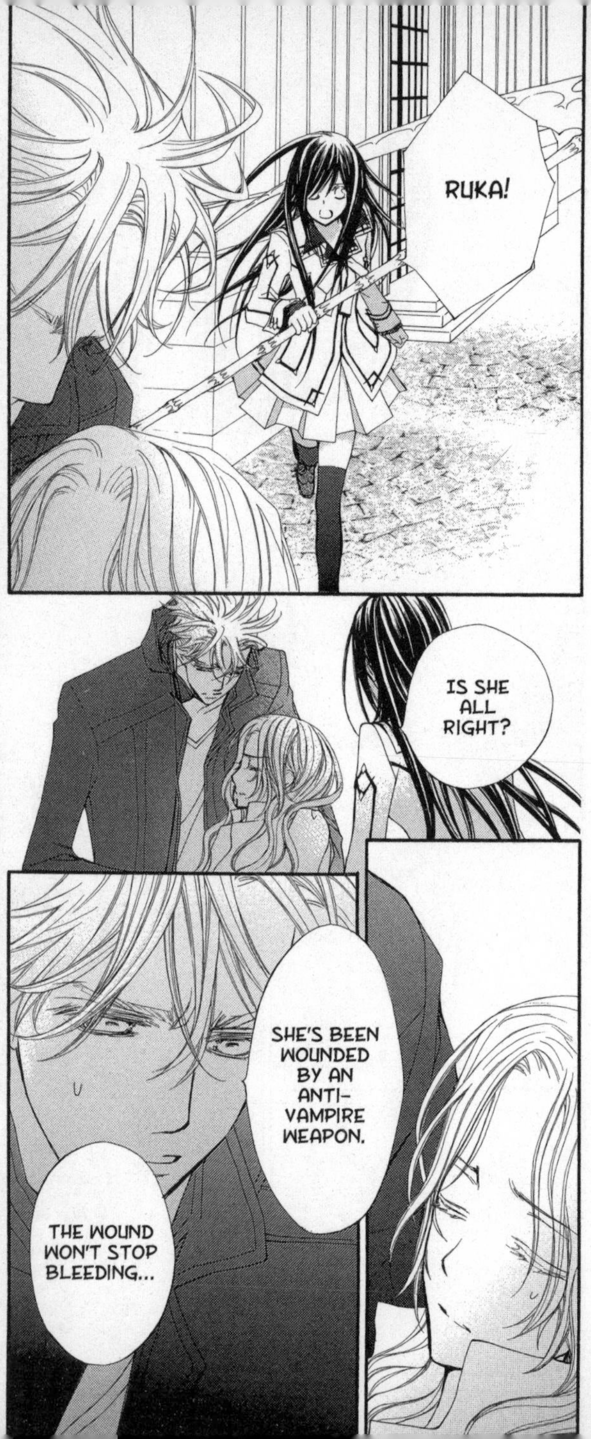
RUKA!
IS SHE ALL RIGHT?
SHE'S BEEN WOUNDED BY AN ANTI-VAMPIRE WEAPON.
THE WOUND WON'T STOP BLEEDING...

III

I'd like to thank everyone. Volume 17 never would have been published without you.

I'd like to thank my assistants...

O. Mio-sama
K. Midori-sama
I. Asami-sama
A. Ichiya-sama

And...
I'd like to thank my editor, my friends and family, and everyone else involved in this work.

And to all the readers...
I'd like to thank everyone from the bottom of my heart.

樋野まつり。
Matsuri Hino

I hope I will see you again in volume 18.

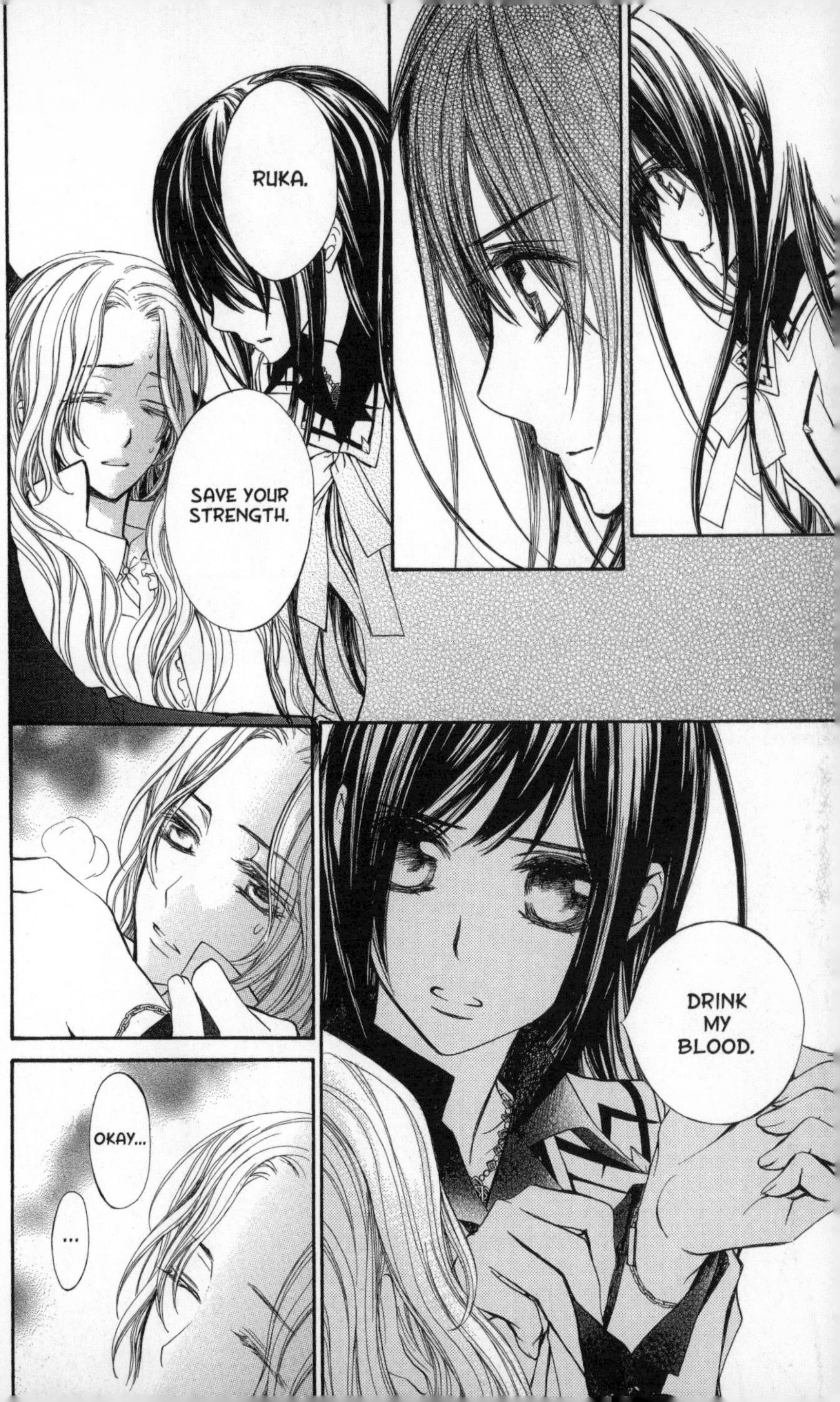
RUKA.
SAVE YOUR STRENGTH.
DRINK MY BLOOD.
OKAY...
...

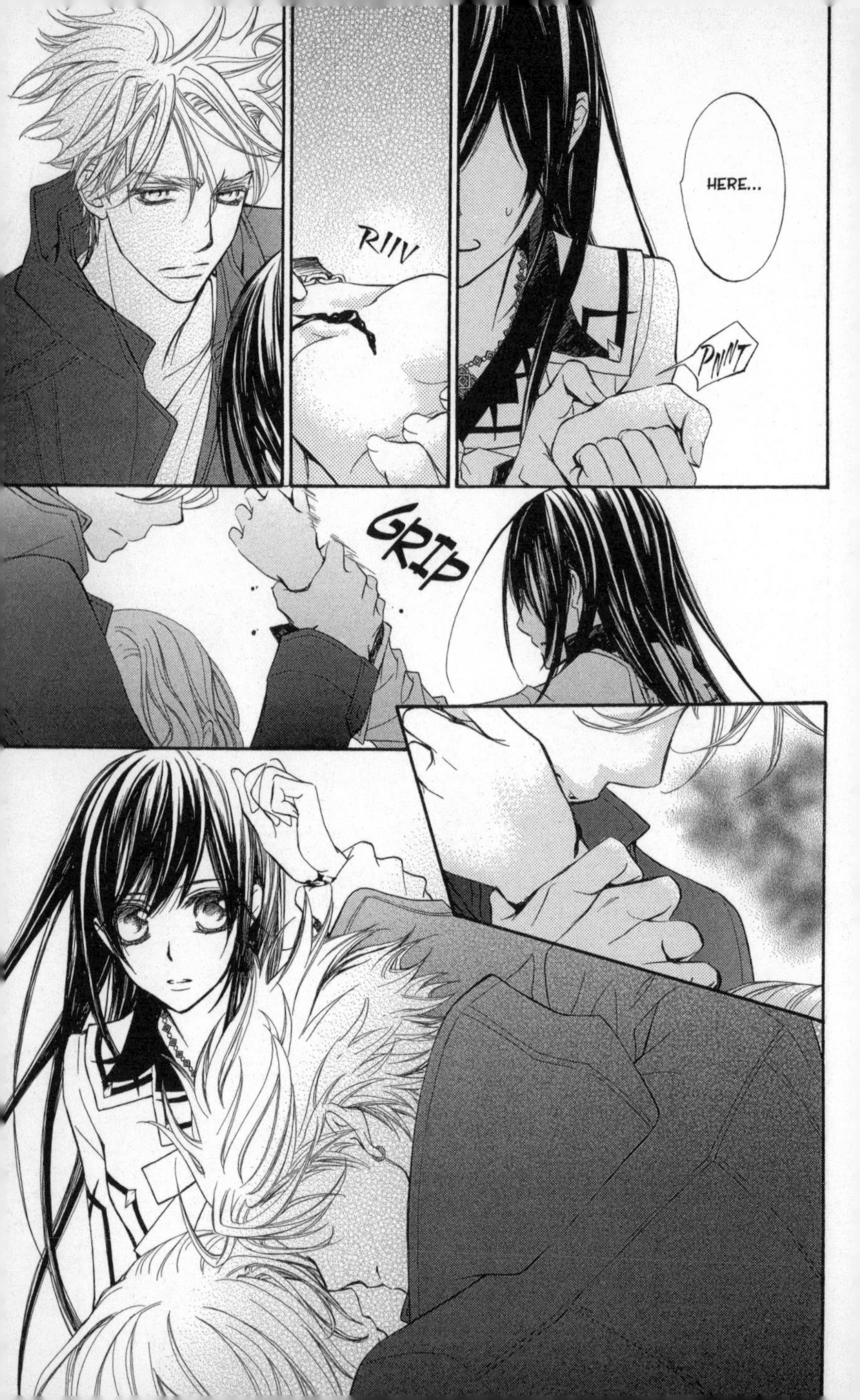
HERE...
PNNT
RIIV
GRIP

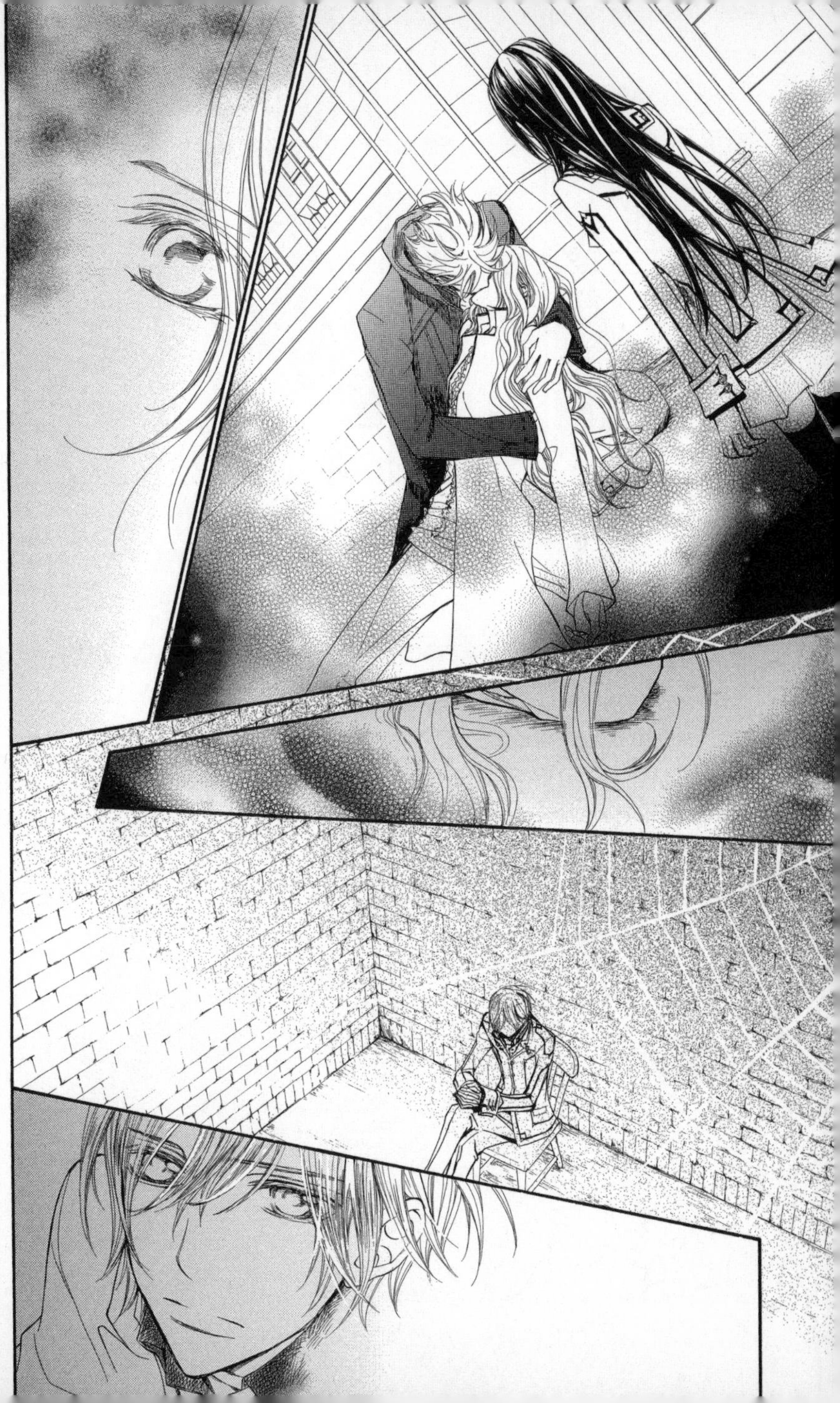

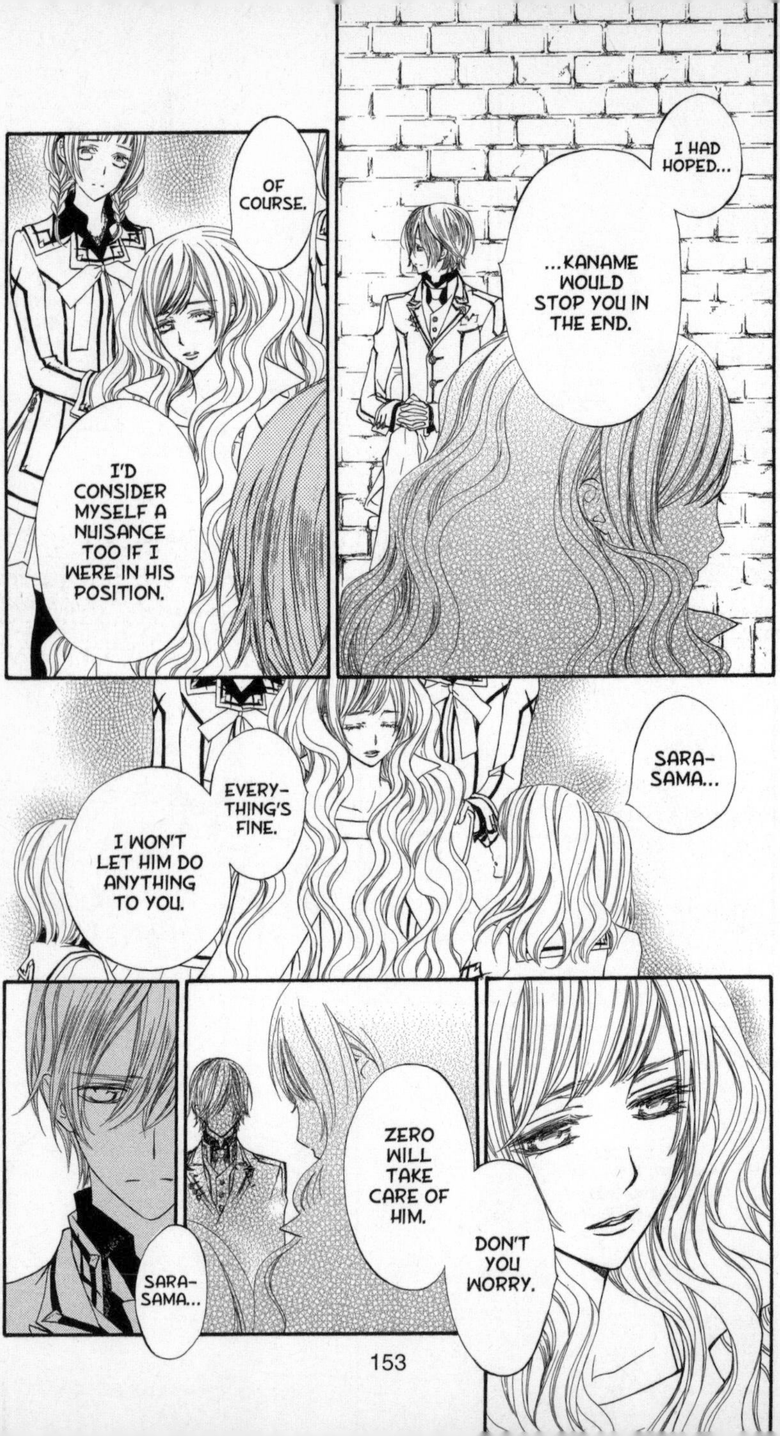
I HAD HOPED...
...KANAME WOULD STOP YOU IN THE END.
OF COURSE.
I'D CONSIDER MYSELF A NUISANCE TOO IF I WERE IN HIS POSITION.
SARA-SAMA...
EVERY-THING'S FINE.
I WON'T LET HIM DO ANYTHING TO YOU.
ZERO WILL TAKE CARE OF HIM.
DON'T YOU WORRY.
SARA-SAMA...

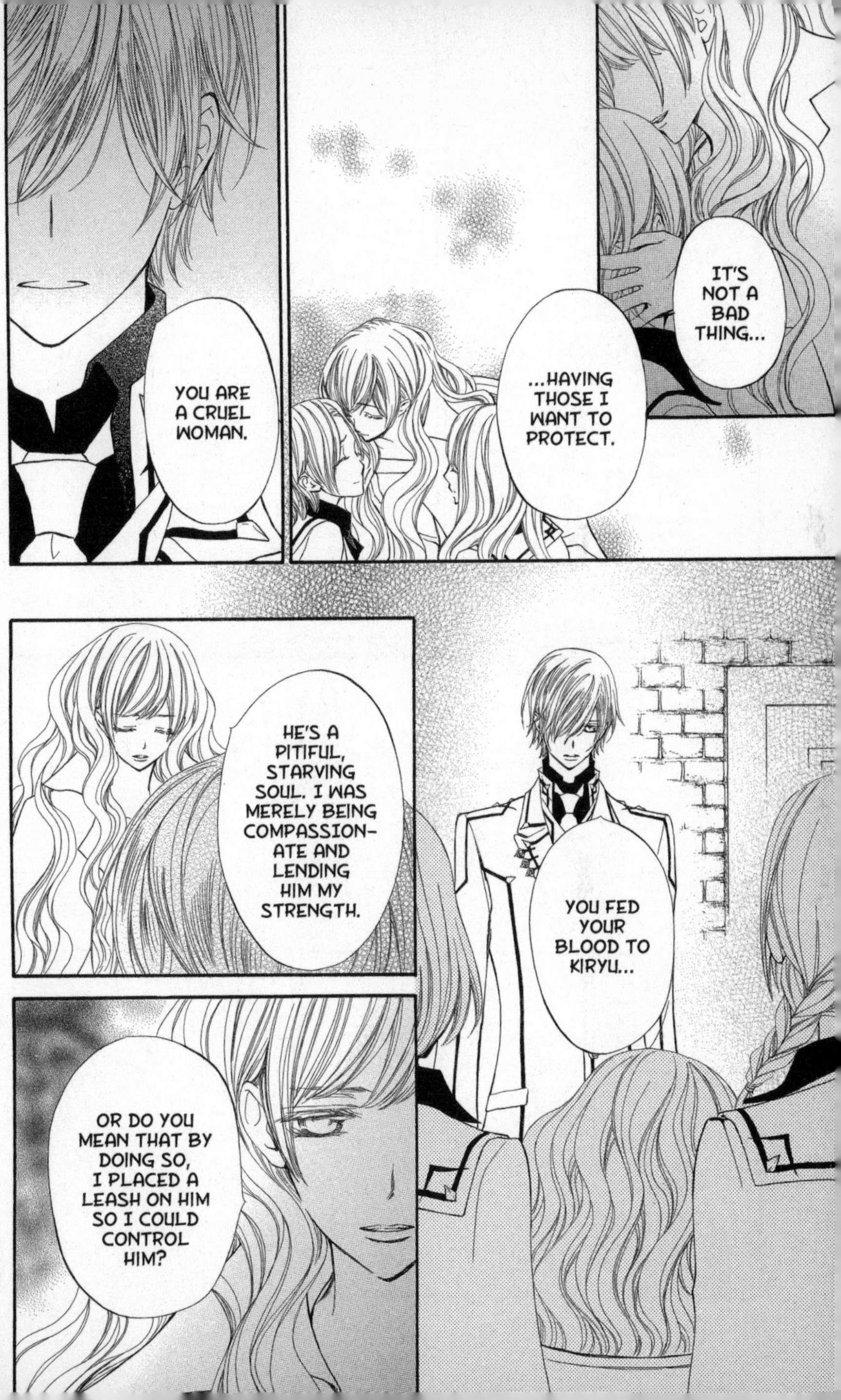
IT'S NOT A BAD THING...
...HAVING THOSE I WANT TO PROTECT.
YOU ARE A CRUEL WOMAN.
YOU FED YOUR BLOOD TO KIRYU...
HE'S A PITIFUL, STARVING SOUL. I WAS MERELY BEING COMPASSION-ATE AND LENDING HIM MY STRENGTH.
OR DO YOU MEAN THAT BY DOING SO, I PLACED A LEASH ON HIM SO I COULD CONTROL HIM?

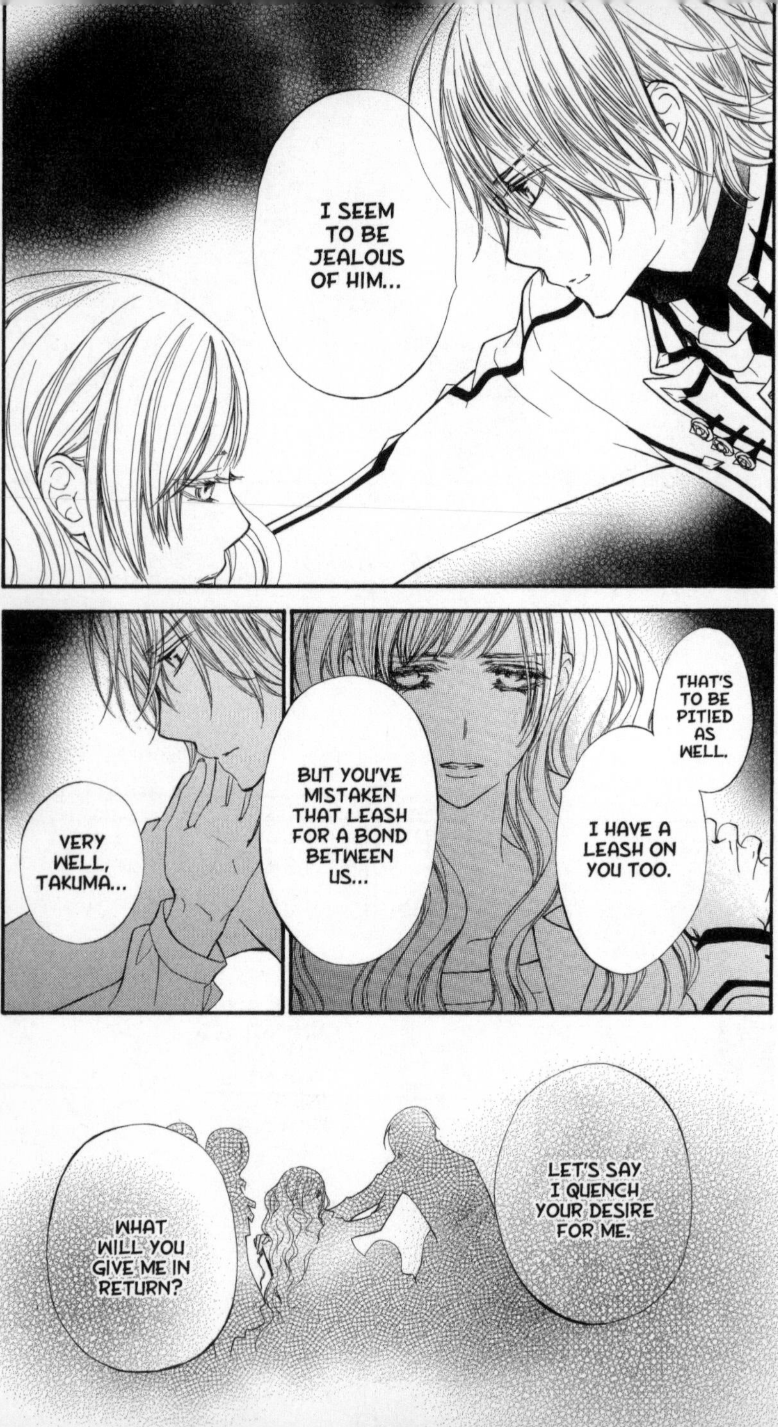
I SEEM TO BE JEALOUS OF HIM...
THAT'S TO BE PITIED AS WELL.
I HAVE A LEASH ON YOU TOO.
BUT YOU'VE MISTAKEN THAT LEASH FOR A BOND BETWEEN US...
VERY WELL, TAKUMA...
LET'S SAY I QUENCH YOUR DESIRE FOR ME.
WHAT WILL YOU GIVE ME IN RETURN?

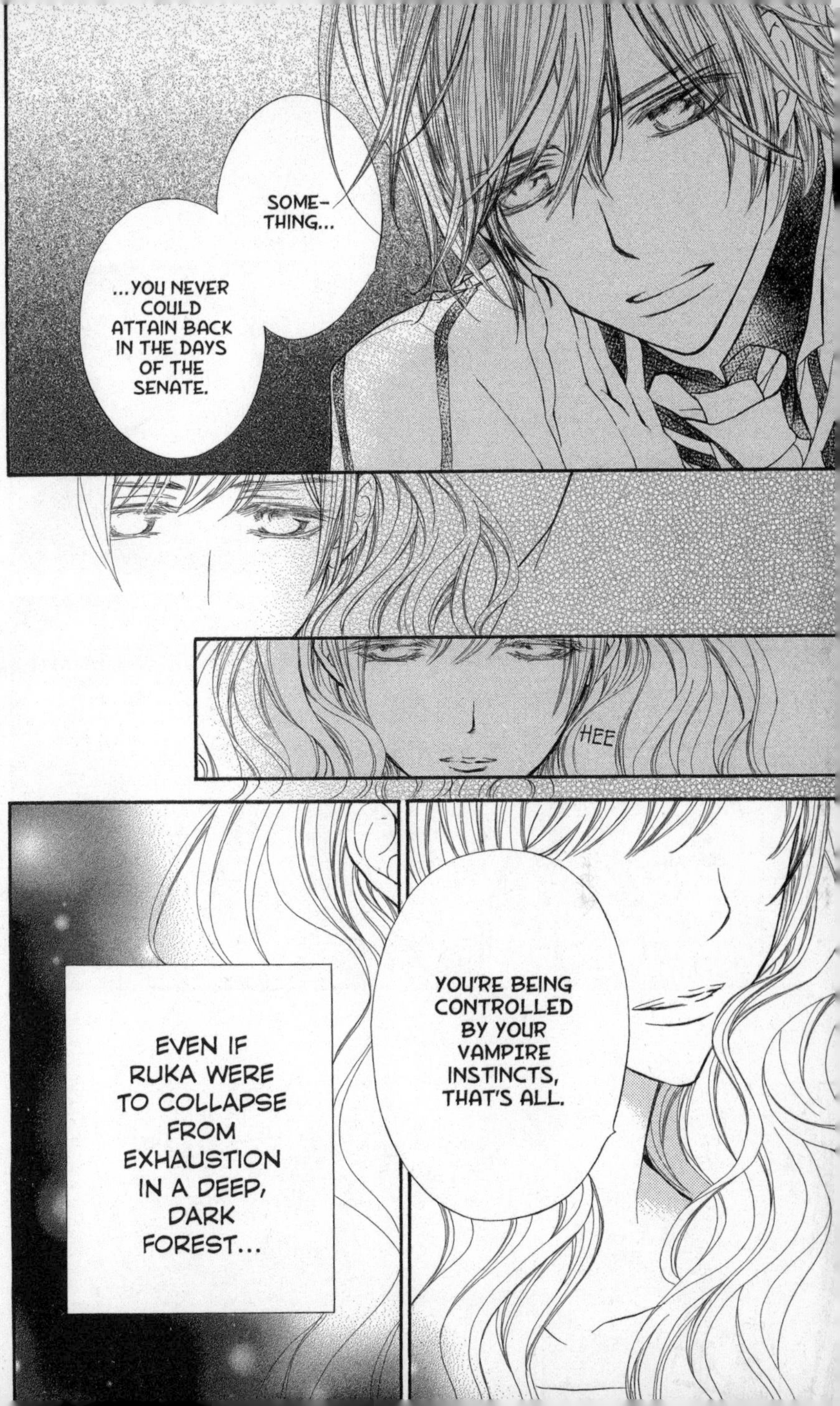
SOME-THING...
...YOU NEVER COULD ATTAIN BACK IN THE DAYS OF THE SENATE.
HEE
YOU'RE BEING CONTROLLED BY YOUR VAMPIRE INSTINCTS, THAT'S ALL.
EVEN IF RUKA WERE TO COLLAPSE FROM EXHAUSTION IN A DEEP, DARK FOREST...

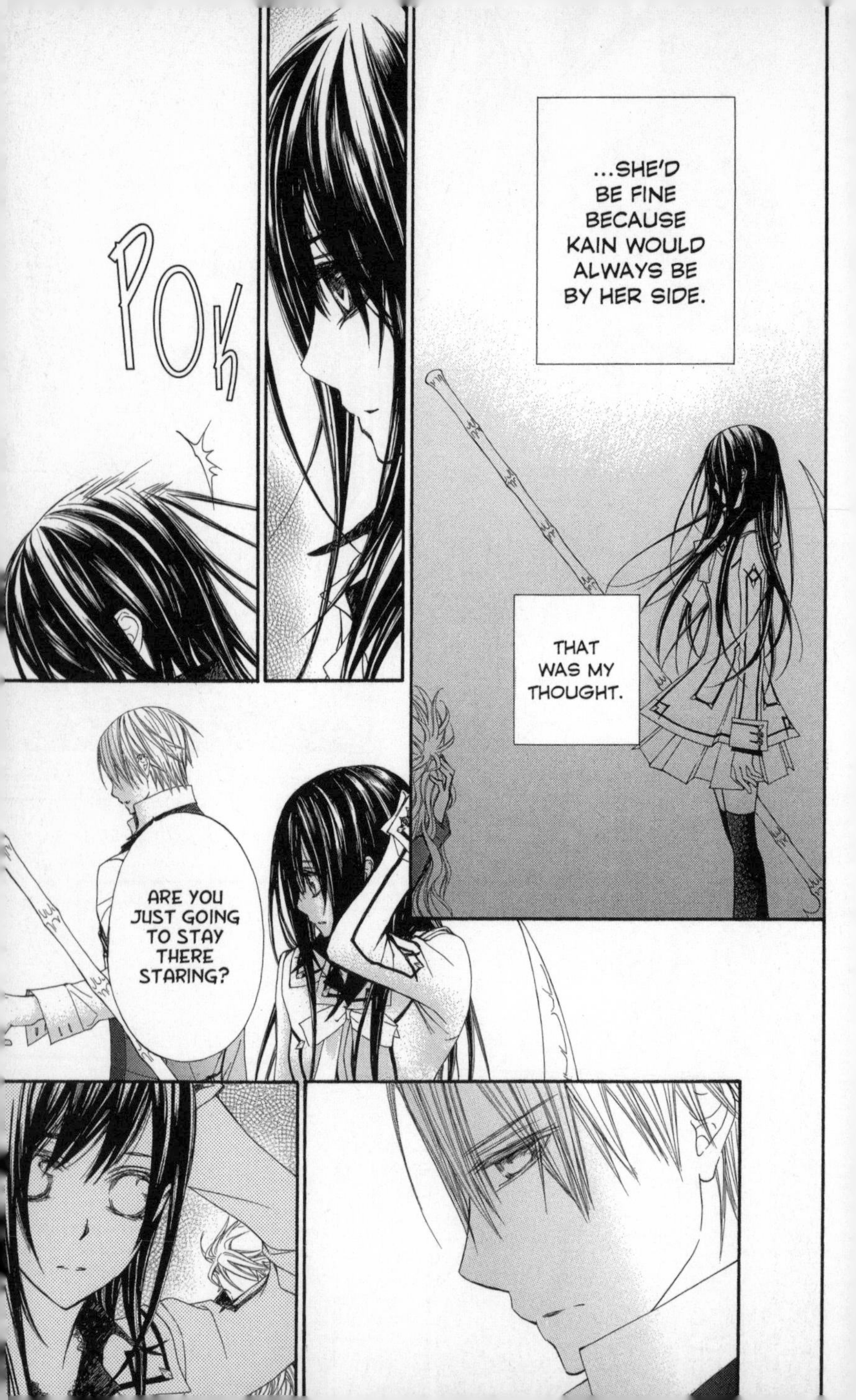
...SHE'D BE FINE BECAUSE KAIN WOULD ALWAYS BE BY HER SIDE.
THAT WAS MY THOUGHT.
POK
ARE YOU JUST GOING TO STAY THERE STARING?

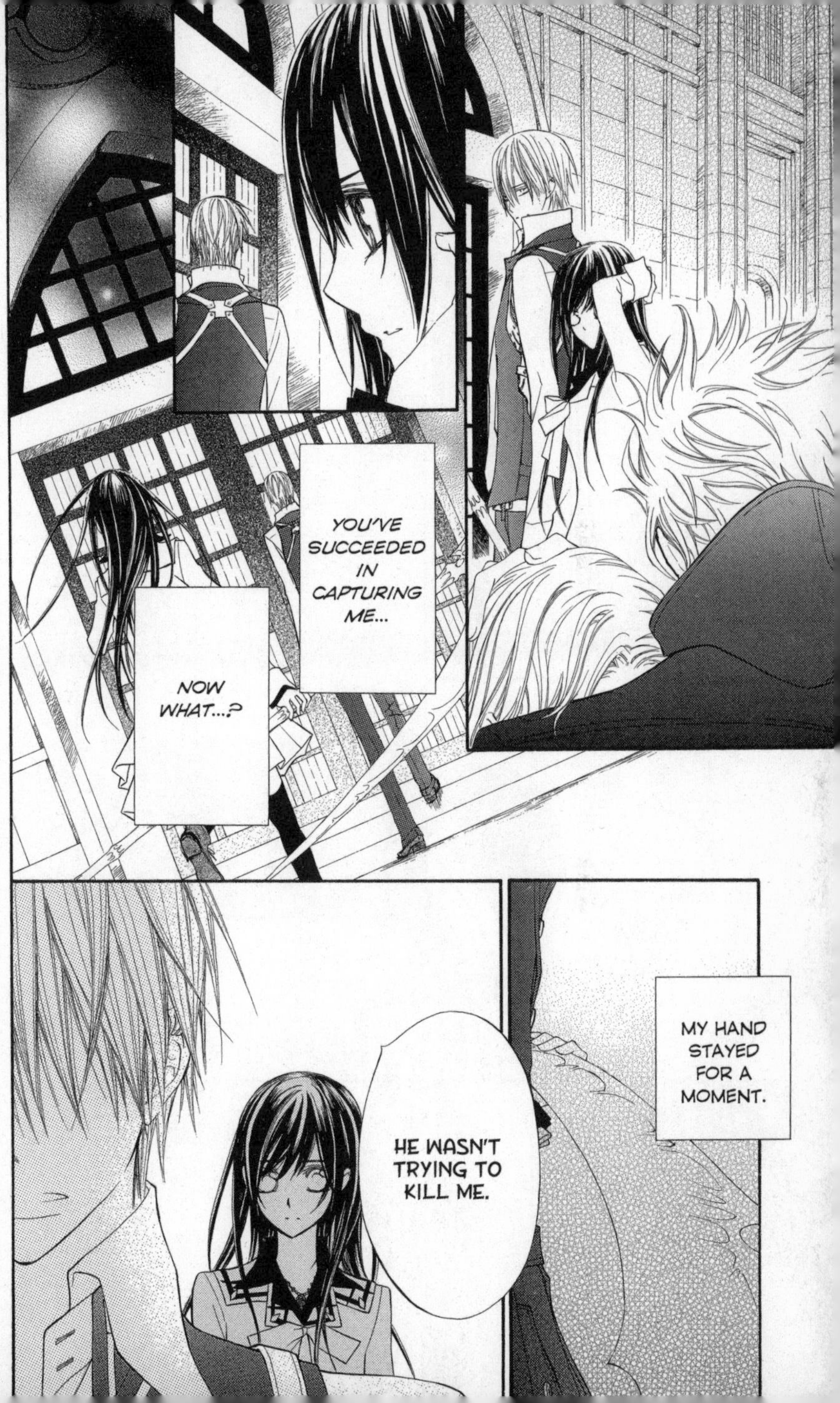
YOU'VE SUCCEEDED IN CAPTURING ME...
NOW WHAT...?
MY HAND STAYED FOR A MOMENT.
HE WASN'T TRYING TO KILL ME.

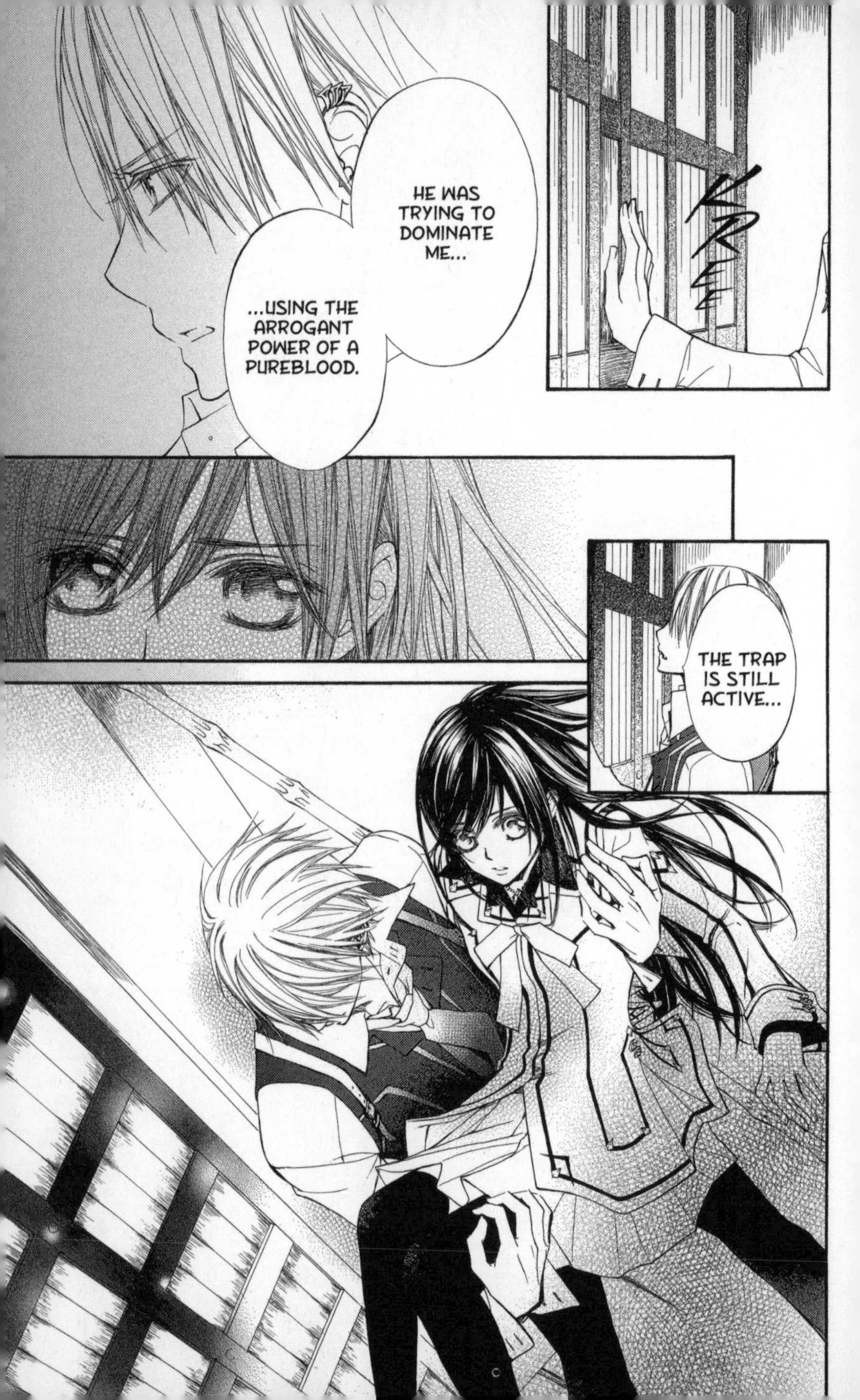
KREE
HE WAS TRYING TO DOMINATE ME...
...USING THE ARROGANT POWER OF A PUREBLOOD.
THE TRAP IS STILL ACTIVE...

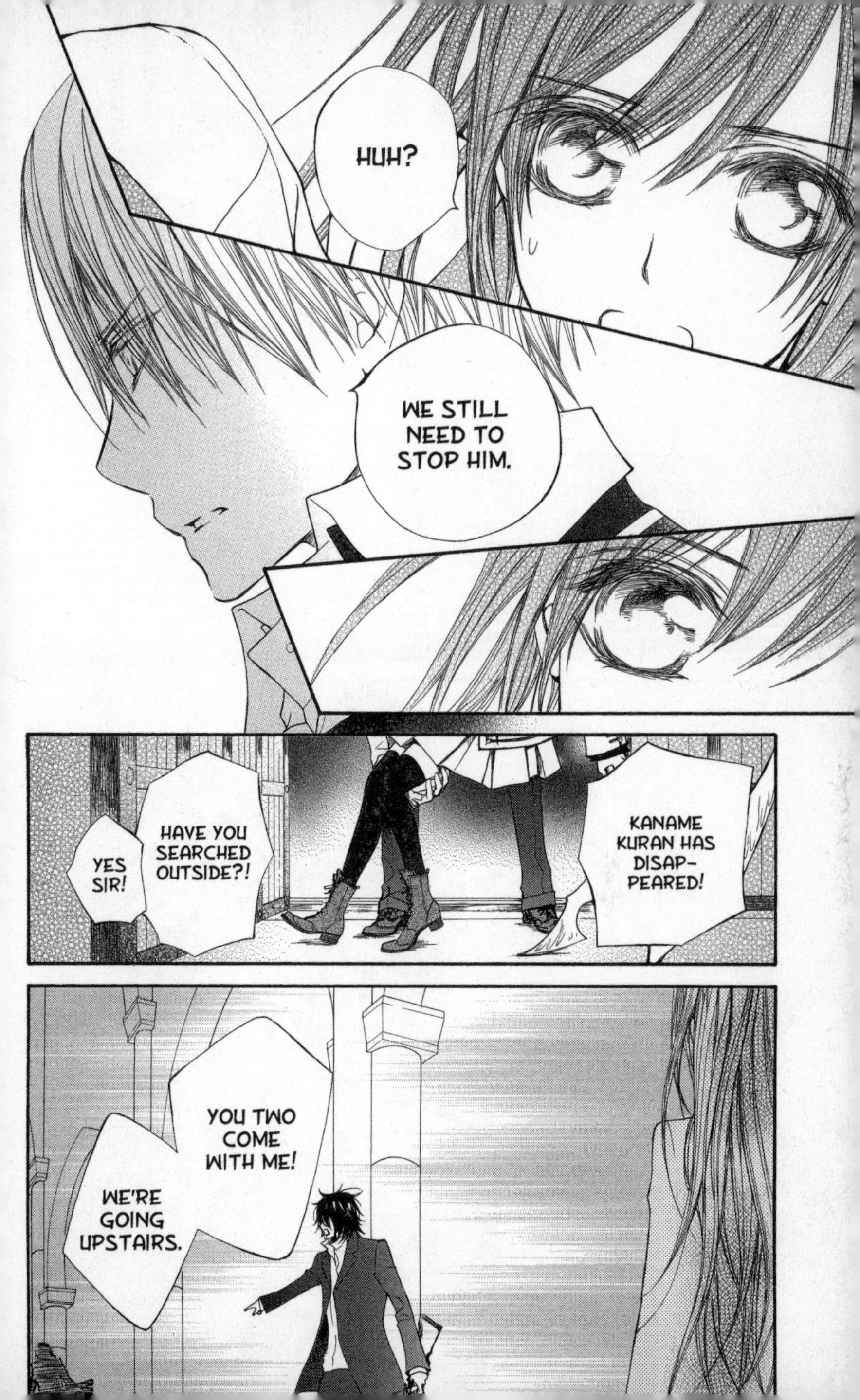
HUH?
WE STILL NEED TO STOP HIM.
KANAME KURAN HAS DISAP-PEARED!
HAVE YOU SEARCHED OUTSIDE?!
YES SIR!
YOU TWO COME WITH ME!
WE'RE GOING UPSTAIRS.

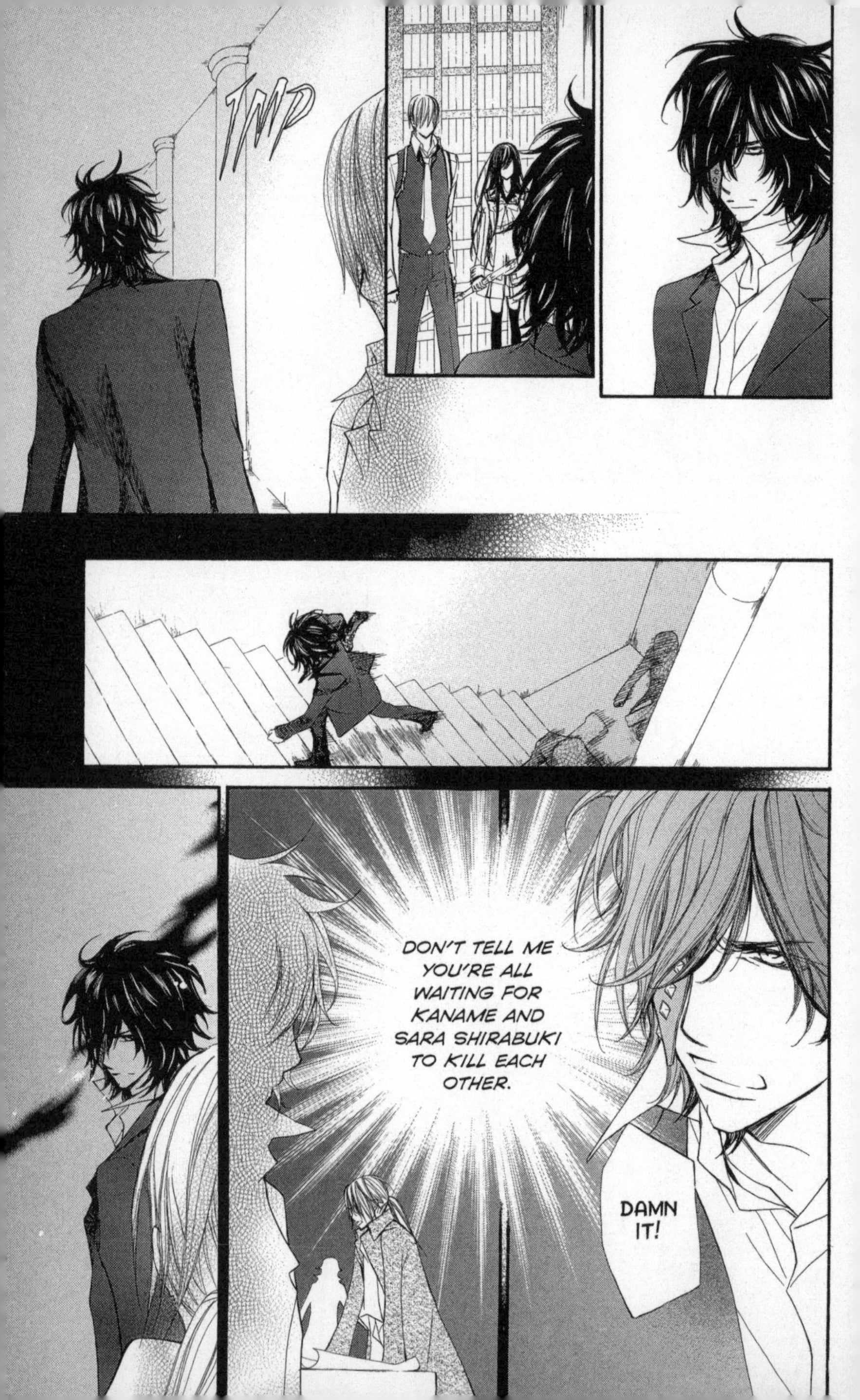
DON'T TELL ME YOU'RE ALL WAITING FOR KANAME AND SARA SHIRABUKI TO KILL EACH OTHER.
DAMN IT!

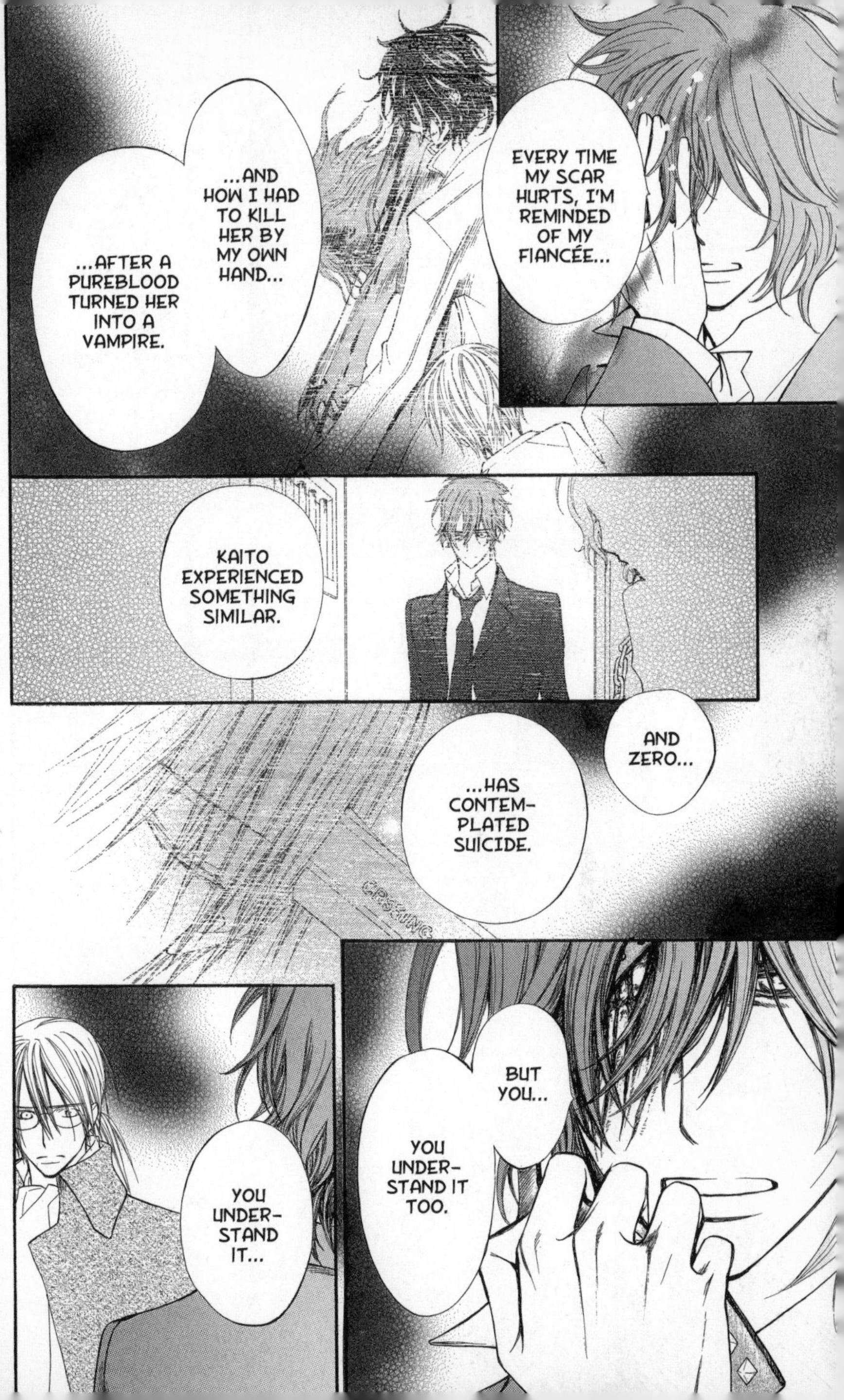
EVERY TIME MY SCAR HURTS, I'M REMINDED OF MY FIANCÉE...
...AND HOW I HAD TO KILL HER BY MY OWN HAND...
...AFTER A PUREBLOOD TURNED HER INTO A VAMPIRE.
KAITO EXPERIENCED SOMETHING SIMILAR.
AND ZERO...
...HAS CONTEM-PLATED SUICIDE.
BUT YOU...
YOU UNDER-STAND IT TOO.
YOU UNDER-STAND IT...

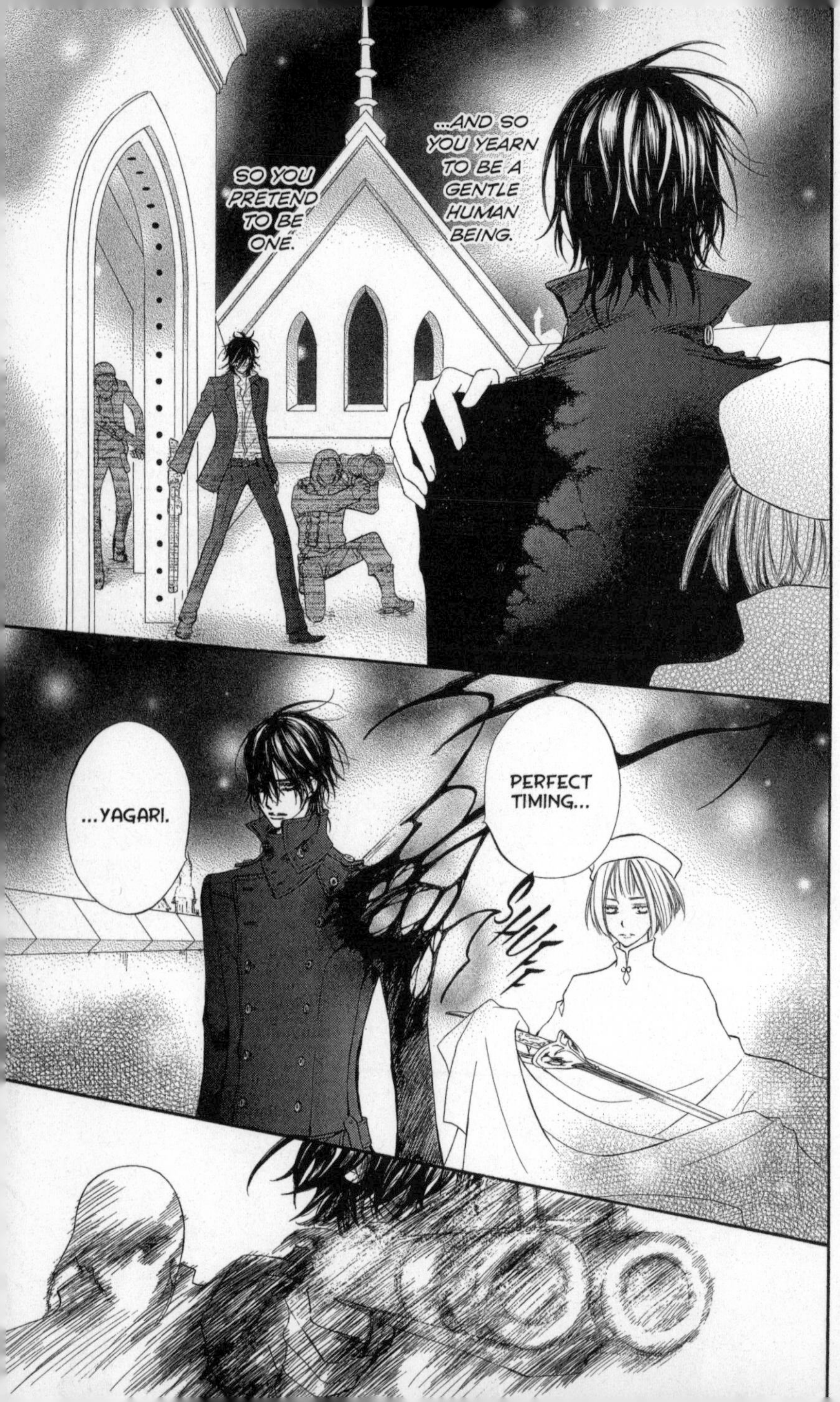
...AND SO YOU YEARN TO BE A GENTLE HUMAN BEING.
SO YOU PRETEND TO BE ONE.
PERFECT TIMING...
SHUFF
...YAGARI.

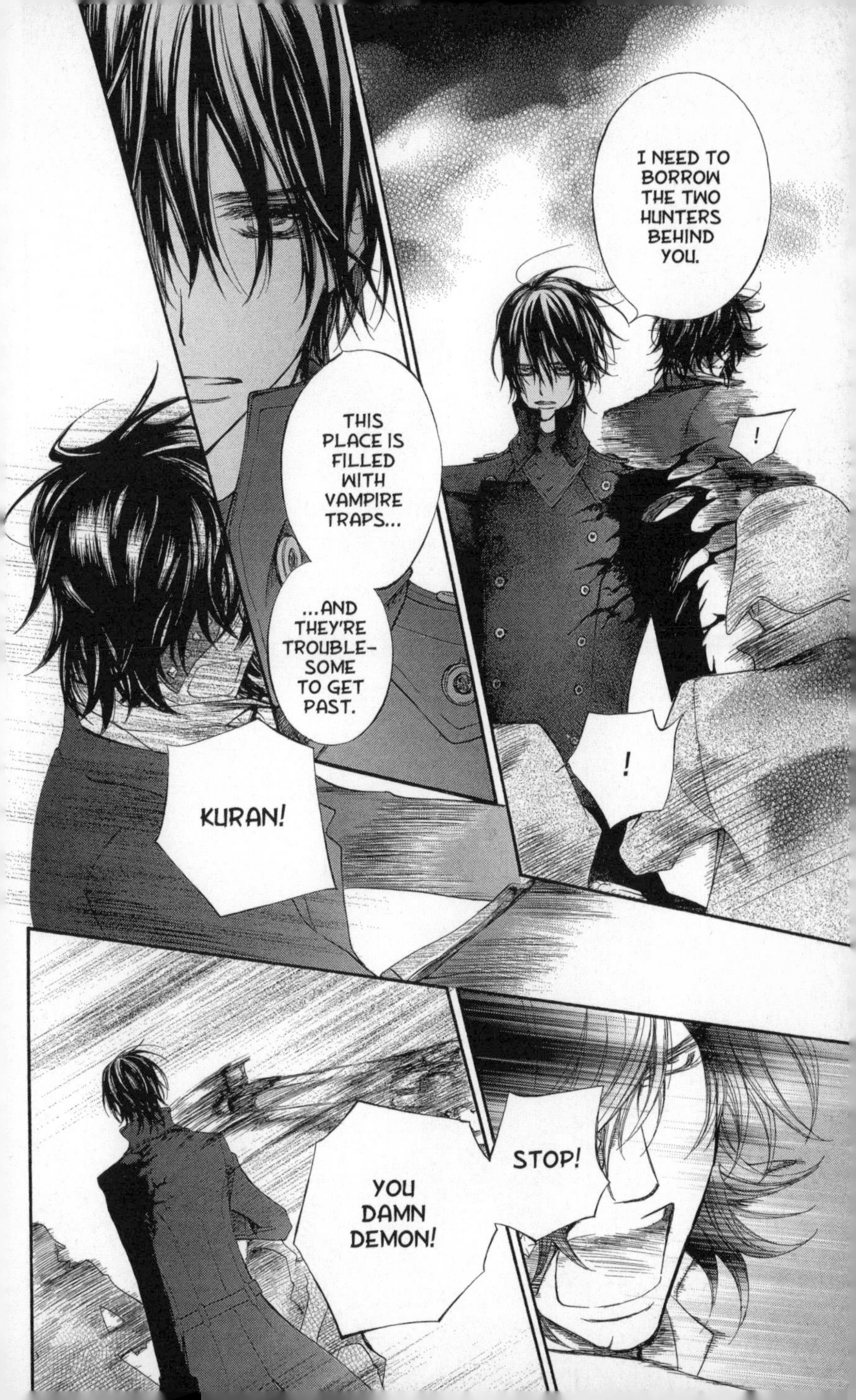
I NEED TO BORROW THE TWO HUNTERS BEHIND YOU.
!
!
THIS PLACE IS FILLED WITH VAMPIRE TRAPS...
...AND THEY'RE TROUBLE-SOME TO GET PAST.
KURAN!
STOP!
YOU DAMN DEMON!

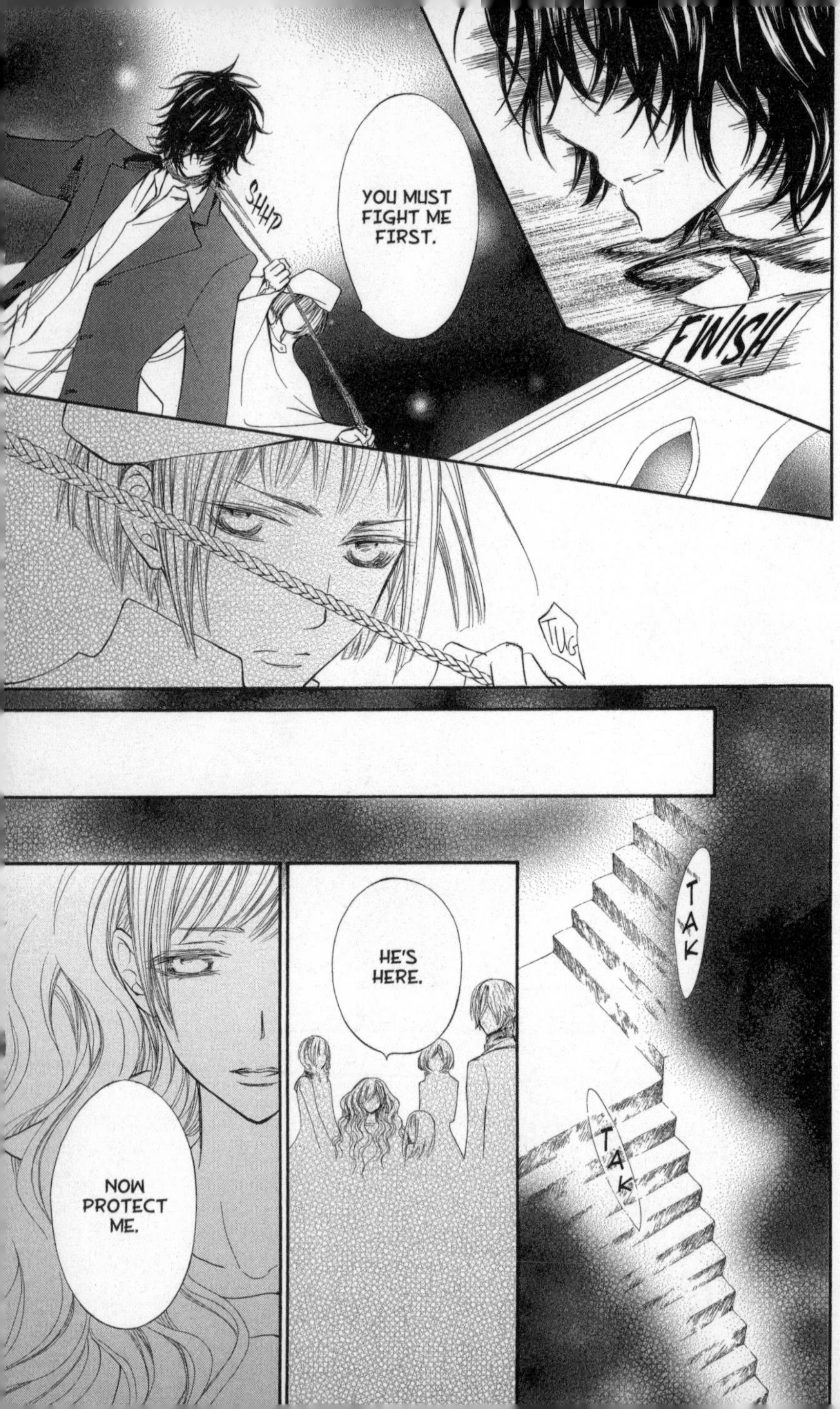
FWISH
YOU MUST FIGHT ME FIRST.
SHHP
TUG
TAK
TAK
HE'S HERE.
NOW PROTECT ME.

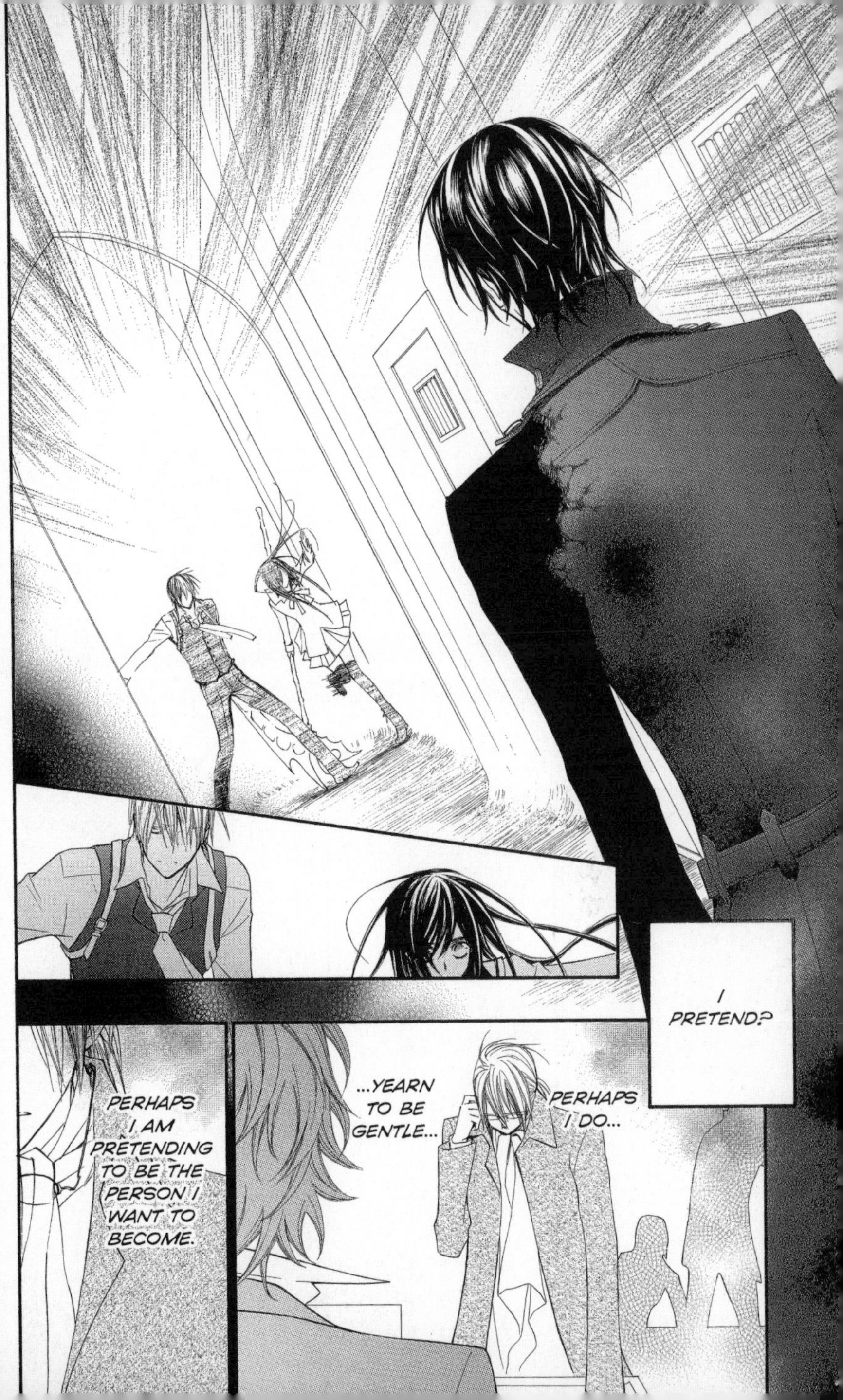
I PRETEND?
PERHAPS I DO...
...YEARN TO BE GENTLE...
PERHAPS I AM PRETENDING TO BE THE PERSON I WANT TO BECOME.

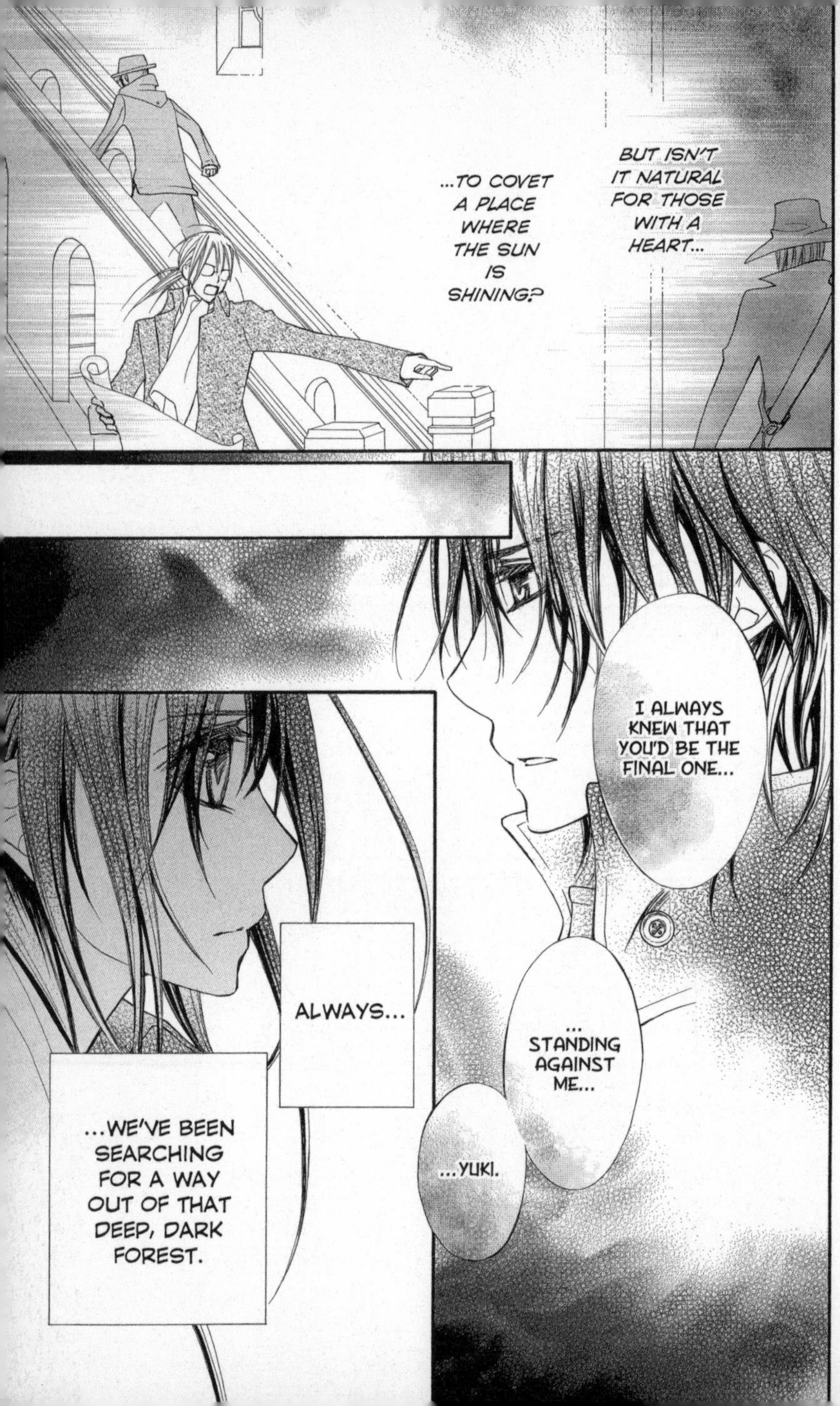
BUT ISN'T IT NATURAL FOR THOSE WITH A HEART...
...TO COVET A PLACE WHERE THE SUN IS SHINING?
I ALWAYS KNEW THAT YOU'D BE THE FINAL ONE...
... STANDING AGAINST ME...
...YUKI.
ALWAYS...
...WE'VE BEEN SEARCHING FOR A WAY OUT OF THAT DEEP, DARK FOREST.

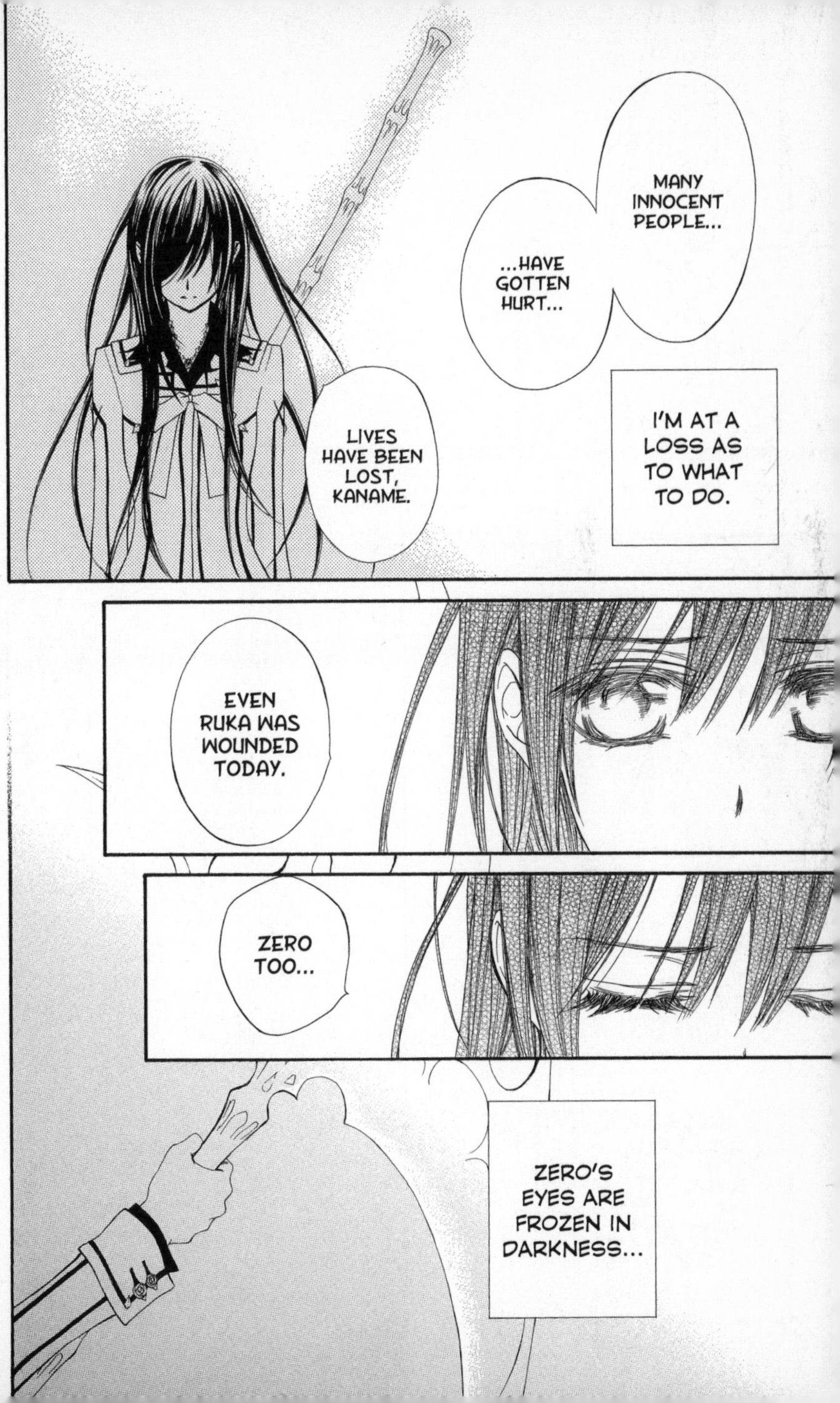
MANY INNOCENT PEOPLE...
...HAVE GOTTEN HURT...
I'M AT A LOSS AS TO WHAT TO DO.
LIVES HAVE BEEN LOST, KANAME.
EVEN RUKA WAS WOUNDED TODAY.
ZERO TOO...
ZERO'S EYES ARE FROZEN IN DARKNESS...

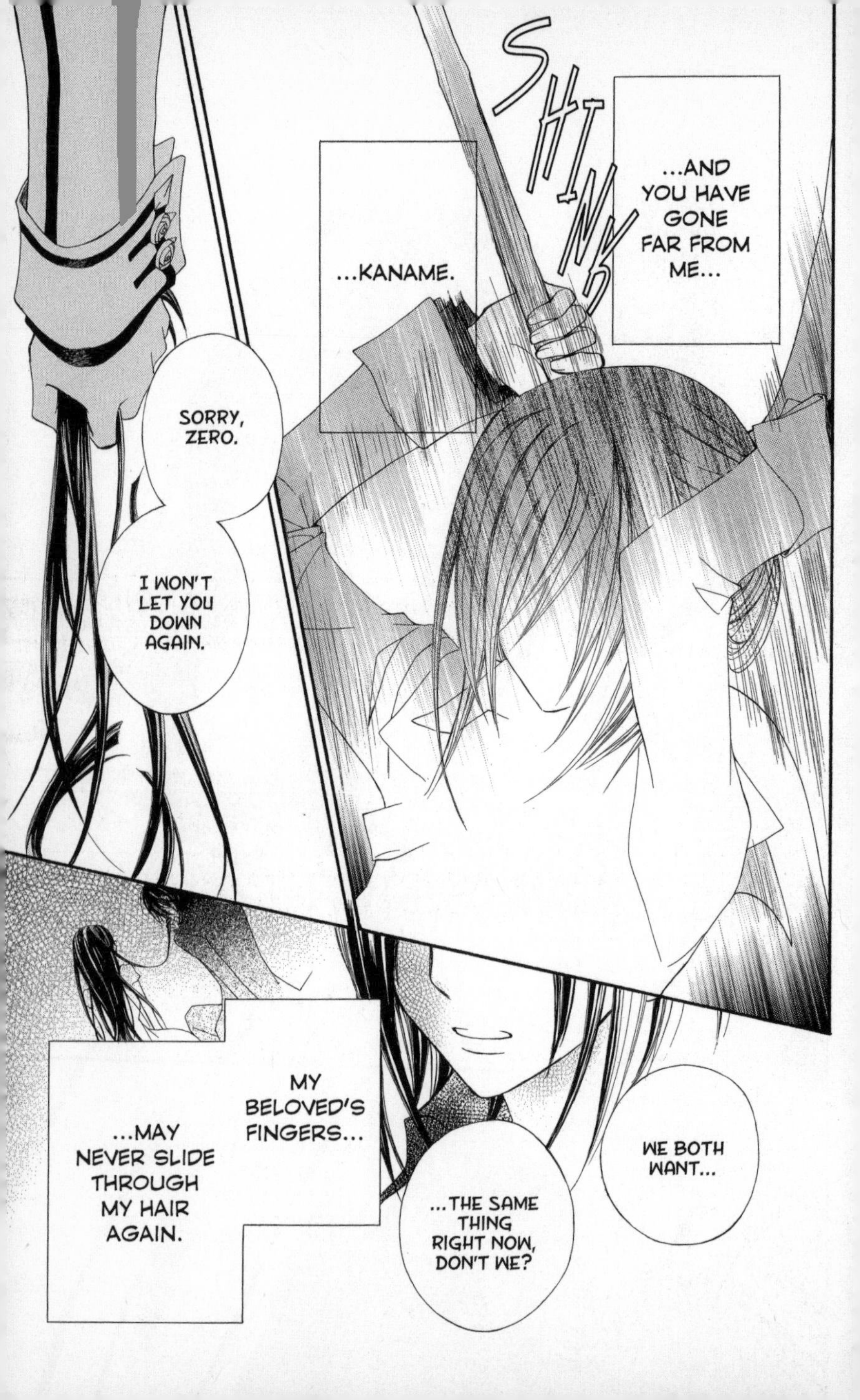
SHINK
...AND YOU HAVE GONE FAR FROM ME...
...KANAME.
SORRY, ZERO.
I WON'T LET YOU DOWN AGAIN.
WE BOTH WANT...
...THE SAME THING RIGHT NOW, DON'T WE?
MY BELOVED'S FINGERS...
...MAY NEVER SLIDE THROUGH MY HAIR AGAIN.

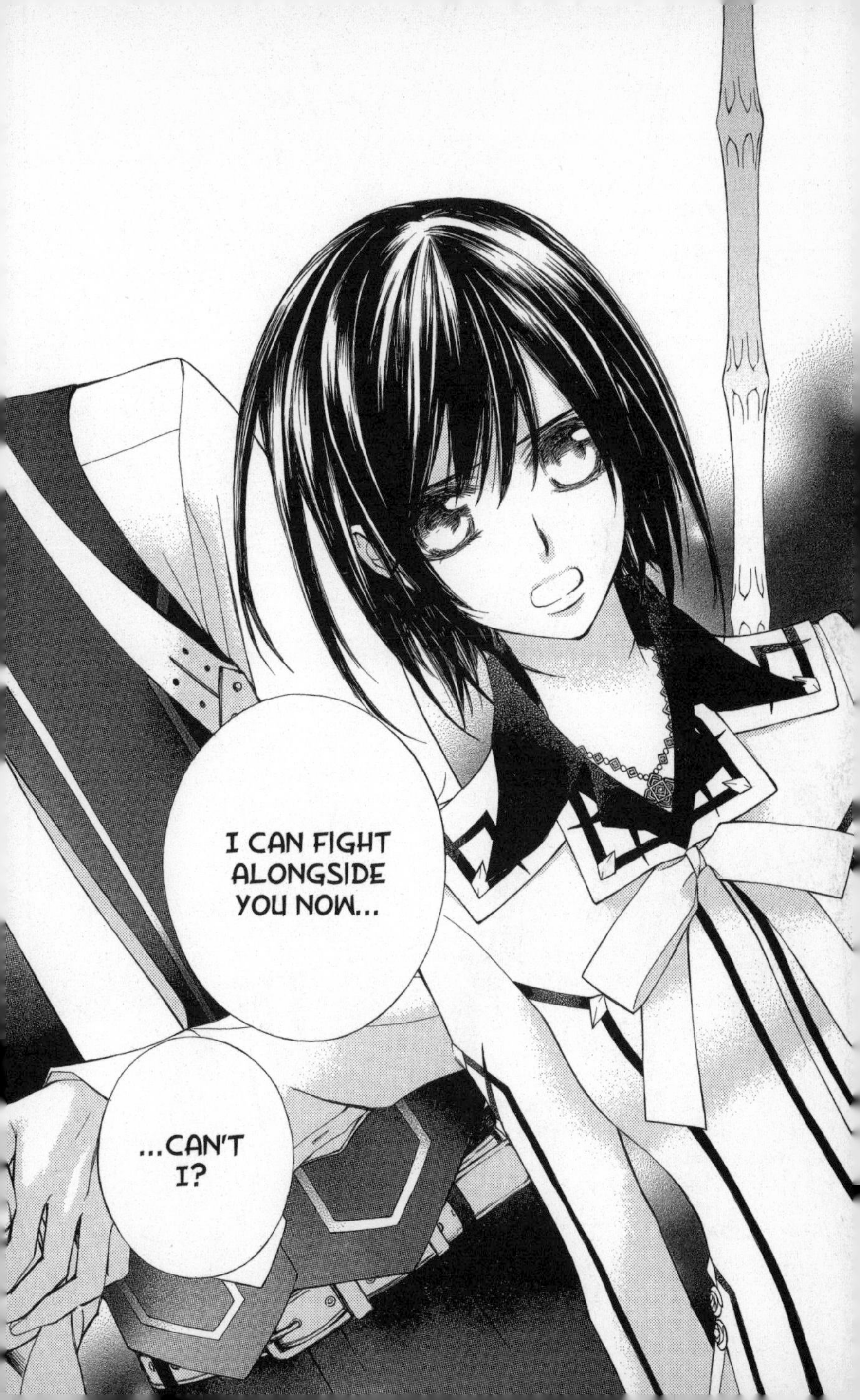
I CAN FIGHT ALONGSIDE YOU NOW...
...CAN'T I?

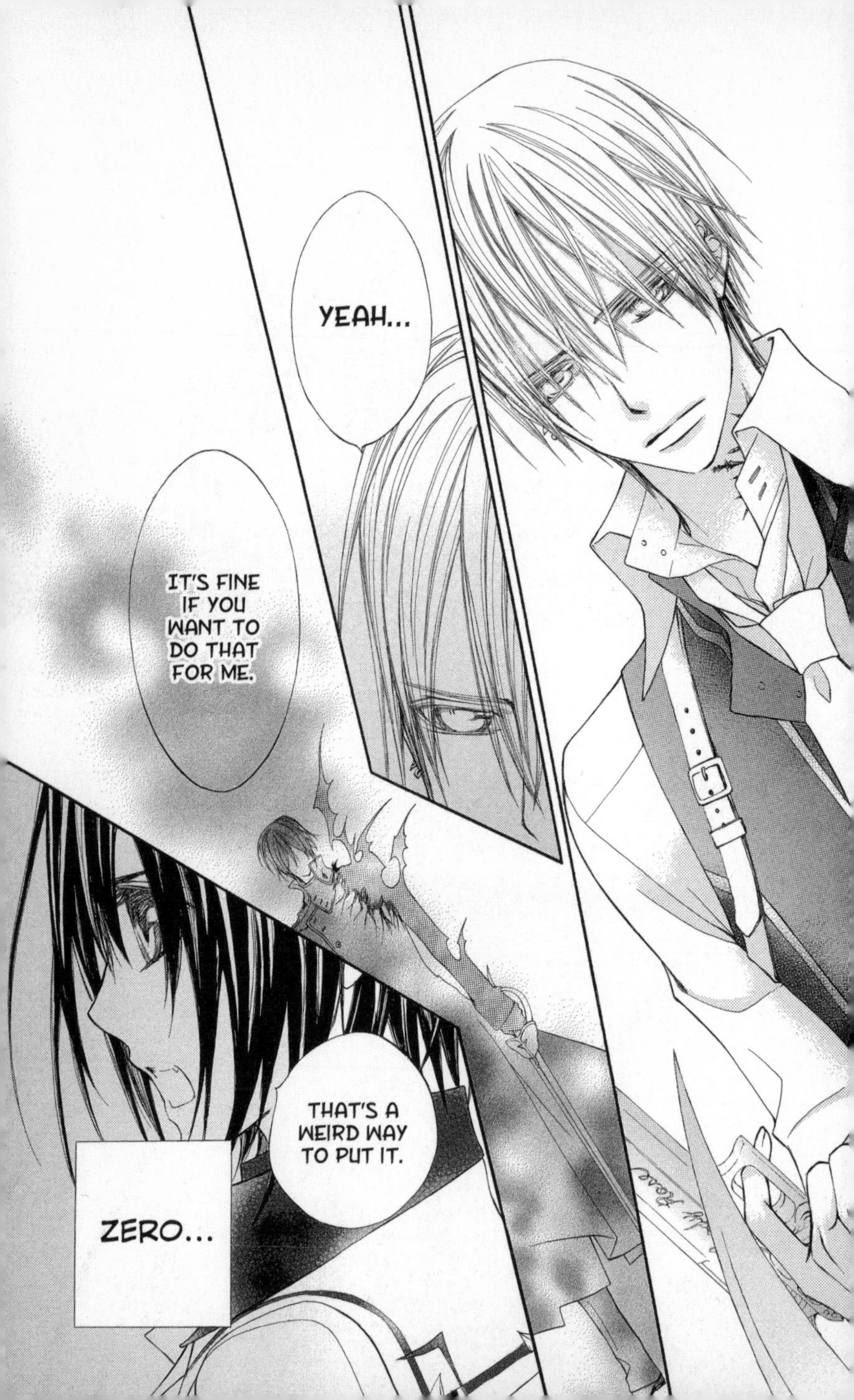
YEAH...
IT'S FINE IF YOU WANT TO DO THAT FOR ME.
THAT'S A WEIRD WAY TO PUT IT.
ZERO...

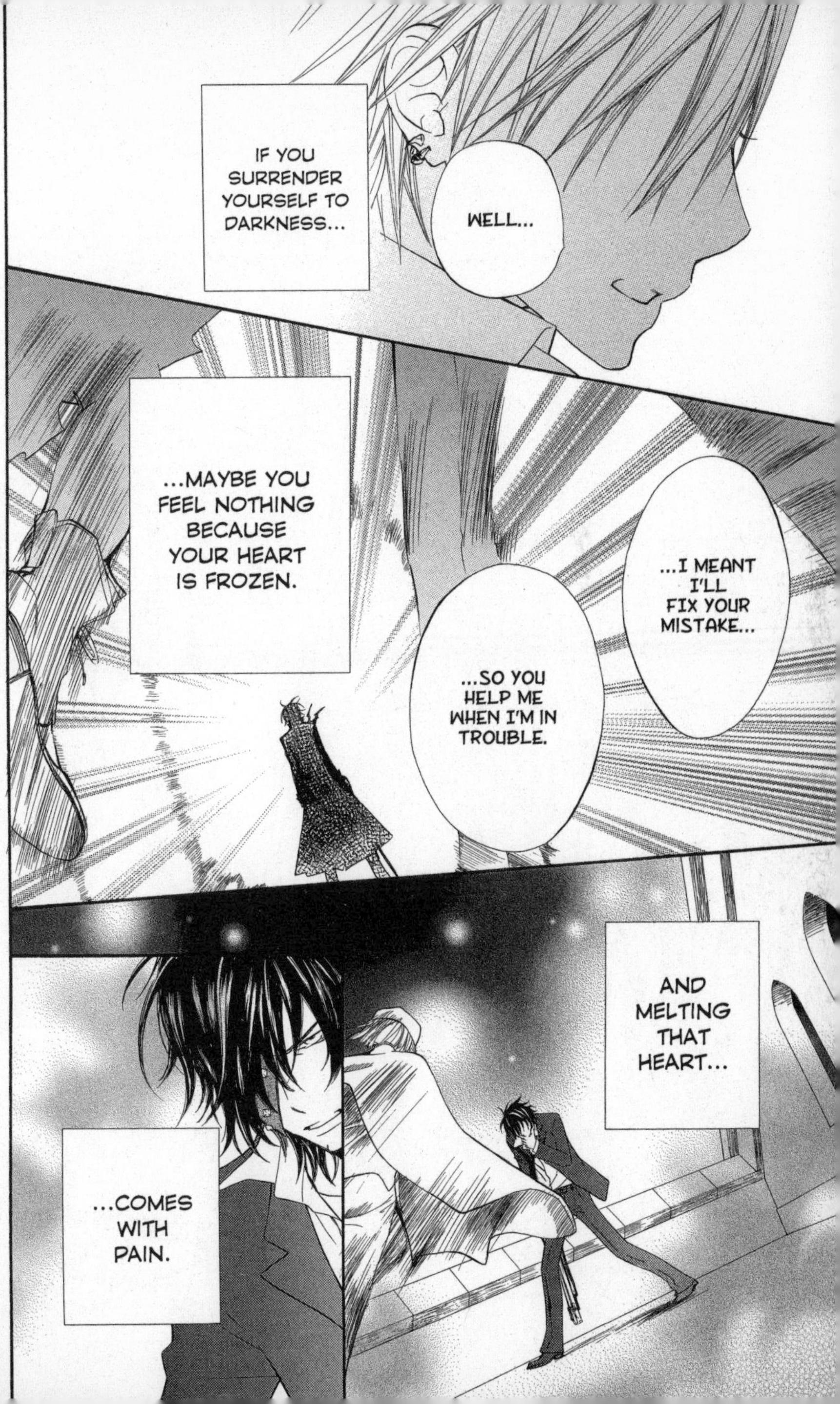
WELL...
IF YOU SURRENDER YOURSELF TO DARKNESS...
...I MEANT I'LL FIX YOUR MISTAKE...
...SO YOU HELP ME WHEN I'M IN TROUBLE.
...MAYBE YOU FEEL NOTHING BECAUSE YOUR HEART IS FROZEN.
AND MELTING THAT HEART...
...COMES WITH PAIN.

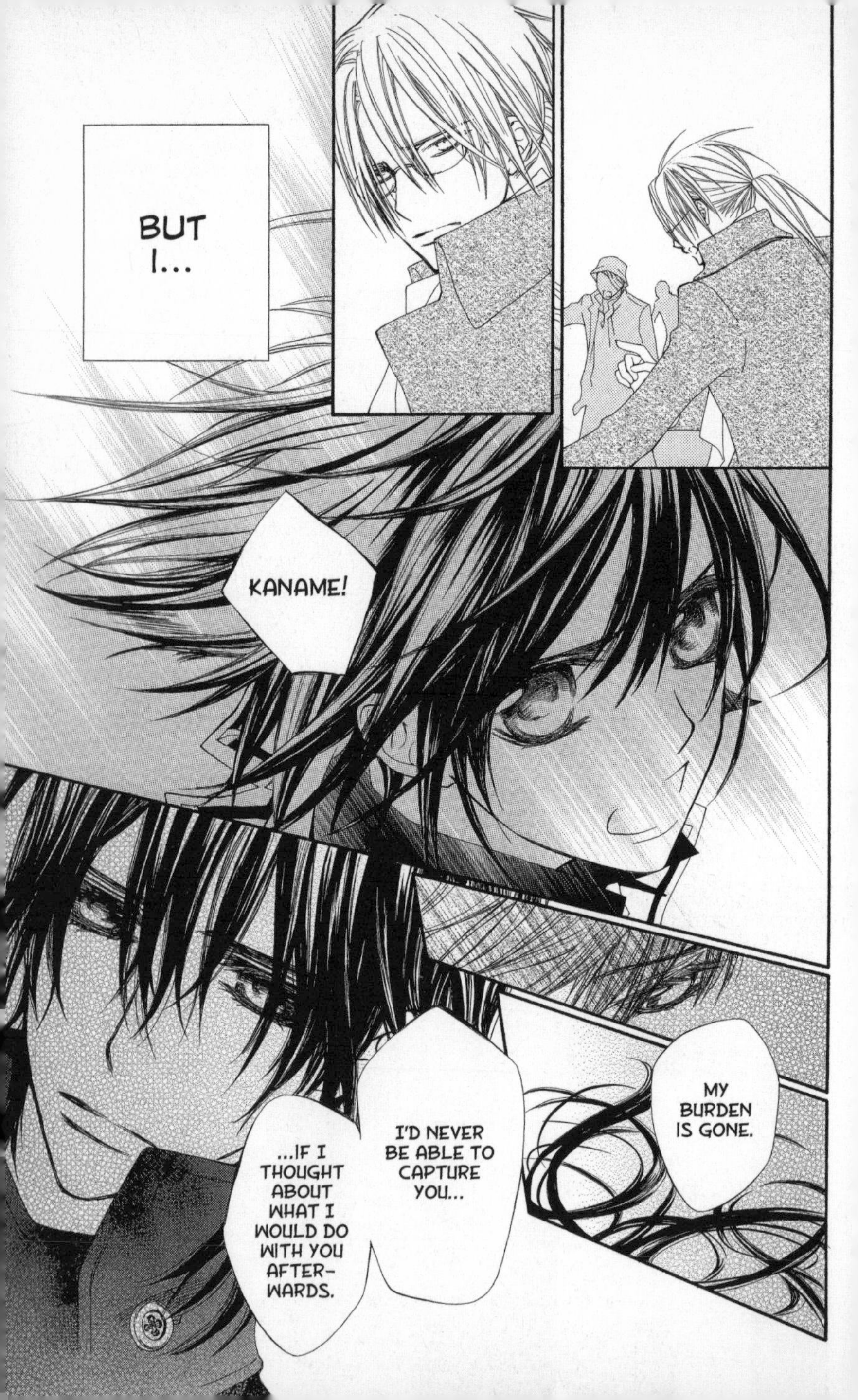
BUT I...
KANAME!
MY BURDEN IS GONE.
I'D NEVER BE ABLE TO CAPTURE YOU...
...IF I THOUGHT ABOUT WHAT I WOULD DO WITH YOU AFTER-WARDS.

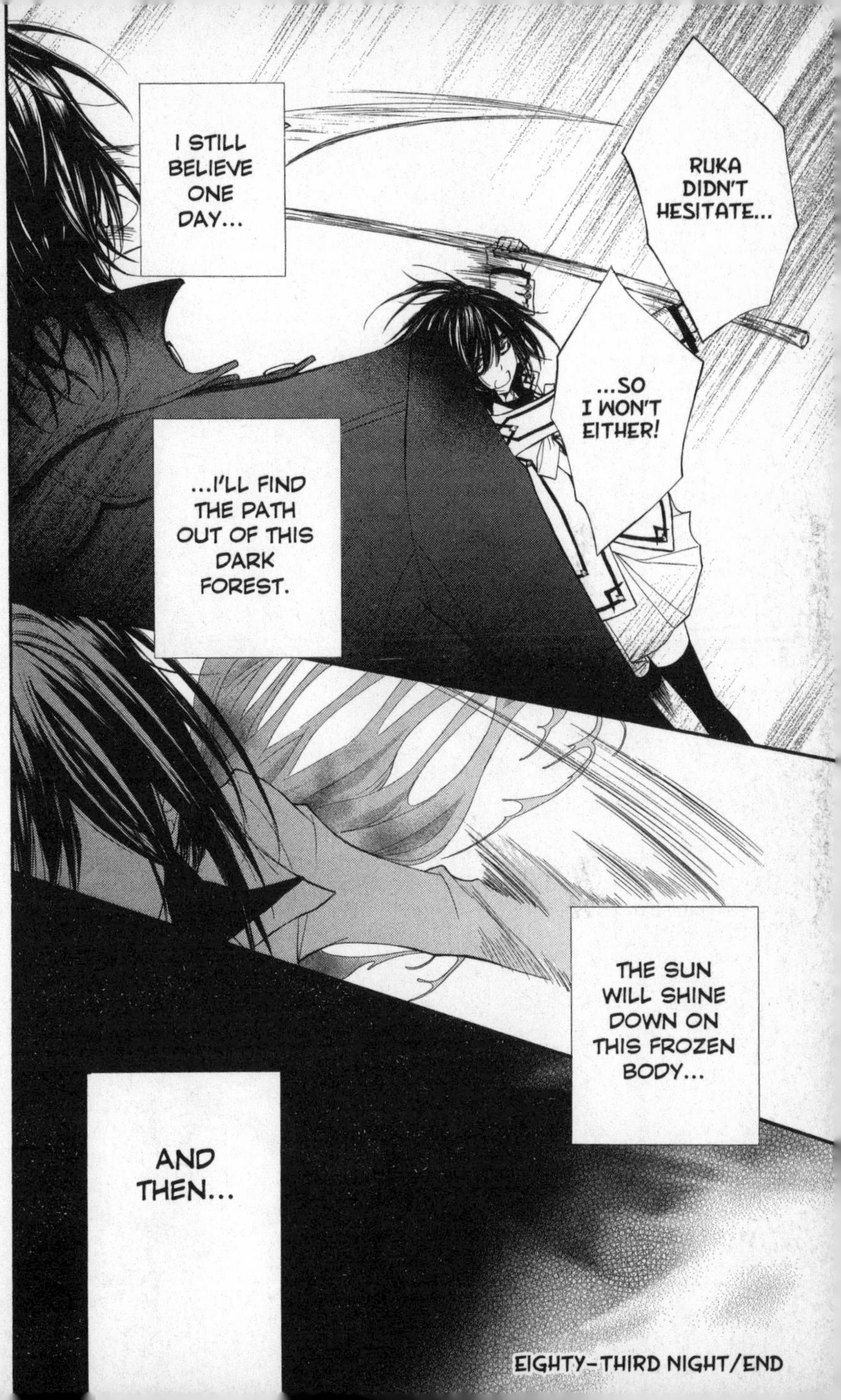
RUKA DIDN'T HESITATE...
...SO I WON'T EITHER!
I STILL BELIEVE ONE DAY...
...I'LL FIND THE PATH OUT OF THIS DARK FOREST.
THE SUN WILL SHINE DOWN ON THIS FROZEN BODY...
AND THEN...
EIGHTY-THIRD NIGHT/END

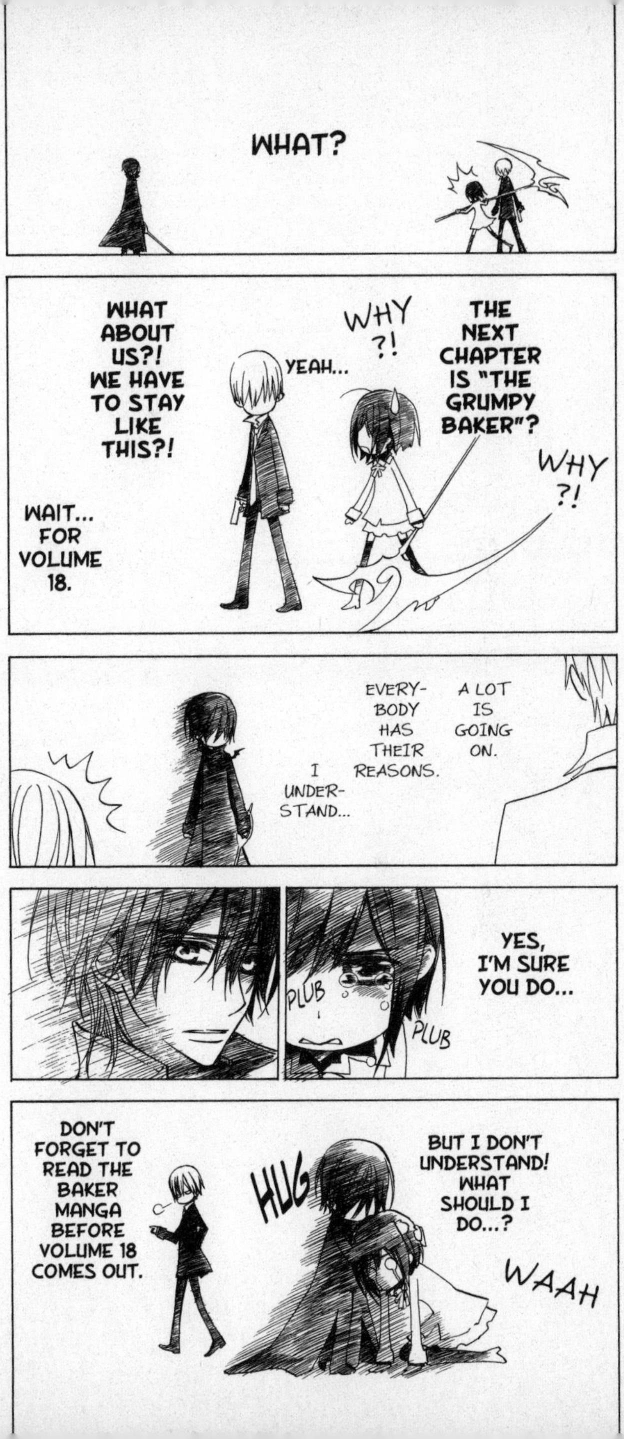
WHAT?
THE NEXT CHAPTER IS "THE GRUMPY BAKER"?
WHY ?!
WHY ?!
YEAH...
WHAT ABOUT US?! WE HAVE TO STAY LIKE THIS?!
WAIT... FOR VOLUME 18.
A LOT IS GOING ON.
EVERY-BODY HAS THEIR REASONS.
I UNDER-STAND...
YES, I'M SURE YOU DO...
PLUB
PLUB
BUT I DON'T UNDERSTAND! WHAT SHOULD I DO...?
WAAH
HUG
DON'T FORGET TO READ THE BAKER MANGA BEFORE VOLUME 18 COMES OUT.

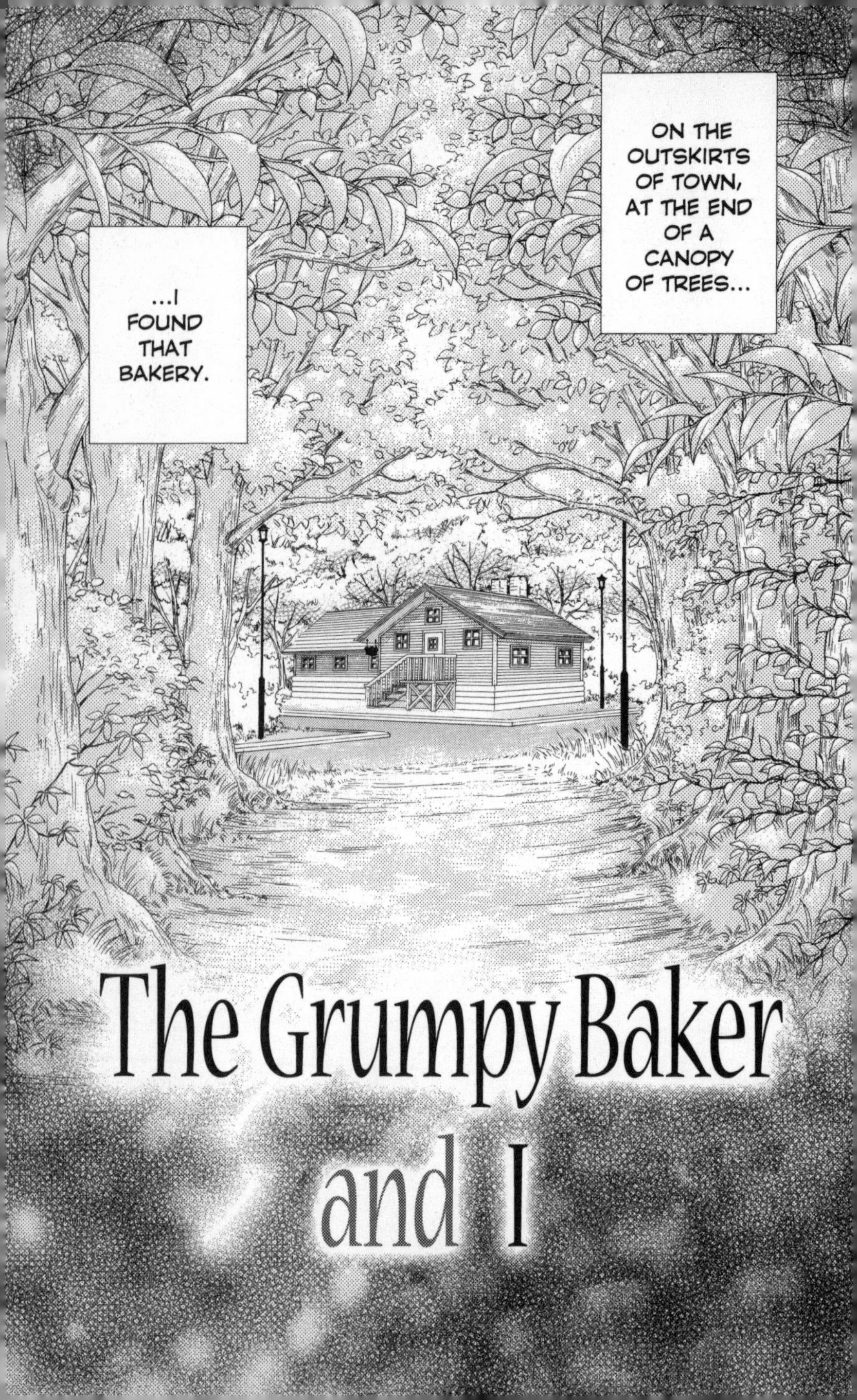
ON THE OUTSKIRTS OF TOWN, AT THE END OF A CANOPY OF TREES...
...I FOUND THAT BAKERY.
The Grumpy Baker and I

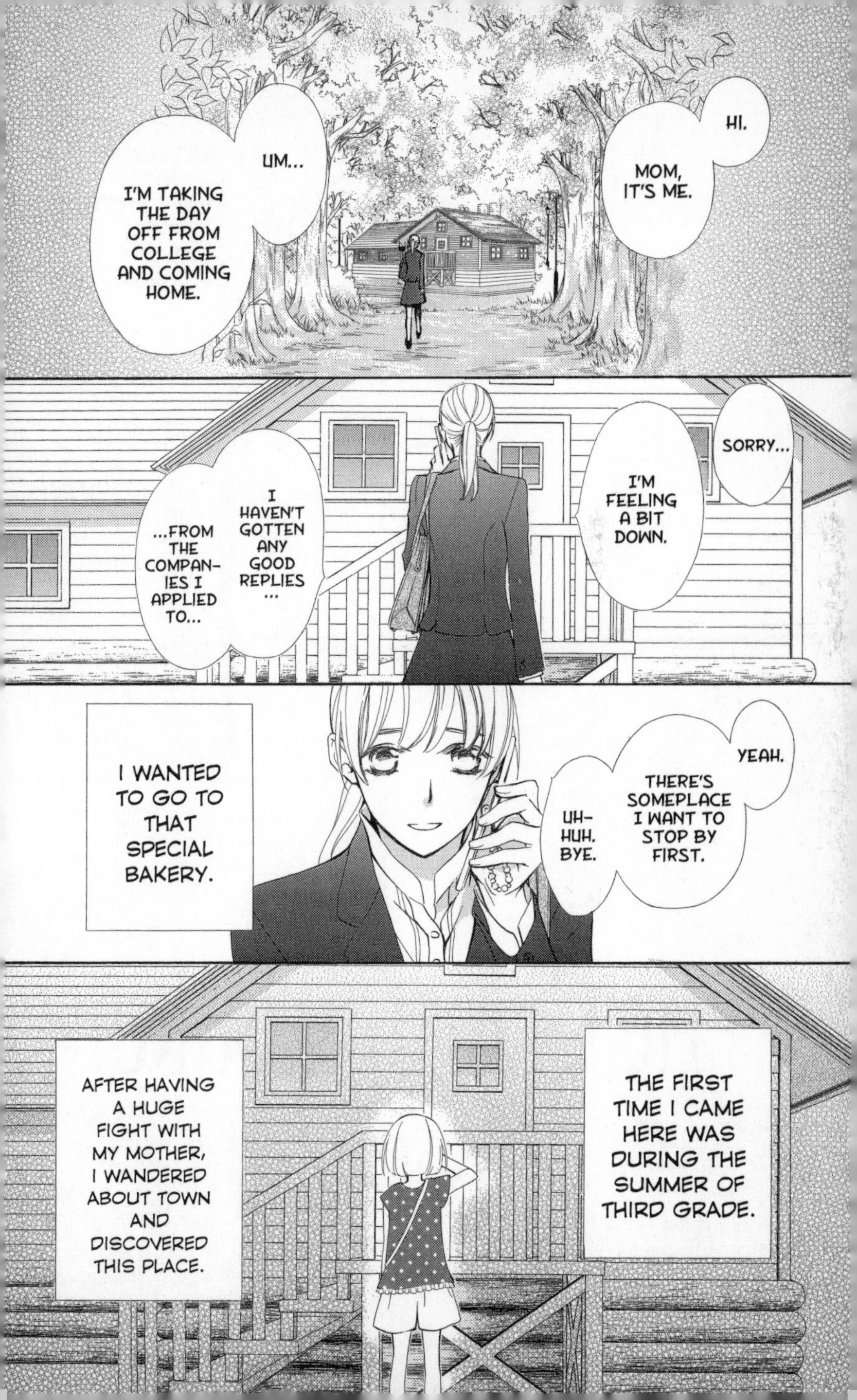
HI.
MOM, IT'S ME.
UM...
I'M TAKING THE DAY OFF FROM COLLEGE AND COMING HOME.
SORRY...
I'M FEELING A BIT DOWN.
I HAVEN'T GOTTEN ANY GOOD REPLIES...
...FROM THE COMPANIES I APPLIED TO...
YEAH.
THERE'S SOMEPLACE I WANT TO STOP BY FIRST.
UH-HUH. BYE.
I WANTED TO GO TO THAT SPECIAL BAKERY.
THE FIRST TIME I CAME HERE WAS DURING THE SUMMER OF THIRD GRADE.
AFTER HAVING A HUGE FIGHT WITH MY MOTHER, I WANDERED ABOUT TOWN AND DISCOVERED THIS PLACE.

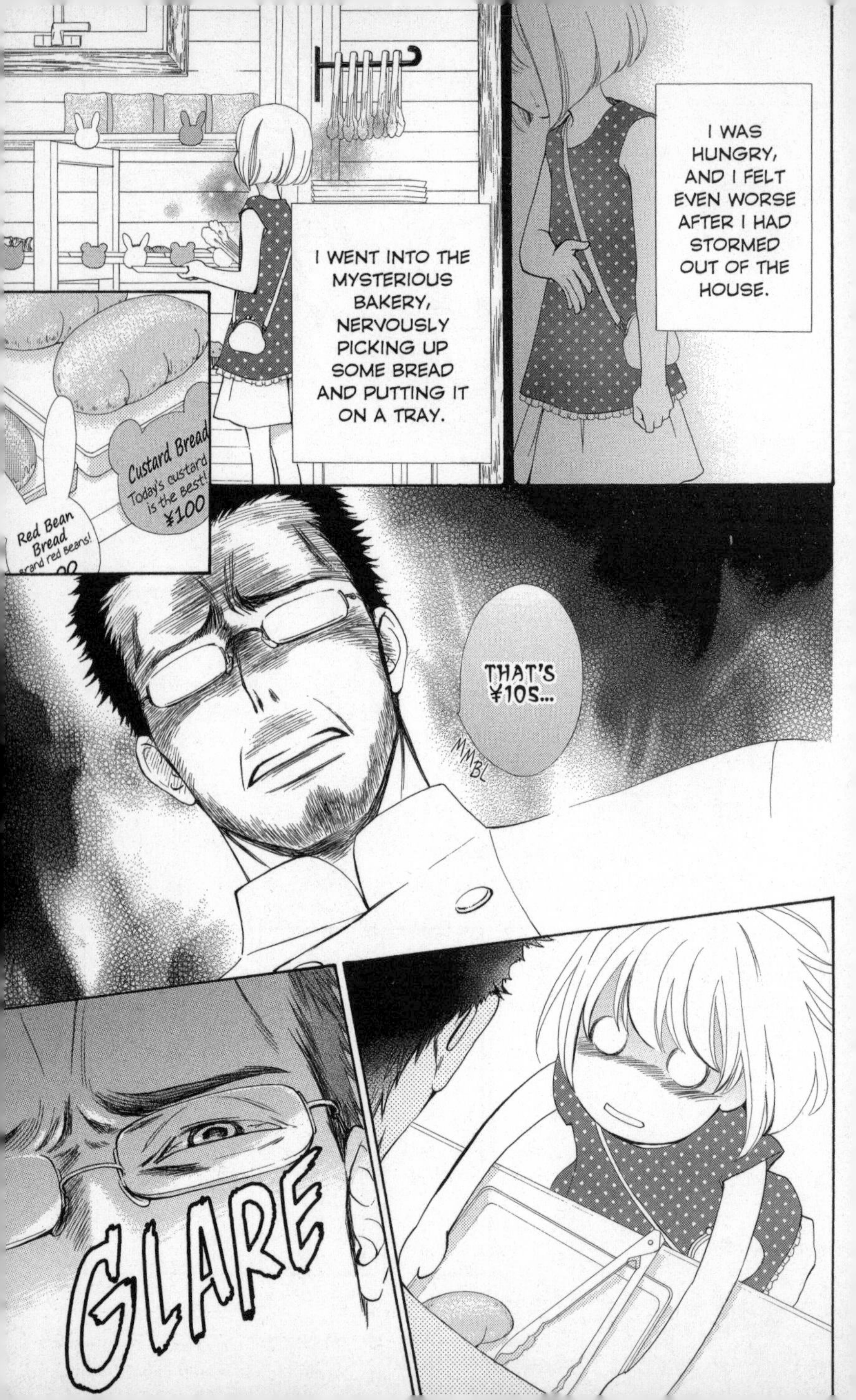
I WAS HUNGRY, AND I FELT EVEN WORSE AFTER I HAD STORMED OUT OF THE HOUSE.
I WENT INTO THE MYSTERIOUS BAKERY, NERVOUSLY PICKING UP SOME BREAD AND PUTTING IT ON A TRAY.
Custard Bread
Today's custard is the Best!
¥100
Red Bean Bread
THAT'S ¥105...
MMBL
GLARE

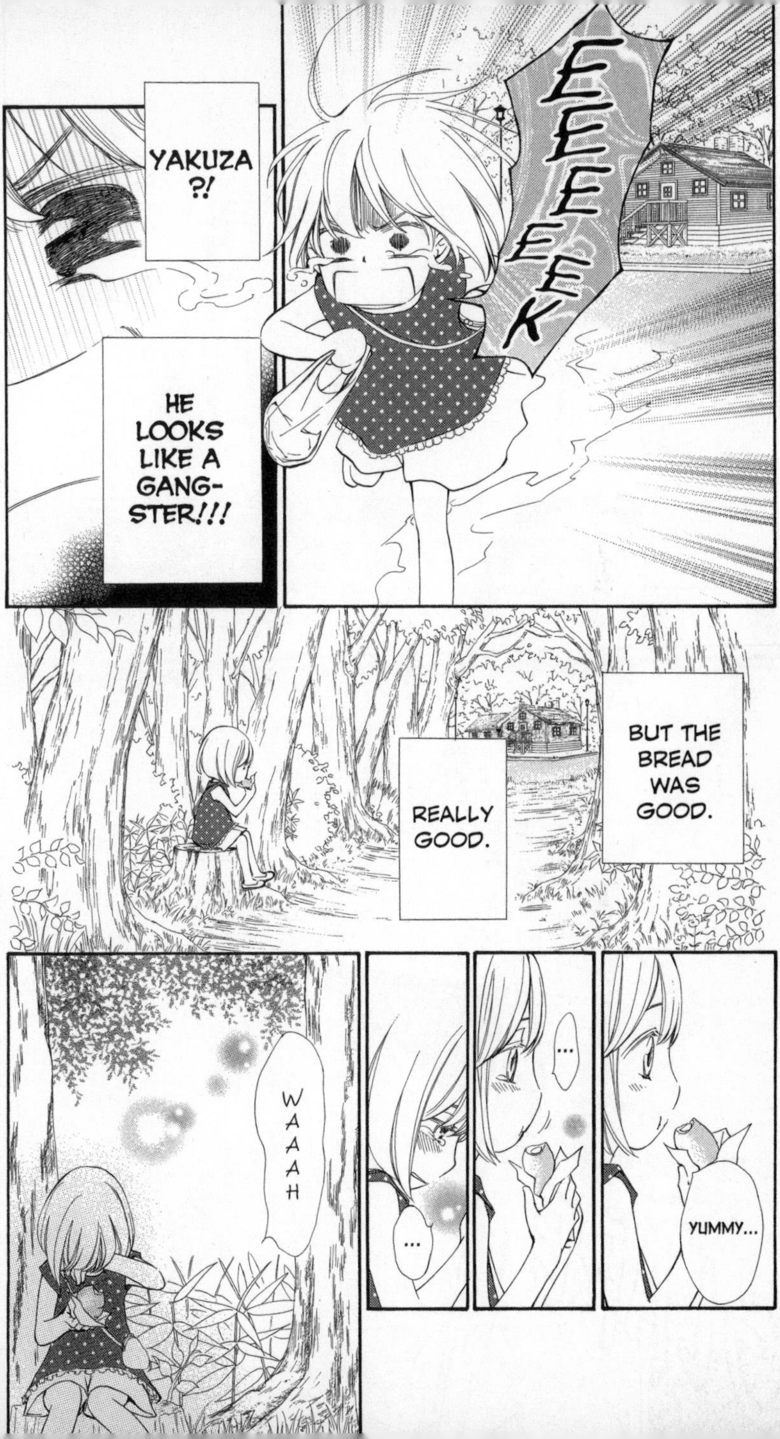
EEEEEEK
YAKUZA ?!
HE LOOKS LIKE A GANG-STER!!!
BUT THE BREAD WAS GOOD.
REALLY GOOD.
YUMMY...
...
...
WAAAAH

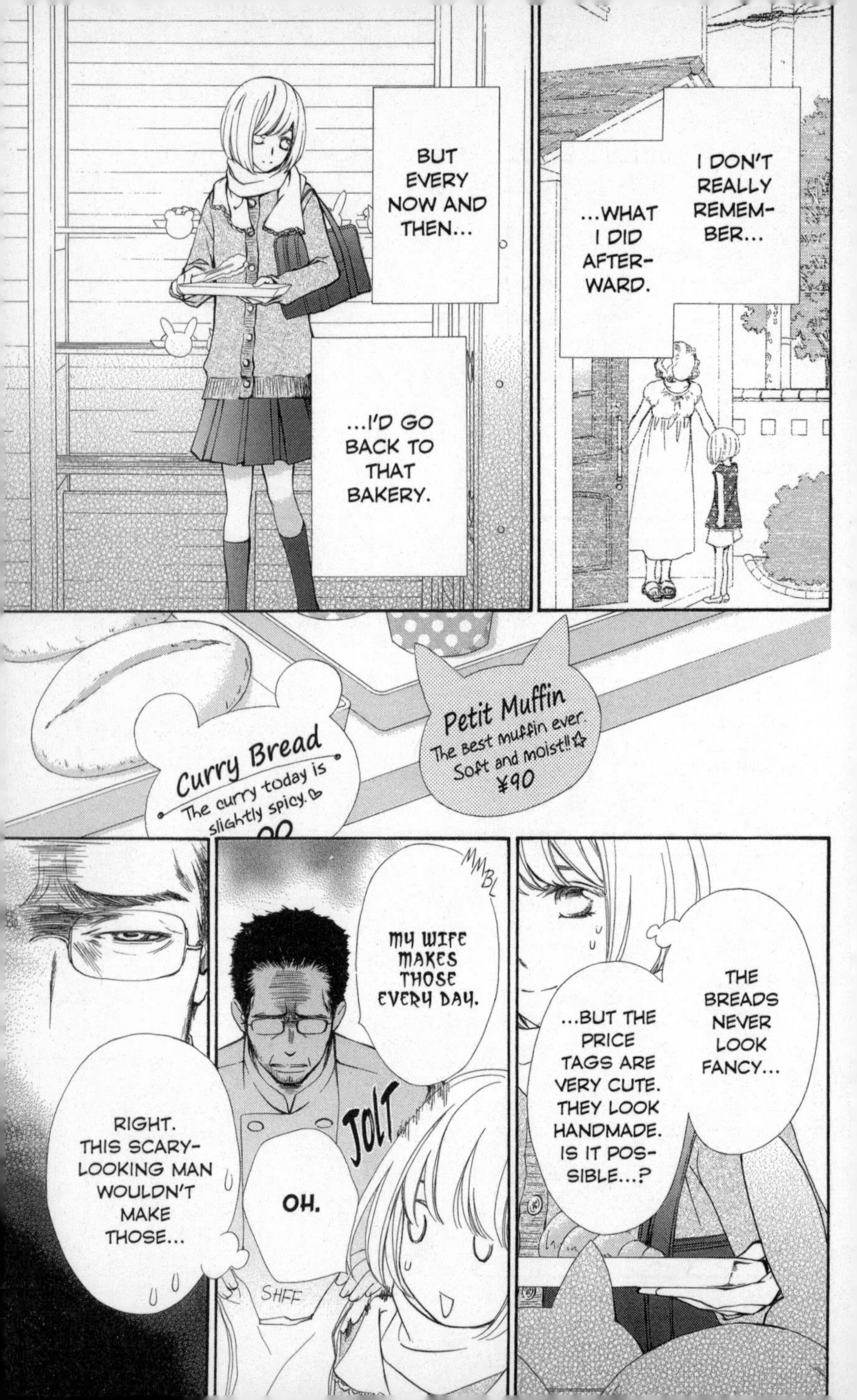
I DON'T REALLY REMEM-BER...
...WHAT I DID AFTER-WARD.
BUT EVERY NOW AND THEN...
...I'D GO BACK TO THAT BAKERY.
Petit Muffin
The best muffin ever. Soft and moist!!
¥90
Curry Bread
The curry today is slightly spicy.
THE BREADS NEVER LOOK FANCY...
...BUT THE PRICE TAGS ARE VERY CUTE. THEY LOOK HANDMADE. IS IT POS-SIBLE...?
MMBL
MY WIFE MAKES THOSE EVERY DAY.
JOLT
OH.
SHFF
RIGHT. THIS SCARY-LOOKING MAN WOULDN'T MAKE THOSE...

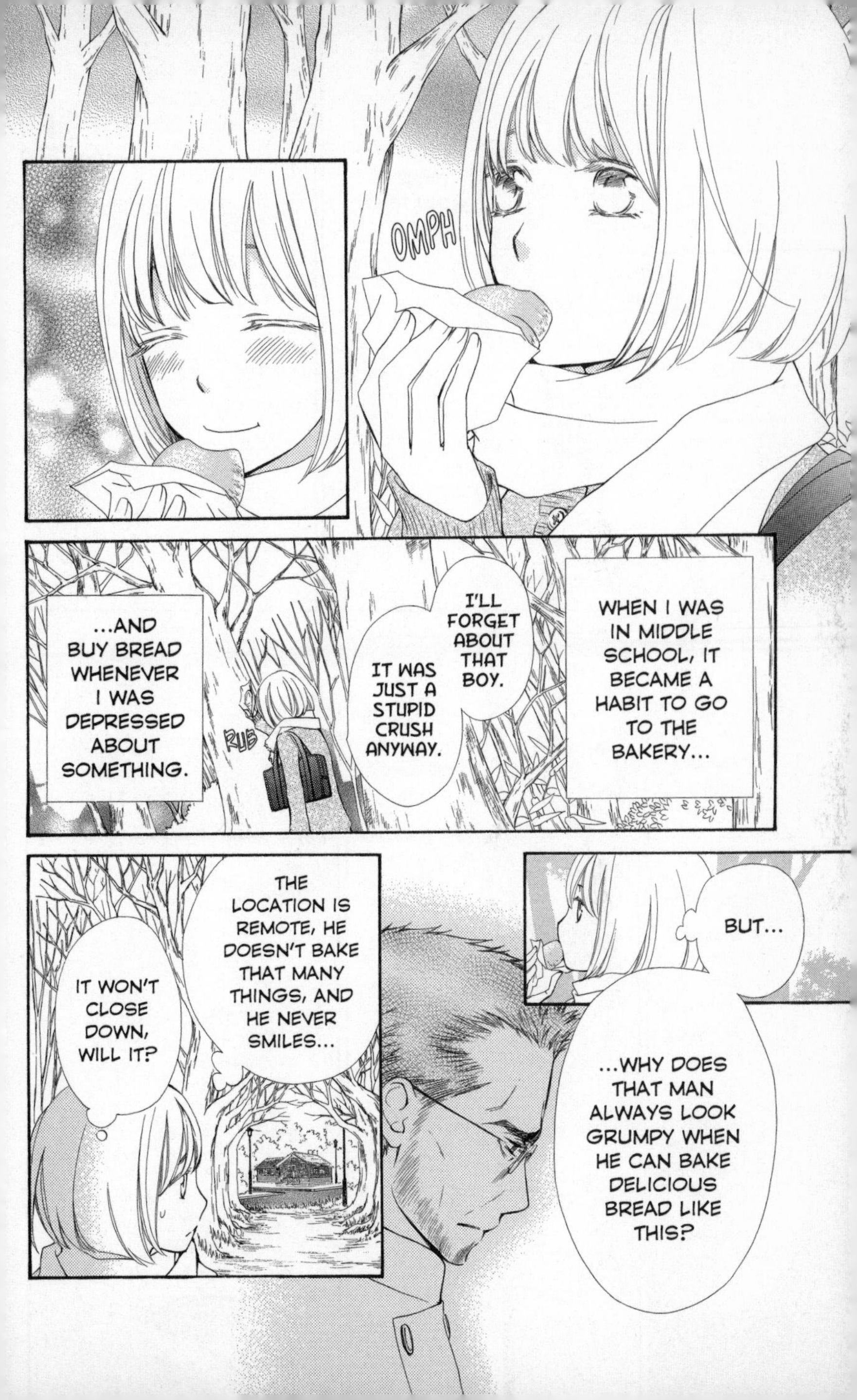
OMPH
WHEN I WAS IN MIDDLE SCHOOL, IT BECAME A HABIT TO GO TO THE BAKERY...
I'LL FORGET ABOUT THAT BOY.
IT WAS JUST A STUPID CRUSH ANYWAY.
RUB
...AND BUY BREAD WHENEVER I WAS DEPRESSED ABOUT SOMETHING.
BUT...
...WHY DOES THAT MAN ALWAYS LOOK GRUMPY WHEN HE CAN BAKE DELICIOUS BREAD LIKE THIS?
THE LOCATION IS REMOTE, HE DOESN'T BAKE THAT MANY THINGS, AND HE NEVER SMILES...
IT WON'T CLOSE DOWN, WILL IT?

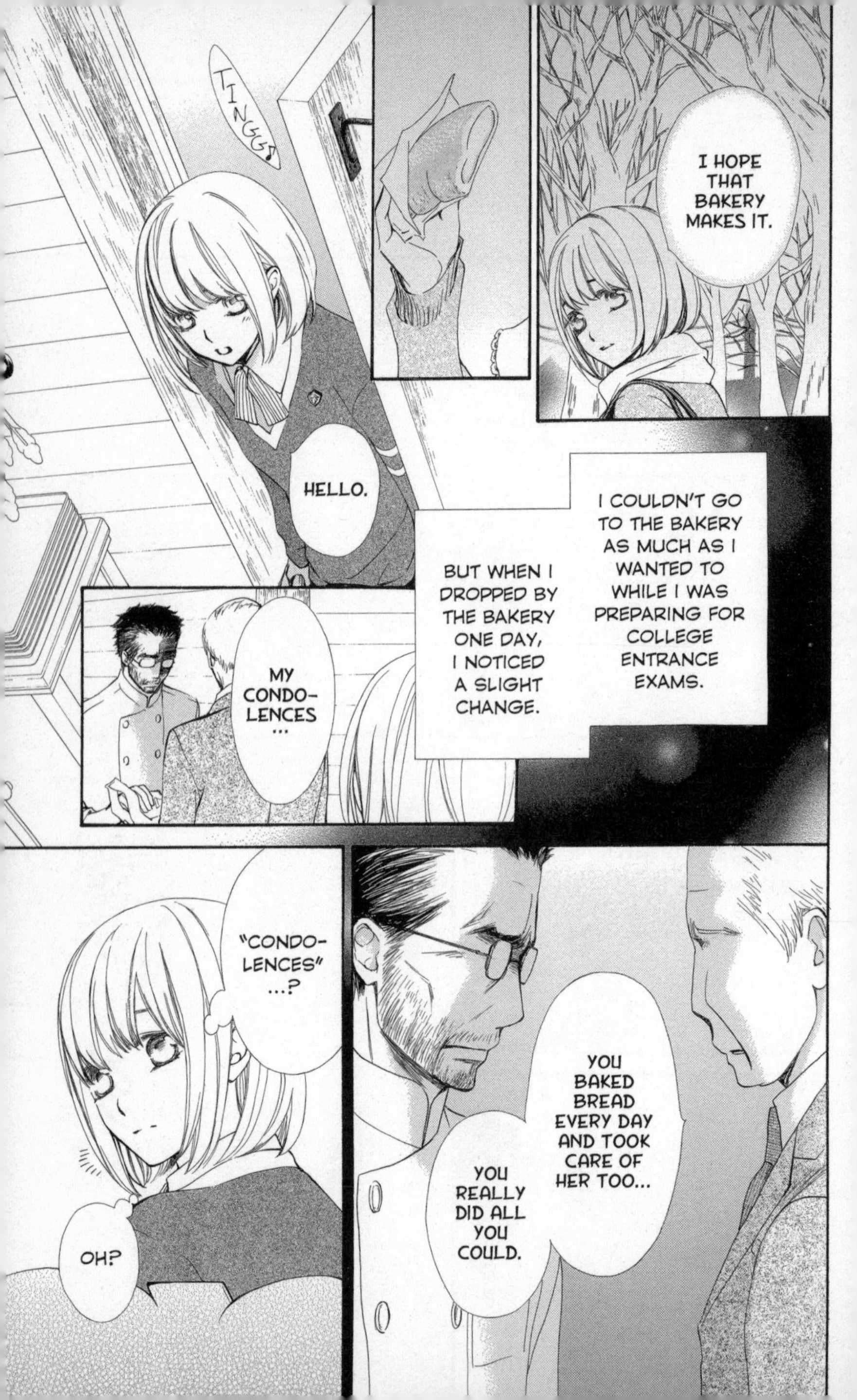
I HOPE THAT BAKERY MAKES IT.
I COULDN'T GO TO THE BAKERY AS MUCH AS I WANTED TO WHILE I WAS PREPARING FOR COLLEGE ENTRANCE EXAMS.
BUT WHEN I DROPPED BY THE BAKERY ONE DAY, I NOTICED A SLIGHT CHANGE.
TINGG♪
HELLO.
MY CONDOLENCES...
YOU BAKED BREAD EVERY DAY AND TOOK CARE OF HER TOO...
YOU REALLY DID ALL YOU COULD.
"CONDOLENCES"...?
OH?

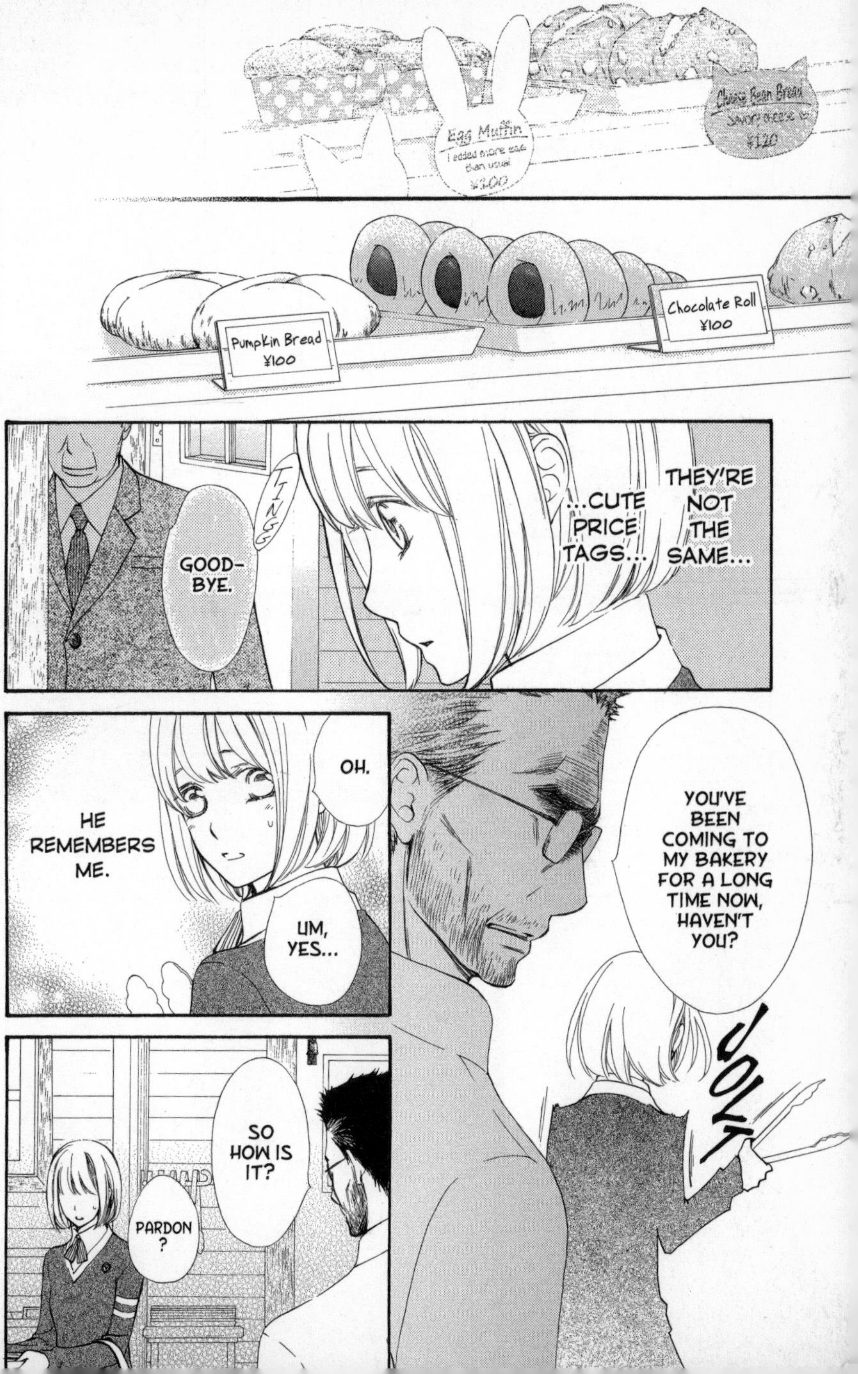
Savory cheese
¥120
Egg Muffin
I added more egg than usual
Chocolate Roll
¥100
Pumpkin Bread
¥100
THEY'RE NOT THE SAME...
...CUTE PRICE TAGS...
TING
GOOD-BYE.
YOU'VE BEEN COMING TO MY BAKERY FOR A LONG TIME NOW, HAVEN'T YOU?
JOLT
OH.
HE REMEMBERS ME.
UM, YES...
SO HOW IS IT?
PARDON?

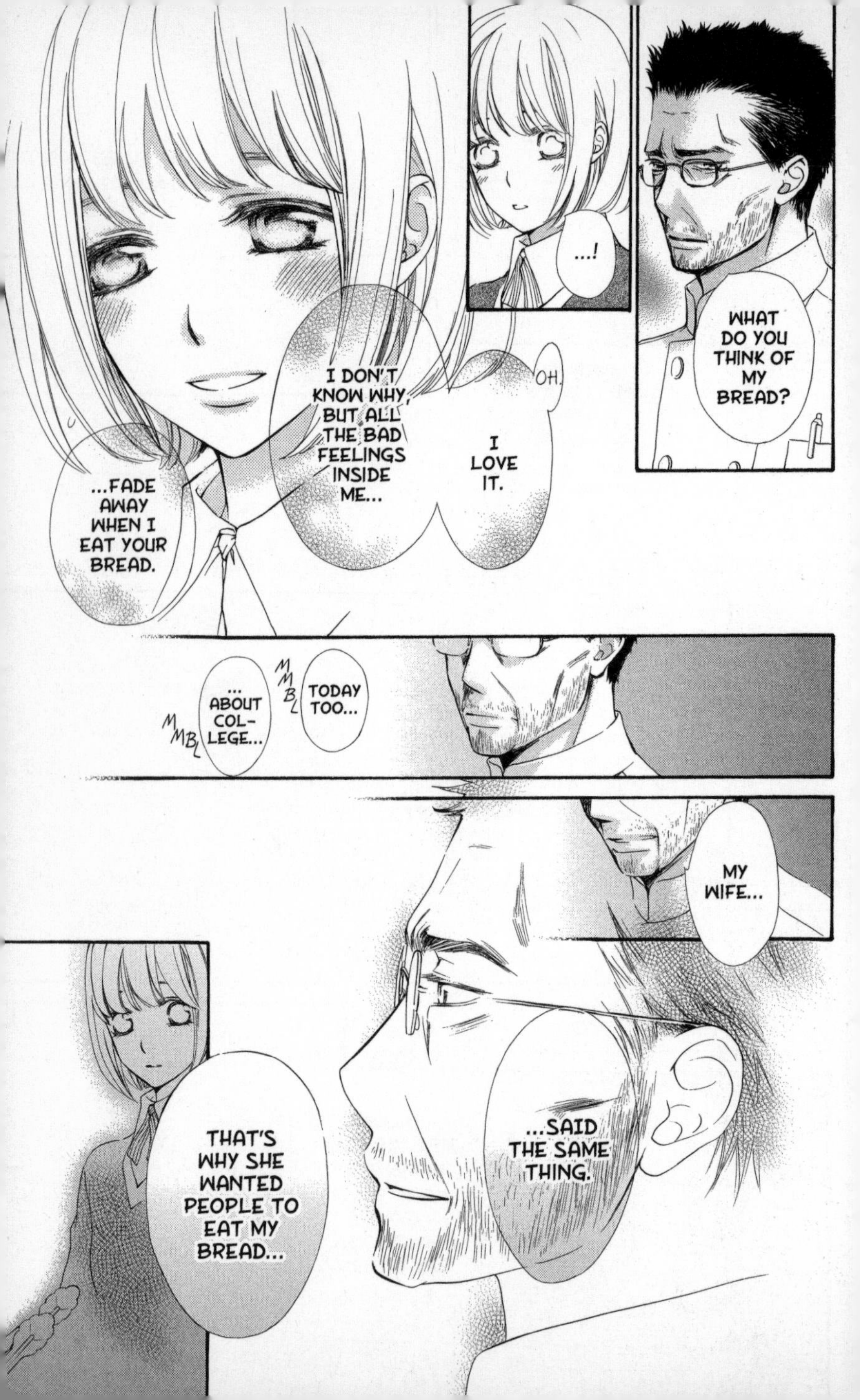
WHAT DO YOU THINK OF MY BREAD?
...!
OH.
I LOVE IT.
I DON'T KNOW WHY, BUT ALL THE BAD FEELINGS INSIDE ME...
...FADE AWAY WHEN I EAT YOUR BREAD.
TODAY TOO...
MMBL
... ABOUT COL-LEGE...
MMBL
MY WIFE...
...SAID THE SAME THING.
THAT'S WHY SHE WANTED PEOPLE TO EAT MY BREAD...

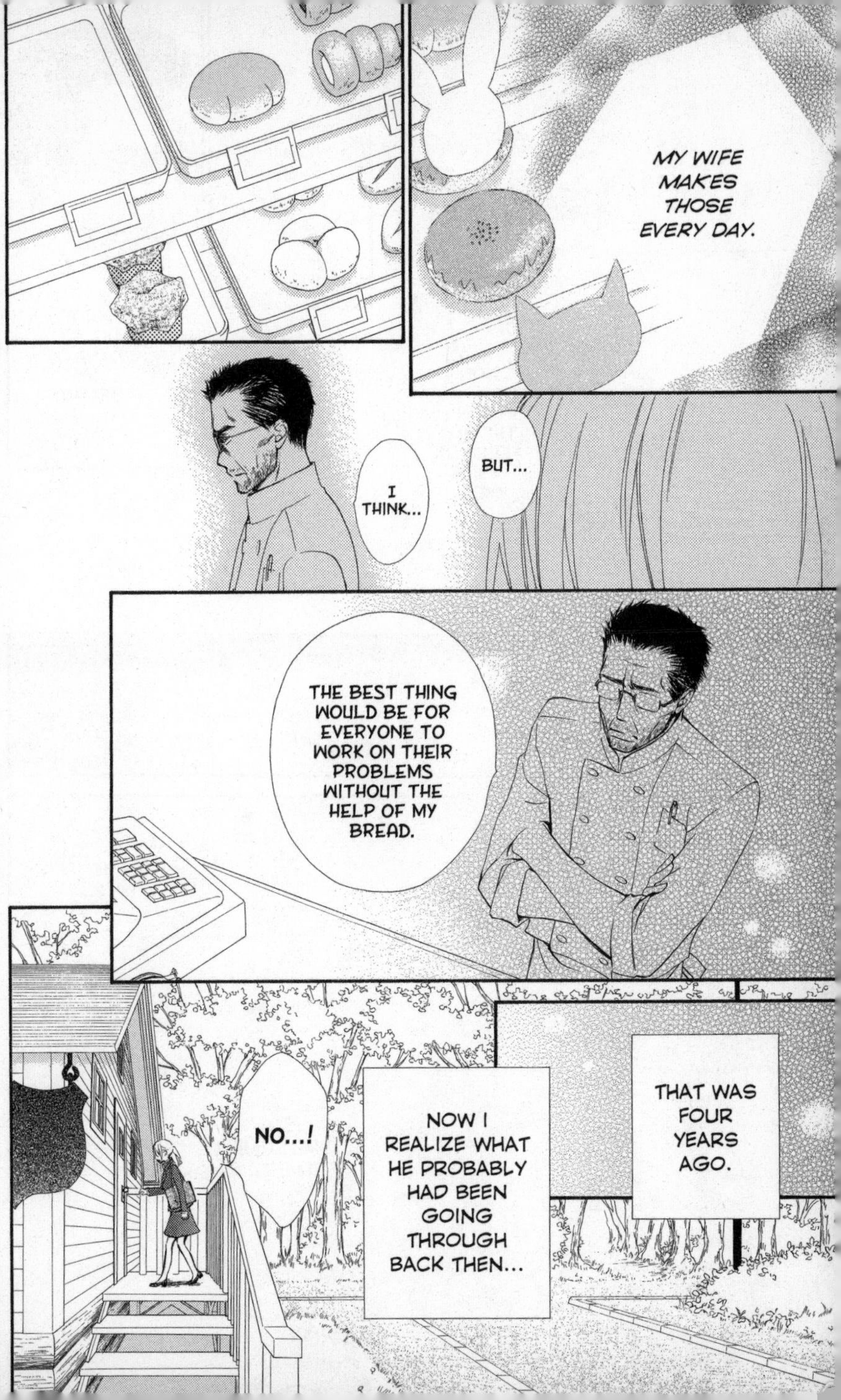
MY WIFE MAKES THOSE EVERY DAY.
BUT...
I THINK...
THE BEST THING WOULD BE FOR EVERYONE TO WORK ON THEIR PROBLEMS WITHOUT THE HELP OF MY BREAD.
THAT WAS FOUR YEARS AGO.
NOW I REALIZE WHAT HE PROBABLY HAD BEEN GOING THROUGH BACK THEN...
NO...!

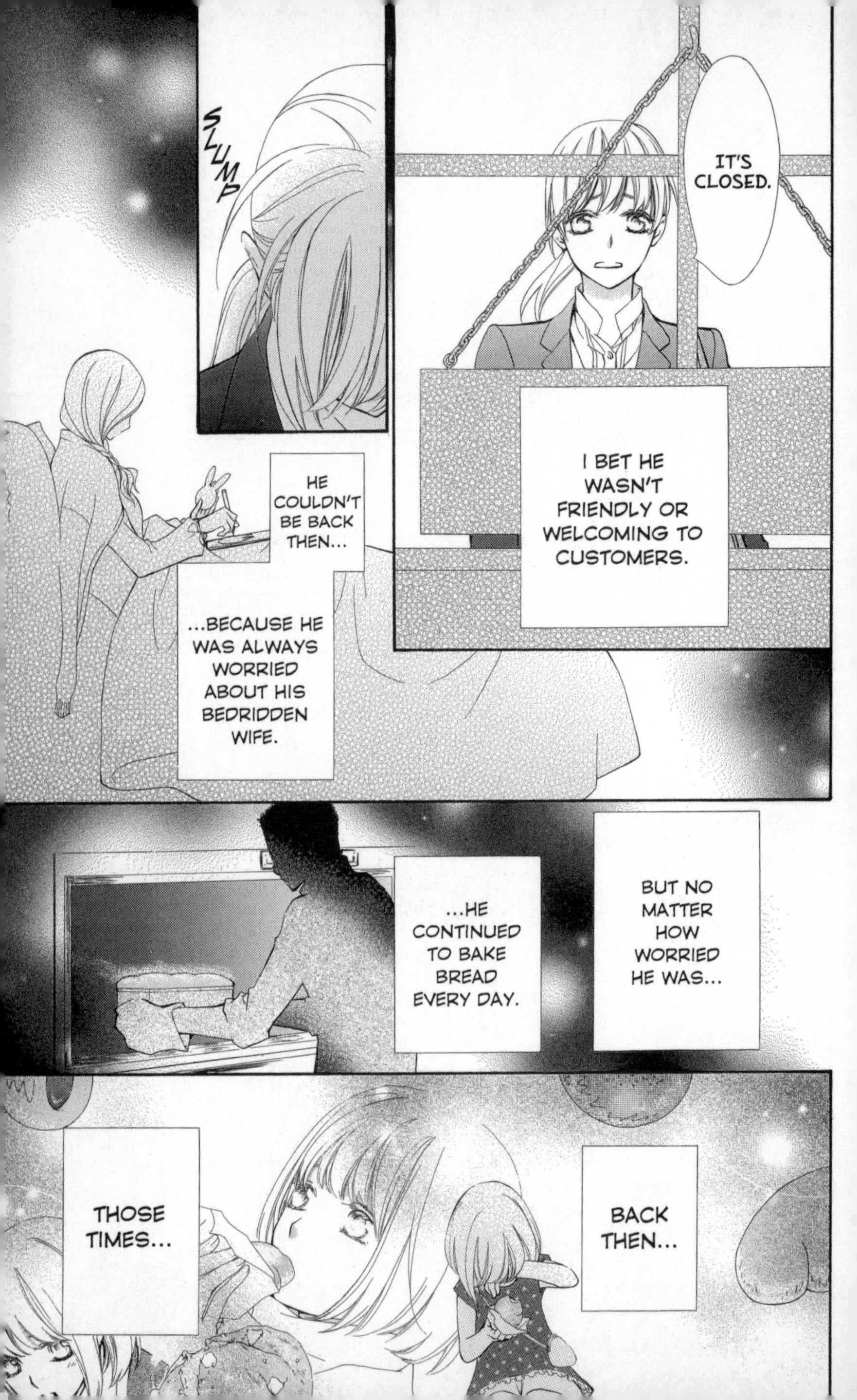
IT'S CLOSED.
I BET HE WASN'T FRIENDLY OR WELCOMING TO CUSTOMERS.
SLUMP
HE COULDN'T BE BACK THEN...
...BECAUSE HE WAS ALWAYS WORRIED ABOUT HIS BEDRIDDEN WIFE.
BUT NO MATTER HOW WORRIED HE WAS...
...HE CONTINUED TO BAKE BREAD EVERY DAY.
BACK THEN...
THOSE TIMES...

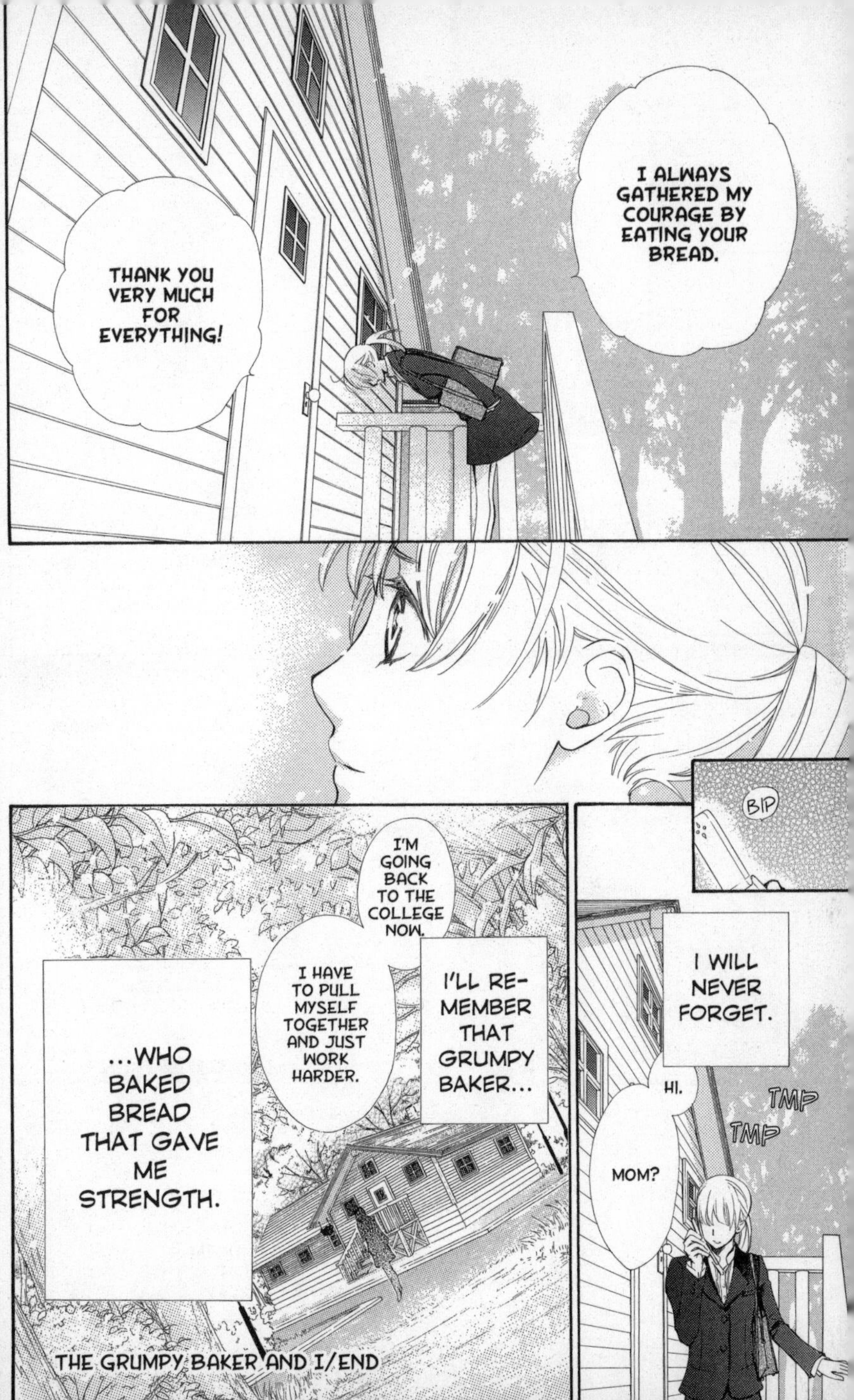
I ALWAYS GATHERED MY COURAGE BY EATING YOUR BREAD.
THANK YOU VERY MUCH FOR EVERYTHING!
BIP
I WILL NEVER FORGET.
TMP
TMP
HI.
MOM?
I'M GOING BACK TO THE COLLEGE NOW.
I'LL RE-MEMBER THAT GRUMPY BAKER...
I HAVE TO PULL MYSELF TOGETHER AND JUST WORK HARDER.
...WHO BAKED BREAD THAT GAVE ME STRENGTH.
THE GRUMPY BAKER AND I/END

EDITOR'S NOTES

Characters

Matsuri Hino puts careful thought into the names of her characters in *Vampire Knight*. Below is the collection of characters through volume 17. Each character's name is presented family name first, per the kanji reading.

黒主優姫

Cross Yuki

Yuki's last name, *Kurosu*, is the Japanese pronunciation of the English word "cross." However, the kanji has a different meaning—*kuro* means "black" and *su* means "master." Her first name is a combination of *yuu*, meaning "tender" or "kind," and *ki*, meaning "princess."

錐生零

Kiryu Zero

Zero's first name is the kanji for *rei*, meaning "zero." In his last name, *Kiryu*, the *ki* means "auger" or "drill," and the *ryu* means "life."

玖蘭枢

Kuran Kaname

Kaname means "hinge" or "door." The kanji for his last name is a combination of the old-fashioned way of writing *ku*, meaning "nine," and *ran*, meaning "orchid": "nine orchids."

藍堂英

Aido Hanabusa

Hanabusa means "petals of a flower." *Aido* means "indigo temple." In Japanese, the pronunciation of *Aido* is very close to the pronunciation of the English word *idol*.

架院暁

Kain Akatsuki

Akatsuki means "dawn" or "daybreak." In *Kain, ka* is a base or support, while *in* denotes a building that has high fences around it, such as a temple or school.

早園瑠佳

Souen Ruka

In *Ruka*, the *ru* means "lapis lazuli" while the *ka* means "good-looking" or "beautiful." The *sou* in Ruka's surname, *Souen*, means "early," but this kanji also has an obscure meaning of "strong fragrance." The *en* means "garden."

一条拓麻

Ichijo Takuma

Ichijo can mean a "ray" or "streak." The kanji for *Takuma* is a combination of *taku*, meaning "to cultivate" and *ma*, which is the kanji for *asa*, meaning "hemp" or "flax," a plant with blue flowers.

支葵千里

Shiki Senri

Shiki's last name is a combination of *shi*, meaning "to support" and *ki*, meaning "mallow"—a flowering plant with pink or white blossoms. The *ri* in *Senri* is a traditional Japanese unit of measure for distance, and one *ri* is about 2.44 miles. *Senri* means "1,000 *ri*."

夜刈十牙

Yagari Toga

Yagari is a combination of *ya*, meaning "night," and *gari*, meaning "to harvest." *Toga* means "ten fangs."

一条麻遠, 一翁

Ichijo Asato, aka "Ichio"

Ichijo can mean a "ray" or "streak." Asato's first name is comprised of *asa*, meaning "hemp" or "flax," and *tou*, meaning "far off." His nickname is *ichi*, or "one," combined with *ou*, which can be used as an honorific when referring to an older man.

若葉沙頼

Wakaba Sayori

Yori's full name is Sayori Wakaba. *Wakaba* means "young leaves." Her given name, *Sayori*, is a combination of *sa*, meaning "sand," and *yori*, meaning "trust."

星煉

Seiren

Sei means "star" and *ren* means "to smelt" or "refine." *Ren* is also the same kanji used in *rengoku*, or "purgatory."

遠矢莉磨

Toya Rima

Toya means a "far-reaching arrow." Rima's first name is a combination of *ri*, or "jasmine," and *ma*, which signifies enhancement by wearing away, such as by polishing or scouring.

紅まり亜

Kurenai Maria

Kurenai means "crimson." The kanji for the last *a* in Maria's first name is the same that is used in "Asia."

錐生壱縷

Kiryu Ichiru

Ichi is the old-fashioned way of writing "one," and *ru* means "thread."

緋桜閑, 狂咲姫

Hio Shizuka, Kuruizaki-hime

Shizuka means "calm and quiet." In Shizuka's family name, *hi* is "scarlet," and *ou* is "cherry blossoms." Shizuka Hio is also referred to as the "Kuruizaki-hime." *Kuruizaki* means "flowers blooming out of season," and *hime* means "princess."

藍堂月子

Aido Tsukiko

Aido means "indigo temple." *Tsukiko* means "moon child."

白蕗更

Shirabuki Sara

Shira is "white," and *buki* is "butterbur," a plant with white flowers. *Sara* means "renew."

黒主灰闇

Cross Kaien

Cross, or *Kurosu*, means "black master." Kaien is a combination of *kai*, meaning "ashes," and *en*, meaning "village gate." The kanji for *en* is also used for Enma, the ruler of the Underworld in Buddhist mythology.

玖蘭李土

Kuran Rido

Kuran means "nine orchids." In *Rido*, *ri* means "plum" and *do* means "earth."

玖蘭樹里

Kuran Juri

Kuran means "nine orchids." In her first name, *ju* means "tree" and a *ri* is a traditional Japanese unit of measure for distance. The kanji for *ri* is the same as in Senri's name.

玖蘭悠

Kuran Haruka

Kuran means "nine orchids." *Haruka* means "distant" or "remote."

鷹宮海斗

Takamiya Kaito

Taka means "hawk" and *miya* means "imperial palace" or "shrine." *Kai* is "sea" and *to* means "to measure" or "grid."

菖藤依砂也

Shoto Isaya

Sho means "Siberian Iris" and *to* is "wisteria." The *I* in *Isaya* means "to rely on," while the *sa* means "sand." *Ya* is a suffix used for emphasis.

橙茉

Toma

In the family name *Toma*, *to* means "seville orange" and *ma* means "jasmine flower."

藍堂永路

Aido Nagamichi

The name *Nagamichi* is a combination of *naga*, which means "long" or "eternal," and *michi*, which is the kanji for "road" or "path." *Aido* means "indigo temple."

縹木

Hanadagi

In this family name, *Hanada* means "bright light blue" and *gi* means "tree."

影山霞

Kageyama Kasumi

In the Class Rep's family name, *kage* means "shadow," and *yama* means "mountain." His first name, Kasumi, means "haze" or "mist."

Terms

-sama: The suffix *sama* is used in formal address for someone who ranks higher in the social hierarchy. The vampires call their leader "Kaname-sama" only when they are among their own kind.

Matsuri Hino burst onto the manga scene with her series *Kono Yume ga Sametara* (When This Dream Is Over), which was published in *LaLa DX* magazine. Hino was a manga artist a mere nine months after she decided to become one.

With the success of her popular series *Captive Hearts* and *MeruPuri*, Hino has established herself as a major player in the world of shojo manga. *Vampire Knight* is currently serialized in *LaLa* magazine.

Hino enjoys creative activities and has commented that she would have been either an architect or an apprentice to traditional Japanese craft masters if she had not become a manga artist.

VAMPIRE KNIGHT
Vol. 17
Shojo Beat Edition

STORY AND ART BY
MATSURI HINO

Adaptation/Nancy Thistlethwaite
Translation/Tetsuichiro Miyaki
Touch-up Art & Lettering/Inori Fukuda Trant
Graphic Design/Amy Martin
Editor/Nancy Thistlethwaite

Vampire Knight by Matsuri Hino © Matsuri Hino 2012. All rights reserved.
First published in Japan in 2012 by HAKUSENSHA, Inc., Tokyo. English
language translation rights arranged with HAKUSENSHA, Inc., Tokyo.

Printed in the U.S.A.

Published by VIZ Media, LLC
P.O. Box 77010
San Francisco, CA 94107

10 9 8 7 6 5 4 3 2 1
First printing, November 2013

www.viz.com

www.shojobeat.com

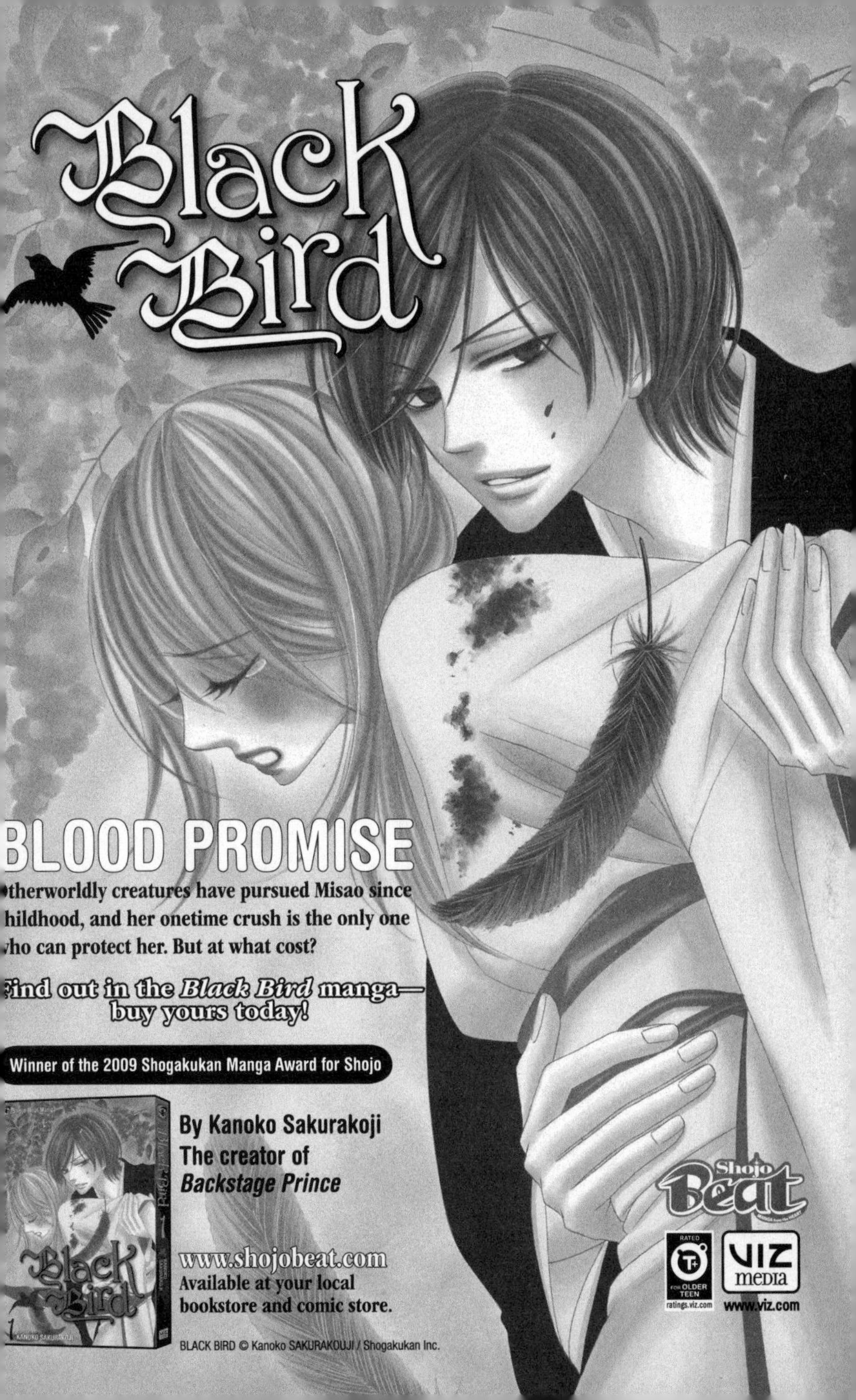

Black Bird
BLOOD PROMISE
therworldly creatures have pursued Misao since
hildhood, and her onetime crush is the only one
ho can protect her. But at what cost?
ind out in the Black Bird manga—
buy yours today!
Winner of the 2009 Shogakukan Manga Award for Shojo
By Kanoko Sakurakoji
The creator of
Backstage Prince
www.shojobeat.com
Available at your local
bookstore and comic store.
BLACK BIRD © Kanoko SAKURAKOUJI / Shogakukan Inc.
Shojo Beat
RATED T+ FOR OLDER TEEN
ratings.viz.com
VIZ media
www.viz.com

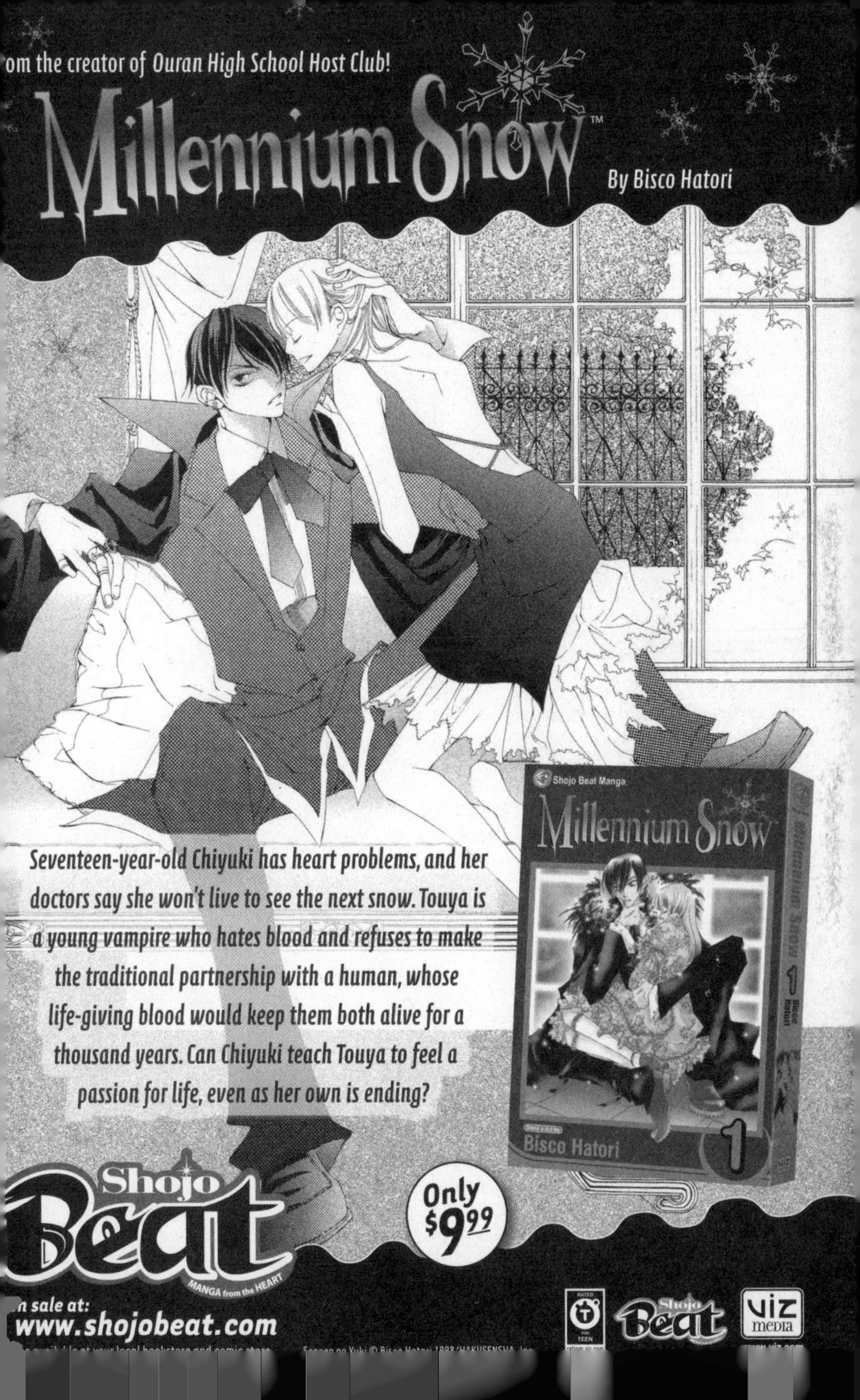

om the creator of Ouran High School Host Club!
Millennium Snow™
By Bisco Hatori
Seventeen-year-old Chiyuki has heart problems, and her doctors say she won't live to see the next snow. Touya is a young vampire who hates blood and refuses to make the traditional partnership with a human, whose life-giving blood would keep them both alive for a thousand years. Can Chiyuki teach Touya to feel a passion for life, even as her own is ending?
Shojo Beat Manga
Millennium Snow
1
Bisco Hatori
Shojo Beat
MANGA from the HEART
Only $9.99
n sale at:
www.shojobeat.com
RATED T FOR TEEN
Shojo Beat
VIZ media

SURPRISE!

You may be reading the wrong way!

It's true: In keeping with the original Japanese comic format, this book reads from right to left—so action, sound effects, and word balloons are completely reversed. This preserves the orientation of the original artwork—plus, it's fun! Check out the diagram shown here to get the hang of things, and then turn to the other side of the book to get started!

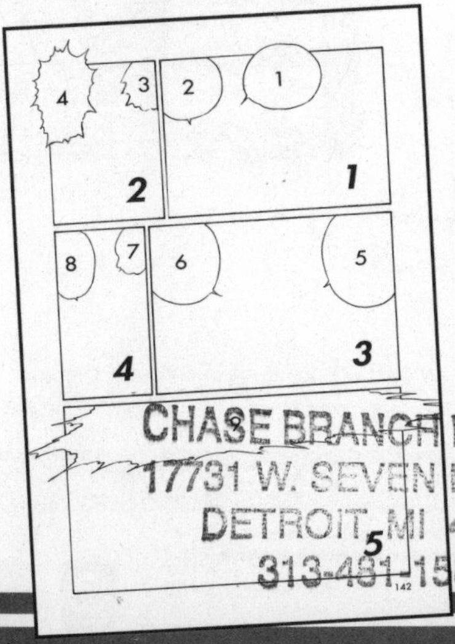
1
2
3
4
1
2
5
6
7
8
3
4
9
5
142

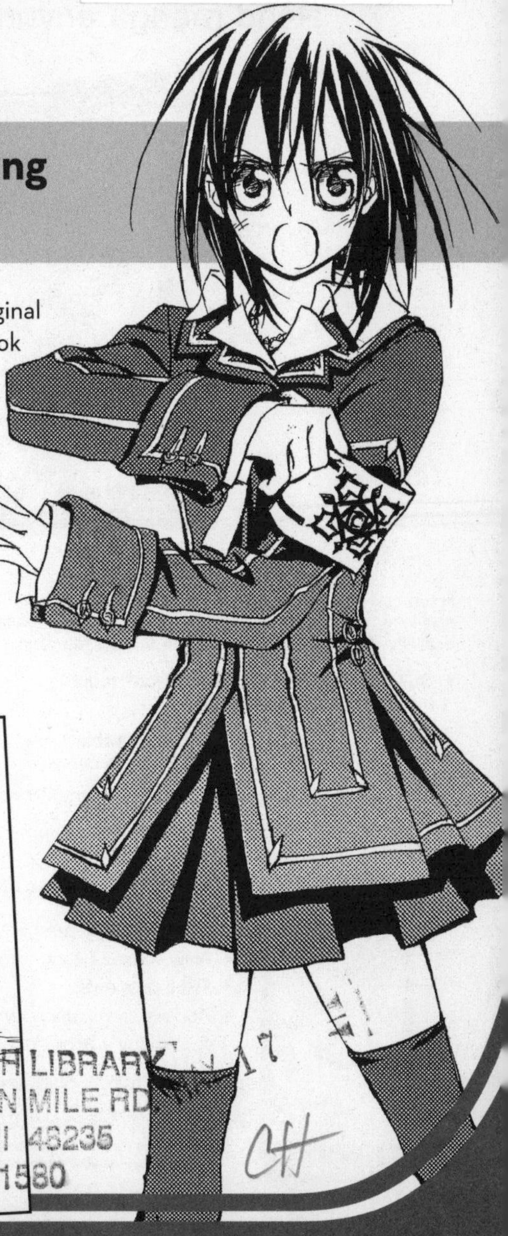